The French Menu Cookbook

The food and wine of France
—season by delicious season—
in beautifully composed menus
for American dining and entertaining
by an American living in Paris and Provence

RICHARD OLNEY

The Original Edition with a
New Introduction by *PAUL BERTOLLI*

TEN SPEED PRESS
Berkeley

 Published in the United States by Ten Speed Press, an imprint of the Crown Publishing Group, a division of Random House, Inc., New York.
www.crownpublishing.com
www.tenspeed.com

Originally published in hardcover in the United States by Simon and Schuster, New York, in 1970. Subsequently published in hardcover with a new introduction by Ten Speed Press, Berkeley, in 2002.

Library of Congress Cataloging-in-Publication Data
Olney, Richard.
The French menu cookbook: the food and wine of France—season by delicious season—in beautifully composed menus for American dining and entertaining by an American living in Paris and Provence / Richard Olney.
p. cm.
Originally published: New York: Simon and Schuster, 1970. With new introd. by Paul Bertolli.
1. Cookery, French. 2. Menus. I. Bertolli, Paul. II. Title.
TX719.O45 2002
641.5944- dc21

ISBN 978-1-60774-002-5

Printed in the United States of America

Jacket design by Colleen Cain
Original design by Eve Metz

10 9 8 7 6 5 4 3 2 1

First Paperback Edition

INTRODUCTION TO THE NEW EDITION

Every aspiring chef needs at least one mentor. Richard Olney was mine. Before I had the pleasure of meeting him in person, I knew him through his early books, *The French Menu Cookbook* (1970) and *Simple French Food* (1974), both of which influenced me more profoundly than any culinary writing of the time and any I have since encountered. These books occupy my culinary consciousness. Their spirit lives in the spirit of what I do.

It was altogether fortunate that the first publication of *The French Menu Cookbook* coincided with my awakening as a cook. Without it I would be much less of a cook now, perhaps no cook at all. Some ten years later, my interest in this book became intense. At the time, as the new chef of Chez Panisse restaurant, I had the responsibility of creating the nightly changing prix fixe menu, and *The French Menu Cookbook* seemed personally addressed to me. Olney, a friend to Chez Panisse and guest author of several of its special menus devoted to French wine and food, also instructed me by handwritten notes sent from abroad on a few occasions. It was my honor to cook for Richard several times, and his generous estimations of the menus I prepared freshened my confidence and bolstered my pride. I cannot say I knew him well, and in this respect my relationship with his words and his thinking was, and still is, pure. I like it that way. In my five or six encounters with Richard both here and in France during the later years of his life, I found him to be a man of few words, a surprising revelation given how large his writing loomed in my imagination. It was from others that I learned of his charmed life on the herb-scented Provençal hillside he called his home. Olney had frequent visitors who would often stay for days, sometimes weeks, in thrall to his cooking and the seductions of his cellar. His appearance was as unabashed as his cooking. I am told he received summer guests wearing no more than a loincloth. To those who kept his close company, Olney was a curious blend of cultured gentleman and lusty sybarite, a disciplined intellectual with the appetites of a beast. He did not suffer fools or foolishness. He was often irascible. On topics of food and wine he was a brilliant reductionist, caustically opinionated, infuriatingly right. Despite his steady habit of Gauloise cigarettes and a dizzying capacity for wine and spirits, he possessed an acutely discerning palate. This quality was ever-present during our shared moments at the table and is everywhere evidenced in *The French Menu Cookbook* and in all of his books that followed.

It is a testament to the enduring quality of a book that one can revisit it after thirty years and find it to be in every way as revealing and vital as it was upon first opening it, if not more so. Influence is something that can only be understood fully in retrospect. Re-reading *The French Menu Cookbook* reminds me of what I was looking for some thirty years ago when I was struggling to find my way as a chef, and what it was that I found in Richard Olney's words. In some important respects, we shared similar sensibilities, perhaps even a parallel path to discovering our passion for food and wine. I had moved away from the pursuit of a career in another art form, music, while Olney had started out as a painter. The transition was not easy for me. While the world of food and wine proved far more accessible and rewarding to my efforts, I missed the quiet intensity, the emotional gratification, and the enduring reward of music making. Before my introduction to *The French Menu Cookbook* I had worked in a number of local restaurants and had spent a grueling year of restaurant apprenticeship abroad. I knew even after I had landed a more comfortable job at Chez Panisse that I would have to find some higher purpose if I were to sustain the profession and the life. Restaurant cooking was fast, loud, hot, late, dirty, imprecise, exhausting, and joyful. What satisfaction could be had from a day's preparation was sadly fleeting. In my worst moments, I viewed the fruit of my hard work, so many beautifully styled plates, reduced to sewage in a matter of hours.

I floundered for nearly a decade trying to find the metaphor in cooking that would reconcile my passion for the elegance of music with the rough kitchen work that was pulling me strongly. *The French Menu Cookbook* was the poem that released me from turmoil. It embodied the purpose I sought and was critical in helping me legitimize my choice to become a chef. In it, I found an artist's eye for the telling detail and for the beauty of food, and a craftsman's patience with process. Olney's menus for all seasons and moods were luminous examples of the possibilities for achieving economy and harmony of form. Olney was a classicist, yet he maintained a relaxed relationship with tradition. Aware of the folly of prescriptions for wine etiquette, menu planning, and food pairing, he warned that "one must not take all of this too seriously . . . it is great fun to make up rules and then disprove them, or attempt to." Beyond his carefully reasoned approach, and the trouble he took to conceive and prepare a meal, was a clear sight of the goal: Food was to be celebrated, raucously enjoyed.

As a writer, Olney forged a melodious, often delicious language that is intimately matched to the sensual language of cooking. His natural powers of description stemmed, I believe, from his own highly developed "tactile" sense, what he considered to be

> a sort of convergence of all the senses- the awareness through touching, and also through smelling, hearing, seeing, and tasting that something is 'just right'—to know by seeing the progression from the light, swelling foam of an initial boil to a flat surface punctuated by tiny bubbles, by hearing the same progression from a soft, cottony, slurring sound to a series of sharp, staccato explosions, by judging from the degree of syrupiness or the smooth, enveloping consistency on a wooden spoon when a reduction has arrived at the point, a few seconds before which it is too thin, a few seconds after which it will collapse into grease or burn; to know by pinching and judging the resilience of a lamb chop or a roast leg of lamb when to remove it from the heat; to recognize the perfect amber of a caramel the second before it turns burnt and bitter; to feel

> the right fresh-heavy-cream consistency of a crêpe batter and the point of light but consistent airiness in a mousseline forcemeat that, having absorbed a maximum of cream to be perfect, would risk collapsing through any further addition. . . .

This "convergence of the senses" remains the most important lesson I took from *The French Menu Cookbook*. As Olney emphasizes on nearly every page, exercising one's sensual powers is what the act of cooking really is. By extension, it is just this sort of attention on the part of the cook that lies behind the transforming pleasure of a fine meal, the very noticeable difference between one prepared by a rote recipe follower and a responsive cook. The sensual language of cooking is what I set about to learn and which I still work to refine today.

By Olney's own description, *The French Menu Cookbook* is a "gastronomic manifesto," a reflection of his life in the kitchen and at the table over the course of the twenty years he lived in France prior to its publication. In this sense it is a culmination. It is also highly personal. We are invited directly into Olney's life to learn of his culinary initiation in the kitchen of his Iowa home ("the rock on which my church was built"), and the inspiration he gained from reading and practicing Escoffier. We meet his colleagues and the chefs he admired. We venture into his home kitchen in Provence, where he worked, cooked, and received. It will soon be evident to the reader that this is not merely a cookbook, but rather a diary of how a uniquely gifted cook lived, thought, and sensed. This sets it apart from better known, if to my mind less important books of the period. Look to *Mastering the Art of French Cooking* by Child, Beck, and Bertholle (originally published nine years prior to *The French Menu Cookbook*), and you will find a book of recipes applied to occasions. For Olney, the occasion is the recipe for the meal, and the meal bears the mark of a place, a season, a tradition relived in a resonant, new moment around the table. Set in this broader context, Olney's recipes are removed from abstraction and find their proper habitat in the aesthetic experience of a meal.

I suspect that at its first publication, many found *The French Menu Cookbook* to be a difficult, offbeat book, one that perhaps asked too much of the reader. To be sure, Olney proposes no shortcuts, is demanding in his insistence on prime ingredients and is not interested in instructing Americans on the best way to resurrect canned peas if fresh peas are not available. He offers no apologies for his predilection for traditional foods that were, and still are, unappreciated by Americans—lambs' tripes, pigs' tails, and calves' ears and brains, among others—even in these enlightened times. Nevertheless, the reader is never stranded. Olney offers words of caution when the preparation of a menu might "represent a heavy expenditure that may . . . not justify the result, no matter how glorious." Most useful is his sensitivity to the position of the cook who, he understands, must often double as host. The workload of the menus is organized and distributed in such a way as to avoid endless or nerve-wracking last-minute preparations. Apart from its broad and foundation-building message, *The French Menu Cookbook* is so full of tips and concise practical advice that it should be made an indispensable part of any cook's education. I need only list a few examples to give the flavor:

ON ROASTING PEPPERS:

"A heat that is too intense will char the skins before the flesh becomes soft; one that is too gentle will dehydrate the flesh before the skins are loosened."

ON TIMING:

"It is far better to wait for a roast partridge than to risk making it wait."

ON THE FIRST STAGES OF BRAISING:

"The slightest fragment of onion that remains in the pan at this point will inevitably burn while the meat is coloring and leave a bitter taste in the sauce."

ON ADJUSTING THE TEMPERATURE OF THE STOCK POT:

"Even if you are on intimate terms with your stove, unless you are accustomed to this kind of preparation and know the precise intensity of flame necessary, this regulation will require 15 minutes to ½ hour of turning the fire slightly up or down and rechecking a few minutes later."

ON COMPATIBILITY:

"Serve the cèpes *toward the end of the* salmis *service. They marry very well indeed, but the subtlety of each risks being muted by the other's rich presence. One may, by serving in this way, appreciate them together and enjoy them apart."*

ON THE ESSENTIALS OF MENU PLANNING:

"The only thing to remember is that the palate should be kept fresh, teased, surprised, excited all through a meal. The moment there is danger of fatigue, it must be astonished, or soothed into greater anticipation, until the sublime moment of release when one moves away from the table to relax with coffee and an alcool."

For those who wish to simply read, imagine, or drool about food, *The French Menu Cookbook* is an exemplar of evocative, lyrical, and informative food writing. You may read with fascination of dishes of a bygone era, such as woodcock soufflé; calf's liver with truffled *cèpe* purée; marinated, rolled boar's belly hung in the chimney to smoke over smoldering olive wood; pike dumplings; and of "the thrush, whose flesh is as lovely as its song . . . roasted rare, unemptied but for the gizzard, which may be replaced by a juniper berry." Discover how to clean a live sea urchin, draw a crayfish, cool your wine, work a drum sieve; learn that the French distinguish three types of skimming of stocks and sauces; and salivate over scrambled eggs with truffles slowly stirred in a *bain-marie* and venison, spit-roasted over a fruitwood fire. What becomes clear in Olney's compelling descriptions of these dishes and techniques is that they are pertinently real, not merely part of a past mythology.

Although his influence will probably never be felt as strongly as it was in the '70s and '80s, those formative years of California's awakening to its culinary promise, we should be reminded that it was because of Olney's intense convictions that chefs everywhere now respect the seasons, plant their own gardens, shop at local farmer's markets, roast in the fireplace, make from scratch, flower their salads, and that by sensing while cooking, have discovered their art.

Paul Bertolli
February 2002

THE

ORIGINAL EDITION

The French Menu Cookbook

THE FOOD AND WINE OF FRANCE
—SEASON BY DELICIOUS SEASON—
IN BEAUTIFULLY COMPOSED MENUS
FOR AMERICAN DINING AND ENTERTAINING
BY AN AMERICAN LIVING IN PARIS AND PROVENCE

RICHARD OLNEY

Drawings by Gösta Viertel

For Georges Garin

CONTENTS

Preface 11
French Food and Menu Composition 17
French Wine 27
Kitchen Layout and Equipment 51
Shopping Sources 67
Basic Preparations 71

AUTUMN MENUS • 97

Two Formal Autumn Dinners

MENU I, 104: Crayfish Mousse, 107 Ravioli of Chicken Breasts, 111 Roast Leg of Venison with Poivrade Sauce, 113 Sweet Potato Purée, 118 Molded Coffee Custard, 118

MENU II, 120: Sorrel Soup, 122 Fritto Misto, 124 Pheasant Salmis, 126 Sautéed Cèpes à la Bordelaise, 129 Orange Jelly, 130

Two Informal Autumn Dinners

MENU I, 132: Baked Trout Stuffed with Sorrel, 134 Sautéed Veal Kidneys with Mushrooms, 135 Lamb's Lettuce and Beet Salad, 137 Charlotte with Crêpes, Sabayon Sauce, 137

MENU II, 140: Pike Quenelles à la Lyonnaise, 142 Veal Cutlets à la Tapenade, 144 Stewed Tomatoes, 146 Artichoke Purée, 146 Apple Mousse with Peaches, 147

A Festive Autumn Meal for Two

MENU, 150: Cucumber Salad in Cream Sauce, 152 Baked Lobster Garin, 153 Braised and Roast Partridge with Cabbage, 155 Fresh Figs with Raspberry Cream, 158

Four Simple Autumn Menus

MENU I, 159: Grilled Pepper Salad, 160 Lamb Stew with Artichoke Hearts, 161 Pears in Red Wine, 164

MENU II, 165: Composed Salad, 166 Boiled Pigs' Tails and Ears with Vegetables, 167 Périgord Pudding, 170

MENU III, 172: Fennel à la Grecque, 173 French Moussaka, Watercress, 174 Orange Cream, 176

MENU IV, 177: Garlic Soup, 178 Grilled Lambs' Hearts and Baby Zucchini, 179 French Pancake Jelly Rolls, 180

WINTER MENUS • 183

A Note on Truffles, 188

Two Elegant Winter Suppers

MENU I, 190: Caviar, 192 Scrambled Eggs with Fresh Truffles, 192 Lobsters à la Nage, 195 Pineapple and Frangipane Fritters, 197

MENU II, 200: Foie Gras, 202 Fresh Egg Noodles with Truffles, 203 Striped Bavarian Cream, 205

An Elaborate Formal Dinner Party

MENU, 208: Cream of Artichoke Soup with Hazelnuts, 210 Grilled Fish with Sea Urchin Purée, 212 Timbale of Sweetbreads and Macaroni, 214 Rum Sherbet, 218 Roast Guinea Fowl with Bacon, 218 Chestnut Purée with Celery, 221 Blanc-manger, 222

Two Informal Winter Dinners

MENU I, 224: Gratin of Stuffed Crêpes, 226 Stuffed Calves' Ears, Béarnaise Sauce, 227 Molded Tapioca Pudding, Apricot Sauce, 232

MENU II, 234: Terrine of Sole Fillets, 236 Beef Stew à la Bourguignonne, 238 Floating Island, 242

Three Simple Winter Menus

MENU I, 245: Celeriac in Mustard Sauce, 246 Cassoulet, 247

MENU II, 252: Soufflées à la Suissesse, 254 Skewered Lambs' Kidneys, 255 Saffron Rice with Tomatoes, 257 Crêpes à la Normande, 258

MENU III, 259: Poached Eggs à la Bourguignonne, 260 Beef Tripe à la Lyonnaise, 262 Composed Salad, 263 Pineapple Ice, 264

SPRING MENUS • 267

Two Formal Spring Dinners

MENU I, 272: Shellfish Platter, 274 Turban of Sole Fillets with Salmon, Sorrel Sauce, 275 Roast Saddle of Lamb with Herbs, 279 Green Bean Purée, 282 Artichoke Bottoms with Mushroom Purée, 283 Frozen Strawberry Mousse with Raspberry Purée, 284

MENU II, 286: Crayfish Salad with Fresh Dill, 288 Spring Stew, 291 Poached Chicken Mousseline, 293 Crusts with Fresh Morels, 298 Pineapple Surprise, 300

Two Informal Spring Dinners

MENU I, 302: Crudités, 305 Shrimp Quiche, 305 Coq au Vin, 308 Flamri with Raspberry Sauce, 312

MENU II, 314: Marinated Sardine Fillets, 316 Grilled Steak, Marchand de Vin, 316 Gratin of Potatoes, 319 Apple Tart, 320

Four Simple Spring Menus

MENU I, 321: Pot-au-Feu, 322 (also Salad, Cheese and Fruit)

MENU II, 327: Garden Peas à la Française, 328 Blanquette of Veal, 329 Molded Chocolate Loaf with Whipped Cream, 331

MENU III, 333: Terrine of Poultry Livers, 334 Deep-fried Beef Tripe, Rémoulade Sauce, 336 Dandelion and Salt Pork Salad, 339 Strawberries in Beaujolais, 340

MENU IV, 341: Warm Asparagus Vinaigrette, 342 Calves' Brains in Red Wine, 343 Cauliflower Loaf, 345 Molded Apple Pudding, 347

SUMMER MENUS • 349

Two Elegant Summer Dinners

MENU I, 354: Artichoke Bottoms with Two Mousses, 357 Sole Fillets with Fines Herbes, 361 Stewed Cucumbers, 365 Spitted Roast Leg of Lamb, 365 Buttered Green Beans, 368 Peach Melba, 369

MENU II, 372: Calves' Brains in Cream Sauce, 375 Squid à l'Américaine, 377 Jellied Poached Chicken, 379 Apricot Fritters, 384

A Semi-formal Summer Dinner

MENU, 386: Braised Stuffed Artichoke Bottoms, 388 Grilled Lambs' Kidneys with Herb Butter, 390 Potato Straw Cake, 392 Peaches in Red Wine, 394

Four Simple Summer Luncheons à la Provençale

Provençal Cooking, 395

MENU I, 397: Provençal Fish Stew, 398 Cervelle de Canut, 403

MENU II, 405: Fresh Sardines in Vine Leaves, 406 Lambs' Tripes à la Marseillaise, 407 Strawberries in Orange Juice, 410

MENU III, 411: Warm Salad of Small Green Beans, 412 Daube à la Provençale, 413 Macaroni in Braising Liquid, 416 (also Cheese and Fruit)

MENU IV, 417: Cold Ratatouille, 418 Blanquette of Beef Tripe with Basil, 420 Steamed Potatoes, 422 Cherries and Fresh Almonds, 422

General Index 427

Recipe Index 439

PREFACE

Until I came to France in 1951, my knowledge of French cooking was mainly academic. I had practiced with a passion what could be gleaned from books—Escoffier, in particular. But the rock on which my church was built was the provincial kitchen of my home in Iowa—not too bad a background, inasmuch as I grew up at a time when eggs were still fresh, Jersey milk was unpasteurized and half cream, chickens were from the back yard, packaged cake mixes and frozen foods were unknown, and garden fruits and vegetables were eaten in their proper seasons. Fortunately for me, my mother, who had eight children to raise and little enthusiasm for cooking, was delighted by my willingness to experiment in the kitchen. Pot roasts, sage-and-onion dressing, and angel-food cakes were more in order at that time than the sort of preparations that occupy me now. But even in those early days I learned to rely on Escoffier for inspiration.

My life in France has been more or less equally divided between Clamart, a Parisian suburb, and Solliès-Toucas, a village in the south of France.

In 1953, Clamart was still a provincial town at the edge of a forest to which a handful of Parisians brought their picnic lunches of a summer Sunday. The bordering cafés recalled, in every detail, the *guinguettes* of impressionist paintings with their cheerful patrons enjoying meals at outdoor tables. The house in which I then let an apartment was surrounded by an unkempt garden and hidden from the street and from neighbors by high stone walls. Although in an advanced state of decay, it was a handsome piece of architecture and, like most nineteenth-century French houses, its cellar was well designed to receive wines, which I began promptly to collect. (After a bit of experimentation, I settled on a formula of bottling three kegs of wine annually—usually a Pouilly-Fumé, a Beaujolais-Villages, and a first-growth Beaujolais—for daily use, and supplementing these by occasional cases of fine Bordeaux and Burgundies.)

In 1961, in love with the light, the landscape, and the odors of Provence, I bought an abandoned property near Solliès-Toucas. The house, perched halfway up a hillside, its only access from below a somewhat precarious footpath (four men and a dolly spent six hours delivering the cookstove while I spent the day running back and forth with bottles of white wine to keep up their spirits), was a total ruin. Stretching above, the several acres of stone-walled terraces planted to olive trees, once meticulously cared for, are grown wild to all those herbs—rosemary, wild thyme and savory, oregano, fennel, lavender, and mint—whose names are poetry and whose mingled perfumes scent the air of Provençal kitchens and hillsides alike.

The definitive move south followed the construction, with the help of my brothers, James and Byron, during the summer of 1964, of the great fireplace that dominates my kitchen and, in part, the pattern of my daily life.

In 1961, Georges Garin, having sold the Hôtel de la Croix Blanche in Nuits-Saint-Georges and having abandoned the kitchens of the Château du Clos Vougeot, opened his own restaurant, Chez Garin, in Paris. A great chef, he surpasses in his culinary knowledge anyone I have ever known, and his appetite and passion for eating are equaled only by my own. My enthusiasm for his cooking and our common passion for discussing anything culinary have cemented a friendship, generously truffled, over the years, by divine and often fantastic meals, in Paris Chez Garin, in Clamart, and in Solliès-Toucas.

Garin's first visit to Clamart marked the only time that I have ever been terrified by the notion of preparing a meal. To avoid the possibility of errors, I opted for simple preparations and fine wines:

A COLD DISH—*Artichoke Bottoms with Two Mousses*
Château Bouscaut blanc, 1959

A RAPID SAUTE—*Ortolans*
Château Grand-Mayne, 1955

SALAD

CHEESES
Château Ducru-Beaucaillou, 1947

Tepid Apple Charlotte
Château d'Yquem, 1950

The meal was a success.

Madeleine Decure (who is, alas, no longer) shared with Garin the distinction of having the other most intelligent and analytic palate I have known. She was one of the two founders, in 1947, of the monthly gastronomic review *Cuisine et Vins de France*. The other was Curnonsky (born Maurice Sailland in Anjou), the remarkable personality who was acclaimed *Prince élu des Gastronomes* by a jury of professional chefs and gastronomic journalists. His eightieth birthday was celebrated by a now famous meal organized by his eighty preferred Paris restaurants, each of which then reserved with a bronze plaque his preferred table in the restaurant—in perpetuity!

I met Madeleine Decure in 1961 (but not Curnonsky, regrettably; he had died five years earlier) at the same time that I met Odette Kahn, then associate director of the magazine, and the gastronomic journalists Michel Lemonnier and Simon Arbellot. Our meals together, exchanged and re-exchanged, individually and as a group, were punctuated by wine-tasting excursions to all corners of France.

Garin, tied to his kitchens, established an annual tradition of inviting us as a group to dinners, at the composition of whose menus I delightedly assisted. Among the preparations—all memorable—were: partridge consommé garnished with tiny partridge mousseline *quenelles*, whole braised calf's liver with a truffled *cèpe* purée, fresh salmon braised in champagne, gratin of crayfish tails, fresh *foie gras*, roast saddle of venison, and that rarity, a perfect *coq au vin*, not to mention a repertory of astonishing soufflés—lobster, pike, woodcock, fresh asparagus, wild strawberry, etc.

The last seriously organized meal that I served in Clamart was in the autumn of 1964. The champagne, a Clos des Goisses, dated from nine years earlier. Madeleine and Odette had asked me to present a menu as a regular monthly feature in *Cuisine et Vins de France*, the recipes for each preparation to be explained in simple and nonprofessional language. The first of my menus to be published in the magazine was the one I served that evening:

Raw Baby Artichokes, Poivrade

Pike Mousseline, Turban of Sole and Salmon Fillets,
Nantua Sauce (garnished with a sauté of truffles and crayfish tails and crayfish shells stuffed with pike mousseline)
Mercurey blanc, 1962

Boned Stuffed Chicken, Glazed in Its Jelly
Pernand-Vergelesses, 1960

Composed Salad

Cheeses
Clos de la Roche, 1955

Pineapple Frangipane Fritters
Château Rieussec, 1947

My menu series in *Cuisine et Vins de France* was entitled (to my dismay) *Un Américain (gourmand) à Paris*. The rubric continues.

In the south, my patterns are different from those of Clamart. Friends are not invited to dinner—they come for a few days or a few weeks. Menus tend to be simpler. Living mostly out of doors for well over half the year, one becomes acutely aware of the swift seasonal cycle, and the table follows suit. The shortest days of the year—the gloom of winter and a dormant garden—are soon brightened by banks of yellow mimosa, and narcissus perfumes the air. Truffles turn blackest and richest from this moment, olives are ripe, and the glorious thick, murky, newly pressed olive oil, unsettled and unfiltered, appears. The first simple country wines of the year, slightly green, a tiny edge of fermentation remaining to tickle the tongue, fresh and fruity, are the perfect accompaniment to rough and robust nourishing winter dishes. In no more than a few weeks the almond trees are already in blossom, the first young fava, or broad beans, too delicate to be eaten other than raw, appear on the market, rapidly followed by violet artichokes, sweet white onions and tiny peas. By the end of March the hillsides are scattered with the tender shoots of wild asparagus, the exquisite morel will soon make its brief appearance, wild thyme is in flower, green beans, cherries, strawberries, peaches, follow in rapid succession, the rich, sweet tomato crowns the summer season, oregano must be gathered, and, with tree-ripe figs, wild mushrooms, game birds, green olives, and the reappearance of young artichokes and sea urchins, the plunge is taken into autumn and the shortest days are again in sight. Fish is fresh the year round, and often can be bought alive; snails are gathered, starved, and sacrificed to the *courtbouillon*, fresh goats'-milk and sheeps'-milk cheeses enrich the cheese platter, and the olives, prepared without chemicals each autumn, garnish the luncheon hors d'oeuvre.

The pages of this book are a loyal reflection of my life in the kitchen and at table over the last twenty years. The seasonal form into which it has been cast emphasizes my intense conviction that, despite midwinter tomatoes, strawberries, asparagus and green beans, and the plethora of "fresh" frozen products on the market, one can only eat marvelously by respecting the seasons; each is sufficiently rich to afford a perfect table the year round, and the excitement of eating a freshly picked fruit or vegetable at the peak of its seasonal richness is forever deadened by the dull and listless year-round absorption of its shadow.

No recipes are given which involve products unavailable in America. Certain American products for which I have a particular affection and which may advantageously be incorporated into French menus (sweet corn, avocados, wild rice, for instance) are not treated, simply because, although the book is essentially a personal gastronomic manifesto, I have preferred that it not stray from traditional French cooking. Some favorite and typically French preparations have been eliminated, victims of the menu formula—for they are nearly all first courses and the presentation of each would have necessitated an accompanying menu, which space did not permit.

Classical appellations have not been tampered with (it would be a pity to deprive Melba of her peaches and ice cream), but, when posciful, I have stuck to simple, descriptive titles and have avoided the fanciful.

Emphasis throughout the book has been placed on the importance of "tactile" sense, which I consider to be a sort of convergence of all the senses—the awareness through touching, and also through smelling, hearing, seeing, and tasting that something is "just right"—to know by seeing the progression from the light, swelling foam of an initial boil to a flat surface punctuated by tiny bubbles, by hearing the same progression from a soft, cottony, slurring sound to a series of sharp, staccato explosions, by judging from the degree of syrupiness or the smooth, enveloping consistency on a wooden spoon when a reduction has arrived at the point, a few seconds before which it is too thin, a few seconds after which it will collapse into grease or burn; to know by pinching and judging the resilience of a lamb chop or a roast leg of lamb when to remove it from the heat; to recognize the perfect amber of a caramel the second before it turns burnt and bitter; to feel the right fresh-heavy-cream consistency of a crêpe batter and the point of light but consistent airiness in a mousseline forcemeat that, having absorbed a maximum of cream to be perfect, would risk collapsing through any further addition. . . .

Happily, cooking of quality is, in addition to everything else, an expression of the personality of the cook, and a recipe followed to the letter by two individuals, in each of whom may be a finely developed tactile sense, will produce, thanks to individual sensibilities, two different dishes, both of which may be excellent.

French Food and Menu Composition

Good and honest cooking and good and honest French cooking are the same thing. Details differ, although climate is probably a greater factor than nationality (the molasses in a New England winter bean-pot seems as bizarre to a French palate as do the tropical excesses of red-hot pepper to French and American alike). Certainly there are national dishes, just as there are regional dishes—sage-and-onion stuffing and apple pie will remain forever English and American (although there is nothing unique about the former except for the choice of herb, and the latter is nothing but a *tarte aux pommes* with a lid), as will *beurre blanc* remain French—but it is comforting to realize that the principles of good cooking do not change as one crosses frontiers or oceans, and that the success of a preparation depends on nothing more than a knowledge of those principles plus personal sensibility.

A meat stew, for instance, is a preparation of pieces of meat seared in fat, enough flour added to bind the sauce, one or several aromatic elements, and liquid, all gently cooked until done. It may, in France, depending on the meat, the fat, the liquid, the aromatic elements, and finally—which has nothing at all to do with its preparation—on specific garnishing elements, assume anyone of dozens of names. Color some onions in lard, remove them and fry floured pieces of chuck in their place, return the onions and moisten with water—in short, reduce each element to its simplest (and most economical) possible version, and you have old-fashioned American beef stew (probably

English, Dutch, German and Swedish, also). The steps in its preparation are identical to those for *boeuf bourguignon*, *carbonade*, *sauté de veau Marengo* or *coq au vin*. American scalloped potatoes have much in common with *gratin dauphinois*, creamed eggs with *oeufs à la tripe*, pot roast is really *boeuf à la mode*. And, of course, corned beef and cabbage, boiled dinners, and the endless soups that our grandmothers prepared are to be found in the French cuisine as *potées and garbures*.

A menu composed of preparations that are not in themselves French may remain totally French in spirit, for it is the degree to which it is based on a sensuous and aesthetic concept that differentiates a French meal from all others. It may be served under the simplest and most intimate of circumstances, but its formal aspect is respected and its composition—the interrelationships and the progression of courses and wines—is of the greatest importance.

There exists a bastard cuisine that is too often assumed to be real French cooking. It patterns itself superficially on the classical *grande cuisine*, but, leaning heavily on the effects of spectacular presentation, it ignores the essential sobriety and integrity of the classic cuisine which becomes its victim. It is not *grande cuisine* but "Grand Palace"—or international hotel cooking. It has, however, many enthusiasts. Perhaps, having never encountered the genuine, they are nonetheless impressed by the presentation and complication of the false. Tragically, it is responsible for the attitude of those who, confusing Grand Palace with *grande cuisine*, innocently become detractors of the latter.

Grand Palace, typically, fails to respect the qualities basic to a product or a preparation. All dishes, for example, are tainted by the same basic sauce (generally a false *espagnole* made up of bones, carcasses and leftovers, overly thickened with flour or cornstarch, and improperly reduced). Crêpes are presented with flames reaching to the ceiling and served floating pathetically in dark pools of half-burned, indifferent brandy. Calves' kidneys are brought, half-cooked, to table and toughened in a blaze of that same alcohol. And roasts (which in order to be perfect must be subjected to a continued cooking process, precisely controlled) are half-cooked, cooled, rolled in pastry and rebaked.

It is interesting—and instructive—to note that in Escoffier's *Guide Culinaire*, out of forty-five recipes for roast fillet of beef, not one is served in pastry. The only lamb recipe suffering this treatment is a leg of baby lamb. Because the flesh of baby animals, cooked rare, is indigestible and must be well done, baby lamb is, therefore, not treated in the same manner as a roast of "grass" (older) lamb, mutton, or beef, which should be kept rose or rare throughout, at the same time that it is heated through). Out of fifteen recipes for calves' kidneys and thirteen for lambs' kidneys, not one is "flamed." (One, foreign in origin, requires the addition of a bit of juniper-flavored alcohol which is flamed to rid it of its alcohol *before being added to the preparation.*) Again, none of Escoffier's recipes for crêpes are flamed, including crêpes Suzette—whose distinguishing characteristic, after all, is the presence, not of flames, but of tangerine juice. (In the English edition, which has been edited and "arranged by other hands" for another public, crêpes Suzette do receive the flaming treatment.)

Classical French cooking—that which, from the beginning (not so long ago), made France's reputation abroad—is naturally eclectic. It was, and is, created by men—professional chefs. It is refined and, in execution, often involved. In the hands of a good, honest chef it can be very good indeed; in the hands of a great chef, it can be sublime.

The entire concept—of the cooking itself, and of a menu, as we know it today—was formed by Carême (1784–1833), genius, egomaniac and scholar. His life seems like a fantastic parody of the success story. Born into a poor family of twenty-five children, he was, as a child, put into the streets with nothing but his father's blessing and told to seek his fortune. He never again saw his family. *Aide de cuisine* at fifteen, head pastry chef for Paris's leading pastry caterer at seventeen, he spent the rest of his life in the service of "the great." He was chef to Talleyrand, to England's Prince Regent, to Czar Alexander I, to the Rothschilds, and during this time he produced the body of technical literature, brilliantly illustrated by himself, which became the basis of all professional training of chefs throughout the nineteenth century. Until Carême, all dishes were placed on the table at the same time; a menu was nothing but a collection of unrelated dishes, more or less elegantly or fantastically dressed, the most sumptuous being placed close to the guests of highest rank. Carême borrowed from the Russians the practice of serving courses separately, so that each, finding its place in a logical sequence, could at the same time be served at its correct temperature.

The concept of a great meal in France has been tremendously altered since the nineteenth century, when menus sometimes counted twenty or thirty courses and a dozen wines. Around the turn of this century a refining and a simplifying force worked hand in hand. Escoffier was no doubt influential, and his great manual, *Le Guide Culinaire*, first published in 1902, remains the professional's standard reference book today. Later, simplification took another leap (though this time, the refining element was less in evidence) when people slowly pulled themselves together again after World War II, not to take up life where it had been left off in 1939, but to plunge into a nervous, active world that occasionally bordered on hysteria. After the war the elaborate leisurely luncheon disappeared, and a simple dinner became the important meal of the day. Today, a meal organized at a great Paris restaurant by the Club des Cent or the Académie des Gastronomes may begin with an hors d'oeuvre or directly with a fish course, followed by meat, cheese and dessert, and accompanied by three wines. Thirty years ago this would have been unthinkable.

In contrast to *grande cuisine* are the traditions in regional cooking—as various as the provinces are numerous, but all related in character in the sense that each is the direct outgrowth of the combined wealth or poverty and the specialties of the immediate countryside and the limitations of the kitchens. It is essentially peasant cooking, elaborated by generations of women who were never far from the kitchen and whose imaginations were forced into flower through necessity and limited means.

Nearly all French country cooking traditions are based on the unique use of the fireplace. Quantities of utensils were designed to be embedded in hot ashes, recipes *en papillote* were originally conceived to be cooked under hot ashes, and those preparations which, one reads, should cook very slowly and regularly over a period of from eight to ten hours are dishes which at one time were simply embedded in hot ashes in the fireplace the night before and forgotten until it was time to serve them (more often than not, the lid of the utensil was hermetically sealed with a strip of flour-and-water paste). As the fire never went out from autumn until spring, a bed of coals was always ready if there were meats or vegetables to be grilled, and it was merely a question of adding a couple of logs to the fire to produce the heat necessary to turn a roast on a spit before the flames. Rapid gratins and glazes were produced by heating a shovel in the hot coals and then holding it directly over the surface of the dish for a few moments (the ancestor of the "salamander"). *Crème brulée*, in certain provinces, is still known as *crème à la pelle*–shovel custard. Slow gratins were made in special dishes designed to be placed on tripods or grills over the coals, their high-sided lids, concave at the top, to be filled with hot coals.

The only ovens were bread ovens, built behind great fireplaces, the door to the oven opening from the back wall of the fireplace. Enormous, igloo-shaped, lined entirely with refractory bricks, they were heated by beds of coals, constantly renewed inside the ovens over a period of several hours. When the bricks were sufficiently heated, the ovens were then swept clean; they retained sufficient heat for many hours of baking. One generally profited from a bread-baking day to prepare other dishes. Each farm had its own oven, but many small villages had a community oven that was heated once a week, to which the entire village brought their risen bread dough and other preparations to be baked.

Today regional recipes have, in large part, passed into the hands of professional cooks, for the provincial housewife, like her American counterpart, now cooks with gas, and her aspirations on the whole separate her from the kitchen. Those few "backward" areas that still cling to old traditions—parts of Auvergne and Brittany, for instance—have, unhappily, never been rich in gastronomic tradition.

The term *cuisine bourgeoise* nowadays is used to describe a certain kind of preparation. As a rigidly defined element of a way of life it no longer exists as a category apart. It is richer than regional cooking in the sense that it uses more expensive products, yet it is also less imaginative. It is based on stock; hence the kitchens were always full of boiled meats, and it was accepted tradition, even for elegant receptions, to place an enormous platter of boiled meats on the table at the same time as the soup and leave it throughout the entire service. (In restaurants it was the kitchen help who were obliged to nourish themselves daily on boiled meats.) Braised dishes like *boeuf à la mode* are typical. "Vulgar" ingredients such as variety meats were eschewed.

Veal liver and sweetbreads were, however, considered elegant, and, curiously, a stew of calves' eyes was acceptable. It is, like regional cooking, also a "woman's cooking" (though it was not the mistress of the house but women cooks who executed it), and the elaborations were to some extent influenced by *la grande cuisine.*

MENU COMPOSITION

A perfect meal can be many things—a plate of lentils with a boiled sausage, a green salad, a piece of cheese and a bottle of cool young Beaujolais—or nothing but a composed salad and any light, young wine.

A dinner that begins with a soup and runs through a fish course, an entrée, a sherbet, a roast, salad, cheese and dessert, and that may be accompanied by from three to six wines, presents a special problem of orchestration. The desired result is often difficult to achieve. Each course must provide a happy contrast to the one preceding it; at the same time, the movement through the various courses should be an ascending one from light, delicate and more complex flavors through progressively richer, more full-bodied and simpler flavors. The wines, too, should be flattered by—and should flatter—each accompanying course while relating to each other, as well in a similar kind of progression.

A semiliquid sherbet, more tart than sweet, usually with a champagne base, refreshes the palate halfway through this progression, and a green salad serves the same purpose before relaxing into the cheese course, which will be accompanied by the fullest-bodied of the red wines—and finally the dessert, neither heavy nor cloying and oversweet, but light and delicate, slightly less sweet than the intricate and voluptuous Sauternes that may accompany it.

This is obviously not the only way to conceive a menu. Essentially the only thing to remember is that the palate should be kept fresh, teased, surprised, excited all through a meal. The moment there is danger of fatigue, it must be astonished, or soothed into greater anticipation, until the sublime moment of release when one moves away from the table to relax with coffee and an *alcool.*

In the past it was *de rigueur* to begin a luncheon with hors d'oeuvre and a dinner with soup. Today the evening meal of a simple peasant or working-class family habitually consists of soup, with a piece of cheese often the only other element—and a very elegant dinner party, conceived in terms of the old precepts, always begins with a soup. Between these two poles lies most of French eating, and in this realm few rules are left. This may, in a sense, be a liberating force although with it come such misfortunes as the sandwich eaten standing up and cigarettes smoked throughout the meal. But despite the precepts of tradition there should be no fast rules. A meal need not always include a salad or cheeses (although Brillat-Savarin's famous and foolish maxim, "A meal without cheese is like a beautiful woman who is missing one eye," reminds us of the contrary)—or fish or a roast. Certain white wines are splendid with certain cheeses. In that part of the Loire Valley that produces Sancerre and Pouilly-Fumé, the hard, nutty-flavored little goat cheeses known as *crottins de Chavignol* are always accompanied by the dry, slightly metallic white wines of the region. In Alsace, Traminer is drunk with Münster cheese, and the Sauternais drink Château d'Yquem with Roquefort—and with *foie gras!*

In organizing a menu, one must consider its presentation—it is nearly as important to flatter the eye as the palate. *Don't* serve tomato sauces in red plates or spinach on a green platter. *Never* serve a roast's garnish on the same platter—a good roast is sufficiently handsome to be presented alone, and, should it slip while being carved, artichoke bottoms and stuffed mushrooms should not be there to fly in all directions. *Don't* sprinkle large handfuls of parsley indiscriminately over everything. *Don't* follow one white-colored sauce by another, or a gratin of fish by a gratin of meat, even though the underlying sauces may be very different in character. Rustic preparations are generally best, and look best, served in the earthenware pots they are cooked in. Elegant preparations should be elegantly presented—on condition that the quality in no way suffers as a result.

A menu must be conceived also in terms of one's time and work. Never try to serve a meal in which every course requires endless last-minute preparations. When a dish requires the addition of a number of ingredients at different times, combine in advance all those elements that are to be added at the same time. In this way you have only one article to think of rather than five or six, a couple of which might otherwise be forgotten in last-minute confusion. Many dishes are at least as good reheated—prepare these the preceding day. Others can be cooked ahead of time except for finishing the sauce. Think everything out ahead of time. When preparing something that is new to you, don't read over the instructions once; memorize them in advance before attacking.

Most important, of course, is the organization of a menu in terms of what may be called a "gastronomic aesthetic." Whether a meal begins with an hors d'oeuvre or a soup (except for the *potées* or *garbures* that are entire meals in themselves), this course must be conceived to heighten—not quench—the appetite. It should be light of body and not overabundant. From that point on, the movement should be from fish or other white delicacies, such as brains or sweetbreads, into meats, and from light meats into dark meats, from light butter or cream sauces into rich dark sauces drawn from stocks and red wines. By this I do not mean to suggest that a dark meat may not be prepared in cream or a fish in red wine, but I do think that it would be a mistake to include these two preparations in the same menu. In the last century it was not unusual to serve fish after meats and chicken after game. To most people today this would seem outlandish.

Repetition should be avoided in a menu. The French claim that the truffle alone may be respectably allowed to appear in more than one dish at the same meal. Though that seems like nonsense, if there are mushrooms in the fish sauce, don't garnish the meat with mushrooms; if one of the main dishes is rich in cream, don't serve a dessert based on whipped cream; nor a custard sauce with the dessert if another sauce is thickened with egg yolks. Don't serve rice with the fish and potatoes with the meat, or watercress with the roast and a green salad after. Don't serve a gratin based on Swiss cheese and include the same cheese on the cheese platter.

The juxtaposition of cold and hot, crisp and creamy, rough and smooth, sauced and dry, should be considered. Rare venison accompanied by *poivrade* sauce, which requires hours, if not days, of preparation, is sublime.

On the whole, it seems to me best for a simple meal to contain only one sauce, and for a more complex menu to be limited to two, which should be very different in character, or perhaps three if one includes a sauced dessert.

The cheese course I think of largely as an excuse (and a good one) to drink another wine. In France, if one serves a single cheese, it is invariably a Camembert. I prefer to serve a cheese platter that may include a fresh goat-type cheese, a Swiss Gruyère, a blue, and a soft-ripened variety. One's guests are happier with a choice.

About desserts, one should remember that heavy desserts should only follow the simplest of meals. Heavy desserts are a tradition only in those countries where a single main dish is also habitual. Something light and playful in spirit is best. Lots of air, perhaps in the form of a soufflé, or a mousse, is usually appreciated. If you want to serve a dessert wine, avoid chocolate at all cost. Ice creams and ices kill wines also (one of the more surprising habits in France is that of drinking *brut* champagne with desserts—often ice cream). With simple meals, many people are happy with a piece of fresh fruit for dessert.

French Wine

Wines are of two sorts. The one whose consumption is the greatest—that known as *gros rouge* in France (its white equivalent is often called *pousse au crime*), the American counterpart of which would be those gallon jugs of cheap red wine—is a product essentially of the laboratory: a knowledgeable mixture of a number of inferior wines, more or less high in alcohol content. It has been subjected to violent clarification processes (known as "defecatory"), often involving the injection of horse's blood into the wine. This is less shocking than it seems, for the blood, high in albumin content, acts merely as a precipitant for the impurities contained in suspension in all young wines. (Most fine wines are clarified also—but by the addition of the gentle egg white.) It has been "stabilized" by heating and by the addition of bacteria-killing chemicals. It is not a living thing.

The other wine lives and grows, and although in recent years technicians and winegrowers have come to understand a great deal more about the life of a wine and the different factors responsible for its development, it retains its mysterious autonomy, and even those old men who have nursed the vines and the wines of their fathers since childhood are constantly surprised by turns taken in a wine's development, whether it be over a period of months as the new wine is refining in kegs or in the course of its life span in bottles. Although, in the large picture, a single wine develops along the same lines from one bottle to another, it rarely happens that two bottles of a very old wine—even though they be from the same keg, bottled at the same time, and laid side by side in the same cellar—present identically the same characteristics when opened one after the other.

The wine one drinks from one's glass depends on a vast number of things that make it precisely what it is at that moment. The basic personality of a wine depends, for one thing, on the grape variety; certain varieties seem to be meant for the climate and soil of certain regions–their qualities are either lost or transformed when they are transplanted elsewhere. The age of the vines is also significant. They must be eight to ten years of age before producing a wine of maximum quality (grapes from younger vines are often harvested separately to make a lesser wine) and are usually replaced at the age of seventy or eighty years). Important, too, are the exposure (hillsides or inclines exposed to the south and east being considered the best), the care and pruning of the vines, the weather of the particular year, the care and rapidity with which the grapes are harvested and the weather at that time, the method of vinification and the cleanliness of the vessels in which it takes place (vinification is that part of a wine's preparation related to the fermentation processes and succeeding purifications). That personality may or may not be developed to its fullest extent, depending on the age of the wine, the care it has received, the temperature at which it is served, the amount of time it has been allowed to breathe and expand between the opening of the bottle and the drinking of the wine, the shape of the glass in which it is drunk, the preparation it accompanies, the condition of one's palate, and so on.

Not only is vinification an extremely complex process, but, methods vary from one region to another, and the following discussion must, necessarily, be very general in nature.

RED WINE

All the grape varieties used for making fine red wines are whitefleshed and give a transparent juice. The coloring matter comes from the skins. (Certain grape varieties known as *teinturiers* are red-fleshed and are used to strengthen the color of inferior wines.) The grapes, once picked, are usually passed through a machine that crushes them at the same time that it separates them from the stems. In the past, the stems were left and the grapes were crushed by treading them with one's bare feet. This is still done on certain small properties, and if economically practicable would still, no doubt, be the best method, for in this way the seeds do not risk being crushed and lending their bitterness to the wine. The removal of the stems is useful in producing wines that are more supple (the tannin contained in the stems does not go into it), and slightly higher in alcoholic content and color, since the water from the stems is eliminated. The crushed grapes are then put into enormous vats, which may be either open or closed; these are traditionally wooden, but today very often of glass-lined cement or stainless steel, which are much easier to clean and maintain. In these vats the juice and the pulp ferment together, the color is transferred to the juice because of the molecular transformation in the pulp, and the sugar is transformed into alcohol. In a normal year—neither too hot nor too cold—the fermentation begins easily and the temperature in the vats does not rise too high (if it goes beyond approximately 95° F., the bacteria are paralyzed and the fermentation is arrested before all the sugar has been transformed into alcohol). In cold years it is often necessary to heat a certain quantity of crushed grapes (*pied de cuve*), which, when in full fermentation, is then added to the vat in order to launch the bacteria rendered sluggish by the cold. In hot years the fermentation is often too active. The must (grape juice) is aerated and special cooling apparatuses installed in the vats are put into operation to prevent the temperature from rising beyond 85° F. (In the past, all that could be done was to throw in a few blocks of ice—far from the ideal solution.) Normally, the alcoholic fermentation is terminated after five or six days, the wine is left to cool in the vat, then drawn off and put into barrels. In the earlier part of this century, it was standard practice to leave the wine and pulp together in the vat for as long as three weeks to a month, producing a wine richer in tannin. Today, the average length of time is more likely to be from five to ten days. The pulp remaining in the vat is then pressed and the resulting liquid (*vin de presse*) is, in most instances, mixed with the wine that has been drawn off, but sometimes it is kept apart to make an inferior wine. Certain great wines may gain by not receiving the addition of the pressed wine, but most wines depend on this addition to give them more body. Red wines remain in kegs for from six months (Beaujolais, for instance) to three years (certain of the great Bordeaux), one and one-half or two years representing the average. During this period the kegs must be regularly refilled to compensate for evaporation and protect the wine from contact with air, the wine must be regularly drawn from one keg to another (*soutirage*) to separate the clear wine from the deposits at the bottom of the keg, and most wines are clarified just before the last *soutirage* or two by the addition of egg white or another albuminous substance.

A secondary fermentation—once thought to have been the tail end of the alcoholic fermentation, thrust back into action by the presence in the air of the pollen from the grape flowers in the spring following the harvest—has in recent years been identified as a completely separate process, which, however, rarely takes place until the alcoholic fermentation is finished, and because of the cold winter months, without the interference of the technician, waits until spring to go into action. It is known as the "malolactic" fermentation and produces a deacidification essential to the quality of the wine. Nowadays, vinification techniques often permit the rapid termination of the malolactic fermentation immediately after the alcoholic fermentation (by drawing the still warm wine from the vat directly into another vat and keeping the vinification cellar—*chais*—heated, for instance).

WHITE WINE

The white grapes, used in making white wines, are pressed immediately after having been picked, and the unfermented juice is put directly into kegs where the fermentation takes place—much more slowly and over a longer period than with red wines because of the smaller size of the kegs. Many experiments have been made with rapid fermentation of the juice in large vats, but the quality of the wine always suffers; however, this is the way in which cheaper white wines are made. White wines, with a few exceptions (such as the great Sauternes, for instance, and Château-Chalon, which is discussed further on), never remain in kegs more than a year and a half, and, more often than not, are put into bottles after six months. They receive the same kind of care in kegs as the reds, and, being more susceptible to disease, are treated with sulphur, often, unfortunately, to excess.

ROSE WINE

Rosé wines are made from red grapes or a combination of red and white and are vinified like white wines. A few start out their career in a vat like the red wines, which lends them a deeper color, but then are pressed after a few hours and run off into barrels or other vats to finish their fermentation. The bulk of them are treated like cheap white wines—pressed immediately, fermented in large vats, and stored in vats, as well.

GENERAL CONSIDERATIONS

Since World War II, a great deal of experimentation in techniques of vinification has taken place, and most, although not all, wine-growers have altered their methods in order to produce less tannic wines that mature more rapidly both in kegs and in bottle. On the whole, the results are satisfactory, the general level of quality, year after year, bad or good, being higher than before, but it is to be feared that the sublime peaks of the past may never again be reached, and that thirty or forty years hence, the wines of great recent years will bear no comparison with the '26s, '28s, '29s, and '34s, whose beauty at present is often so astonishing.

The world has changed, and economic pressures force the wine-grower to change his methods in order to satisfy a wine-buying public far larger, and far more modest in income and wine knowledge, than their predecessors. Few have cellars and fewer still are willing to invest in wines that must be put to rest for ten or twenty years. Even with "improved" methods that bring rapid maturing, most of the great wines are drunk before they are ready, engendering disappointment in those consumers who had hoped to find more than a famous label and who do not understand the reasons for their disappointment. More than once, friends have told me apologetically that perhaps they are wrong, but they prefer a Beaujolais to one wine or another of prestigious reputation; this is not astonishing, even though Beaujolais are nearly always drunk too old in America!

The vintage, or year, counts for a great deal in the aging of a wine and constantly deals surprises even to the most accomplished of winegrowers. Different years develop more or less rapidly and often in an unpredictable way. At the moment of this writing, for instance, the '61 Bordeaux are not ready to drink, nor are many '57s (both in Bordeaux and Burgundy), whereas, most '58s and some '59s are on the downward path, and the '62s are at their peak, in many instances, with a few declining. Many '37s remain young, but astringent (probably they never will develop), and, while most '47s and '49s have long since taken the fall, the '45s remain generally solid, and many '48s (which everyone thought to be a nasty, thankless vintage) have begun to open out beautifully.

Wines freshly bottled often suffer from "bottle sickness" (*maladie de bouteille*) and any shipment, as well, temporarily unsettles a wine's equilibrium. Put to rest in a good cellar, these wines regain all their qualities after a few months and then continue to develop in a normal way.

Wines that have traveled, or that have been kept in a poor cellar, or that have been changed often from one cellar to another, age more rapidly and less perfectly. Thus a fine wine from a recent year, opened and drunk at the vineyard, may still have the cool, deep color of youth, retain a great deal of fruit, and remain tannic and jealous of its bouquet, whereas the same wine bought from an American dealer is apt to be lighter and warmer in color, suppler, with its bouquet in full bloom. Its qualities at this early peak, although characteristic, will lack the depth eventually to be achieved by the companion wine that has never left the home cellar.

A good cellar is not a luxury or a fantasy but an absolute necessity for anyone who loves wine. In city apartments, where such a cellar may be out of the question, one has no alternative but to buy wines in small quantities at a time from a dependable dealer who has a good cellar and store them in the darkest, coolest corner of the apartment. If the central heating equipment is in the cellar, an old-fashioned "cave," like that in which our grandmothers kept preserves, may be the best solution. It is relatively simple of construction. Many Americans are experimenting with air-conditioned cellars. This, too, might be interesting for those who can afford such an installation. The ideal temperature is 50–55° F., but a cellar that is cooler is better than one that is too warm. Above all, the temperature should not vary more than a few degrees from one time of year to another. It should neither be too humid nor too dry, but an excess of humidity is less harmful than too little. There should be some ventilation. Foods that may lend an odor to the air should never be kept in a wine cellar, for the gentle development of a wine depends on a slow breathing process through the cork (it is for this reason that half-bottles, bottles and magnums—different capacities related to identical corks—age more or less rapidly, other circumstances remaining the same). Bottles must always be stored lying down. A cork that is not constantly in contact with the wine loses its resiliency and allows too much air to enter, and the wine spoils.

TEMPERATURE AND SERVICE

The myth that all red wines should be served at "room temperature" has ruined more great wines than any other single mistreatment. It dates from the nineteenth century, when, for venerable wines, it was a valid dictum, as central heating did not exist and room temperature was closer to 60° F. than to 80° F. Small red wines, drunk young, gain by being served slightly cooler than cellar temperature. Fairly young Burgundies are perfect drunk at cellar temperature. In general, Bordeaux should be served slightly warmer than Burgundies and older wines slightly warmer than young, but never should they be reduced to that horrible, tepid brew that wine stewards regularly blackmail their clients into accepting.

White wines should, of course, always be chilled, but never iced. They should be chilled as rapidly as possible; the classic ice bucket is still the best method. A couple of hours in the refrigerator or a half hour in the freezer (provided one does not forget it is there) will do the trick; but a prolonged stay in the refrigerator will rob a wine of all its qualities—it is *cassé*—broken.

Any old wine, white or red, should be uncorked a couple of hours before serving. If this is not feasible, it should be decanted before serving, for the aeration or "breathing" is essential to the development of the bouquet. Even in restaurants, if I know in advance what I want to drink, I always telephone several hours ahead to ask that the wine be uncorked in time, for I have too often known a great wine to begin to open out only as the bottle was being finished.

White wine rarely contains sediment other than an occasional deposit of tartar crystals, which, being relatively heavy, do not disturb the wine. A red wine that contains a certain amount of sediment must be handled very gently from the moment it leaves the cellar to the moment the last drop is poured. (Often, in restaurants, one sees bottles turned upside down, shaken, tossed around, before being thrown into their wicker cradles, then poured with the greatest of "loving" care and ceremony before the client; the liquid that comes out, of course, is mud.) If possible, the bottle should be stood upright for a couple of days before it is to be served; otherwise, a cradle into which it may be slipped sidewise without disturbing the sediment is the best solution. If it is not decanted, it should be poured slowly and regularly without ever returning to an upright position until all glasses have been filled. To decant a wine, a candle or a small light bulb should be placed behind the decanter and slightly to the right (for a right-handed person) so that, while pouring, the light is directly behind the neck of the bottle. Tilt the bottle slowly with a steady hand and pour steadily, watching the transparency through the neck of the bottle. The moment the wine becomes troubled, stop pouring. Properly poured, the wine in the decanter will be completely limpid and only one-third to one-half glass of liquid and residue will remain in the bottle.

The glass from which one drinks should be uncut, undecorated and uncolored, so that the color of the wine may be properly admired. It should be stemmed and large enough to hold approximately one-half cup when less than half filled. The form may be that of a tulip or a *ballon*; the essential thing is that the circumference of the lip be somewhat smaller than that of the rest of the glass, so that when the glass is from one-third to one-half full, the bouquet may develop in the space above. It is attractive, but not necessary, to serve white and red wines in differently shaped glasses. Traditionally, Burgundy and Bordeaux (as well as many other wine regions) have their own glasses, but, in practice, "claret" glasses are too small to serve for anything but water and Burgundy glasses are too large to avoid ostentation.

To taste a wine properly, I do not feel that it is too indiscreet to pucker one's mouth (the French say that one forms one's mouth in a *cul de poule*) and suck air through the wine before letting it spread to all corners of the mouth and tongue (although, admittedly, one's table companions may be surprised at this performance).

In selecting wines for a meal, it is logical to begin with the lightest and driest of whites (they are also perfect as apéritifs and do not paralyze the palate as do, for instance, dry martinis), which may accompany hors d'oeuvre, light seafood dishes, etc., and work through richer, though still dry, white wines with hot sauced fish dishes and certain other white meats, vegetable gratins, cheese soufflés (fish cooked in red wine are, preferably, accompanied by red wine). In moving from a white to a red wine, neither should suffer by comparison (thus, it would be a pity to leap from a Muscadet into a Lafite or to serve a Beaujolais after a Corton-Charlemagne), and the red wine that follows another should be bigger of body and older. In short, work from white to red, small to large, and young to old. But one must not take all of this too seriously; and it is great fun to make up rules and then disprove them, or attempt to. In general it is easier to marry wines from the same region than those of disparate character, but it is often amusing, and sometimes exciting, to switch from Bordeaux to Burgundy, or from old to young, or from Burgundy to Bordeaux (which is severely disapproved!). Assuming the dessert to be of the right character, one's pleasure is always enriched by finishing a meal with a great Sauternes. (The name Sauternes when referring to the region in France or wines from that region is always spelled with a final *s*. The *s* has been dropped in English when the name refers to American-made wines).

Some French Wines

With some rare exceptions, the finest wines of France are produced in the Rhône Valley, Burgundy, the region of Bordeaux, and the Loire Valley—Champagne being a world apart, although it does produce lovely still white wines, *blancs de blancs natures.* The term, *blanc de blancs* distinguishes any white Champagne wine, made uniquely of white grapes, from other Champagnes made of red grapes (*blancs de noirs*) or of a mixture of white and red grapes. When found on wine labels from other regions, where *all* white wines are made from white grapes, the term is merely a bit of pretentious nonsense designed to flatter snobbish instincts through its associations with champagne and "elegance."

Central and southern France produce vast quantities of small wines, many of which carry the V.D.Q.S. (*Vins Délimités de Qualité Supérieur*) label of quality. Their qualities are best appreciated in the regions that produce them (although I cannot take too seriously the notion that certain wines cannot travel—no wines travel well, but all wines travel. It is, rather, I think, those circumstances that render these little wines pleasant that refuse to travel with them—the abrupt coolness of a cellar on a sweltering, thirsty day and the appeasement lent by a light, young, cool wine, combined with the teasing perfume of the earthen floor, impregnated with wine spilled and spit there by tasters for decades, if not centuries).

The few wines discussed on the following pages are among the best known in France and the most widely exported. They nearly all fall under the control of the French Institut National des Appellations d'Origine (hence, the term *Appellation Contrôlée* to be found on the labels). When referring to an *Appellation Contrôlée d'Origine*, I shall, for simplicity's sake, often use the abbreviation "A.O."

The order of presentation is unrelated to respective qualities, but follows, rather, a geographical logic. The descriptions of the various wines are, inevitably, vague, and in any case one may come to know wines only through tasting (although it does not follow that those far more experienced than myself can always pinpoint a wine tasted blindly).

THE RHÔNE VALLEY

The southern part of the Rhône Valley, near Avignon, produces one splendid red wine, Châteauneuf-du-Pape, whose qualities are sometimes masked by an excess of alcohol content. A good Châteauneuf acquires a great deal of elegance with age. A few of the Châteauneuf vineyards make a small quantity of white wine—that of the Domaine de Mont-Redon is particularly successful. Tavel, Chusclan, and Lirac produce rosé wines, highly perfumed, with perhaps too high an alcoholic content to drink with the abandon that, well chilled, they incite.

Traveling north, the wines of Crozes-Hermitage and Hermitage, both red and white, are remarkable, less overpowering than their southern neighbors, and finally, as one approaches Lyons, the Côte-Rôtie is perhaps the subtlest of the Côtes-du-Rhône reds. All are made with a number of different grape varieties, of which the Syrah dominates in the Côte-Rôtie and the Grenache (a variety useful in raising the alcohol content of a wine) too often dominates in the Châteauneufs. All are, at best, ideal red meat, game and cheese wines.

A famous white wine, the Château Grillet, is made in the Côte-Rôtie area, but so limited is its production that it belongs, essentially, to the realm of wine literature.

THE BURGUNDIES

North of Lyons is Beaujolais country. Lyons itself claims to be fed by three rivers, of which the third is Beaujolais—in fact, wine to a Lyonnais means Beaujolais, and I have never drunk a bad one in that city—nor one that was over a year old. The wines of Beaujolais are made from the Gamay grape (a small amount of white Beaujolais wine has been produced in recent years—it is of interest mostly as a curiosity), and when honestly vinified in the traditional Beaujolais manner, drunk cool and young, they are glorious. Light and fruity, the French say of them that they are *gouleyants*, which means essentially that they slide down the throat with ease and in great quantity. The finer ones come from strictly limited areas that take the village names. If one were to construct a "ladder" of the different *crus* and the perfect age at which to drink them (not, however, to be taken too seriously), Beaujolais and Beaujolais-Villages might occupy the months of December through March; Chiroubles, Brouilly, Côte de Brouilly and Morgon, April through June; and Fleurie, Saint-Amour, Juliénas and Chénas would finish out the year nicely. Moulin-à-Vent occupies a place apart, as it has more *grand vin* pretensions and should be allowed to age a bit. Those who "adore" Beaujolais wines know that these should neither be drunk at room temperature nor iced. Brought directly up from the cellar and kept in an ice bucket for five minutes or in the refrigerator for half an hour, they are perfect. They are the ideal accompaniment to simple, rustic dishes (*potées*, tripes, *poule au pot*, *charcuterie*) and grilled meats and poultry.

Many decent table wines, both red and white, issue from the Mâconnais, but the Pouilly trinity (-Fuissé, -Vinzelles, -Loché) are the only Mâcon wines in a class apart. Made from the Pinot Chardonnay grape (the same responsible for the Côte de Beaune whites and for *blanc de blancs* champagne), they are the ideal "all-purpose" white wines; neither too dry nor too rich nor excessively alcoholic, they have a fresh and exciting fruit when young, and after two or three years in bottle they develop a suave elegance that lifts them easily into the "great wine" category.

A bit before arriving at the southernmost tip of the Côte d'Or, Mercurey and Rully both produce white wines, about which, although each has its distinct personality, the same general remarks may be made as about Pouilly-Fuissé. Mercurey reds are light-bodied and, after a couple of years in bottle, develop a very pretty bouquet. They will keep much longer, but are never better than when drunk two or three years old and at cellar temperature.

All the greatest wines of Burgundy are produced from a strip of land hardly more than thirty miles long, known as the Côte d'Or. It stretches from Santenay to Fixin (just south of Dijon) and is divided into two sections, the southern half of which is known as the Côte de Beaune and the northern as the Côte de Nuits. A mere recital of the names of the villages covering that stretch will excite the papillary glands of a wine lover.

The greatest whites come from the Côte de Beaune (although a few, none the less impeccable, made from the Pinot Blanc grape, are produced in the Côte de Nuits) and are made from the Pinot Chardonnay grape. Montrachet, it is said, finds its peer only in Château d'Yquem. The Puligny-Montrachets, Corton-Charlemagnes and certain Meursaults (-Perrières, -Genevrières, -Charmes, etc.) certainly run close competition and, perhaps by virtue of being slightly less "heady," are easier to place in a menu. Another beautiful white, less well known, is the Clos des Mouches at Beaune. All of these wines superbly accompany richly sauced fish dishes and chicken in white wine or cream sauces, and they happily precede great red Burgundies.

The Côte d'Or reds are made from the Pinot Noir grape. Those from the Côte de Beaune, with the Volnays heading the list (Corton, which is near the borderline, has a distinctly "Nuits" personality), are lighter in body than the Côte de Nuits, suppler, and on the whole mature more rapidly. They are faultless and often suffer unfairly from the inevitable comparison with the Côte de Nuits.

On the Côte de Nuits side, great red wines are numerous. The wines of the Domaine de la Romanée-Conti are universally thought to be the finest of all, and, of course it is true that they are breathtaking, but with such glories as Musigny and Chambertin (in whose bouquet, many people claim to find traces of the barnyard—that is possible, but it comes about as close as anything I know to Heaven) in the running, it seems unfair to give a place apart to one tiny group of vineyards. Many beauties, besides those mentioned, come from Vosne, Chambolle and Gevrey (which most often add the names of their most distinguished growths to those of the villages). Nor are Echezeaux, Vougeot (these two are both very close in character to the Vosne-Romanées), Fixin, or Nuits-Saint-Georges to be snubbed. The latter have a character apart—perhaps less sophisticated, not so elegant, more "earthy," a bit harder—it is difficult to touch with words the soul of a wine. As for La Romanée, famous in oenological literature, I have never tasted it, nor even ever seen a bottle of it. One of Gevrey-Chambertin's best known winegrowers told me recently that he had seen it and tasted it for the first time only a few months earlier on a trip to England!

The *Appellation Contrôlée* system is particularly complicated for the wines of the Côte d'Or, for not only is each of a number of communities distinguished by the right to an A.O. (see page 36), but each community is broken up into a number of so-called *climats*, each named and many with A.O. rights, in which case the name of the community need not be mentioned on the label (La Tâche, for instance, is a Vosne-Romanée, Le Clos de Tart a Morey-Saint-Denis, etc.). Others with A.O. rights mention the community in conjunction with the *climat* and still others, with no A.O. rights beyond the name of the community, print in small letters beneath the *Appellation Contrôlée* the name of the *climat*. To complicate things even further, many *climats*, though they may represent tiny plots of land, are shared by a number of different proprietors, who, naturally, do not all vinify their wines in the same way or with the same care. Many are bought by *négociants*, sometimes before the vinification, sometimes after, and, of course, *négociants*, too, are more or less honest. Certain *négociants*' practices, strictly forbidden but difficult to control, such as adding large quantities of sugar to the crushed grapes before fermentation to bring up the alcohol content or mixing heavier, more alcoholic wines from the Côtes-du-Rhône and Algeria with the Burgundy base, have done tremendous harm to Burgundy's reputation. Many people are convinced that the best of the Burgundies are powerful, heavy, inky-colored wines that leave mangled systems in their wake, whereas, in fact, the best are light in color (a wonderful, transparent ruby, turning "tile-colored" with age), contain no more than 12½% alcohol, are delicate and rich with nuance on the palate, and, to quote the Bourgignons, "They leave the breath clean and the head clear."

A label tells everything. Indifferent wines tend to lean on grandiose and meaningless phrases—Grand Vin d'Origine, for instance. The finer the wine, the more specific the information. One may know the vintage (wines that bear no year or the mention V.S.R.—Very Special Reserve*—are a mixture of several years designed to produce a rounder, smoother—and more anonymous—product), the specific vineyard (*climat*, *cru*, growth), whether the wine was made, cared for, and put into bottles by a private winegrower, or bought, cared for and bottled by a *négociant* (who may be an owner as well, and wine that is produced from his own property will be so indicated on the label—or he

* Said by some to mean *Vins Spécialement Recommandés.*

may have exclusive rights to buy the entire production of a specific vineyard, and this, too, will appear on the label).

This information will no doubt seem rather dreary to many readers, but, when buying Burgundy wine, unless one simply settles on a Romanée-Conti, it is absolutely essential to be able to read the label correctly. The name of the American importer will also appear on the bottle, and, for those whose knowledge of the source is limited, that, too, may be an indication of relative quality.

CHAMBERTIN CLOS DE BÈZE

APPELLATION CONTRÔLÉE

Domaine Armand Rousseau Père et Fils

GEVREY-CHAMBERTIN (CÔTE D'OR)

MISE AU DOMAINE **Product of France**

Clos de Bèze is the most prized section of the climat *of Chambertin, itself the first growth of the community of Gevrey-Chambertin; other vineyards with special A.O. rights beside the community appellation, but not within the Chambertin climat, incorporate the name of Chambertin also, but their modifying names (Charmes-, Mazoyères-, etc.) precede that of Chambertin. The label indicates the name of the proprietor and that the wine was put into bottles on the property* (Mise au Domaine).

GRANDS VINS  DE BOURGOGNE

1964

Joseph Drouhin

RÉCOLTE DU DOMAINE

BONNES-MARES

APPELLATION CONTROLÉE

MONOPOLE DE VENTE

JOSEPH DROUHIN

Maison fondée en 1880

NÉGOCIANT A BEAUNE, COTE-D'OR

AUX CELLIERS DES ROIS DE FRANCE ET DES DUCS DE BOURGOGNE

Bonnes-Mares is a border climat, *part of which is within the community boundaries of Morey-St.-Denis, the other part in Chambolle-Musigny. Since the* climat *enjoys its own A.O. rights, it is unnecessary to mention either of the community names. The label specifies* Récolte du Domaine, *which indicates that the vineyard is the property of the firm. It does not say* Mise au Domaine *or* Mise à la Propriété, *since for practical reasons a* négociant *must care for all his wines in a central cellar (in this instance in Beaune) where they are also put into bottles. The* Monopole de Vente (*exclusive sale rights*) *refers only to the* domaine, *for there are many other proprietors in the* climat *of Bonnes-Mares.*

Récolte 1962

Musigny

Appellation Contrôlée

Ets Leroy. Négociants à Auxey-Meursault (Côte d'Or)

Musigny is the first growth in the community of Chambolle-Musigny (the village having added to its own name that of its first growth, as have Gevrey and Vosne). As the label describes the firm only as négociants, *it is understood that the wine has been bought from a winegrower whose vines are in the* climat *of Musigny, and "raised" and put into bottles in the* négociant's *cellars.*

Far to the north in Burgundy, midway between the Côte d'Or and Champagne, Chablis (which produces four categories of wine: *Grand cru*, *Premier cru*, Chablis—with no modifier—and Petit Chablis), makes dry, nutty white wines of great quality. They are not flamboyant and they need to be known intimately to be appreciated at their true value.

BORDEAUX

There is an endless and foolish quarrel between Burgundy and Bordeaux enthusiasts. It would seem that for many people it is impossible to love the one without detesting the other. Clichés concerning the opposing characters of the one and the other abound. It is claimed that Burgundy wines are "sensual" and beloved by brash youth, whereas the wines of Bordeaux are "intellectual" and that the wisdom that comes only with age is essential to an understanding of their full beauty. Mostly foolishness, of course, although in a general way I think that one might claim for the wines of Bordeaux—in particular for the reds of Graves and Médoc—that they are drier and more reserved in personality (though never sardonic).

Bordeaux age more slowly than Burgundies and live longer, a Burgundy being most often perfect to drink when it is from four to ten years of age, whereas the great Bordeaux attain their maximum qualities between the ages of ten to twenty. This is all approximate, and both count many exceptions (I have drunk forty-year-old Burgundies that were at the height of their glory and five- or six-year-old Bordeaux whose decline had already set in).

Bordeaux wines often suffer in the judgment of the uninitiated because they are drunk too young. The great red wines of Bordeaux, and in particular those of Graves and Médoc, have an extremely high tannic content, which renders them harsh and often unpleasant in their youth. The greater the château (the "first growths" start out each year's production of wine in new oaken kegs, supplementing the wine's natural tannin with that of the wood), and the better the year, the more tannic the wine. It is precisely this tannin that forms, in a manner of speaking, the structural support for the body of the wine, and permits it to age elegantly without collapsing, while at the same time the harshness of the tannin disappears, and the tannin itself, in part, withdraws into the sediment that is found in old wines.

The outlying regions of the Bordelais number among the largest wine-producing areas in France. Most make good table wines and many benefit from special *Appellations Contrôlées.*

The great Bordeaux red wines come from Médoc (in which the villages of Pauillac, Saint-Julien, Saint-Estèphe, Margaux, Moulis and Listrac claim their own A.O.), Graves, Saint-Emilion and Pomerol, and the great whites from Graves, Sauternes and Barsac.

The white wines are made principally from the Sauvignon and the Semillon grapes, and the reds from Cabernet Sauvignon, Cabernet Franc, Merlot and Malbec. The last is used less now than in the past and other varieties have been almost completely eliminated. In the Haut-Médoc and among the finest Graves, the proportion of Cabernet Sauvignon is high—50 percent to 75 percent, and up to 95 percent for the greatest vineyards. Saint-Emilion and Pomerol contain generally about one third Cabernet Sauvignon and 50 percent Merlot. The finest wines are grown in soil so poor that to raise anything else in their place would be unthinkable (Graves means gravel and is so named because of the makeup of its soil).

Among the wines of Bordeaux, it is easier to know what one is buying than in Burgundy, for each vineyard (or château) is the property of a single person or society, and in most instances the labels are marked *Mise en Bouteilles au Château*, an assurance to the buyer that the wine has been cared for and put into bottles by the proprietor. The role of the *négociant* is thus more often minimized to that of distributor.

The best of the wines from the Haut-Médoc are, when drunk under the right conditions, probably the most subtle of all red wines. (Practically no white is produced.) Château Margaux makes a small quantity of pleasant, nonvintage white wine, marketed under the name of Pavillon Blanc du Château Margaux. Those from Pauillac are generally the "biggest," "fullest," "roundest," but the wines from Saint-Estèphe (Cos d'Estournel, Montrose, Calon-Ségur) have a special elegance of their own, those from Margaux (Margaux, Malescot-Saint-Exupéry, Rauzan-Gassies), a particular earthy flavor, and the Saint-Juliens (Ducru-Beaucaillou, the Léovilles, Talbot), a direct, clean quality that is nonetheless not lacking in nuance.

The famous 1855 classification of the wines of Médoc remains essentially dependable. Two wines from outside of Médoc (Haut-Brion from Graves and Yquem from Sauternes, the latter the only white wine mentioned in the entire classification) are included among the five first growths. Of the others, two are from Pauillac, Latour and Lafite (a third, Mouton-Rothschild, classed as a second growth, is now considered by everyone to be equal in quality), and the other is Château Margaux. These wines are respectfully referred to as *les Grands Seigneurs.*

Graves is the victim of a curious misconception, as widespread in France as elsewhere. It is generally believed to produce only white wines, all of which are thought to be sweet, whereas, in fact, some of Bordeaux's most elegant reds are Graves, and its finest whites are an dry and exquisitely perfumed.

Of the reds, those who have drunk old vintages of Château Haut-Brion (in recent years, I suspect the makers of having experimented too heavily with modern techniques of vinification) will not soon forget them. Perhaps my most "transcendental" wine-drinking experience is related to a 1926 Château Bouscaut, whose delicate and complicated bouquet—that of a great wine whose gentle decline has begun—recalled dried rose petals, field mushrooms, decayed leaves and quantities of other autumn odors impossible to define, combined with elusive memories of fresher, fruitier qualities. The beauty of such a wine is elaborated in one's memory—more precisely defined in retrospect–but brings no deception on retasting. Other particularly fine red wines from Graves are: Pape-Clément, Haut-Bailly, La Mission Haut-Brion, Malartic-Lagravière, Carbonnieux, and Domaine de Chevalier.

The white wines of Graves, unlike many dry white wines, age gracefully and live long, and, although it is rare to find on the market any that are over ten years of age, the chance should not be missed to try one, should an older one present itself. Among the best of the Graves whites are the Châteaux: Bouscaut, Laville Haut-Brion, Couhins, Domaine de Chevalier and Carbonnieux.

The wines of Saint-Emilion and Pomerol—all reds—have a great deal in common; they are generally less aristocratic in personality than those just discussed, although certainly not lacking in elegance. They are often heavier of body. Less complicated, both in bouquet and on the palate, in youth they are more supple than the Médocs and Graves, and they mature more rapidly. The Pomerols, in particular, are often ready to drink after a couple of years in bottle (four years of age), but take age well, also. Each has its *grand cru.* Château Cheval Blanc is considered to be the greatest of the Saint-Emilions, and Château Petrus heads the Pomerols. Other great and good Saint-Emilions are the Châteaux Figeac, La Gaffelière-Naudes, Ausone, Canon, Grand-Mayne, and Monbousquet. Vieux Château Certan and the Châteaux l'Evangile, Nenin, La Conseillante and Beauregard are among the Pomerols that demand a particular respect.

The wines of Sauternes and Barsac are sweet, and the fashion today is, unhappily, antisweet wine (with the pathetic result that even Château d'Yquem now markets a dry little white wine called Ygrec).

The richness of these wines depends on whether or not the summer is hot enough for the grapes to ripen early, before the autumn rains set in. When fully ripened, they are attacked by a fungus known as *la pourriture noble* (the English translation, "noble rot," somehow sounds rather foolish to me), which dehydrates them, concentrating the rich fruit sugars in the withered, moldy pulp, and, of course, the mold itself gives a characteristic flavor. The separate grapes are clipped from the grape clusters as they are sufficiently altered by the *pourriture noble*, which may necessitate four or five passages through the vines before the entire harvest is realized. The bit of juice extracted from these grapes produces a wine rich in glycerine and alcohol (the fermentation of any must containing such a high natural sugar content stops automatically before all the sugar is transformed into alcohol, with the result that, in rich years, a high sugar content remains in the wine—which nonetheless counts a full 18% alcohol), whose natural enveloping sweetness is never sugary or cloying, whose bright gold turns deep amber with age, and which, in great years, outlives by far the men who make it. Its depth of bouquet and its expansion on the palate can be breathtaking. It should be sipped, sensuously analyzed for a long time in the mouth, but drunk in small quantities. Therein lies its greatest drawback, for, in order to justify sacrificing a bottle of old Sauternes, there should be at least five or six people at table. Drunk well chilled, with a warm butter-crust apple pie (for which I do not intend to give the recipe in this book), both take on unforgettable dimensions.

Apart from Château d'Yquem (of which it has too often been said that it is the greatest white wine in the world), the Châteaux Rieussec,

Suduiraut, La Tour Blanche, Gilette and Rayne-Vigneau, among others, produce wines of perfect quality whose prices are generally far more interesting than that of their famous neighbor.

THE LOIRE VALLEY

The Loire Valley is not, technically, a region, for the Loire River begins far to the south, winds all the way up through central France and across, to empty out into the Atlantic at the southern border of Brittany. The finest wines come from four distinctly different regions, and it follows that certain of them have little in common apart from their proximity to the same river. They are predominantly white.

Beginning at the mouth of the river, Muscadet (the Nantais region), made from the Muscadet grape (transplanted from Burgundy where it is known as "Melon"), is a light and very dry wine, best when drunk very young—one of the best with raw oysters. Its slight acidity renders it a useful and refreshing thirst quencher, but may perhaps proscribe it for certain stomachs. The same region produces a slight little wine from the Gros Plant grape which is a favorite among collectors of the little known.

Savennières (Anjou) makes good white wines from the Pineau grape (spelled differently to distinguish it from the Burgundy Pinots), the best known of which comes from a tiny vineyard, the Coulée de Serrant. Formerly a sweet wine, it has, for the last ten years, been vinified as a dry wine; the grapes are picked before being attacked by the *pourriture noble*. A suave, delicate wine with a slightly "peppery" taste, it improves greatly with age and is probably best, depending on the year, when five or six years old. It is splendid with smoked salmon, fish in sauce, and such dishes.

Vouvray (Touraine) now vinifies much of its production "dry" also, with less success, it seems to me. The Vouvrays are also made from the Pineau grape. The 1921s are still remembered with reverence. When made in the traditional way, they are perfect apéritif and dessert wines. A certain part of the production is treated like champagne to make a sparkling wine.

Farther along the Loire, Sancerre and Pouilly-Fumé are made from the Sauvignon grape, known in that part of the country as Blanc Fumé because of the wines' delicate, smoky taste, partly a result of the grape variety and partly of the earth in which it is grown. The Pouilly-Fumés (from Pouilly-sur-Loire–unrelated to Pouilly-Fuissé) have the more pronounced *fumé* taste of the two. The same vineyards make a wine from the Chasselas grape, which takes the name of the village (Pouilly-sur-Loire)—delicious when drunk very young, but of little interest once it is a year old. Sancerre produces also a small amount of rosé wine, which, like Bouzy and Gros Plant, is much cherished by curiosity seekers.

Close neighbors, but on the banks of the Cher, Quincy and Reuilly (not to be confused with Rully) are light and lovely mid-morning thirst quenchers (Sauvignon).

Three beautiful red wines come from the Loire Valley: Bourgueuil (of which the best is Saint-Nicholas de Bourgueuil), Chinon and Saumur-Champigny (the first two are from the Touraine, the third, from the Anjou). All are made from the Cabernet Franc grape and experts claim to discern in them the odor of violets and the flavor of raspberry. When young, they have an astonishing deep purple-red "robe" and an exhilarating fruit. They share with the wines of Beaujolais the beauty of youth (and, like them, should be drunk slightly cool), but they age with more grace and eventually come to resemble certain old Bordeaux.

OTHER REGIONS

Alsace, all of whose wines (with the exception of Zwicker, a mixture) are named after grape varieties, produces one, made from the Riesling grape, which, at best, is in a class apart—a splendid wine with light fish dishes and far better than beer with sauerkraut. Gewürztraminer enjoys great popularity, but its fruit and perfume are so overpowering that, despite its being relatively dry, I cannot imagine it being drunk with anything but a dessert.

The Jura makes a great white wine of a totally different character than that of any other French wine: Château-Chalon. Tastewise it falls somewhere between a fine sherry and the great white Burgundies. It remains in kegs for about six years, evaporation loss is never replaced, and thanks to this particular process of vinification, a layer of special bacteria forms on the surface of the wine that gives it its unique quality. It is powerful and, although very dry, has a rich fruit. It accompanies well certain rich, strongly flavored fish dishes (lobster in various sauces in particular) and can occasionally replace advantageously a red wine—with certain game birds, duckling, or pork dishes whose sauces are slightly sweet, for example. The Jura also produces a very small quantity of *vin de paille* ("straw wine"), the grapes of which are partly dried on layers of straw before being fermented. I have never seen this wine on the American market.

The Mediterranean coast produces few wines of quality. The white wines of Cassis are pleasant, though a bit alcoholic. (Cassis is the name of the village, and the wine must not be confused with cassis—blackberry liqueur—particularly since one of the favorite apéritifs in Burgundy is *vin blanc cassis*, a white Aligoté sweetened by the addition of a bit of blackberry liqueur. To an inexperienced ear it sounds much the same as *vin blanc de Cassis*.) At Bandol, the Domaine Tempier makes a rosé wine as good as any I know and a fine red wine that takes age well. All of the wines of southern France are made from a large number of grape varieties: Grenache, Picpoul, Clairette, Tibourin, Ugni and others. The quality of the Tempier red is due, in part, to the presence of the *mourvèdre* grape.

Near the Spanish border, in Catalan country, Banyuls enjoyed a great reputation in the past, but a time came when the product had sunk to an indifferent quality. Shortly after World War II, an energetic and impassioned major of Banyuls took the winegrowers in hand, organized impressive installations for vinification and storage, revised vinification techniques, and today the various Banyuls Grand Cru wines are again of splendid quality. They are not "table wines," although they accompany nicely certain dishes in the preparation of whose sauces they have played a part, but are, rather, of the same family as the great ports, and the vinification is similar. It begins as for red table wines, but the fermentation is "muted" before completion by the addition of an eau de vie, thus raising the degree of alcohol and imprisoning a certain amount of the natural sugar in the wine. Banyuls is aged in kegs out of doors, exposed to the sun. These wines are extremely useful (as is port) in many culinary preparations, and are fine apéritif and dessert wines.

Kitchen Layout and Equipment

My kitchen I love, but would recommend to no one else. It contains more equipment and fewer conveniences than most home kitchens, and the organization of space is totally impractical. The largest room in the house, it is the one in which I live, work, cook and receive.

Weather permitting, meals are served out of doors, but during a good half of the year the dining table automatically finds its place before the immense fireplace, which dominates the room and is the only source of heat. Before it, all roasts are turned on a spit; in it, meats, fish and vegetables are grilled. Buried in its ashes, such vegetables as potatoes, beets and eggplant are baked, and often an earthenware pot is half buried in the ashes to pass the night. From time to time, when intense heating is not necessary, I climb to the rooftop and suspend a marinated, rolled boar's belly or other delicacy in the chimney to be smoked, and over a period of several days I regularly nourish the smoldering olive wood with bundles of rosemary.

Beside the fireplace is a small professional cookstove. Its top is a cast-iron plate heated from beneath by a system of gas flames and refractory bricks, permitting one to move pans all over the surface, exactly as with old-fashioned wood- or coal-burning cookstoves, in order to find the precise degree of heat desired. To the side are two open gas flames, and the oven, deep, solid and hermetic, is also heated on the same principle as that of the old-fashioned cookstove. The flames are beneath, but the heat is circulated through hollow walls that encircle the oven.

MY KITCHEN FIREPLACE

The work table, chopping boards and refrigerator—alas—are at the other side of the room, the heart of which is blocked by the dining table and, worse still, beyond the table, by a huge and encumbering pillar that supports the main beam of the room. Despite the size of the room, space is lacking. Earthenware casseroles are piled seven or eight deep, the mantel of the fireplace is hung heavy with omelet and crêpe pans, the copper pans, for lack of a better place, are hung the length of the room, including above the stove (which prompts rapid tarnishing), the soup tureens and sauceboats are kept on shelves so high that a ladder is necessary to reach them, and the largest of the marble mortars, far too heavy to be easily displaced, has never found a permanent place and needs constantly to be shifted.

The following suggestions, then, often represent, in terms of organization, that which my kitchen lacks and which I miss bitterly. As to small equipment, I have contented myself with describing a selection from my own kitchen, excluding those articles common to all kitchens.

A kitchen should be as spacious and as light as circumstances permit. A basic work table or surface and a chopping board should ideally be placed between the sink and the stove, but should, in any case, be as near to the stove as possible. The surface of the chopping board should be at such a level that, standing before it, one may without either straining or bending one's elbows easily place one's hands flat on it (thus, the height of the table should be conditioned to the individual who will most often be working in the kitchen). Most table tops and chopping boards are too high, and one's work is consequently less efficient and more tiring.

Electric ovens, well regulated, are very good for pastries, slow gratins and so-called casserole dishes, and ideal for the many preparations that require a very slow cooking process over a period of many hours. They are suitable for roasts, though I prefer a spit before an open fire. For rapid gratins and grilled meats they are less than satisfactory. As to cooking on top of the stove, I personally find electricity impracticable. A naked gas flame is imperfect, but with the use of asbestos pads and other insulating devices one can arrive at a fairly delicate regulation. A small professional or semiprofessional gas cookstove, similar to that described above, is, to my way of thinking, the most satisfactory solution. A system, whether it be incorporated into the stove or apart, of intense overhead heat for rapid gratins and glazing is useful. The broiler common to most American household stoves never gives a sufficiently intense heat for glazing. There should be some arrangement for heating plates.

In most home kitchens a fireplace such as mine is out of the question. Nevertheless, a small fireplace built into the wall at tabletop or stovetop level is altogether conceivable in a modern kitchen. Several of my friends have built such fireplaces in their kitchens, and others, impressed by the simplicity and the practicality of the arrangement, are in the process of doing so. They are people who are not city dwellers but live in comfortable, centrally heated houses equipped with small modern kitchens, and who, unlike myself, have no desire to recapture living patterns of the past with an of the attendant discomforts. They simply understand that the superiority of a roast on a turnspit before an open fire or of fish and meats grilled over fruitwood embers is pertinently real and not merely part of a past mythology.

Such a fireplace should be large enough to contain a small grill or to permit a spitted chicken or leg of lamb to be turned before it. An opening 25 inches wide by 20 inches high with a depth of 20 inches is sufficient. A platform approximately 15 to 18 inches deep—large enough to easily support the turnspit (*tournebroche*) and dripping pan (*lèchefrite*)—should extend outward from the fireplace floor. The corresponding space beneath the fireplace is used for storing wood.

Accompanying equipment (for Shopping Sources, see page 67) should include: a heavy WELDED-IRON GRILL for meats and poultry, a large DOUBLE-FACED GRILL of heavy hinged steel wire for small fish, and

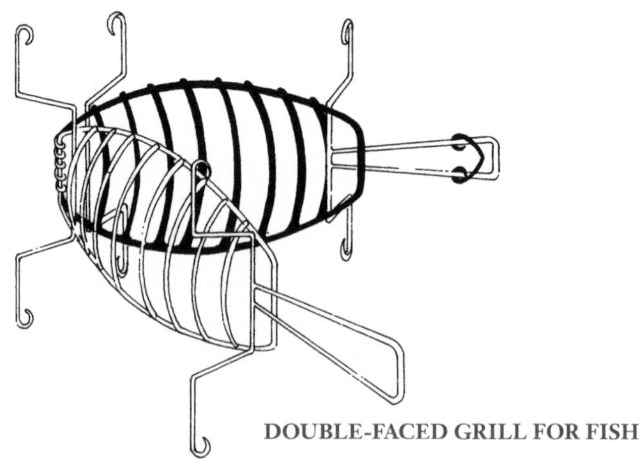

DOUBLE-FACED GRILL FOR FISH

MODERN VERSION OF KITCHEN FIREPLACE

a SPECIAL DOUBLE-FACED GRILL, oval and swelled in shape, for large fish, a TURNSPIT (the most practical are electrically operated), a selec-tion of SPITS, and a DRIPPING PAN designed to be placed beneath the roast to collect the drippings with which it is basted and from which the sauce or juices are prepared. It should be of a heavy material—steel or cast iron rather than the flimsy, tinned affair most often found on the market. I have opted for a huge steel frying pan—a large skillet, propped slightly higher at the fire side with a fragment of brick or stone, will do.

SMALL EQUIPMENT

The CHOPPING BOARD should be large (2½ by 3 feet is a good size), thick (1½ to 2 inches), absolutely flat, and unjointed. It should have its place near the stove and always be in place. It should be kept impeccably clean and occasionally scraped. A butcher's chopping block is a handsome object but expensive, and must be bought new or its surface will not be flat. Small boards are impractical, except for serving cheese or cutting sausage, and frustrating.

One should have at least six or seven good razor-sharp knives (the single most exasperating thing about most kitchens is that they almost never contain a single knife that cuts): a couple of small PARING KNIVES (*couteaux d'office*), a BONING KNIFE (*couteau à désosser*), a medium-sized knife for fine slicing (*couteau à émincer*), at least one of those knives commonly called FRENCH CHEF'S KNIVES with a blade approximately 10 inches long (*couteau à hacher*), one larger of the same form, and a long, narrow CARVING KNIFE (*couteau à trancher*). A SHARPENING STEEL should be kept in place near the knives so that it becomes an automatic thing to sharpen knives regularly as one uses them. The most practical place to keep the knives is in a rack behind one's work table so that they are constantly in view and at hand and do not risk being rubbed against. Magnetic knife racks are dangerous and impractical. Knives should be rinsed or merely wiped clean as one uses them, then replaced in the rack. Until recently, stainless steel knives were generally flimsy and impossible to sharpen, and most cookbooks rightly discouraged their use, but it is now possible to find

good, solid stainless steel knives that take well to sharpening, are much easier than carbon steel to keep clean, and do not blacken certain foods (notably artichokes) on contact as do the carbon steel knives. Good professional knives under the brand "Sabatier-Trumpet" and described as "full-forged stainless steel" are available in America.

A good, heavy pair of KITCHEN SHEARS is necessary for preparing fish and often useful for cutting poultry.

Nothing can replace heavy tinned COPPERWARE in a kitchen, and certain preparations can never be successfully realized without it. But note that copper should not be used on electric stove tops. The best—made for professional use—has heavy iron handles. The brass-handled articles are always lighter in weight and comparatively more expensive. A good selection would be: a *sauteuse* (sometimes called *plat à sauter*), a saucepan with low, straight sides, large enough to hold a cut-up chicken at ease (approximately 12 inches in diameter); a *sautoir*–to confuse things, this is sometimes also called a *sauteuse* (slanting sides, higher than a *sauteuse*), somewhat smaller; at least four more saucepans (casseroles) of varying sizes; and an oval *cocotte* with a tight-fitting lid, large enough to contain a trussed chicken. Copper is not difficult to clean (in any case it is the substance itself,

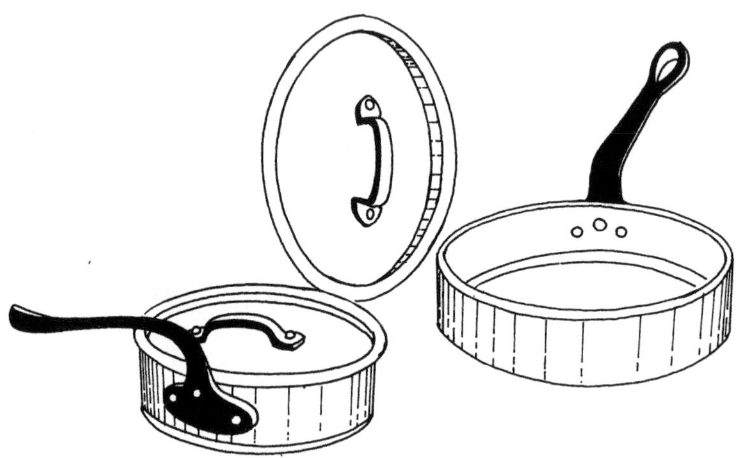

HEAVY TIN-LINED COPPERWARE

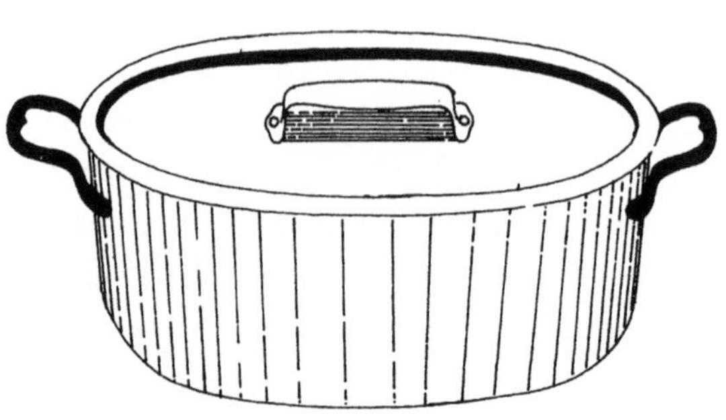

and not its exterior appearance, that renders it useful). When copper utensils are rubbed on the outside with an abrasive cleaning pad and scouring powder each time they are washed, they retain their clean, mat copper color—it is only when copper is not used regularly that it becomes tarnished and unsightly. There are copper-cleaning products on the market that work rapidly and easily and do no harm to the utensils; for those interested, a home recipe, a paste made of a couple of cups of marble dust, an egg white, about 3/4 cup of flour, 1/3 cup vinegar, and a handful of salt, may be prepared and kept indefinitely in a sealed container. Copper occasionally must be retinned, although for rapid sautés tinning that has gone thin will do no harm. When a copper pot contains liquids, the flame may be quite high, but for frying or sautéing the heat must not be too intense or the tin will melt.

EARTHENWARE

Though many serious cooks are able to do without EARTHENWARE, and even disapprove of it on the grounds that it retains odors, I find it indispensable, particularly for the many rustic dishes that require many hours of slow, even cooking. These dishes are never quite so good prepared in anything else, for no other material takes the heat and holds the heat in quite the same way. Over a gas flame, earthenware should always be protected by an asbestos or other insulating pad. New earthenware should be rubbed inside and out with garlic, filled with water and left to boil for several hours. Earthen *poêlons*, low, wide, and round in form, with bulging sides, find many uses, and an oval *cocotte* of 4- to 5-quart capacity with a closely fitting lid is particularly valuable.

Although hardly an article of daily use, a FISH COOKER (*poissonière*) and its accompanying TRIVET are essential to poach and properly present a large fish. It may be used as well for braising whole fish, whole stuffed rabbits, hares, etc. It need not be of copper.

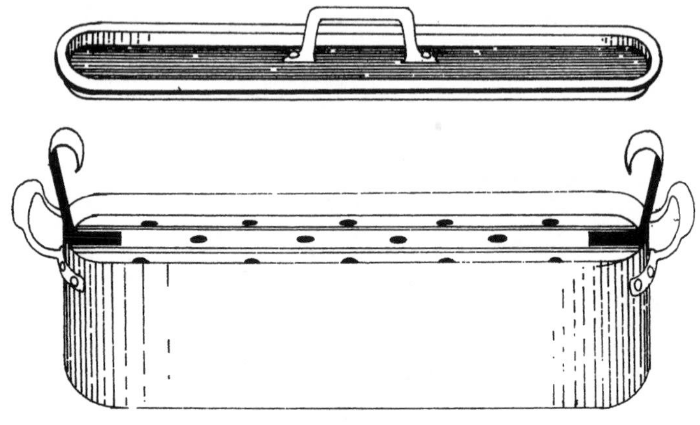

FISH COOKER

A large IRON SKILLET is useful, and heavy steel OMELET and CREPE PANS (the latter have very low, sharply slanting sides) are indispensable. When new, these should be seasoned by heating cooking oil in them over an intense heat until the metal darkens and turns bluish in color, then emptied and wiped with a dry cloth. Omelet and crêpe pans may be used interchangeably or for semi-deep-frys or any other preparation that involves no addition of liquid and does not risk sticking to the pan. After use, they should be wiped out with a dry cloth—never washed. Nothing will stick to them if they are properly treated, but should they suffer mistreatment, wash them in warm soapy water with an abrasive pad or fine steel wool, rinse well, dry them with a cloth, then heat over a high flame and rub well with an oiled cloth.

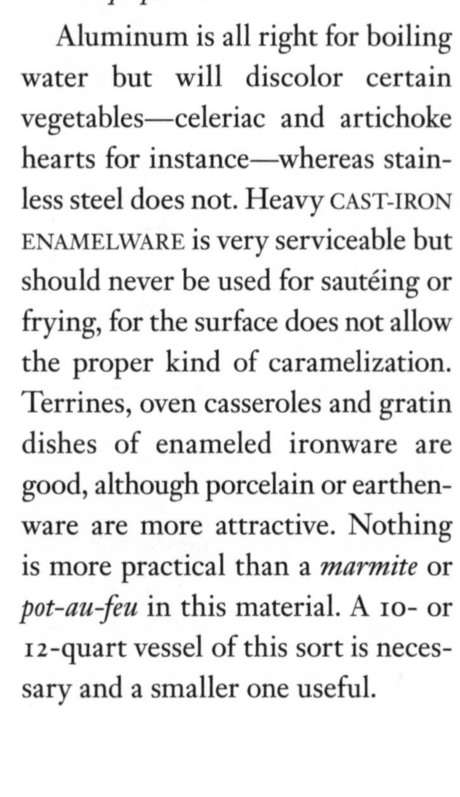

Aluminum is all right for boiling water but will discolor certain vegetables—celeriac and artichoke hearts for instance—whereas stainless steel does not. Heavy CAST-IRON ENAMELWARE is very serviceable but should never be used for sautéing or frying, for the surface does not allow the proper kind of caramelization. Terrines, oven casseroles and gratin dishes of enameled ironware are good, although porcelain or earthenware are more attractive. Nothing is more practical than a *marmite* or *pot-au-feu* in this material. A 10- or 12-quart vessel of this sort is necessary and a smaller one useful.

CAST-IRON ENAMELWARE

One should have WOODEN BOARDS cut to the dimensions of those terrines destined to be used for pâtés, so that the pâtés can cool under a weighted board.

Two MARBLE MORTARS, one with an interior diameter of approximately 12 inches for pounding forcemeats, and one about half that size which serves multiple purposes (reducing dried herbs to powder, making bread crumbs rapidly, preparing stuffings and forcemeats in small quantity, etc.). The pestle for the larger one has, classically, a head on either end.

MARBLE MORTAR AND PESTLE

Also essential are:

WOODEN SPOONS and WOODEN PESTLES, one of which, the *champignon* (mushroom-shaped), is particularly useful, for its form fits exactly to that of a rounded screen sieve.

Several SCREEN SIEVES (*passoires*) of different dimensions, rounded and conical (the latter are called *chinois*) and NYLON DRUM SIEVES (*tamis*). These sieves were formerly woven of horsehair, but nylon is better, because horsehair had a tendency to shed fragments into the food. Nylon drum sieves are useful for passing raspberries and other acid fruits that suffer from contact with metal, and are essential for the passing of fine forcemeats. A FLEXIBLE, OVAL PLASTIC DISK (*corne*, so called because in the past it was made of horn), about five inches across (to be held between the thumb and the four fingers and scraped firmly and flatly against the sieve) is needed for passing material through a drum sieve—pestles are not only ineffectual but hard on the sieve.

WIRE WHISKS for sauces and beating egg whites, and an UNTINNED COPPER BASIN, in which egg whites mount more firmly and with greater volume.

A VEGETABLE MILL (*moulinette*) for passing soups, puréeing vegetables, and making rough purées to facilitate their final passage through the *tamis*, and a *mouli-julienne*, a small, simple and miraculous machine with several changeable blades for reducing raw vegetables into anything from thread-sized julienne strips to fine slices. It may also be used for grating cheese.

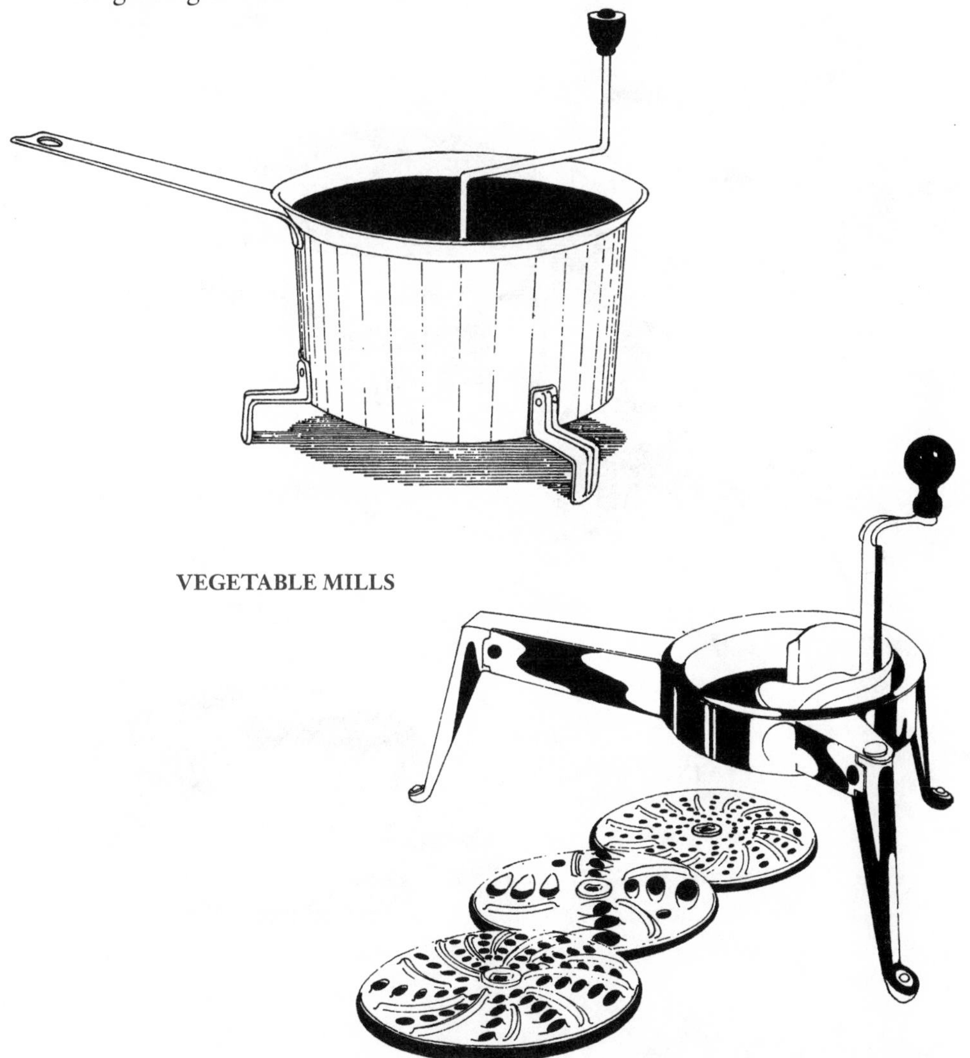

VEGETABLE MILLS

A MEAT-GRINDER.

A selection of MOLDS including SAVARIN (a low, round mold with a thick central tube), JELLY (small, high mold, generally with a geometric surface décor and a narrow central tube), CHARLOTTE (a simple round, flat-bottomed mold, the bottom of which is slightly smaller in circumference than the top), and DOME (or, lacking that, a ROUND-BOTTOMED, TIN-LINED METAL BOWL, *cul de poule*, designed for pastry cooks).

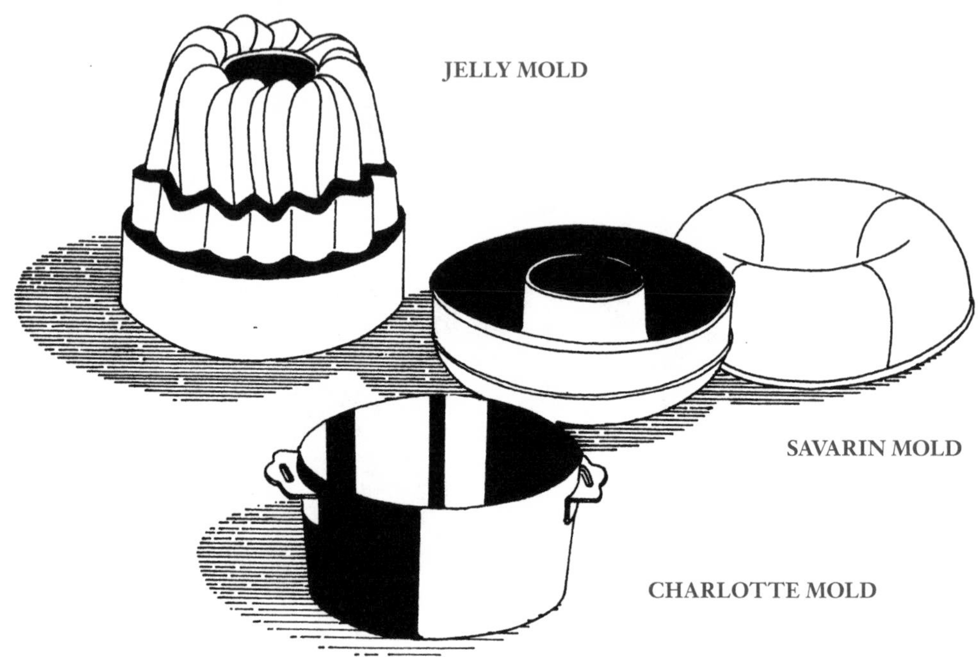

A LARGE WIRE SKIMMING SPOON (*araignée*), useful for lifting anything out of liquid and better than a wire basket for deep frying, for not only does the basket take up needed space in the frying basin, but articles dipped in batter often stick to it and their browned surfaces are torn open in turning them.

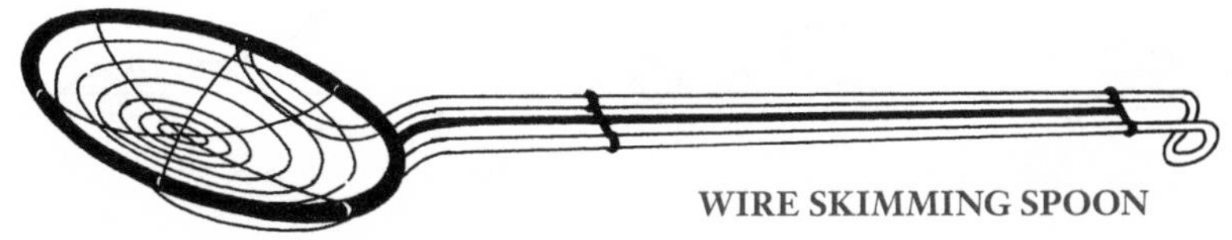

NEEDLES for sewing up stuffed and/or boned fowl, rabbits, fish, etc.: one straight needle about five inches long and a curved upholsterer's needle; a LARDING NEEDLE for larding surfaces with strips of fresh fat pork.

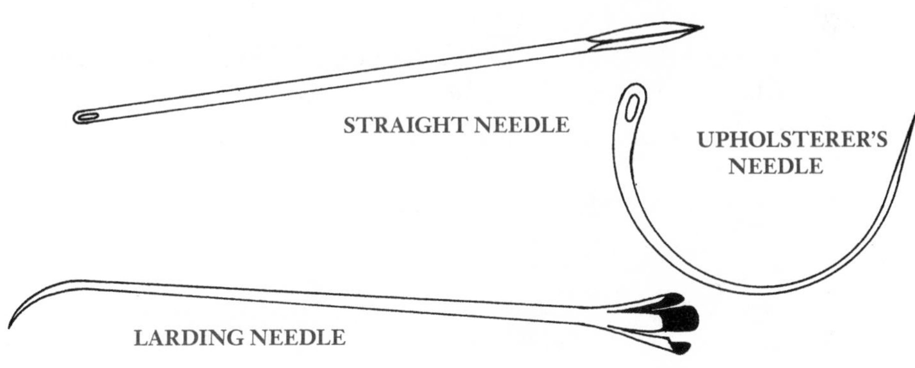

A ROUND WIRE GRILL for steamed vegetables and WIRE PASTRY GRILLS.

Manche à gigot, a handle designed to be screwed or clamped onto the leg bone of a leg of lamb (or venison). Without it, a leg of lamb cannot be correctly carved at table.

A MARBLE SLAB for rolling out pastry is attractive and useful in a large kitchen, but in this refrigerated age perhaps no longer indispensable.

A classic pastry-cook's ROLLING PIN, without handles, which is longer and thinner than the standard American type and, once one is accustomed to it, more convenient.

SALAD BASKET, GRATERS for cheese, nutmeg, etc., BRUSHES for buttering, basting, brushing pastry with egg, etc., SKEWERS, LADLES, LONG-HANDLED FORKS, COFFEE-GRINDER, PEPPER GRINDERS, and lots of TOWELS and PAPER TOWELS.

ELECTRIC MIXERS and BLENDERS are certainly useful and energy-saving, but they cannot, as many people believe, do everything, and should be used only if the quality of the preparation will in no way suffer as a result.

Shopping Sources

With the ever-increasing popularity of French cuisine in the United States, it is possible to buy imported cooking equipment much more widely than ever before. Many department stores now carry a good stock of French utensils, as do specialty shops in large metropolitan centers. Bazar Français, 666 Avenue of the Americas, New York 10010, is one such specialty shop; it has an excellent catalogue and will ship mail orders to any part of the country.

The following suggestions include also some special addresses for those who would like to order from France, or shop there when traveling.

Fresh Truffles

Mr. Paul A. Urbani
Tel.: 609-394-5851
130 Graf Avenue
P.O. Box 2054
Trenton, New Jersey 08607

Mr. Urbani will airmail fresh truffles to any place in the United States. The season for white truffles is from September through October, and for black truffles from December through February.

The supply differs greatly from one year to another and the prices differ accordingly. Truffles are always expensive.

Copperware and Other Kitchen Equipment

E. Dehillerin
18–20 rue Coquillière
Paris, 1er

This famous Paris restaurant-supply house (metal and wood—no earthenware, porcelain or glass) will send its catalogue on request. It contains no prices, but, by comparison with those in America, they are astonishingly low. Copper utensils are sold by weight and not by the piece.

Tourists in Paris should not overlook a trip to Dehillerin. It is a living museum of marvelous and useful objects. Attractive and decorative brass-handled copperware is displayed on the ground floor. Heavy utilitarian iron-handled copper utensils are all in the basement.

Jacquotot
77 rue Damesme
Paris, 13ème

Another kitchen-supply firm, particularly interesting for a wide choice of copper utensils. They have no catalogue—which is perhaps as well—since prices fluctuate constantly, so the address is of interest essentially to those readers who may be visiting Paris. They will ship, and those buyers whose addresses are outside of France are spared the recent heavy taxes (19 percent) imposed by the French government. They go out of their way to be helpful and to please the client in any way possible, which is not always the case with firms accustomed to dealing only with professionals.

Seeds

Vilmorin-Andrieux
4, Quai de la Mégisserie
Paris, 1er

Vilmorin will furnish a catalogue on request. Many seeds that are difficult to obtain in America are listed. Among those particularly useful in a kitchen garden are:

Field Salads

Rocket (*roquette*)
Lamb's lettuce (*mâche*)—7 varieties
Cultivated dandelion (*pissenlit*)
Purslane (*pourpier*)
Mixed wild salads (*mesclun*)
Garden cress (*cresson du jardin*)

HERBS

Basil (*basilic*)—the large-leafed variety is less "peppery" and more delicate in flavor
Chervil (*cerfeuil*)
Common or Italian parsley (*persil commun*), finer of flavor than the curly variety
Burnet (*pimprenelle*)
Angelica (*angélique*)
Hyssop (*hysope*)
Oregano (*marjolaine*)
Savory (*sarriette*)—annual and perennial are both listed; the latter is finer

MISCELLANEOUS

Sorrel (*oseille*)—3 varieties
Leeks (*poireaux*)—11 varieties
Broad beans (*fèves*)—3 varieties
Gray shallots (*échalotes ordinaires*)—bulbs
Wild strawberries (*fraisiers de quatre-saisons*)

To import broad-bean seeds or shallot bulbs, one must fill out a form (furnished either by Vilmorin-Andrieux or by the United States Department of Agriculture at the address given below) to be sent to the following address (requesting, at the same time, special mailing labels to be enclosed, along with the permit number, in the order):

Permit Section, Plant Importation Branch
Plant Quarantine Division
209 River Street
Hoboken, New Jersey

None of the other seeds listed above require a formal importation permit.

TURNSPITS AND ACCESSORIES

Ets. Giraudon
144, Avenue Paul Vaillant Couturier
Sainte-Geneviève des Bois 91
France

This old-fashioned firm deals only in turnspits, grills and related material. Although they specialize in made-to-order installations, they also stock a number of standard articles. They willingly ship to the United States and will furnish complete documentation on request.

The type of small portable turnspit likely to interest most readers exists in 3 electric models: one capable of turning to approximately 8 pounds (about $50); one up to 16 pounds (about $54); one up to 30 pounds—strong enough to turn a suckling pig or milk lamb (about $72). A single clockwork model exists (10-pound strength, at about $76). Each includes a single standard spit. A number of others are available. The *broche-filet* (a cagelike spit that avoids piercing) comes to about $10. An asbestos construction (*parefeu*) designed to protect the mechanism from the direct flame costs about $4.

Their standard dripping pans are constructed of thin tinned sheet metal and are totally impractical. In my kitchen I have substituted a huge skillet, which I prop at a slight tilt, permitting the juices to collect at the far side from the fire. Giraudon manufactures stainless steel dripping pans, but no prices are quoted.

The prices quoted above do not include packing and shipping charges.

General Shopping

Italian neighborhoods are particularly useful for shopping. Elsewhere it is difficult to find such items as bouquets of dried oregano, dried *cèpes* (wild mushrooms), salted anchovies, fresh basil, field salads (lamb's lettuce, arugula), *fines herbes*, broad beans, celeriac, decent bread, and good-quality olive oil. I have had no success trying to persuade small producers in the south of France of the virtue of exporting their exquisite products, but decent olive oils may be bought in tins on the American market—a good Italian brand is Filippo Berio and a good French oil, from Marseilles, "fruitier" than most Italian ails, is James Plagniol.

The fancy-food sections in large department stores often furnish such rarities as good butter and quality *charcuterie*.

Search out the best butcher in your neighborhood and make friends with him. Ask questions and discuss cuts and qualities of meat. It is natural to give one's best service to those clients who are knowledgeable, interested—and faithful. Each time one buys an indifferent cut of prepackaged meat in a supermarket, one misses an opportunity of solidifying relations with one's butcher and ensuring good service when something special is needed. In any case, even his hamburger, chopped to order, fat removed, will also be of superior quality.

Basic Preparations

Any French cooking manual contains a comprehensive chapter on basic preparations. Only those recurrent in this book are presented here. Those that occur only once are relegated to specific recipes.

VEAL STOCK

(Fonds de Veau, Fonds Blanc, Blond de Veau)

A pure veal stock, properly executed, is the only impeccable, all-round basic stock. Ideally, a braising liquid or a sauce base should be an essence of the basic element in the preparation (woodcock glaze for woodcocks, venison stock for venison, etc.), but this leads us into theoretical cooking, for only past royalty was able to permit itself such luxury. A Beef Stock (*pot-au-feu*, page 322) remains the best braising stock for beef, and its full-bodied flavor, less marked in personality than that of furred game, renders it satisfactory as a braising liquid for the latter. By the same token, chicken stock may be used in certain preparations of feathered game. Only veal stock, by virtue of the essentially anonymous character of the meat, can lend body and support to all other flavors without altering their basic personalities. It is a solid vehicle and catalyst that is never self-assertive. It serves also as a base for other stocks for, although one may not be able to sacrifice several pheasants to the preparation of an essence for one pheasant *salmis*, one may very easily enrich a veal stock by the addition of leftover carcasses (or heads, necks, giblets) from roast birds. The many recipes for braised vegetables may be properly made only with veal stock. Covered, it may be kept indefinitely in the refrigerator if one is careful to boil it every few days and transfer it to a clean container. I have never tried freezing it but see no reason why it should suffer from this treatment.

The specific quantities of ingredients, although given, are of no importance. The important thing is that the result be as concentrated in aromatic essence as possible. For this reason, anything that takes up room in the stock pot without lending flavor should be eliminated—bones, in particular, with the exception of veal hock, which gives readily of its gelatin. For bones to be serviceable, one must make, first, a stock of bones which is allowed to cook for a good eight to ten hours, then use this liquid for moistening the veal.

A veal stock that is moistened with another veal stock rather than water is, naturally, that much finer. A veal half-glaze (*demi-glace de veau*) is clear veal stock reduced to a light syrupy consistency. A veal glaze (*glace de veau*) is the half-glaze reduced (with regular changes to smaller saucepans) to its ultimate intensity. Although valuable, even essential, for certain preparations, these refinements, because of the time and expense involved, do not occur in the recipes in this book.

Veal Stock

about 4 *pounds inexpensive gelatinous cuts of veal* (*rib tips, shank, neck, trimmings*)
1 *veal hock* (*knuckle*), *broken into pieces*
about 1 *pound carrots*
2 *large onions, one stuck with* 2 *cloves*
1 *leek* (*or* 3 *or* 4 *small—if not available, do without*)
1 *large sprig fresh thyme* (*or* 1 *teaspoon dried thyme leaves*)
1 *branch celery*
1 *bay leaf*
1 *large bouquet parsley* (*including roots, if possible*)
1 *small handful coarse salt* (*salt lightly because of the eventual reduction*)
3–4 *quarts water, depending on the form of the stock pot*

Ask your butcher to break up the veal hock with a cleaver. Keep the meat in fairly large pieces. Peel the carrots and the onions, leaving them whole (if the carrots are very large, cut them across in two). Stick one onion with the cloves. Slice off the roots of the leek, remove the tough, dark-green sections of the leaves and, with a small, sharply pointed knife, pierce the flesh halfway down, slitting upward through the tips of the leaves. Repeat this procedure two or three times so that the upper half of the leek is coarsely shredded but well intact. Wash well, swishing it around in a basin of water. Wash the celery branch and the parsley (scraping the roots, if there are any). Tie the leek, doubled in two, the branch of celery, the bay leaf and the parsley (plus the thyme, if it is in branches) into a bundle.

Put the bones into the stock pot (preferably one of heavy enameled ironware or earthenware). Place the pieces of veal on top, and add enough cold water to cover generously (about 1½ inches above the meat). Place over a medium flame (if using earthenware, protect it with an asbestos mat and place over a high flame) and when just below boiling point, begin to skim. The scum will continue to rise to the surface. You may help it along from time to time by displacing slightly the pieces of meat and bones with a wooden spoon, but without stirring. Continue to skim as it rises. When a full boil is reached and no more scum rises, pour in a small glassful (about ⅓ cup) of cold water. Scum will begin to rise again. Continue to skim until the boil is reached again and pour in more cold water. Repeat the process twice more, or until no more scum rises after the addition of cold water. Add all the other ingredients, making certain that everything is submerged. Continue skimming until the boil is reached again, and regulate the heat so that, with the lid slightly ajar, the tiniest suggestion of a simmer is constantly maintained. (Even if you are on intimate terms with your stove, unless you are accustomed to this kind of preparation and know the precise intensity of flame necessary, this regulation will require 15 minutes to ½ hour of turning the fire slightly up or down and rechecking a few minutes later.) Leave to cook for a good 4 hours. Skim off the surface fat 3 or 4 times during this period, but never stir the contents or otherwise disturb them in any way.

Gently pour the contents of the stock pot into a sieve lined with a couple of layers of cheesecloth, which has been placed over a large mixing bowl. Do not press or mash the debris in the sieve, but allow to drain well so that all the clear liquid passes through. Leave the broth to cool, and skim off all traces of fat from the surface.

BEEF STOCK

Because the *pot-au-feu* produces a stock that is one of the basic elements in other culinary preparations and is also a meal in itself, the recipe is given in the main body of the book (page 322). If it is prepared essentially for use as beef stock, cabbage and the refinement of adding tender spring vegetables will find no place in its preparation, nor need it undergo the double preparation recommended in the recipe. It may be made exactly like the veal stock, substituting gelatinous pieces of beef (tail, shank, chuck) for the veal.

The *petite marmite*, or *poule au pot*, one or the other sometimes garnished by the appellation "Henri-IV," is merely a *pot-au-feu* to which a hen has been added. A classical consommé is a *petite marmite* moistened with a *pot-au-feu* bouillon, completely degreased, and clarified by an additional couple of hours' cooking with a mixture of egg whites and lean ground beef. Although it is truly ambrosial in character, none of the soup recipes in this book will require an equivalent expenditure of time or material.

MIREPOIX

Plats cuisinés (which means, vaguely, those preparations that contain a number of elements and require a more or less involved cooking process—the term might be translated, "dishes cooked with art") rest generally on an aromatic foundation of onions, carrots, thyme and bay leaf. Other aromas, quite as valuable, may too often be excluded, but these mentioned, in any case, lend the primary support to all stocks, *court-bouillons* and braised preparations, and, although the latter often require a stock as braising liquid, it is nonetheless reinforced by a new addition of these same elements. For those preparations in which the carrots remain as part of the garnish, the vegetables are simply cut up, but for the many dishes that are garnished otherwise, or only sauced, a *mirepoix* (or *matignon*, which is the same thing except that the vegetables are finely sliced rather than chopped) is used as the aromatic base. Some recipes (none in this book) call for an addition of chopped ham or salt pork. For preparations in which the sauce is passed separately, the vegetables may be chopped more coarsely. If the *mirepoix* is to remain in the body of the sauce, the vegetables should be chopped very finely and the woody core of the carrots should be first removed. The *mirepoix* may be prepared in quantity and kept in the refrigerator, but the preparation is so simple that it seems hardly worthwhile. I personally feel that it gains by a substitution of mixed herbs for thyme, but that is an affair of taste, and the following recipe is classic.

Mirepoix

2 *large carrots (approximately* 4–5 *ounces) with cores removed*
2 *onions (equivalent weight to the carrots)*
1/2 *bay leaf and a large pinch of thyme, ground to powder in a mortar, or merely crumbled if the sauce is to be passed through a sieve. (Do not use herbs already powdered—they have no flavor)*
1 *heaping tablespoon finely chopped parsley (including roots, if possible)*
4 *tablespoons (*2 *ounces) butter*
pinch of salt

Peel the carrots and the onions and chop them finely. To chop the carrots, cut them in two lengthwise, pry out the core with the help of a small knife, and slice each half lengthwise as finely as possible. Flatten these slices out on the chopping board and continue slicing through them lengthwise until they are reduced to tiny sticks, then, holding them together, slice finely crosswise. Rechop this mass several times until very fine. For those who dislike chopping there is a useful device, a *mouli-julienne*, through which the carrots may first be passed, then chopped through a couple of times.

Melt the butter in a small, heavy saucepan, add all the ingredients and cook very gently, stirring regularly, for about 1/2 hour. The *mirepoix* should be thoroughly cooked, but absolutely not browned. If it is to be stored in the refrigerator, pack it into a glass or small jar, pressing well with a fork to eliminate all air pockets, and cover the surface with a buttered round of kitchen paper, aluminum foil or wax paper.

DUXELLES

Duxelles is occasionally used, like *mirepoix*, as an aromatic braising element, but more often as a stuffing, either alone or as one of several ingredients in a forcemeat, and as the base for *sauce duxelles* (boiled with white wine, reduced, brought to consistency with tomato purée and half-glaze and buttered away from the heat). It, too, may be prepared in advance and kept in the same way as *mirepoix*, if desired. To save time and effort, the mushrooms are often passed through a grinder. The result is still flavorful, but the fine, clean texture that may be attained only by chopping with a sharp knife is sacrificed to that of a mashed, coarse purée.

Duxelles is usually made with cultivated mushrooms, but they may be replaced advantageously by any wild mushroom. For reasons of economy, stems alone may be used (the heads, if not designed to serve immediately, may be boiled for 3 or 4 minutes with 1/4 cup of water, a chunk of butter, salt, pepper, and a bit of lemon juice, and kept in their cooking liquid, which is also a valuable flavoring agent). A particularly elegant *duxelles* is that made of truffle peelings. It should be subjected to a shorter and less violent cooking process.

Duxelles

1 *large onion, finely chopped*
2 *tablespoons* (1 *ounce*) *butter and* 1 *tablespoon olive oil (or* 4 *tablespoons butter)*
1/2 *pound mushrooms or mushroom stems, finely chopped*

salt, freshly ground pepper
1 heaping tablespoon finely chopped parsley
nutmeg
a few drops of lemon juice

Cook the chopped onion in the fat until it is soft and yellowed in color. Add the mushrooms and turn the flame up. Stir and toss until their liquid has evaporated and the mixture is fairly stiff. Turn the flame low again, salt and pepper to taste, stir in the parsley, and continue to cook for a minute or two, stirring regularly. Grate in a tiny bit of nutmeg, add the lemon juice and remove from the heat. If the *duxelles* is to be stored, eliminate the lemon juice, which may be added just before using.

THE PREPARATION OF ARTICHOKE BOTTOMS

Artichoke bottoms may be cooked and kept submerged in their cooking liquid for several days before using (if they are to be canned, the cooking time should be reduced to a minimum since they must be sterilized afterward). Served cold, the following recipe represents the complete cooking process. Served hot, artichokes always gain in flavor by a final cooking in butter. (If one has the luck to find them young and tender, they may be cooked directly in butter after having been rubbed with lemon.) The lemon—both the rubbing and its presence in the cooking liquid—is designed to keep them from turning dark, but should not be overdone, for although a slight lemon flavor is agreeable, a delicately flavored grayish artichoke is preferable to one that is acid in flavor, though impeccable in color. Also, to avoid discoloration, artichokes should not be cooked in any metal except stainless steel or enamelware, nor "turned" (pared in spiral fashion) with a carbon knife.

(*Recipe follows*)

Artichoke Bottoms

artichokes
lemon halves for rubbing them

Cooking liquid:
for 1 quart water, the juice of 1/2 lemon, pinch of thyme, salt

Break off the stems, which permits any fibrous strings to be pulled out. If the stems are sliced off, the strings remain in the bottom. Tear off all the tough outer leaves, pulling each backward, then down toward the base. When the leaves appear white and tender at the base, cut across the artichoke, leaving the tender bases attached to the bottom. Using a small, well-sharpened stainless steel knife, neatly pare the bottoms where the stem has been torn off, then continue, in a spiral fashion, all the way round to the top, removing all dark green parts. The finished product will be a pale-green and white flattened sphere. The pared surface of an artichoke darkens rapidly in contact with air, and, unless one's work methods are extremely efficient, it is best to rub it with the cut surface of a half lemon several times during the process. Don't worry about the chokes at this point.

Plunge them into the boiling liquid and cook, covered, at a simmer. The cooking time may vary from 10 to 40 minutes depending on the qualities of the artichokes. They are done when the flesh no longer resists a sharply pointed knife. They should remain firm, for they will continue to cook slightly while cooling in their liquid and, unless they are to be served cold, they will be subjected later to an additional cooking. Cool them in their liquid and keep them well submerged, the receptacle covered, refrigerated, until ready for use. Before using them, carefully remove the chokes, using a teaspoon to gently pry them loose, and sponge the artichoke bottoms dry with a towel.

MOUSSELINE FORCEMEAT

A mousseline forcemeat is the ultimate in a stuffing. It is most often made from fish (such as pike, sole, flounder, whiting, salmon, lobster), chicken, veal, feathered game, wild rabbit, or hare. The first time one launches oneself into its preparation it may seem complicated, but the basic principles are simple. It is a fine purée of raw flesh, bound by a bit of egg white and mounted with heavy cream.

The younger and fresher the flesh, the less albuminous support is required in the form of egg white. The less egg white used and the more cream—up to a certain point—the finer the result. The trick is to find the point at which the *farce* still holds, and the usual method is to decide on a given amount of egg white, and to then test it 2 or 3 times while adding the cream by poaching a tiny *quenelle* in a pan of simmering water that is kept ready. As long as the little dumpling poaches firmly, more cream can be added. With an excess of egg white, all the delicacy is lost, and the stuffing is heavy and rubbery. With too little egg white, or too much cream, it collapses during the poaching process. *Quenelles* that are poached in hot water require more egg white than those that are poached "dry" in a gentle oven, or than a molded mousseline forcemeat. Fish can support more egg white than chicken—a young chicken, freshly killed, needs none at all.

The testing method will, no doubt, seem discouraging to the reader, as it often does to me, and the following recipe is a good, standard one that takes no chances. There is, perhaps, particularly for chicken or veal, a bit too much egg white, and most materials may support a bit more cream than the quantity given. Assuming the cream to be absolutely fresh, which is no problem in America, and the instructions followed to the letter, it cannot go wrong.

Mousseline Forcemeat

1/2 *pound raw meat, fish or poultry*
salt, freshly ground pepper, nutmeg
1 *egg white*
1 *cup heavy cream*

Remove any traces of skin or fat from the flesh, scrape strips or fillets with the blade of a sharp knife, holding the tip with the other hand

and scraping away from you, with the grain of the flesh, removing all the ligaments and membranous material possible—it is impossible to eliminate it entirely, but the more is removed at this point, the easier will be the final passage through the sieve. After scraping it to shreds, pound the flesh in a mortar until it is completely reduced to a purée—the more it is pounded, the better. Add salt, pepper and the slightest suspicion of freshly grated nutmeg, and continue working the purée with a pestle, adding the egg white, in very small amounts at a time. When the final addition has been completely incorporated into the mixture, start passing it, about a tablespoonful at a time, through a fine-meshed nylon drum sieve, using the plastic disk (*corne*); scrape all the debris (nervous, membranous material) from the surface after each passage.

Pack the purée into a bowl (if time presses, it will chill more rapidly in a metal bowl—an hour on cracked ice is sufficient), smooth the surface of the purée, cover the bowl and embed it in cracked ice. Put into the refrigerator until needed.

Mount the purée, keeping the bowl still on ice (having poured off the water and replaced it by more ice, if necessary), by adding the cream, well chilled, in small amounts at a time and working it vigorously with a wooden spoon. At first it is hard to work, for the mixture is very stiff, then it becomes somewhat more supple, and, though it is still firm, it is possible to beat it. After the addition of about 1/2 cup of cream, it should be quite malleable. At this point, whip the remaining cream until fairly firm, but not stiff, and stir and fold it gently into the mass until the whole is intimately combined. It is ready to use.

RICE

Plain rice is the automatic accompaniment to numerous stews or other dishes whose sauces are generally either tomato-flavored or creamed, and often thickened with egg yolks. Assuming the rice to be of quality, any of the methods of preparation are good. Do not use precooked or "treated" rice. The latter, in particular, is slippery-textured and distinctly chemical in flavor. A rice with a large, long grain and a mat surface usually seems to be the best. In France, the best riceavailable comes from Madagascar; in America, Carolina rice may be the best on the market. The short, round-grained Piedmont rice can be of excellent quality, but requires a special *risotto* treatment. For my purposes, I have found a pilaf type of preparation to be the simplest and the most satisfactory: The rice need neither be washed before cooking nor dried (steamed) after; its natural flavor remains intact and its grains separate; it may be kept warm for long periods of time without suffering any loss in quality. Classically, chopped onion is first cooked in the butter to heighten the flavor, and the rice is moistened with a bouillon or stock, but these seem questionable supports, for they mask the delicate natural flavor of a good rice. Different rices are capable of absorbing slightly different quantities of water and may require a few minutes more or less of cooking time, but this is no problem, for a rice that is slightly undercooked or overcooked is not bad as long as it is dry and the grains remain separate; after a couple of tries your timing and liquid measure will adjust themselves to your rice. Acceptable results may be produced in a thin aluminum pot with a plate for a cover, but a pilaf is perfect only if prepared in a heavy saucepan, preferably copper, with a tight-fitting lid. Count one cup of rice for four people.

Rice Pilaf

1 *tablespoon* (1/2 *ounce*) *butter*
1 *cup dry, unwashed rice*
salt
2 *cups boiling water*
4 *tablespoons* (2 *ounces*) *butter*

Melt the tablespoon of butter in the saucepan over a low flame, add the rice, sprinkle with salt, and allow it to cook gently in the butter, stirring regularly with a wooden spoon, for a couple of minutes, or until the grains lose their slightly translucent quality and become milky and opaque. Add the boiling water, stir once to be certain no grains are sticking (done correctly, no grains will be browned andnone will stick), and cover tightly. Leave to cook, undisturbed, for about 25 minutes, either on top of the stove or in a preheated slow oven. If left on top of the stove, it may be necessary to use an asbestos mat underneath the pot to help regulate the heat—the liquid should present only the slightest suggestion of a surface movement. The rice is done when the water has been completely absorbed. Mix in the remaining butter, cut into small pieces, manipulating the rice delicately with the prongs of a fork so as not to break or crush the grains, and turn it out immediately into a warmed serving dish (or, if it is prepared some time in advance, into another saucepan which will then be kept, covered, in a warm, but not hot, place).

CREPE BATTER

Crêpes are unleavened, paper-thin pancakes. Depending on the use to which they are put, they may be called "crêpes" or *pannequets.* They form the "shirts" in *en chemise* preparations and the crisp surfaces of some *cromesquis* when stuffing enveloped in a crêpe is fried in deep fat. Under certain circumstances, they may replace the sheet of paste used to enrobe *cannelloni.*

The following recipe will serve for all the preparations in this book. For unsweetened dishes, the sugar should be eliminated. One may count on 18 to 20 small crêpes or 10 to 12 large with these proportions.

It is not terribly important to remain loyal to precise ingredients or measurements. Crêpes are good made with milk or beer, with or without the addition of cognac or liqueur, and perfectly acceptable made with water. The batter may be enriched by the addition of cream, may contain more or fewer eggs, and olive oil may replace the butter. Finely chopped *fines herbes* added to an hors d'oeuvre or main-course crêpe batter is an attractive refinement.

The batter should be thin—the consistency of very fresh cream. The pan should be in impeccable condition. If a large number of crêpes must be made, one may save a great deal of time by working with 2 or 3 pans over different burners. Crêpes may be made in advance, in which case they must be stacked on a plate neatly, one on top of the other, and covered with a towel, to avoid their drying out.

Crêpes

2 heaping tablespoons flour
1 heaping tablespoon sugar (include only in dessert crêpes)
small pinch salt
3 eggs
1 cup milk
1 tablespoon cognac
3 tablespoons (1½ ounces) melted butter

Sift the dry ingredients into a mixing bowl, make a well in the center, and break in the eggs. Stir, keeping to the center, until all the flour is gradually absorbed into the eggs, then slowly add approximately ⅔ cup of milk, stirring all the while. Stir in the cognac and melted butter and thin the batter with milk until it is no thicker than fresh cream. I do not find it essential to let the batter stand before cooking, but this may of course be done.

A small ladle of a capacity of about 3 tablespoons is practical for pouring. For large crêpes (approximately 7 inches in diameter at the bottom of the pan), count about 3 tablespoons of batter, for small (5 inches), about 2 tablespoons. If the batter refuses to cover the bottom of the pan, it is too thick, and more milk should be added.

Heat the pan, lightly buttered (it need be buttered only once, assuming the batter to be sufficiently lubricated), over a low to medium flame (after the first 2 or 3 crêpes, adjust the heat if necessary). If the pan does not sizzle at contact with the batter, it is not hot enough. Lift the pan from the flame and, holding it with one hand, pour in the batter with the other. At the same time, give the pan a rolling motion, turning it rapidly in all directions, so that the batter spreads immediately over the entire surface. Return it to the flame, and after 30 seconds or so, delicately lift an edge of the pan cake with the rounded tip of a table knife to check its progress (after one or two times, you will have the feeling and everything will go automatically). Ease the knife blade all the way under and flip the crêpe over. Toss it if you prefer—it is a pretty piece of theater, but requires a certain amount of practice, and the result is the same. After about 15 seconds, remove the pan from the flame, lift the crêpe out with the knife and begin the operation all over again. It is essential to remove the pan from the flame for several seconds each time, for, with the flame at the correct intensity for cooking the crêpes, the pan heats progressively and rapidly becomes too hot. The batter should be stirred each time just before being poured, as the flour has a tendency to settle to the bottom and the butter to rise to the top. If, partway through, the batter is noticeably thicker, more liquid may be added.

HERBS

For my own purposes, I have settled, finally, on the following herbs. Among those to be used fresh: parsley, chives, tarragon, chervil (the traditional *fines herbes*, alone or in combination), basil, dill, wild fennel, and savory.

Those to be used dried: thyme, bay leaf, rosemary, oregano (wild marjoram), savory and wild fennel.

Others are in my garden, but usually remain untouched. Hyssop I occasionally use—sparingly—when receiving erudite curiosity seekers. Borage, sage, and mint find their place mostly in bouquets (not *garnis*), and coriander (whose seeds are essential in many brine and vinegar conserves) I planted only once (its tender green leaves, known in French as *persil chinois*, and in the United States as Chinese parsley, are much used in Arab and Oriental cooking); I found the odor so intensely repellent that I could never bring myself to try it. The only two that I regret not having are cultivated marjoram, neither the seeds nor plants of which I have been able to find in France, and *serpolet*, a variety of wild thyme, the perfume of which resembles savory more than thyme but is more fragile and delicate than either. In the past, the mountainsides of Provence were covered with it, but for a reason that none can explain it is rapidly disappearing.

A *bouquet garni* is a bundle of herbs tied together in order to simplify their removal from a dish at the end of its cooking process.

For those who are in a position to raise or collect their own herbs, the following things should be kept in mind:

1. Thyme flowers are finer in flavor than the leaves, but at the moment that the plant is in flower (April through June, depending on the climate), the leaves also have a stronger and more characteristic perfume. The year's provision is best made at this time.

2. Oregano must be collected when in full flower (July and August). It may be bought in dried bouquets from Italian grocers and, in this form, is always fresher and more fragrant than that found in jars or cans.

3. Perennial savory has a more pungent but finer flavor than the annual variety, which, although useful in the absence of the former, has a vague suggestion of kerosene to its scent.

4. Rosemary is always powerful and may be collected at all times of the year. Although delicious, it should be used with circumspection. Curiously, the smoke of burning or smoldering rosemary is a far more voluptuous and delicate incense than that of any other herb. Any fish, meat, fowl, or vegetable grilled over coals is enhanced if, during the last few moments of the grilling process, a small handful of rosemary leaves is sprinkled over the coals.

A jar of mixed herbs of one's own confection (for not only does one not know what is contained in the commercial mixtures, but they are always too old, with the result that they lend only a vague, powdery, peppery quality) is practical. Nearly all recipes that call for a complicated dosage of several different herbs are happily supplied by a single pinch of the mixture. The mixed herbs should be dry, but as nearly as possible of the year's production. Do not be tempted by the miraculous blender to reduce your mixture to powder—the flavor will very rapidly be lost. For those recipes that require a pinch of powdered herbs, it is much the best to pound them in a mortar at the last minute.

(Recipe follows)

Mixed Herbs

1 *heaping tablespoon savory*
1 *heaping tablespoon thyme*
1 *heaping tablespoon oregano*
1 *teaspoon finely crumbled rosemary*
1 *bay leaf, finely crumbled*

Cultivated marjoram may, by all means, be added and, if one likes, a couple of leaves each of sage and dried mint, crumbled finely. Store in a small tightly closed jar.

KITCHEN GARDENS

A garden can alter the entire aspect of one's kitchen and table. Even without a garden, most herbs can still be raised in pots or window boxes, but with a few square yards of garden space, one can plant such hard-to-find and easy-to-grow things as chervil (in French, *cerfeuil*). For constant production it should be planted every two or three weeks from early spring to early fall—in a shady corner at the hottest part of the season. Sorrel (French, *oseille*) requires no particular care or special soil, and with a bit of protection during the winter, will produce all year round for four or five years. Wild fennel (*fenouil*) is another good garden possibility, as are all the semi-wild salads: rocket (*roquette*), lamb's lettuce (*mâche*), burnet (*pimprenelle*), purslane (*pourpier à salade*), basil (*basilic*), borage (*bourrache*) and many others. In France, seed packages of mixed wild salads (*mesclun*) are commonly sold. In the list of useful addresses (page 68) I have given the name of a French seed house that mail-orders to America.

If space allows, a few artichoke plants (the violet variety, if possible) will permit the discovery of the marvelous raw artichoke, eaten with a vinaigrette at a tender young age before the choke is even developed. Other useful plants are the common gray shallots (*échalotes grises*)—I have substituted onions for shallots in most recipes in this book, for the only shallot that I have ever found on the American market is the ugly, coarse-flavored red shallot. Also useful are leeks (*poireaux*), and broad beans (*fèves*)—one of the most exquisite of all vegetables, hard to find and nearly always too mature when offered for sale. To import the seeds, a customs permit is necessary. And, of course, there are green beans, which are never picked young enough and never sold fresh enough. Nasturtiums will grow anywhere with no care, and the flowers are as pretty as they are useful in salads. A rich soil will produce too much foliage and few flowers.

SALADS

The indications for salads in these menus is deliberately vague. With the exception of iceberg lettuce, all easy-to-find salad materials such as romaine, Boston lettuce, leaf lettuce, chicory, escarole and endive are possible in salads described as "tossed green" or "mixed green." A salad garnished with *fines herbes* should be light in flavor, hence escarole or chicory are excluded from the choice. These light salads occur often in the more elegant menus, with the exception of those menus in which game is the climactic point. Chervil is the most delicate of the *fines herbes* and may be used in quantity. A light lettuce caressed by its ephemeral scent provides the perfect accent after a *suite* of more or less intricate and subtly flavored dishes, but only a fairly pungent green can hold its own after the rich savor of game.

Robustly flavored, rustic dishes are marvelous followed by salads flavored with "wild" or uncultivated greens, such as watercress, field cress, purslane, burnet, lamb's lettuce, young dandelion greens, wild chicory, *arugula*, rocket—alone or in mixture. Chopped fresh savory and fresh basil leaves add a splendid accent. Tender young nasturtium leaves and nasturtium buds and flowers have a fine, cleansing, peppery taste, and a décor of the multicolored flowers against the dark-green leaves of wild salads is, to say the least, ravishing. A salad for which I have a particular affection is composed of approximately half lettuce and half rocket with a healthy handful of fresh basil leaves added, decorated with nasturtium flowers. Rocket (in French, *roquette*) is a "wild" salad that one may cultivate—and which I am never without.

It resembles somewhat the green called *arugula* handled by Italian greengrocers, but is spicier and more "personal" in flavor. When planted in rich soil and kept watered, it grows rapidly and is never too strong.

Any salad must be well dried. Nothing is more repulsive than a bowl of salad dripping in water and vinegar with a few globules of oil floating here and there. A salad basket is useful for drying tougher leafed greens, but lettuce should be carefully dried between two towels. Many of the wild or semi-wild greens are small-leafed and escape from the whirling salad basket. They, too, must be dried in a towel, but may be treated with less care. Nasturtium flowers should, of course, never be treated with insecticide; they should be freshly picked and used unwashed.

Nothing can replace the fresh, clean, fruity flavor of young, virgin olive oil in a vinaigrette salad dressing. The vinegar should be made of good wine and it should be used sparingly. For a lettuce and *fines herbes* salad, one part of vinegar to five parts of olive oil is about right. Only salt and pepper should be used as seasoning. For the more pungent salads, the bowl may be rubbed with garlic, and a bit of mustard absorbed into the vinegar. These salads can also take a stronger dose of vinegar. The easiest and most attractive way to prepare a salad is to prepare the dressing directly in the salad bowl (not a sticky, wooden one), rubbing the bowl first with garlic (if that is to be included), then adding the seasoning and vinegar, stirring until the salt has been dissolved, and, finally, adding the oil. The serving fork and spoon may then be crossed in the bowl, and the salad leaves arranged on top, so that they do not contact the dressing. In this way, the salad may be prepared before the meal, presented, untossed, the surface sprinkled with *fines herbes* or decorated with flowers, then tossed the instant before serving.

A pleasant occasional change from vinaigrette is a lemon and cream dressing. This, too, may be heightened with a touch of mustard, and gains by an addition of chopped fresh dill leaves or *fines herbes.*

A concentrated aromatic vinegar allows a salad to profit from the basic virtues of a good vinegar without suffering from either the acidity or the excessive moisture that are inevitable with a vinegar of normal constitution. Only a few drops need be used in conjunction with the other seasonings. Although serviceable immediately, it improves with age, and if one makes a certain quantity each year, it is interesting to compare "vintages."

Aromatic Vinegar

1 *quart of good wine vinegar*
2 *crushed cloves of garlic*
1 *bay leaf*
1 *tablespoon of Mixed Herbs* (*page* 86)
a few sage leaves
2 *cloves*
few grains of coriander

Reduce the vinegar by half over a high flame (the fumes are choking—close kitchen do or and open a window). Remove it from the heat, add all the aromatic ingredients and leave it, covered, for several hours or overnight. Place a cloth or several thicknesses of cheesecloth over a funnel and strain the vinegar into a bottle.

AROMATIC PEPPER MIXTURE

So-called "aromatic pepper" is nothing more than the whole grains of allspice. They are slightly larger than peppercorns and reddish-brown in color.

Although black and white pepper come from the same plant (the black being picked before maturity and dried with its hull, the white picked ripe and hulled), they are very different in flavor. About 3 parts of black to 2 of white and somewhat less than 1 of the allspice is a good mixture. For some few preparations, this mixture can replace neither white nor black pepper, but for most things I prefer it. It will, no doubt, not please all readers.

Fresh, tender green peppercorns are now marketed either frozen or canned. They are useful in the preparation of certain game dishes in sauce.

SKIMMING

There are three distinctly different kinds of skimming, for which, in French cooking terminology, there are three verbs: *écumer* (to scum); *dégraisser* (to degrease); and *dépouiller* (to skin). The first two are generally understood and respected. *Dépouillement* (skinning) is too often misunderstood or merely sidestepped, even by professional cooks, in the mistaken belief that it does not make that much difference. It makes, among others, the supreme difference between a sauce that is absolutely digestible and one that is not. It is a combined purification and reduction, traditionally practiced with all sauces based on stock that have been thickened by a *roux*. The flavor and the quality of the thickening are dependent on the flour's being first cooked in butter or another fat, but the fat, cooked over a long period of time and indigestible, inevitably remains in suspension in the sauce. It and other impurities are eliminated by skinning. The duration of time may be from a quarter of an hour to two or three hours, but the process is always the same: the liquid is brought to a boil and the saucepan is placed over a small flame (on a gas stove, the central part of a burner or the smallest burner—on an electric stove, the saucepan is simply pulled partway to the side of the smallest burner) so that one side of the bottom is heated and a steady, but very slight boil is produced at only one point to a far side of the liquid's surface. A thin skin will slowly develop over the remaining surface, collecting and growing thicker at the edge of the saucepan that is farthest from the simmering area. The skin should, at regular intervals (every two or three minutes for a sauce that is *dépouillée* for a short time, every ten or twenty minutes for one that remains in the process over a long period of time) be carefully gathered to the side of the saucepan with the edge of a spoon and removed. Each time, a certain amount of loose, floating fat remains. This, too, should be carefully skimmed off.

Simple stews (lamb ragouts, veal *sautés*, fricassees, *boeuf bourguignon*, *coq au vin*, etc.) are rarely treated in this manner, but they gain in quality and in digestibility if, when the meat is cooked, the sauce is passed through a sieve and subjected to this process rather than to the rapid reduction over an intense heat which is more common. The latter method may bring a sauce to the correct consistency, but the violent boiling throws the fat and other impurities back into an emulsion in the sauce. Often, with dishes of this kind, even the reduction is not respected and the "sauce" is nothing but a watery, greasy, dirty brown beverage—half the restaurants in France have a dish that answers this description on the menu every day.

USING A DRUM SIEVE

Drum sieves come in standard sizes, the most practical of which, for home use, is "08." The inside diameter of the high wall is 9 inches—exactly that of a standard soup plate.

For semiliquid material, place it on a fiat surface, high wall down, with the soup plate underneath to collect the purée. The plastic disk (*corne*) should be held firmly between the thumb and four fingers, with the fingers reaching almost to the lower edge of the disk. The disk should be held flat (at something less than a 45° angle) and firmly against the surface of the sieve and drawn toward oneself in regular repetition while the drum is turned in a circle with more or less regularity by the other hand. The thicker the food substance, the less regularly the drum need be turned, until, finally, when working with a small quantity of stiff substance, it is no longer useful to turn the drum. Fairly liquid materials pass easily and are no problem. The stiffer the material, the greater care should be taken in its preliminary preparation to reduce it into as consistent a purée as possible to facilitate its passage through the sieve, and the smaller quantity one should work with at a time. In passing pounded, raw meat for forcemeats, no more than a tablespoonful at a time should be attempted. A plate is no longer necessary. The sieve may be placed directly on a chopping board or a clean table top. Draw the disk flat across the sieve's outer surface from time to time to spread out the material that collects on its underside. After each passage, scrape the surface of the sieve clean with the disk and discard the residue. Clean off the purée clinging to the underside of the sieve and begin again.

SLICING AND CHOPPING

For slicing, a knife with a blade 5 or 6 inches long is easiest. The article to be sliced should be held in place on the chopping board with the tips of one's thumb and fingers held closely together and turned inward, clawlike, to keep them clear of the blade's edge. The side of the blade should rest constantly against the farthest joint of one's middle finger, which serves as a guide. Articles to be chopped (an onion, for instance) should be first cut in two to create a flat surface against the chopping board, each half sliced through finely, then given a quarter-turn on the board and sliced through again. Thus one has a mass of material already reduced to tiny cubes to start with. To chop it more finely, use a "French chef's" type of knife, holding it in such a way that the tip of the thumb and the curled knuckle of the forefinger touch the base of the blade and rest the fingers of the other hand against the top of the blade toward the tip. This creates an easy leverage and one need not press or force the knife with the chopping hand.

TO PEEL AND SEED TOMATOES

To loosen the skin, dip them first in boiling water (if they are very ripe this may not be necessary), cut out a small cone from the stem end, peel off the skin, and cut them across horizontally. Squeeze the halves to rid them of seeds and excess water (this liquid may be passed through a sieve to be added to a sauce if one likes). If the tomatoes need to be kept whole, remove seeds and liquid with your finger or the end of a teaspoon handle rather than squeeze them.

TO PEEL GARLIC

Unless the clove must remain undamaged (as for rubbing the interior of a casserole or salad bowl), place the clove on the chopping board, hold the blade of a knife on top of it and give the blade a smack with the palm of your hand. The clove will be slightly crushed and the skin may simply be lifted off.

BREAD

Good bread is made of nothing but flour, salt, water and a leavening agent. Its quality depends on the quality of the flour, which should not be over-refined), the quality of the leavening agent (sourdough being the best), and the quality of the oven. A perfect bread oven radiates heat regularly from all points—some professional ovens, like those in old-fashioned cookstoves, are heated by a system of hot-air circulation all around the body of the oven. Most modern home ovens are heated directly from below. With these, it is wise to install a metal plaque in the bottom of the oven to diffuse the heat, encourage an even coloration and prevent burning on the bottom.

One may, with American "all-purpose" flour and dried yeast, make a better bread than anything to be found on the market. To attempt to enrich it in any way will ruin it. Add no sugar, no milk and no shortening. The following recipe will produce one fairly large loaf of firm, crusty bread, which is better a day or two old than fresh from the oven, and resembles country bread (*pain de campagne*).

White Bread

1 *slightly mounded teaspoon dry yeast*
2 *cups water*
5 *cups flour (plus flour for dusting the board, the tray and the loaf)*
something over 1/2 *teaspoon salt*

Put the yeast into 1/2 cup of tepid water and leave for 10 or 15 minutes to ferment slightly.

Sift the flour and the salt into a large mixing bowl, make a well in the center, and pour in the remaining 1 1/2 cups of water, also tepid, and the yeast mixture. First stir out from the center until a thick paste is formed, then work it thoroughly with your hands until all of the flour has been absorbed. Form the dough into a ball in your hands, dust it with flour or roll it in flour, sprinkling a bit of flour inside the bowl also; put dough back into the bowl, cover with a towel, and place in the warmest part of the kitchen (but not on the stove). When it has more than doubled in size (after an hour, more or less, depending on the temperature of the kitchen), turn the ball out onto a floured board, punch it down to force out all the air, kneading it well, form it again into a ball, and leave it, floured, in the bowl as before. When again risen (it should rise a bit faster the second time), repeat the punching down and kneading process, form it into a ball (or a thick sausage shape, depending on the form of loaf desired), and place it on a lightly floured (but not greased) heavy metal baking sheet. Cut deeply into the surface of the loaf with a sharp, pointed knife, forming a simple design (a deep, central slash with rays cut out to either side, for instance, or, for a round loaf, curved slashes cut out from the center, or repeated diagonal slashes for a long loaf). This not only makes a more attractive loaf, but creates a greater surface to be transformed into crust. Dust the loaf with flour and leave it on the baking sheet, covered with a towel, to rise again for about 1/2 hour.

Bake it in a preheated oven, adjusted to medium-low (about 325° F. at the moment of putting the loaf in) for 1 hour and 10 minutes to 1 hour and 15 minutes. Check its progress after about 50 minutes after the first time, you will know exactly how to adjust the oven. Baked for 1 hour and 10 minutes at an even, regular heat, the crust should be an evenly colored, rich golden brown and should resound when thumped.

ALMOND COOKIES

One of a variety of simple cookies (petits-fours), although never mentioned on a menu, are as automatic an accompaniment to most desserts (with the exception of pastries or crêpes or particularly starchy puddings) as is bread to the main body of a meal.

Tuiles (literally, "tiles," a reference to their flat, thin, "warped" shape) are good, all-around dessert cookies and permit one to dispose of leftover egg whites. The cookies may be kept crisp in a tightly closed tin box.

Almond Cookies

Tuiles

1/2 cup sugar
3 *egg whites*
1 *heaping tablespoon flour*
1 *small pinch salt*
2 *tablespoons cream*
4 *tablespoons* (2 *ounces*) *melted butter*
1/2 cup slivered almonds

Whisk the sugar and the egg whites together in a mixing bowl, add the flour and the salt and continue whisking until well mixed. Incorporate the cream and the melted butter. Stir in the almonds.

Butter a *heavy* cookie sheet, cast iron if possible (the cookies are more easily removed from a heavy sheet), dust it with flour and give it a smart rap, upside down, to rid it of excess flour. Distribute the batter on the sheet in teaspoonsful, leaving enough space between each mound to allow for spreading, and bake in a gentle oven (about 325° F.) for about 10 minutes, or until they are golden brown around the edges and the center is only slightly yellowed.

They must be removed from the sheet the moment they leave the oven, to avoid sticking. Scoop each up with a deft, clean movement of the spatula and press it onto a rolling pin, or other cylindrical object, to give it its characteristic form. While still hot, the cookie is soft and pliable, but turns crisp upon cooling. After a few minutes on the rolling pin, remove the cookies to a cake rack and leave them till completely cooled.

Autumn Menus

Appropriate wines for each menu are suggested on the pages indicated below, which mark the beginning of each menu and its recipes.

Two Formal Autumn Dinners

I

PAGE 104

Crayfish Mousse with Champagne
Ravioli of Chicken Breasts with Fines Herbes
Roast Leg of Venison with Poivrade Sauce
Sweet Potato Purée
Endive and Lamb's Lettuce Salad
Pont l'Evêque Cheese
Molded Coffee Custard

II

PAGE 120

Sorrel Soup
Fritto Misto
Salmis of Pheasant
Wild Mushrooms à la Bordelaise
Rocket Salad with Nasturtium Flowers
Cheeses
Orange Jelly

Two Informal Autumn Dinners

I

PAGE 132

Baked Trout Stuffed with Sorrel
Sautéed Veal Kidneys with Mushrooms
Rice Pilaf
Lamb's Lettuce and Beet Salad
Cheeses
Charlotte with Crêpes, Sabayon Sauce

II

PAGE 140

Pike Dumplings à la Lyonnaise
Veal Cutlets à la Tapenade
Artichoke Purée
Cheeses
Apple Mousse with Peaches

A Festive Autumn Meal for Two

PAGE 150

Cucumber Salad, Cream Sauce

Baked Lobster Garin

Braised and Roast Partridge with Cabbage

Cheeses

Fresh Figs with Raspberry Cream

Four Simple Autumn Menus

I

PAGE 159

Salad of Grilled Sweet Peppers
Lamb Stew with Artichoke Hearts
Rice Pilaf
Wild Salad
Cheeses
Pears in Red Wine

II

PAGE 165

Composed Salad
Boiled Pigs' Tails and Ears with Vegetables
Goat Cheeses
Périgord Pudding

III

PAGE 172

Fennel à la Grecque
French Moussaka
Fresh White Cheeses
Orange Cream

IV

PAGE 177

Garlic Soup
Grilled Lambs' Hearts and Baby Zucchini
Cheeses
French Pancake Jelly Rolls

Autumn Menus

Autumn in France means wild mushrooms (in particular, *cèpes—Boletus edulis*) and game. In Italy, it also means the glorious white truffle, which is best raw, and shaved generously at the moment of serving over a hot preparation, such as pasta and butter or chicken breasts rapidly sautéed in butter. It is not true, as some pretend, that the white truffle is better or less good than the black truffle—it is a divinity apart.

From mid-September to just before Christmas (when fancies turn to *foie gras* and truffles), the French open markets far outdo the Dutch still-life painters in their festive display of game. A wild boar or deer is usually the centerpiece, and rows of pheasant, partridge and woodcock are strung around, punctuated by an occasional splash of wild-duck color. Hare, wild rabbit, garlands and piles of thrush, larks and "blackbirds" (unrelated to the American blackbird) enter into the composition, and, at this season, guinea fowl is often left in its feathers simply to keep it in the spirit of things.

Unless hunters number among one's family or friends, the problem of game in America is difficult, for that killed within the country may not be commercialized. Songbirds are protected by law so no recipes are given for the thrush, whose flesh is as lovely as its song (should one pass by the kitchen of an unscrupulous reader, it, like the woodcock, should be roasted rare, unemptied but for the gizzard, which may be replaced by a juniper berry).

Gastronomic growing pains, at least among those of loyal academic inclination nourished on the literature of Brillat-Savarin and Grimod de la Reynière, inevitably include experiences with "high" game. I have, fifteen years later, a painfully vivid memory of an extremely well-seasoned pheasant that I dutifully stuffed with fresh truffles a day in advance to "permit all the fumes to intermingle." When the creature was put to roast, the odors that escaped from the kitchen were unbelievable. Before coming to table, everyone was slightly uneasy, and after we all poked a bit at the food, queasiness took over. I doubt if any of my guests ate pheasant again that season. I did not. Knowledgeable analyses treating the difference between the aging of meat and putrefaction cannot change the fact that a dead animal when hung for several weeks is rotten. I do not suggest that one eat the thing while still in the throes of rigor mortis. The flesh must be somewhat aged, just as any other meat, or it will be dry, tough and tasteless.

Any bird that has been badly damaged by gunshot, particularly in the intestinal region, should be plumed and cleaned immediately. In other cases, a pheasant will be much improved if hung for about four days (a partridge for three days) in a cool, dry, well-ventilated place. These birds should be plumed, cleaned and dressed only shortly before being put to use, although, dressed, they may be kept in the refrigerator for a day or so without suffering. Wild duck and quail are at their best when eaten the day after having been killed or, at least, freshly cleaned and dressed immediately and kept refrigerated for only a short time.

Venison should be hung, whole, for from five days to a week. If cut up when freshly killed, the unskinned legs may still be hung, providing the open flesh is protected from contact with air and insects (rubbing with oil and covering with plastic wrap should do the trick—I have never had the opportunity to try it). The hind legs and saddle of young deer are best roasted slightly rare, unmarinated—or, at most, marinated for only a few hours in nothing more than a bit of white wine, olive oil and a pinch of herbs. The remaining parts may be prepared in identically the same way as *Daube à la Provençale* (page 413) or *Boeuf à la Bourguignonne* (page 239). The last method is incorrectly called *civet.*

Two Formal Autumn Dinners

with appropriate wines

MENU I (FOR 6)

CRAYFISH MOUSSE WITH CHAMPAGNE
[MOUSSE D'ECREVISSES AU CHAMPAGNE]

*A champagne blanc de blancs,
either effervescent or nature*

RAVIOLI OF CHICKEN BREASTS WITH FINES HERBES
[PELLMENES DE BLANCS DE VOLAILLE AUX FINES HERBES]

*A dry but full-bodied white wine:
Riesling or white Burgundy
(Corton-Charlemagne, Clos des Mouches,
Puligny-Montrachet, etc.)*

ROAST LEG OF VENISON WITH POIVRADE SAUCE
[GIGUE DE CHEVREUIL A LA SAUCE POIVRADE]

*A robust red wine: Côtes-du-Rhône
(Châteauneuf-du-Pape, Hermitage,
Côte-Rôtie) or Burgundy
(Nuits-Saint-Georges)*

SWEET POTATO PUREE
[PUREE DE PATATES DOUCES]

ENDIVE AND LAMB'S LETTUCE SALAD

[SALADE D'ENDIVES ET MACHE]

PONT L'EVEQUE CHEESE

[FROMAGE DE PONT L'EVEQUE]

A finer and older wine than the preceding but in the same spirit

MOLDED COFFEE CUSTARD

[CREME RENVERSEE AU CAFE]

A champagne demi-sec or a Vouvray of respectable age

The crayfish mousse and the *poivrade* sauce served with the venison belong to a realm of restaurant cooking that unhappily is of the past. Restaurants today capable of serving either may be counted on the fingers of one hand; for such dishes to be practicable, such elements as game stock or half-glaze, fish *fumet*, calf's-foot jelly and *mirepoix*—plus a number of competent workers–should automatically be at hand. Today restaurants often serve *poivrade* sauces that are basically boiled-up, flour-thickened mixtures of vinegar, pepper, water, and bouillon cubes—equivalent recipes have even appeared in more or less respectable French publications. It is not surprising that *la grande cuisine* has so many detractors. I can only hope that readers will try these recipes once before deciding that "nothing is worth that much trouble" and, for those who cannot afford such a heavy expenditure of time, that one or another of them be incorporated into simpler menus.

A roast leg of venison needs a sauce, but may obviously be accompanied by any of a number of very simple sauces (for instance, the roasting pan may simply be washed out with Madeira and the reduction finished with heavy cream). Currant jelly is often added to game sauces.

A sweet potato purée is hardly the usual French fare, but in this context its delicately sweet flavor and light texture are more satisfactory than the traditional heavy chestnut purée.

The juxtaposition of hot and cold, of textures, flavors and colors, follows a logical pattern, and a rich, "heady" cheese finds its perfect expression here (although many wine lovers prefer, no matter what the circumstances, to nibble at an anonymous cheese in order to best savor the wine). A wine powerful enough not to suffer by comparison with that designed to accompany the venison is, by the same token, able to support a Pont l'Évêque—one of the soft fermented cheeses most easily bought in good condition, neither too salty nor smelling of ammonia. Its delicacy of flavor comes often as a surprise after the sometimes rather terrifying odor.

The basic preparations for the *poivrade* sauce should be begun the preceding day; it would be a good thing to treat the family to a *pot-au-feu* a day or so in advance in order to have a good stock on hand. The dessert and the mousse may be finished and forgotten on the morning of the chosen day, and the ravioli may be prepared ahead of time. The final preparations, then, consist only in poaching and gratinéing the ravioli, roasting the leg of venison, finishing the sauce and preparing the sweet potato purée—in short, precisely the same amount of time and work involved as if one were to insert some prepared frozen food in the oven for a first course and serve a roast beef, mashed potatoes and gravy afterward.

The ravioli, the roast and the sweet potatoes should all be put into the oven just before the meal begins—that is to say, about twenty minutes before the ravioli are to be served and an hour before the roast. Ordinarily the ravioli should be finished in an oven less hot than that at which the roast should be begun, but that is not too serious—watch it carefully, and when the gratin is perfect, remove it from the oven. If the cream remains in large part unabsorbed, place the dish over a gentle heat on top of the stove for a few minutes. If your oven is not large enough to take both the gratin and the roast, start the former ten minutes earlier—it may be kept in a warm place until ready to serve—and the roast ten minutes later. Encourage your guests to linger over each course—a pleasure, as long as there is no scarcity of wine.

THE CRAYFISH MOUSSE

Crayfish abound in American streams, but are little eaten. Like lobsters, they must be alive when cooked, and they rank among the very great delicacies.

Writers at the turn of the century were already bitterly complaining that French streams were rapidly being emptied of crayfish. Today the French market is supplied by importations from Italy, Holland, Germany or Poland.

The white wine used in cooking the *fumet* should be of good quality (I most often use a Pouilly-Fumé), but, unlike the champagne, which remains unaltered by cooking, it need not be of the class of great wines.

If calf's-foot jelly is preferred to commercial gelatin the foot need only be parboiled, rinsed and put to simmer in water, covered, for seven or eight hours. The resultant jelly, cleansed of all fat, replaces the water in the fish *fumet*. If, on the other hand, one were to omit the *fumet* and the jelly from the preparation, the *velouté* might be replaced by a stout *béchamel* to which a tablespoon of dissolved gelatin has been added.

Crayfish Mousse

Mousse d'Ecrevisses au Champagne

1/3 cup Mirepoix (page 75)
2 dozen good-sized, lively crayfish
salt, tiny pinch of Cayenne
1 cup dry white wine
4 tablespoons (2 ounces) butter, plus small lump

Fish fumet:
several carcasses of neutral-flavored fish (flounder, lemon or grey sole)
1 1/2 cups dry white wine
1 1/2 cups water
1 onion, coarsely chopped
thyme, bay leaf, parsley, fennel seeds
salt
2 tablespoons unflavored gelatin

Velouté:
1 tablespoon (1/2 ounce) butter
1 tablespoon flour
1 cup of the fish fumet

1 cup whipping cream
1 egg white
1 tablespoon chopped fresh chervil
1 tablespoon chopped fresh tarragon
1 small glass champagne

Crayfish Mousse

THE FISH FUMET

Chop or break up the fish carcasses into small pieces. Bring the wine and water to a boil, add the fish carcasses and all other ingredients except the gelatin, and simmer, covered, for 1/2 hour. Add the gelatin, which has been softened in a bit of cold water, a couple of minutes before removing from the heat, stir to dissolve, and pass the liquid through a sieve, pressing bones and flavoring to extract the juices.

THE VELOUTE

Melt the butter, stir in the flour, cook for a couple of minutes, continuing to stir, over a low flame. Remove the saucepan from the heat and slowly pour in the cup of *fumet*, stirring all the while to avoid lumps. Bring to a boil, still stirring, and leave over a tiny flame, a bit to the side, to barely bubble for about 20 minutes, occasionally removing the bit of skin that forms on the surface.

THE MOUSSE

Melt a small lump of butter in a large skillet or *sauteuse*, add the *mirepoix* and heat over a low to medium flame. As rapidly as possible, beginning with the largest, rinse each crayfish and holding it firmly in the left hand (with a towel to avoid being pinched), tear loose, with a tiny, abrupt motion to each side, the central tail flap, or fin. Pull the tail flap gently in order to ease out the thread of intestine without breaking it and drop the crayfish into the *mirepoix*. The intestine, if not removed, lends a bitter taste, but once removed, the animal should be put to cook as rapidly as possible to prevent the loss of its juices.

When all are in the pan, turn the flame high, add the seasoning, toss and stir them around until they have turned red, add the cup of wine, bring to a boil, lower the flame, and leave to cook, covered, for 7 or 8 minutes. Select the handsomest and most regularly formed of the crayfish—one for each guest—and put them aside. Tear the others in two, carefully remove (and discard) the shells from the tails and put the latter aside with the whole crayfish. Pound the carapaces (that is to say, the entire upper part of the crustacean, including the pincers), 3 or 4 at a time, in a mortar (or reduce them to a rough purée in a blender, adding a bit of the cooking liquid), then thoroughly work in the 2 ounces of butter, pounding and turning the mixture with the pestle.

Add this *pommade*, along with the *mirepoix* cooking juices, to the *velouté*. Bring to a boil, mixing and stirring well, remove from the heat, and pass the contents of the saucepan through a food mill or *moulinette*, using the medium blade—this will eliminate the coarser debris of the carapaces. Pass this purée, in small quantities at a time, through a fine drum sieve, cleaning the surface well after each passage, discarding the residue, and collecting the purée into a large mixing bowl.

Embed the bowl in cracked ice and stir the purée continuously until it begins to thicken or "set." Whip the cream until semi-firm but not stiff, and mix it in thoroughly but gently. Pour into a deep platter or a shallow crystal dish, large enough to easily contain the bed of mousse and later the final decoration of tails, crayfish and jelly without giving a crowded effect. Put to set in the coldest part of the refrigerator, or embed in ice, but do not put in the freezer.

Combine the remaining *fumet*, the chopped chervil and tarragon and the egg white, beaten stiff, in a saucepan, bring to a boil, whisking all the time and, when the boil is reached, lower the flame and simmer for 4 or 5 minutes, whisking from time to time. Pour into a sieve placed over a bowl and lined with a kitchen towel or other finely textured cloth. When the filtered jelly is nearly cold, stir in the champagne.

THE DECORATION

Truss the reserved whole crayfish by pulling the tip of the tail upward in an arc toward the head—gently, without forcing—and, with equal care, easing the pincers back to meet it. Pierce the tail near the base, on each side, with the immobile point of each pincer. Arrange the trussed crayfish on the surface of the solid mousse. Place the additional shelled tails around in a decorative pattern and add something green (parboiled tarragon leaves or small bouquets of chervil) to the composition. Coat everything with the jelly (turning it, small quantities at a time, into a small bowl embedded in cracked ice, and rapidly spooning it over the décor as it begins to stiffen), repeating the process a few times on the trussed crayfish, which will require a heavier coating. Chill well. It is both practical and attractive, for the service, to embed the serving dish in cracked ice.

THE CHICKEN RAVIOLI

A particularly happy variation is the substitution of a couple of tablespoonfuls of finely chopped truffle peelings for the *fines herbes*, but possibilities are endless. *Duxelles* (page 76) can also be a useful addition.

Ravioli of Chicken Breasts

Pellmènes de Blancs de Volaille

Noodle dough:
- *2 cups flour*
- *1/2 teaspoon salt (about)*
- *2 whole eggs and 3 yolks*

Filling:
- *6 tablespoons (3 ounces) butter*
- *2 good-sized chicken-breast halves (1 whole breast)*
- *salt, freshly ground pepper*
- *1 tablespoon each parsley and chervil, and a few leaves of tarragon, all finely chopped*

Final preparation:
- *3 tablespoons (1 1/2 ounces) butter*
- *3 tablespoons (1 1/2 ounces) freshly grated Parmesan cheese*
- *1 cup heavy cream (approximately)*

THE NOODLE DOUGH

Sift the flour and salt into a large mixing bowl, add the whole eggs and the yolks and mix together thoroughly. The paste should be fairly firm but malleable (perhaps slightly firmer than short paste). If it does not seem stiff enough, sprinkle in a bit more flour, or if it is too stiff, add a bit of the extra egg white. Knead it with the palms of the hands on a lightly floured board, roll into a ball, wrap in wax paper and put into the refrigerator to "relax" its elasticity for an hour or so.

THE FILLING

Allow the butter to stand at kitchen temperature for an hour or so to soften. Remove the skin and bones from the chicken breasts, scrape the flesh with a small sharp knife, following the grain and removing all nerve tissue as you proceed. Chop finely until it forms a unified mass of coarse purée. Mix the chicken thoroughly with the butter, the seasoning and the *fines herbes* and refrigerate until ready for use.

Divide the dough into 4 equal parts and roll each out thinly on a lightly floured board to form an approximately square shape, turning it over regularly and sprinkling with flour, if necessary. Imagining the sheet of paste to be lined both horizontally and vertically at 2- to 2½-inch intervals, place a small teaspoonful of filling in a mound at each intersection. Using a small brush, repeatedly dipped in water, moisten wide lines in both directions between the mounds of filling, place another sheet of paste on top and press well all along the moistened areas with the side of the hand so that each bit of filling is completely sealed in. Cut along the center of each sealed line with a wooden pastry wheel or a knife. Make certain that each "package" is well sealed on all sides. The ravioli may equally well be made by cutting the sheet of paste into circular or square sections, placing filling in the center of each, moistening the edges, and folding each into a half-circle or triangle. They may be prepared hours ahead of time, in which case they should be kept spread out on a lightly floured board.

THE FINAL PREPARATION

Drop the ravioli, a few at a time (to avoid their sticking to one another), into a large pot of salted, boiling water. When it returns to a boil, reduce the heat, cover, and leave to barely simmer for about 6 minutes. Slowly and carefully pour the contents of the pot into a colander, so that none may be damaged. Pour some hot water over the ravioli to rinse the starch from their surface and leave to drain.

Butter a large gratin dish or shallow baking dish with 1 tablespoon of butter, sprinkle the bottom with half the grated cheese, arrange the ravioli on top, pour over enough cream so that they are just covered, sprinkle the surface with the remaining cheese, and distribute over the surface 2 tablespoons of cold, firm butter, cut into thin slices with a small sharp knife, repeatedly dipped in cold water. Bake for about 20 minutes in a medium oven, or until the cream is about two-thirds absorbed and the surface a golden brown.

THE LEG OF VENISON

If rare or medium-rare meat is looked upon with displeasure, roast venison may as well be discarded from one's repertoire. Well done, it is dry and savorless. The leg should be cut like a leg of lamb, the pelvic bone removed and the leg bone cut just above the lower joint so that a *manche à gigot* (see page 65) may be attached to facilitate the carving at table.

Roast Leg of Venison with Poivrade Sauce

Gigue de Chevreuil à la Sauce Poivrade

1 *leg of venison*
about 5 *ounces fresh fat side pork* (*for larding*)
salt and pepper
Poivrade Sauce (*page* 115)

Marinade:

3 *tablespoons olive oil*
2 *tablespoons white wine*
1 *small pinch mixed herbs*

THE LARDING

The layer of pork fat next to the skin is the firmest and purest. It is usually sold with the rind attached. (If fresh fat pork is unavailable, do not substitute bacon. If salt pork smells fresh, it may be used.)

The larding needle (hollow, with a very sharp, flexible point, widening toward the other end which is splayed to permit the insertion of the strips of fat) should be bent into a gentle curve at the needle end. The piece of fat, well chilled to ensure its being as firm as possible, should be cut with a sharp knife into long strips about 1/8 inch wide, and each strip cut into 1/8-inch "sticks" (this depends, of course, on the size of the article to be larded and on the dimensions of the needle—the strips must not be so thick that they have to be forced into the splayed end or they will slip out rather than penetrate the meat). The plumpest wide surface of the leg and the two sides (that is to say, the three-quarters of the surface not resting on the bottom of the roasting pan) should be larded.

The only practical and painless way to lard a piece of meat is to seat oneself comfortably in a chair and place the article to be larded on a clean towel on one's knees—in this instance with the leg bone end pointing away from one's person. A *lardon* (lardoon) of fat is inserted into the splayed hollow of the needle, as far as it will go without forcing—something over 1 inch—and, the needle held in the right hand, the flesh is transpierced from right to left. To facilitate the task, the *lardons* should be fairly long, but, once trimmed, each will be about 1 1/2 inches long, the central half of that length being embedded in the flesh and the visible ends protruding an equal distance on either side. For aesthetic reasons, the leg should be neatly larded in closely placed rows from top to bottom, the odd rows falling into one horizontal alignment and the even rows into an alternate parallel intermediate one.

The formal design of golden-brown protrusions on the surface of the roast forms a presentation as attractive as it is essential to the moistness and flavor of the flesh.

THE MARINADE

If the animal is young and tender, one may dispense with the marinade. It should, in any case, be very simple and scant, its object being to tenderize and flatter, without alteration of flavor, the natural qualities of the venison. Cognac should never enter into a marinade.

Place the larded leg on a platter, sprinkle over it the marinade ingredients, turn it so that all surfaces are well moistened and wrap the meat carefully in a moisture-proof wrapping (Saran wrap, aluminum foil, etc.). It may be kept like this for several hours—or a day or two, if necessary.

THE PREPARATION

As nearly as possible, the roasting pan should be of heavy material (cast iron is perfect), shallow, and just the right size to barely contain the roast. I have always been puzzled by the insistence that a roast be placed on a grill to prevent the meat's contacting the roasting juices. Unless the roasting is conducted at a stewing temperature, the fat and the caramelized meat juices inevitably burn with this treatment, are useless as an addition to a sauce or for the preparation of a juice, and the flavor of the meat suffers as well. It is comparable to placing a frying pan containing a piece of butter over a high flame. Left empty, the butter will burn a few seconds later, but if, the moment it is hot, a piece of meat, of a size to contact the entire heated surface, is added, the meat gently browns and the butter does not burn.

The roast should be carefully sponged dry with a towel and the dried surface rubbed or patted with oil. (Any other moisture creates a steaming process, which bleeds the meat of its juices and prevents the rapid browning that seals the surface so that all the juices remain inside. Oiling, on the other hand, hastens this browning process.)

Start the roast in a hot oven (about 400° F.). After 10 minutes, season it with salt and freshly ground pepper and turn the oven down to medium (about 325° F.). After another 15 or 20 minutes begin to baste it regularly.

For an average leg of venison, count about 40 minutes of actual roasting time and an additional 20 minutes for the meat to rest in a warm place (it may be left in the oven, turned off, with the door propped slightly ajar; remove it first for a couple of minutes to arrest the cooking process, then return it).

Present it unadorned on a heated platter, the sauce and sweet potato purée served separately.

THE POIVRADE SAUCE

A *sauce poivrade* is a sharply seasoned essence of meats and aromatic elements. A certain amount of flour gives it body, but its presence, thanks to the long cooking and purifying process, is indiscernible, and the suave consistency of the sauce depends on the reduction of the natural gelatinous elements in the meats to which the final addition of butter lends a velvety finish. It is one of the summits of classical cooking.

The recipe, as it stands here (a step down from the summit), although time-consuming, is practical in a home kitchen, the process being identical to that of an ordinary stew. Respect for the nature of the preparation hardly permits further simplification.

Poivrade Sauce

Sauce Poivrade

2 *medium carrots and* 2 *medium onions, coarsely chopped, or an equivalent amount of previously prepared Mirepoix* (*page* 75)
about 3 *tablespoons mild cooking oil*
1 1/2 *pounds venison stewing cuts—neck, trimmings, etc., cut up as for a stew* (*frozen game may be used*)
2 *tablespoons flour* (*about* 1/4 *cup*)
1 *teaspoon Mixed Herbs* (*page* 86)
1/2 *cup white wine*
1/2 *cup wine vinegar*
1/2 *cup tomato juice*
4 *juniper berries, slightly crushed*
about 2 1/2 *quarts rich, gelatinous stock—a Pot-au-Feu* (*page* 322) *containing, in addition to the usual ingredients, veal knuckle and shin is perfect*
8 *to* 10 *whole peppercorns, slightly crushed*
4 *tablespoons* (2 *ounces*) *fresh, unsalted butter*

No salt should be used, that contained in the stock being sufficient in view of the reduction to which the sauce will be subjected.

Cook the carrots and onions in the oil over medium heat (if using *mirepoix* already prepared, omit this step) using a large, heavy saucepan such as a *sautoir.* (A skillet may be used, but in that case everything should be transferred to a large casserole after the preliminary preparations.) Stir regularly until lightly browned, remove vegetables, and replace them by the pieces of meat. Turn the flame up (add more oil, if necessary) and cook on all sides until well browned; drain off the excess oil, sprinkle with the flour and, lowering the flame, cook for a couple of minutes longer, turning the pieces to permit the flour to brown. Return the vegetables to the pan (or, if already prepared *mirepoix* is used, add it at this moment), sprinkle with mixed herbs, mix everything well together, stirring with a wooden spoon, and add the white wine and the vinegar, stirring and scraping thoroughly the bottom and sides of the pan to make certain that all frying adherents are dissolved into the liquid. Continuing to stir, reduce by two-thirds over a high flame. Add the tomato juice and the juniper berries and stir in 2 quarts of boiling stock. Cook, covered, preferably in a slow oven, or over a tiny flame, for 4½ to 5 hours. Ten minutes before removing from the heat, add the peppercorns.

Pour everything into a fine sieve placed over another saucepan, pick out and discard any bones, and press the debris well with a pestle so as to extract all the juices without passing the solid material into the sauce. Add enough of the remaining boiling stock to bring the sauce to a lightly thickened consistency—that of a fairly thin syrup. Bring to a boil, move the saucepan to the side of a fairly low flame, and "skin" frequently (see Skimming and *Dépouillement*, page 90) for about 45 minutes or until it is reduced to about 2–2½ cups.

Skim all the fat from the roasting pan, deglaze the pan with a bit of white wine, reduce liquid by half and add it to the sauce. Pass the sauce again, this time through a fine nylon drum sieve, helping it through by stirring with a wooden spoon. Reheat, remove from the heat, and add the butter, cut into small pieces. Turn the saucepan in all directions, giving it a "rolling" motion, until the butter is completely absorbed. Pour the sauce into a heated sauceboat.

Sweet Potato Purée

Purée de Patates Douces

2 pounds sweet potatoes
2 large white potatoes
salt, pepper
¼ pound to 5 ounces butter (softened at kitchen temperature)

Bake the white potatoes and sweet potatoes in the oven until well done—45 to 60 minutes, depending on size and variety. Split them in two, remove the flesh with a spoon and pass it through a fine sieve into a saucepan, pressing with a wooden pestle. Avoid a turning, "grinding" motion, which lends an elastic, compact quality to the texture. Season to taste and reheat over a medium flame, stirring with a wooden spoon. Remove from the heat and add the butter—not all at once, for only enough should be added to bring the purée to the desired creamy, but not runny, consistency.

THE COFFEE CUSTARD

The quality of a poached custard depends on its containing only just enough egg for the form to hold at a tremble, once unmolded, and on its being poached at a temperature just below boiling (if the water in the *bain-marie* is allowed to boil, the marvelous velvety "suspension" will collapse into a vaguely rubbery article riddled with tiny holes). Any simple mold will serve. The charlotte is traditional, but the savarin mold may permit a prettier presentation.

Molded Coffee Custard

Crème Renversée au Café

Caramel:
¼ cup sugar
2 or 3 tablespoons water

Molded Coffee Custard

Custard:

½ cup sugar
tiny pinch of salt
1 cup milk
½ vanilla bean (or ½ teaspoon vanilla extract)
2 whole eggs and 3 yolks
1 cup very strong, freshly made drip coffee
almond oil for mold

THE CARAMEL

Bring the ¼ cup sugar and the water to a boil in a small saucepan. Keep at a light boil, watching it all the time, until it turns a deep honey color. Remove immediately from the flame and pour it into the mold, turning it rapidly in all directions in order to coat the bottom and as much of the sides as possible before the caramel solidifies. When thoroughly cooled, lightly oil the sides that remain untouched by the caramel.

THE CUSTARD

Combine the ½ cup sugar, salt, milk and vanilla bean (or extract) in a saucepan, and bring to a boil. Remove from heat and leave to infuse for a few minutes.

Beat the eggs and yolks together in a bowl, slowly add the milk and the freshly made hot coffee, while continuing to beat. Pass the mixture through a fine sieve into another bowl, allow to stand for about 5 minutes, and carefully skim off all the foam that has settled to the surface. Pour it into the mold and cook in a *bain-marie* (place the mold in a larger pan, pour in enough nearly boiling water to immerse the mold by two-thirds and put it in a low to medium oven—325°–350° F.) for about 40 minutes, or until the center is no longer liquid. A solid mold will require a longer cooking time than a savarin, which has a central tube.

Chill. Unmold just before serving, first running the tip of a small knife around the edges of the custard.

Two Formal Autumn Dinners

with appropriate wines

MENU II (FOR 4)

SORREL SOUP

[POTAGE GERMINY]

MIXED FRITTERS

[FRITTO MISTO (BEIGNETS MIXTES)]

A light, dry white wine: Burgundy (Pouilly-Fuissé, Chablis, Mercurey), or Loire Valley (Pouilly-Fumé, Sancerre, Savennières), or Graves

PHEASANT SALMIS

[SALMIS DE FAISAN]

A Médoc or Graves (red), at least 8 to 10 years old

SAUTEED CEPES (WILD MUSHROOMS) A LA BORDELAISE

[CEPES SAUTES A LA BORDELAISE]

Same wine as the preceding

ROCKET SALAD WITH NASTURTIUM FLOWERS
[SALADE DE ROQUETTE AUX FLEURS DE CAPUCINES]

CHEESES
[FROMAGES]

An older Bordeaux from a greater year or a Côte de Nuits

ORANGE JELLY
[GELEE A L'ORANGE]

On the whole, care has been taken to present menus which, despite being in certain instances fairly elaborate, require a minimum of nervous last-minute preparation. This menu involves no particularly complicated preparation, but for the servantless housewife there is a serious snag: the *salmis* must be prepared at the last minute and the final steps require a devoted half-hour. It seemed nonetheless too fine a thing to eliminate, and a pity to present it otherwise than under semiformal circumstances.

The *cèpes* will suffer little from being prepared ahead of time and kept warm for a half-hour or so. As for the other courses, the sorrel soup may, but for the final thickening, be prepared in advance, the fritters require only the incorporation of beaten egg whites into the batter, and the actual frying, and the dessert is of necessity prepared hours ahead.

Nasturtiums persist until the first freeze.

Serve the *cèpes* toward the end of the *salmis* service. They marry very well indeed, but the subtlety of each risks being muted by the other's rich presence. One may, by serving in this way, appreciate them together and enjoy them apart.

The presence of mushrooms in two different preparations (they also appear in the *fritto misto*) may seem bizarre, but their similarity is in name only.

Save the leftover egg yolks from the jelly clarification when you make the orange jelly (immersed in water to prevent their drying out) for thickening in the soup and the whites from the extra yolks, which will be needed for use in the frying batter for the *fritto misto.*

THE SORREL SOUP

With very little cooking, sorrel "melts" almost completely into a purée, and in simpler soups than this one nothing is gained by passing it through a sieve. Its light, refreshing acidity renders it useful in many soups, hot and cold. One sorrel soup, simple in preparation and far less rich, but delicious, is made with water, thickened with potato and lightly buttered before serving—a finely chopped onion is cooked in butter to which shredded sorrel is added, and when it is reduced to a purée, boiling water and finely sliced potatoes are added and cooked until the latter are partially dissolved. A soup prepared like the Germiny but made with water is also possible, but should not, of course, be dignified by that title.

Sorrel Soup

Potage Germiny

about 6 ounces sorrel leaves
1/4 *pound butter*
1 *quart consommé* (*or veal stock*)
3/4 *cup heavy cream*
6 *egg yolks*
salt
handful of chervil leaves (*stems removed*)

Remove the stems from the sorrel leaves, pulling the stems backward to tear out the fibrous threads in the leaves. Wash the leaves in several waters, drain well, and gather them into a compact mass on the chopping board, holding them well together while cutting or chopping them into coarse shreds (*chiffonade*). Melt 2 tablespoons of butter in a heavy saucepan, add the sorrel and cook over low heat, stirring regularly, until it is reduced almost to a purée (about 15 minutes), then pass it through a fine sieve and return to the saucepan. Assuming the stalks and fibrous elements to have been completely removed, it may instead be puréed in a blender with a bit of stock.) Add the stock to the sorrel purée. Mix together, in another receptacle, the cream and the egg yolks. Combine the two mixtures, whisking, and cook over a low to medium flame, whisking constantly, until the liquid turns creamy and velvety in consistency—it is then said to "coat the spoon." It must absolutely not be allowed to come to a boil. Remove from the flame, taste for seasoning and add salt if necessary, whisk in the remaining butter cut into small pieces, pour into a warmed soup tureen and sprinkle with a handful of chervil leaves.

THE FRITTO MISTO

(Mixed Fritters)

The origins of this preparation are respected in both English and French, on the condition that brains and artichoke hearts count among the elements to be fried. Besides those vegetables given in this recipe, others such as small young onions, sliced raw zucchini, parboiled green beans, cauliflower sections, broccoli flowers, may add variety to the mixture.

A simple tomato sauce, served separately, goes well in some instances, but in this framework, it would not be an attractive preface to the *salmis* sauce. The nuances of the marinating liquid and the fried parsley lend sufficient character to permit these fritters to be served without a sauce.

Fritto Misto (Mixed Fritters)

Fritto Misto (Beignets Mixtes)

1 *calf's brain*

Court-bouillon:

3 *cups water*
1/4 *cup wine vinegar*
1 *carrot and* 1 *onion, both peeled and finely sliced*
bouquet of parsley, thyme, bay leaf
salt

3 *medium Artichokes (plus lemon and thyme—see page* 77)
1/4 *pound small firm young mushrooms*

Marinade:

2 *tablespoons olive oil*
1 *tablespoon chopped fines herbes*
salt, pepper
juice of 1/2 *lemon*

Fritto Misto (Mixed Fritters)

Frying batter:

- *3/4 cup flour*
- *1 pinch salt*
- *2 tablespoons olive oil*
- *3/4 cup tepid water*
- *2 egg whites*
- *at least 1 quart frying oil (preferably olive)*
- *1 large handful parsley bouquets (short sections of stem with their leaves attached)*

THE CALF'S BRAIN

Put the brain to soak in cold water. Carefully peel off the fine enveloping membrane, immersing the brain repeatedly in water if the membrane resists (it sometimes helps to hold it under water while removing particularly adherent sections), and leave it again to soak in cold water in order to clear it as nearly as possible of bloodstains.

For the *court-bouillon*, bring the water and the vinegar to a boil, add all the other ingredients and boil gently, covered, for 1/2 hour before using.

Slip the brain into the boiling *court-bouillon* and poach, covered, at a bare simmer, for 20 to 25 minutes. Remove from liquid and drain.

Prepare the artichokes as indicated on page 77, paring them somewhat less radically than for bottoms and keeping them quite firm. Cut each into quarters or sixths, depending on their size, and cut out the chokes.

Pare the mushrooms, if necessary, rinse them rapidly and sponge them dry in a towel. Those whose diameter is no larger than that of a five-cent piece may be left whole; others should be cut into halves or quarters.

Cut the brain into more-or-less cube-shaped pieces measuring approximately 3/4 inch across, combine them in a bowl with the mushrooms and artichokes, sprinkle over them the ingredients of the marinade, and mix together all the elements, lifting with the fingertips and letting them drop back into the bowl. Repeat this two or three times in the course of the marination, always gently, for the brains are fragile. They should be left for 1 hour at least, but may remain for several hours or overnight.

THE FRYING BATTER

Sift the flour and salt into a bowl, make a well in the center, pour in the oil, and slowly add the water, stirring from the center and moving outward in an enlarging circle as the flour is absorbed. Work the batter no more than is necessary to achieve a smooth mixture and leave it to "relax" at kitchen temperature for a good hour to ensure its losing all elasticity. Just before using it, gently fold in the two egg whites, beaten stiff.

Heat the oil until it sizzles at contact with a drop of batter. Do not use a frying basket. Drop several of the elements to be fried into the batter; ladle batter over them with a teaspoon, and drop them, one by one, from the spoon into the hot fat. A void cooking more at a time than may freely float without touching one another. Turn them over in the fat with the prong tips of a fork, taking care not to pierce the crisp surface and, when evenly golden, remove to a kitchen towel, using a large wire skimming spoon to scoop them up. Keep them warm in a folded towel while frying the remaining batches. It may be necessary to regulate the heat to prevent the oil from becoming too hot.

When the last of the fritters are removed from the oil, drop in the parsley and fry until crisp (only a few seconds). Drain it on a towel, but do not try to "sponge" it, for it will crumble. Serve the fritters enclosed in a folded napkin, the parsley sprinkled on top.

THE PHEASANT SALMIS

Pheasant, abundant in American farming regions, is often appreciated more as a hunting target than as a table delicacy. Many American cookbooks treat game birds summarily, suggesting simply that they be dealt with in the same way as domestic fowl. Pheasant hens are often plumper and their flesh less dry than that of cocks, but American law shields them.

A pheasant should be young, hatched in the spring of the same year it is killed. The flesh of the breast will seem tender to the touch and the breastbone flexible; the final and longest wing feather remains pointed. (Older birds may be braised with cabbage or used for stock.)

Pheasant Salmis

Simply roasted, its breast protected by a fine strip of fresh fat pork, young pheasant should be served slightly rare (about 35 minutes in a fairly hot oven) and accompanied by triangles or rounds of crouton spread with *farce gratin* (the pheasant's liver, supplemented by that of a chicken, rapidly sautéed in butter with salt, pepper, and a pinch of herbs, flamed with a spoonful of cognac and passed through a fine sieve).

A *salmis* is a rare-roasted game bird whose sauce is drawn from the carcass and a reduction of white wine and shallots and tempered with stock. In season, the canned truffles are better replaced by fresh, and when the stock is enriched by the addition of another roast pheasant carcass, the preparation achieves ultimate perfection. In a professional kitchen a certain amount of meat glaze would be available to lend additional body and succulence to the sauce. The dish is elegant in concept but, to be enjoyed under perfect circumstances, does not permit of an elegant presentation.

Pheasant Salmis

Salmis de Faisan

Velouté:

1 *tablespoon* (1/2 *ounce*) *butter*
1 *tablespoon flour*
2 *cups Veal Stock* (*page 72—if prepared especially, use* 1 *pound veal, a few chicken necks, and the neck, head and giblets of the pheasant*)
1 *cup dry white wine*
1 *tablespoon chopped gray shallots* (*if only red shallots are available, substitute* 1 *tablespoon chopped white onion and* 1/2 *clove garlic*)
4 *or* 5 *white peppercorns, slightly crushed*
1 *small jar of preserved truffles* (*those in jars are usually better than those in cans—in any case they should be vacuum-packed in a minimum of liquid, not swimming in salt water*)

1 *young pheasant*

(*Continued*)

thin strips of fresh fat pork or, if possible, a single sheet (omit this step rather than substitute bacon)
1 *tablespoon cognac*
few tablespoons white wine
4 *tablespoons* (2 *ounces*) *unsalted butter*

THE VELOUTE

Melt the butter in a heavy saucepan, add the flour and cook gently, stirring regularly with a wooden spoon for two or three minutes. Away from the flame, add the stock slowly, stirring all the while to prevent its lumping. Simmer over a low flame for about 1/2 hour, skimming from time to time. Boil the white wine, chopped shallots and peppercorns over a high flame until only a few spoonfuls of liquid remain. Add it, along with the truffles' preserving liquid, to the *velouté.*

THE PHEASANT

Sprinkle the pheasant inside and out with salt, completely cover the breast with a sheet or strips of fat pork, if you have it, tie with a kitchen string, and place it in a small skillet or other pan just the size to hold it. Roast it in a very hot oven for 25 minutes. Remove from roasting pan, discard the fat pork and any fragments of skin that may be charred. Remove the legs, leaving thighs and drumsticks attached, cut the joint end from the drumstick bone and peel off the skin. Reserve skin. Clip the breast and wings loose from the carcass with heavy kitchen shears. Cut the bird in two the length of the breastbone, remove the breastbone, and cut each half in two lengthwise. Remove the skin and reserve, and any fragments of splintered bone, trim the pieces of pheasant neatly and place them and the legs in a presentable earthenware or copper *cocotte* just large enough to hold them. Distribute the truffles, sliced fairly thickly, over the surface, grind a bit of pepper over and sprinkle with the cognac, which has first been heated and flamed to rid it of its alcohol. Keep covered in a warm place while finishing the sauce.

Pour off the fat from the roasting pan and dissolve the caramelized meat juices in a couple of tablespoons of white wine, stirring, scraping and reducing over a high flame. Chop the reserved skin, trimmings and carcass coarsely, pound in a mortar, add this and roasting juices to the *velouté*, boil for 8 to 10 minutes, and pass the contents of the saucepan through a sieve, pressing the solids firmly with a pestle in order to extract all the juices. Bring the sauce back to a boil and simmer with the heat to one side of the saucepan, skimming regularly (see page 90) for about 10 minutes, or until the sauce is reduced by about one third. Pass it through a very fine sieve, taste for seasoning and reheat. Away from the flame, swirl in the butter, cut into small pieces. Pour the sauce over the pheasant and truffles and serve immediately.

Sautéed Cèpes (wild mushrooms) à la Bordelaise

Cèpes Sautés à la Bordelaise

1 *pound cèpes*
3/4 *cup olive oil*
1 *tablespoon chopped gray shallot (or substitute chopped white onion)*
1 *clove garlic*
1 *tablespoon fine bread crumbs*
2 *tablespoons chopped parsley*
1/2 *lemon*
salt and pepper

Choose small, firm mushrooms that have not completely opened out. Larger ones should be reserved for grilling. Don't wash them, but wipe each carefully with a damp towel after having cut off the stem ends to remove any adhering earth or sand. Remove the stems, slice each in two lengthwise and cut out and discard any parts that may be wormy. Chop about half the stems (the equivalent of a good cupful) fairly fine and put them aside with the chopped shallot or onion and garlic clove. Any heads that are no larger than a small walnut may be left whole. The others should be cut into halves, quarters or thick slices.

Heat the oil in a large skillet or *sauteuse*, add the mushrooms and stem pieces, season and cook them over a high flame for about 10 minutes, tossing them or gently stirring them regularly with a wooden spoon. (At the beginning, the mushrooms must not be too crowded in the pan—if it is not large enough, use two pans and additional oil. After all are browned, they may be put together for the finishing processes.) When they are lightly browned, turn the flame low and leave them to cook, covered, for another 5 minutes or so. Turn the flame high again, add the chopped stems, chopped shallots and the garlic clove, and cook, stirring and tossing, for another 2 or 3 minutes. Drain off as much of the oil as possible. (The large quantity of oil is essential for the first stage in the cooking to be correctly carried out, but must not remain. It may, however, be used again and will lend an attractive flavor to fried potatoes, for instance.) Turn the flame down again, add the bread crumbs and two-thirds of the chopped parsley, stir together and leave over a low heat, stirring regularly, long enough for the bread crumbs to completely absorb the remaining oil. Discard the garlic clove. Sprinkle the mushrooms with a few drops of lemon juice, add salt and pepper to taste, and garnish with the remaining chopped parsley.

THE ORANGE JELLY

The ghastly commercial jellies, symbol of the sordid cafeteria counter, have, understandably, formed a block of prejudice against their highly respectable ancestor. Few people today have ever tasted wine or fresh-fruit calf's-foot jellies. Limpid, trembling, set in old-fashioned jelly molds with their intricate geometric designs and central tubes, their beauty of presentation rivals their delicacy of flavor.

Orange Jelly

Gelée à l'Orange

2 *calves' feet*
5 *pints water*
1 *cup sugar*
juice of 1 *orange and* 1 *lemon, plus several strips of the peel of both (sliced thin to avoid the white)*

Orange Jelly

2 egg whites
$^2/_3$ cup dry white wine
pinch of cinnamon
$3^1/_2$ cups freshly squeezed orange juice

Have the large, upper bone removed from the feet. Soak them in cold water for 2 or 3 hours, then cover them with fresh cold water and parboil them for 10 minutes. Drain and rinse them well, cover with the 5 pints of water, bring to a boil, cover and allow to barely simmer for about 7 hours. Skim the fat from the surface several times during the cooking and as completely as possible at the end. Pass the jelly through a sieve and, when it has cooled until firm, remove all traces of fat, first using a spoon, then wiping the surface with a cloth slightly dampened in hot water. About 1 quart of jelly should remain.

Mix the sugar, the juice of 1 orange and 1 lemon, and the peels together in a saucepan, add the jelly, bring to a boil and leave to cool for 10 minutes. Beat the egg whites with the white wine, add them with pinch of cinnamon to the jelly and bring to a boil, whisking all the time, then simmer for 15 minutes, whisking from time to time. Line a sieve with a tightly woven towel, pass the jelly through, and leave it until nearly cool.

Let the $3^1/_2$ cups of orange juice settle for $^1/_2$ hour after squeezing, pass it through a fine cloth, stir it into the jelly, pour into a mold and chill for at least 4 hours. Unmold just before serving, first dipping the mold for a second in hot water and wiping it dry.

Two Informal Autumn Dinners

with appropriate wines

MENU I (FOR 4)

BAKED TROUT STUFFED WITH SORREL
[TRUITES A L'OSEILLE AU FOUR]

A young, fruity, dry white wine:
Burgundy (Pouilly-Fuissé, Mercurey,
Pinot Blanc) or Loire Valley
(Sancerre, Pouilly-Fumé)

SAUTEED VEAL KIDNEYS WITH MUSHROOMS
[ROGNONS DE VEAU SAUTES AU CHAMPIGNONS]

One of the Beaujolais (Chiroubles,
Morgon, Fleurie, Brouilly)
from the most recent vintage,
or a Loire Valley red wine (Chinon,
Bourgueuil, Saumur-Champigny)
a couple of years old—any of these
served slightly cool

RICE PILAF
[PILAF]

LAMB'S LETTUCE AND BEET SALAD
[SALADE DE MACHE ET BETTERAVES]

CHEESES
[FROMAGES]

The same wine as the preceding, or a Côte de Beaune (Volnay, Pommard, Chassagne-Montrachet)

CHARLOTTE WITH CREPES, SABAYON SAUCE
[CHARLOTTE AUX CREPES, SAUCE SABAYON]

A Sauternes or a sweet Vouvray

THE BAKED TROUT STUFFED WITH SORREL

Whiting, small sea bass, or any white-fleshed, non-fatty fish of the right size to serve as an individual portion may be prepared in this way. The relative firmness of the trout's flesh lends itself particularly well to this preparation. The fragility of the whiting, once cooked, renders the service difficult. A bed of stewed sorrel laid with fish fillets, masked with *béchamel*, sprinkled with cheese, dotted with butter and gratinéed is another happy possibility.

A Mousseline Forcemeat of the same or another fish (page 78) or a tomatoed *Duxelles* (page 76) are other stuffing possibilities for fish boned and baked in this way. The final addition of cream is, in these instances, unnecessary.

Baked Trout Stuffed with Sorrel

Truites à l'Oseille au Four

4 *medium-size trout*
1 *pound sorrel*
1/4 *pound butter*
salt, pepper
1 *small onion, finely chopped*
1/4 *cup dry white wine*
buttered kitchen paper cut slightly smaller than top of baking dish
1/4 *cup heavy cream*

Using a small, sharp pointed knife, slit each trout the length of the back on each side of the spinal column in order cleanly to separate the fillets from the central skeletal structure, taking care not to puncture the skin of the belly. Clip the spinal column at the base of the head and about an inch from the tail, remove it, empty the fish and tear out the gills. Rinse fish inside and out and sponge dry with paper towels.

Pull the stems backward from the sorrel leaves and detach them, pulling with them any fibrous veins from the leaves. Wash the leaves in several waters, drain them, shred them coarsely on the chopping board and stew them gently in half the butter, seasoned with salt and pepper, stirring frequently, until they have "melted" to a near purée.

Spread onions over the bottom of an earthenware or enameled cast-iron baking or gratin dish just large enough to hold the fish comfortably. Season them, inside and out, and arrange them in the dish, belly down. Place a small piece of butter inside each and stuff the cavities with the sorrel purée. Place a thin slice of butter on top of each, sprinkle white wine over and around the fish, gently press the buttered paper on the surface and bake in a hot oven (about 400° F.) for about 15 minutes. Upon removing them from the oven, pour a tablespoon of heavy cream over each and serve immediately in their baking dish.

THE SAUTEED VEAL KIDNEYS WITH MUSHROOMS

Calves' kidneys are less strong in flavor than others and most recipes do not recommend discarding the liquid that is drained from them after the initial cooking. It is, however, this liquid that contains the flavor that many people fear. Prepared in the following manner, kidneys rarely fail to please the wariest of guests.

The following is a recipe "type," and is among the simplest of ways to prepare sautéed kidneys. The many variations depend on different garnishing and flavoring elements, but the process remains identical. In professional kitchens meat glaze usually lends additional body and intensity to the sauce.

Sautéed Veal Kidneys with Mushrooms

Rognons de Veau Sautés aux Champignons

2 *fresh (not frozen) veal kidneys*
4 *tablespoons (2 ounces) butter*

(*Continued*)

salt and pepper
1/2 pound mushrooms, cleaned and thickly sliced
2 gray shallots (or one small onion) finely chopped
2 tablespoons cognac
1/3 cup dry white wine
1 cup heavy cream

Remove the fat and fine surface membrane from the kidneys and cut each symmetrically in two lengthwise. Remove the core of fat and cut each section crosswise into approximately 1/2-inch slices.

Heat the butter in a heavy skillet or *sauteuse* (avoid enamelware), add the kidneys, salt and freshly ground pepper, and cook over a high flame, tossing or stirring regularly with a wooden spoon for 2 or 3 minutes, until they turn grayish in color and are firm and somewhat "rubbery" to the touch—no more; they must remain pink inside. Remove them immediately to a strainer or colander, leaving their cooking butter in the *sauteuse*, and allow them to drain while finishing the sauce. The brief contact with heat will cause them to "bleed" and this liquid should be discarded.

Season and toss the mushrooms in the same butter, still over a high flame, for a couple of minutes, or until their natural liquid has evaporated and they are slightly browned. Remove them and replace them by the chopped shallots or onion. Stir them around for a few seconds, add the cognac and the wine and reduce almost completely, stirring and scraping with a wooden spoon to loosen and dissolve all adhering frying matter; then return the mushrooms to the pan and add 1/2 cup of cream. Reduce, stirring constantly, until the sauce becomes fairly thick, adding a bit more cream if it seems too sparse. Lower the flame and return the kidneys to the sauce, stirring them around for a few seconds to ensure their being thoroughly reheated in the sauce, but under no circumstances allow the sauce to boil again, as this would toughen the kidneys. Remove from the flame, stir in enough additional cream to bring the sauce back to a very lightly thickened consistency. Taste for seasoning and serve at once, accompanied by a Pilaf (page 81).

Lamb's Lettuce and Beet Salad

Salade de Mâche et Betteraves

Lamb's lettuce is found at Italian greengrocers in large cities. It is easy to raise and, in temperate climates, may be picked all winter long.

Bake the beets in the oven (the French more often simply boil them, but they are far better baked, and better still cooked under hot ashes) and, when they are cooled, peel them and cut them into thin slices, large dice, or coarse julienne sticks. They should be allowed to macerate for an hour or two before being served and the vinaigrette should, because of the natural sweetness of the beets, be somewhat more salty than usual. The lamb's lettuce requires a very thorough washing and should be carefully dried by being pressed between two towels. It should be tossed with the beets only at the moment of serving.

THE CHARLOTTE WITH CREPES

"Charlotte" refers only to the mold, and any number of otherwise unrelated desserts formed in this mold, some cooked, others merely chilled in it, may take the name. Non-dessert preparations are, however, never called charlottes. This dessert is a simplified variation of pudding Bohémienne.

Charlotte with Crêpes, Sabayon Sauce

Charlotte aux Crêpes, Sauce Sabayon

1 *tablespoon (1/2 ounce) butter*
9 *dessert Crêpes (page* 83)
jam or jelly, such as apricot, currant, black currant

(Continued)

Custard mixture:

just under 1/2 *cup sugar*
2 3/4 *cups milk*
strip of lemon peel
1 *tiny pinch salt*
3 *whole eggs*
3 *egg yolks*

Sabayon Sauce (*page* 139)

A standard charlotte mold accommodates approximately 3 pints of liquid and measures about 5 inches in diameter at the bottom. The crêpes should be prepared in a small crêpe pan whose bottom diameter is also 5 inches.

Butter the mold generously and line the bottom with a crêpe, pressing it to ensure its adhering. Spread the other crêpes, almost to their edges, with the chosen jam or jelly and fold them, top down, bottom up, and each side inward, in the form of rectangles whose height (slightly over 3 inches) corresponds to that of the mold. Some should be folded slightly wider at the top than at the bottom to compensate for the spread at the top of the mold. Press each gently with the palm of the hand to ensure its holding its shape, then press them side by side against the wall of the mold, folded sides facing in. While preparing the custard, chill the mold in the refrigerator in order to strengthen the adherence of the crêpes.

For the custard, combine the sugar, milk, and lemon peel in a saucepan, and bring to a boil. Remove from heat, leave to infuse for 15 minutes, and discard the lemon peel. Beat the eggs and extra egg yolks together in a large bowl as for an omelet, add salt, then pour in the milk mixture, whisking as you pour. Pass the mixture through a fine drum sieve into another mixing bowl, leave to stand a minute or so, and carefully skim the foam from the surface. Pour the custard into the mold slowly, so as not to displace the crêpes, and place the mold in a *bain-marie*—a larger receptacle into which enough nearly boiling water is poured to immerse the mold by two-thirds. Cook in a slow oven for approximately 40 minutes, taking care that the water never reaches a boil. The pudding is done when the center of the cream is firm to the touch (or when a needle or small pointed knife, plunged into the center, comes out clean).

Leave it to cool, and unmold it while still slightly tepid. (If left to chill in the mold, the hardened butter will resist unmolding.) The mold should, however, be left over the unmolded pudding to act as a cover and protect it from the air until the moment of serving. Serve well chilled, masked by several spoonfuls of chilled *sabayon* sauce, the rest served separately in a sauceboat.

THE SABAYON SAUCE

The principle is the same as the rich, heady Italian *zabaglione*, but, with a light white wine replacing the Marsala, a *sabayon* finds a far wider range of application. It may also be prepared with champagne, Sauternes, etc., but, if a particularly fine wine is used, it would be an error to add an additional flavor such as lemon or vanilla. With a hot dessert, *sabayon* should be prepared at the last minute and served hot. The flavor of a cold *sabayon* may be attenuated by the addition of a certain amount of whipped cream, if one likes.

Sabayon Sauce

Sauce Sabayon

1/2 *cup sugar*
3 *egg yolks*
2/3 *cup dry white wine*
3 *strips of lemon peel (peeled thin to avoid the white), then cut crosswise into tiny threadlike julienne strips*

Beat the sugar and egg yolks together in a saucepan (the sauce doubles in quantity, so choose the saucepan accordingly) until creamy. Add the white wine and the julienne of lemon peel and whisk in a *bain-marie* (in this case, the saucepan is immersed in a larger saucepan of nearly boiling water on top of the stove) over a low flame until thickened. The water should be kept near the boiling point, but should not boil. Lower the flame, if necessary, or raise it if the process seems to take too long.

Two Informal Autumn Dinners

with appropriate wines

MENU II (FOR 4)

PIKE DUMPLINGS A LA LYONNAISE
[QUENELLES DE BROCHET A LA LYONNAISE]

*A soft, dry white wine,
not too "nervous": Cassis or
Côtes-du-Rhône (Châteauneuf-du-Pape,
Hermitage), or a chilled rosé
(Lirac, Tavel, Bandol)
with the entire meal*

VEAL CUTLETS A LA TAPENADE
[ESCALOPES DE VEAU A LA TAPENADE]

*If a white wine precedes,
serve a meridional red wine:
Bandol or Côtes-du-Rhône
(young Châteauneuf-du-Pape,
Cornas, Hermitage)*

ARTICHOKE PUREE

[PUREE D'ARTICHAUTS]

CHEESES

[FROMAGES]

The same wine as the preceding course, or a wine of smilar type but older

APPLE MOUSSE WITH PEACHES

[MOUSSE DE POMMES AUX PECHES]

Sauternes, Banyuls, or port are possible. If a rosé has been served throughout the meal, continue it, or serve nothing with dessert

The work may be organized to eliminate all but a few last-minute details: the pike dumpling mixture may be prepared a day or so ahead and the *quenelles* need only be poached and gratinéed at the last minute; the veal cutlets may be prepared, except for the actual frying, several hours ahead of time; and the artichoke purée merely reheated and buttered at the last minute. The dessert, except for the presentation, is automatically prepared in advance.

THE PIKE QUENELLES A LA LYONNAISE

Pike *quenelles* are often made also from a simple pike mousseline forcemeat, and these are lighter and more elegant in spirit. The hearty, rustic Lyonnaise *quenelles* have more body and are preferred by many people. Any *farce* mixture based on pounded raw meat (usually veal) and incorporating suet is known as *godiveau*. The pike *godiveau* is a specialty of Lyons and may be accompanied by any simple cream or *béchamel* sauce or any fish sauce (*à l'américaine* or *velouté*, for example, containing a garnish of shrimp tails, mushrooms, mussels, scallops, if one likes) that will not separate through contact with heat. After having been poached, these *quenelles* should always be baked in a sauce, during which time they continue to swell.

Pike Dumplings à la Lyonnaise

Quenelles de Brochet à la Lyonnaise

Panade for quenelles:

2 *egg yolks* (*whites will be used later*)
2/3 *cup milk*
3 *heaping tablespoons flour*
salt, pepper, nutmeg
3 *tablespoons* (1 1/2 *ounces*) *melted butter*

1/2 *pound beef suet* (*dry crumbly fat from around the kidney*)
1/2 *pound raw pike* (*bones and skin removed*)

salt, pepper
2 *egg whites*
1 *cup heavy cream*
4 *tablespoons* (2 *ounces*) *butter*
freshly grated cheese (*half Parmesan, half Gruyère*)

THE PANADE

Separate the yolks from the egg whites and put the latter aside. Bring the milk to a boil and leave to cool slightly. Sift the flour into a mixing bowl, add salt, freshly ground pepper, a tiny bit of freshly ground nutmeg, and the egg yolks. Begin mixing, working from the center, add the melted butter, then slowly add the milk, stirring constantly until the mixture is completely amalgamated. Whisk it over a medium flame until thick, spread the resulting paste on a plate and chill.

THE QUENELLES

Crumble the suet in your hands, discarding membranous material, and pound it in a mortar, first alone, then with the chilled *panade*, until they form a well-blended paste. Put this mixture aside. Pound the pike until it is reduced to a purée, then pound the two mixtures together, finally working the pestle in a grinding motion to ensure a total amalgamation. Add salt and pepper, if necessary, then add the egg whites in small quantities at a time, working the paste until each addition of egg white is thoroughly absorbed. Pass the mixture through a fine drum sieve, a tablespoonful at a time, using the plastic disk (page 62). Pack it into a bowl and put to chill in the refrigerator. It may be kept for several days in this state if desired, the surface protected by wax paper or the mixture wrapped in aluminum foil. If it is to be used immediately, pack it in a metal bowl and embed it in cracked ice for an hour before using.

To poach the *quenelles*, use a large receptacle wider than it is deep (an American roasting pan is perfect for this purpose), well filled with boiling, salted water.

Form the *quenelles* on a lightly floured board, using a heaping tablespoonful of mixture for each and rolling them with the palm of the hand into elongated cylinders. Lower the flame so that the water no longer boils and drop the *quenelles* in one by one. Leave to poach for a few minutes, covered. If the water threatens to return to a boil, turn off the flame. The *quenelles* will first sink. When they rise to the surface, they are ready. Gently lift them from the water one at a time with a perforated skimming spoon and put them to drain on a towel or absorbent paper. Arrange them fairly closely in a buttered baking dish, leaving enough space for them to swell during the gratin process. Pour in the cup of cream, distribute the 2 ounces of butter in several thin slices over the surface and sprinkle with the grated cheese. Bake in a medium oven (350° F.) for 15 or 20 minutes—or until the cream is in large part absorbed and the surface colored golden.

THE VEAL CUTLETS A LA TAPENADE

A *tapenade* is a Provençal spread or paste, basically a purée of black olives whose flavor is heightened by the addition of various other aromatic elements. Its marriage with the veal cutlet is not classic—the French might describe it as an "amiable fantasy." Egg noodles tossed with butter and grated cheese are the more usual accompaniment to breaded cutlets, but the fine flavor of the artichoke in juxtaposition to that of the *tapenade* is a happy innovation and the delicate pale green in combination with the golden cutlet, the rich red tomato and the spot of intense parsley green affords a very pretty service.

Veal Cutlets à la Tapenade

Escalopes de Veau à la Tapenade

4 veal cutlets, cut thin but not flattened
marinade of lemon, dried oregano flowers, olive oil
salt, pepper
Tapenade (recipe follows)
2 eggs

bread crumbs made of firmly textured, stale but not dried-out white bread, grated
about 1 *pint of olive oil for frying*
Stewed Tomatoes (recipe below)
1 *tablespoon parsley*

Trim the cutlets, removing any fat or gristle, sprinkle them on both surfaces with lemon juice, oregano and a few drops of olive oil and leave to marinate for an hour or so, turning them from time to time.

Season the cutlets on both sides and spread one side of each with the *tapenade*. Put them to chill for a while. This, although not altogether necessary, renders the *tapenade* firmer and easier to handle.

Beat the eggs as for an omelet. Place each cutlet, *tapenade* side up, in the dish of beaten egg, and scoop egg over it with a spoon. Then lift each cutlet carefully to the crumbs, sprinkle crumbs generously over the surface, and pat or press gently with the palm of the hand to ensure their adhering. Remove to a chopping board or a piece of wax paper sprinkled with crumbs, and leave cutlets to dry out or "set" slightly before frying.

Heat the olive oil (you will need either a very large or two medium-sized frying pans) and cook the cutlets until golden on each side, turning the flame down to a low-medium, once the oil is heated. Turn them carefully without piercing the crust. Drain them on a cloth and transfer to a heated serving plate, a stewed tomato topped by a pinch of parsley on each. Serve the artichoke purée separately.

Tapenade

Tapenade

4 *anchovy fillets, preferably not preserved in oil but salted (soaked in water to desalt them and sponged dry with absorbent paper)*
1 *heaping teaspoon capers, rinsed and well drained*
1/4 *pound pitted black olives (niçoises if available)*

(Continued)

1 *teaspoon cognac*
2 *tablespoons olive oil*

Grind the anchovy fillets and capers together in a mortar until they form a paste, add the olives and pound until the mixture forms a well-unified, coarse purée. Pass it through a fine sieve, using a pestle, and work in the cognac and enough olive oil to form a fairly firm but easily workable paste.

Stewed Tomatoes

4 *canned whole peeled tomatoes (Italian canned "plum" tomatoes are good for this purpose) or* 4 *garden tomatoes if available*
2 *tablespoons* (1 *ounce*) *butter*
1 *crushed garlic clove*

When garden-ripened tomatoes are in season, use them, peeled and seeded. If canned tomatoes are used, press them gently to rid them of extra juice and seeds, retaining their form as nearly as possible. Cook the raw tomatoes, seasoned with salt and pepper, over a tiny flame with the butter and the crushed garlic clove. Do not cook for too long a period or over too high a flame or they will disintegrate. Canned tomatoes need only be heated through with the butter and garlic. The best are, of course, those which you have canned yourself, peeling and seeding them before canning, covered with their own juice, strained, and simply sterilized without any preliminary cooking process.

Artichoke Purée

Purée d'Artichauts

8 *large Artichoke Bottoms, precooked (page* 77)
about 1/4 *pound unsalted butter*
salt, pepper

Stew the artichoke bottoms in half the butter over a low flame, using either a stainless steel or an earthenware dish, the latter protected from the direct flame by an asbestos pad, until very tender. Pass them, along with their cooking butter, through a nylon drum sieve (a metal sieve will blacken them), leaving them first to cool somewhat if the plastic disk is to be used (with a mushroom pestle, they may be passed through immediately). Taste for seasoning and reheat the purée rapidly over a fairly high flame, stirring and beating it constantly with a wooden spoon to prevent its sticking or burning. Beat in the remaining butter, half of which has been melted and cooked until brown, and nutty in odor, the other half fresh, cut into small pieces. The nutty flavor of the brown butter enhances the artichokes' natural flavor. The purée will be fairly thin. For those who prefer more body, a freshly baked, sieved potato may be stirred in and additional butter added.

Apple Mousse with Peaches

Mousse de Pommes aux Pêches

1 *pound apples, cored, peeled and sliced*
1 *tablespoon water*
pinch of cinnamon
2 *cups milk*
1 *vanilla bean or* 1 *teaspoon extract*
2/3 *cup sugar*

Meringue:

2 *egg whites*
tiny pinch of salt
3/4 *cup confectioners' sugar*

4 *egg yolks*
1 *tablespoon unflavored gelatin*
3/4 *cup heavy cream*
3 *home-canned peaches or fresh peaches poached in sugar syrup*
1/2 *cup good port wine*
2 *cups stewed apricots, sugared to taste*

(*Continued*)

Cook the apples with the tablespoon of water and the cinnamon in a saucepan over a medium heat, stirring from time to time, until tender but not cooked into a complete purée. Pass them through a sieve and put them aside.

Boil the milk with the vanilla bean and the sugar. Remove from heat and leave to infuse for 15 to 20 minutes.

For the meringue, add the pinch of salt to the 2 egg whites and beat them until stiff. Sift the confectioners' sugar over them and mix thoroughly but without violence.

Remove the vanilla bean and reheat the milk, regulating the heat to a bare simmer. Drop teaspoonfuls of meringue into the milk, poaching only a few at a time, for they swell and should not be crowded. After a couple of minutes, carefully turn them over in the simmering milk, leave to poach another couple of minutes, and remove them to a nylon drum sieve that has been placed over a mixing bowl to collect the milk that drains from them. Repeat the poaching process until all are done, transferring the meringues to a plate as they are drained.

Combine the poaching milk with that collected from draining the meringues. Beat the egg yolks in a saucepan and slowly pour in the milk, whisking the while. Cook over medium heat, stirring constantly with a wooden spoon, until the mixture coats the spoon. Add the gelatin, first softened in a bit of cold water and combined with 2 or 3 tablespoons of egg-milk mixture. Continue stirring the custard over heat for a few seconds to permit the gelatin to dissolve completely, but do not allow the custard to come to a boil. Mix the custard and the apple purée together and chill, keeping an eye on it, and when the mixture begins to jell, whip the cream until fairly firm, but not stiff, and fold it well into the apple mixture.

Lightly oil a savarin mold (a round mold with a rounded bottom and a central tube) with sweet almond oil (or lacking that, a tasteless vegetable oil), fill it with the mixture, tap the bottom of the mold 2 or 3 times on a table top to settle the contents, and chill, either in the coldest part of the refrigerator or directly in cracked ice for at least 4 hours.

Put the peaches to macerate in the port wine.

Pass the stewed apricots through a sieve, add the wine in which the peaches have macerated, and taste for sugar. A bit of lemon juice may be a useful addition.

Just before serving, dip the mold for 2 or 3 seconds into hot water and unmold the mousse onto a large, round, chilled platter. Pour some of the apricot sauce in a circle around the mousse, distributing the meringues on top of the ribbon of sauce, fill the central cavity of the mousse with the macerated peaches, mask them with a few tablespoonfuls of sauce, and serve the rest of the sauce in a sauceboat.

A Festive Autumn Meal for Two

with appropriate wines

THE MENU

CUCUMBER SALAD, CREAM SAUCE
[CONCOMBRES FRAIS A LA CREME]

If a light, white wine or champagne was drunk as apéritif, continue it, or serve the following wine

BAKED LOBSTER GARIN
[HOMARD AU FOUR, FACON GARIN]

A white Côte de Beaune (Corton-Charlemagne, Meursault, Puligny-Montrachet), or Château-Chalon

BRAISED AND ROAST PARTRIDGE WITH CABBAGE

[PERDRIX AUX CHOUX]

A robust, young red Burgundy (Fixin, Pernand-Vergelesses, Santenay) or a fairly young Pomerol (Vieux Château Certan, La Conseillante)

CHEESES

[FROMAGES]

The same wine as the preceding or an older Côte de Nuits (one of the Gevrey-Chambertin or Vosne-Romanée growths), or, following a Pomerol, an older Saint-Emilion

FRESH FIGS WITH RASPBERRY CREAM

[FIGUES A LA CREME FRAMBOISEE]

A demi-sec champagne or a Sauternes

When faced with the problem of composing a menu for two, one is nearly always tempted to fall back on a simple hors d'oeuvre and a *grillade*, there being few *cuisiné* preparations practicable for a small service. Lobster and partridge both lend themselves by nature to a luxurious concept of eating and, by size, to a meal for two. There is otherwise no reason that this menu may not be conceived for any number of guests.

The cucumber salad does nothing for a wine and, if one were drinking a light white wine or champagne as apéritif, it would be better to continue it during the first course rather than to dissipate the pleasure of beginning a carefully chosen great white wine at the moment the lobster is served.

All preparations, with the exception of the actual baking of the lobster, the roasting of the young partridge, and whipping the cream for dessert, are automatically finished well before the dinner hour (the cabbage and old partridge may even be prepared the previous day and gently reheated without suffering).

The lobster should be put to cook just before going to table and the partridge to roast no earlier than ten minutes after the lobster has been served—lobster is not a thing to eat hurriedly and it is far better to wait for a roast partridge than to risk making *it* wait.

THE CUCUMBER SALAD IN CREAM SAUCE

Cream sauce is occasionally a pleasant change from a vinaigrette for a green salad and nicely accommodates any number of raw vegetable hors-d'oeuvre salads. Raw mushrooms, first marinated in lemon juice and seasoning, the cream added later, are delicious. Lemon juice should always replace vinegar when cream is used. With cucumbers, fresh dill may replace the chervil.

Cucumber Salad, Cream Sauce

Concombres Frais à la Crème

2 medium cucumbers
salt
1 lemon
pepper
1/2 cup heavy cream
1 tablespoon chopped chervil

Peel the cucumbers and rinse them (a precaution against an occasional bitter-tasting skin). They may either be split lengthwise, the seeds removed, and sliced thinly, or, for a prettier presentation, cut into approximately 2-inch lengths, seeded with a coring device, and each section cut into rings. Spread them in layers in a soup plate or bowl, generously sprinkling each layer with salt, leave them for an hour or two to rid them of their excess water, and drain them well, pressing firmly.

Mix the lemon juice (starting with the juice of 1/2 lemon and adding more later, if necessary) and pepper (but not salt) in a bowl and slowly stir in the cream. Mix together with the cucumbers, mound the mixture neatly on the serving plate and sprinkle with the chervil.

THE BAKED LOBSTER GARIN

The simple but ingenious notion of punching a hole in the carapace through which to enrich the flesh of the lobster with herb butter while it cooks eliminates any risk of its drying out. The juices are an retained. The claws lend themselves imperfectly to this preparation and are poached separately *à la nage*.

The preparation of the butter has been slightly simplified for a home service—in the restaurant version, a fish *fumet* (see Sole Fillets with Fines Herbes, page 361) replaces the white wine, the reduction is less intense and is then mounted over a low heat, like a *beurre blanc*. The restaurant presentation may also involve the lobster's being lightly flamed at the moment of service with a bit of preheated pastis.

Baked Lobster Garin

Homard au Four, Façon Garin

Herb butter:

- *1/2 cup dry white wine*
- *2 1/2 tablespoons pastis (or other anise-flavored liqueur)*
- *1 large pinch Mixed Herbs (page 86)*
- *salt, pepper*
- *1/2 pound softened butter*

Anchovy butter:

- *1 anchovy fillet*
- *1 tablespoon (1/2 ounce) butter*

Court-bouillon (for the claws):

- *1/2 cup dry white wine*
- *1/2 cup water*
- *mixed herbs, parsley, bay leaf*
- *1 small onion, sliced*
- *a few carrot slices*
- *salt, 5 or 6 peppercorns*

- *3 tablespoons olive oil*
- *1 lively lobster weighing about 1 1/2 pounds*

THE HERB BUTTER

Reduce the white wine, pastis, and herbs over a high flame until only about 3 tablespoonfuls of liquid remain in the saucepan. Leave until lukewarm, season with salt and freshly ground pepper and whisk vigorously with the softened butter. (Part of this butter will serve for basting and the remainder will accompany the lobster at table.)

THE ANCHOVY BUTTER

Soak the anchovy fillet (preferably salted and not preserved in oil) in water for 1/2 hour to desalt it, sponge it dry in paper toweling, mash it to a fine paste in a mortar, then mash in the butter (ordinarily, it would be passed through a sieve—for this preparation, it is not essential).

THE COURT-BOUILLON

Bring the liquids to a boil, add all the other ingredients, with the exception of the peppercorns, and simmer, covered, for a good 1/2 hour—the peppercorns will be added a few minutes before the lobster claws.

Pour the olive oil into a heavy oval *poêle* or gratin dish, as nearly as possible of just the size to hold the lobster, and heat it in a very hot oven (475°–500° F.). Tear off the claws—a simple twist is all that is necessary—and put them into the court-bouillon to poach, covered; after they have simmered for 10 minutes, remove the saucepan from the flame, leaving them in the cooking liquid, and put the lobster into its oven-heated dish. Turn it around in the hot oil several times over a period of about 10 minutes, or until it is equally reddened on all sides. Lower the heat of the oven to about 325° F., take out the pan and, using the end of the handle of a wooden spoon (for instance), punch a hole in the center (top side) of the lobster shell, which contains the coral and terminates in the head, and insert the anchovy butter and as much of the herb butter as can be forced in. Return it to the oven, and over a period of 20 minutes, regularly force more herb butter into the hole (4 to 5 tablespoons in all).

Split the lobster in two, discard the gravel sack ("queen") to be found at the head's extremity, and serve accompanied by the rest of the herb butter. Serve the claws after.

BRAISED AND ROAST PARTRIDGE WITH CABBAGE

Braised old partridge (*perdrix*) and cabbage usually is served "as is," the bird picked out from its nest of cabbage and presented crowning the mound of cabbage, the garnish of carrots and side pork surrounding it. A sausage is often braised and included in the garnish. (Out of game season, guinea fowl may be treated in the same way.) One must not expect too much of the old partridge, all of whose flavor has gone to enrich the cabbage, but in combination with the young partridge (*perdreau*) roasted slightly rare, just out of the oven, the total experience is perfect.

Should the cabbage-braising liquid remain from a recent *Pot-au-Feu* (see page 322), it will serve splendidly. While it is unlikely that the home cook will use a concentrated stock made exclusively from partridge carcasses, the result, when this essence serves as the braising liquid, is spectacular.

Braised and Roast Partridge with Cabbage

Perdrix aux Choux

1 *medium cabbage* (2 *to* 2 1/2 *pounds*)
2 3/4-*inch slices* (*about* 1/2 *pound*) *lean salt side pork*
    (*substitute slab bacon, if necessary*)
1 *old partridge*
1 *tablespoon* (1/2 *ounce*) *butter*
1/4 *cup white wine*
1/2 *cup Mirepoix* (*page* 74); *if prepared especially, use* 1 *medium*
    carrot, 1 *large onion, and more herbs than usual*
2 *whole, peeled carrots*
about 2 *cups rich, gelatinous Veal Stock* (*page* 72)

Roast partridge:
1 *young partridge* (*hung for* 3 *or* 4 *days but not "high"*)
1 *pinch oregano*
1 *tablespoon* (1/2 *ounce*) *butter*
1 *thin sheet fat side pork* (*not bacon*)

Remove the outer leaves from the cabbage, cut it in two, cut out the core, separate the leaves, and pare the thick ribs from each. Gather the leaves together on a chopping board and shred them coarsely (about 1/2-inch strips). Parboil the cabbage in a large quantity of salted water for 10 to 15 minutes and drain it thoroughly in a colander, pressing the leaves well.

Cover the slices of salt pork with cold water, bring to a boil, simmer for 8 to 10 minutes and drain.

Cook the old partridge in the butter, in a small skillet or heavy saucepan, for about 15 minutes, turning it regularly, keeping the flame low enough to avoid any smoking. When it is lightly colored on all sides, remove it and wash out the pan with the white wine, scraping loose any frying adherents and reducing the liquid to a tablespoon or two.

Line the bottom of a heavy copper saucepan or an earthenware or enameled cast-iron casserole with half the *mirepoix*, spread a bed of cabbage on top, place the partridge in the middle, a carrot and a slice of side pork to either side, pour over the bit of white wine reduction from the partridge's cooking pan, regularly distribute the remaining *mirepoix*, and add the rest of the cabbage, packing it lightly and smoothing the surface. Heat the stock enough to melt it, pour in enough to rise just above the cabbage's surface, bring to a boil over medium heat, and cook, covered, either over a tiny flame or in a slow oven, at a bare simmer, for at least 2½ hours in all. After 1 to 1½ hours, the side pork should be thoroughly cooked. Remove it carefully and put it aside. If at this time the quantity of liquid seems excessive, continue the braising with the lid ajar to permit evaporation; if it seems low, add some boiling stock. After 2½ hours, remove the partridge, lift the flesh from the bones (it will be in a condition to fall off), chop it coarsely, and return it to the cabbage. The braising liquid should be almost completely reduced—if the cabbage is still quite liquid, continue cooking it for 10 to 15 minutes on top of the stove with the lid off, at a sufficient heat to produce a regular, gentle bubbling. (If it is to be reheated, it may remain slightly liquid—it will arrive at the correct state of reduction through a slow reheating.) Return the side pork a few minutes before serving to heat through. Taste for salt; none should be needed, as the stock, the *mirepoix* and the pork are all salted and the reduction should do the rest.

THE ROAST PARTRIDGE

Once cleaned and singed, sprinkle salt, pepper and oregano into the body cavity, insert the butter, salt and pepper the outside, place the sheet of fat pork over the breast, and tie the bird, encircling it 2 or 3 times with kitchen string to keep the slice of fat in place.

It is difficult to give a precise timing or method for roasting partridge—a fresh specimen requires a bit longer than one several days old, and, despite thermostats, ovens differ.

Choose a heavy, shallow roasting pall, just large enough to hold the trussed bird (a small crêpe pan, despite the theory that it should only serve its intended purpose, is just the right size—or a tiny gratin dish), start it out in a very hot oven and, after 5 minutes or so, turn it down to about 350° F. After 10 to 12 minutes in the oven, clip the strings, remove the sheet of fat, and 5 minutes later turn the oven off, leaving the bird in the oven for another 5 or 6 minutes (something over 20 minutes, in all). From the time the slice of fat is removed, it should be basted every couple of minutes. When done, the flesh of the breast should remain slightly rose in color. (A more usual but less satisfactory method consists in roasting it unattended in a 400° F. oven for 18 minutes.)

Mound the cabbage onto a preheated, deep serving platter, split the roast partridge in two, place the halves on the cabbage, and surround them with the slices of side pork, each cut into 4 or 5 sections, and the carrots, cut into thick slices.

Fresh Figs with Raspberry Cream

Figues à la Crème Framboisée

1 *pound fresh figs (tree-ripened and freshly picked, if possible)*
1/2 *pound fresh raspberries*
sugar to taste
2/3 *cup heavy cream*

Peel the figs, leaving them whole (the skin pulls off very easily in strips), arrange them in a serving dish, and chill them well. Pass the raspberries through a nylon (not metal) drum sieve and stir in the sugar. Whip the chilled cream in a chilled bowl until just stiff, mix in the raspberry purée and pour over the figs.

Four Simple Autumn Menus

Each of these menus will be happily served by a single red wine, young, cool, fruity and plentiful. None of the first courses are of a nature to flatter a wine, but if one were drinking a white wine as apéritif, it might be continued with the first course.

MENU I (FOR 4)

SALAD OF GRILLED SWEET PEPPERS
[POIVRONS DOUX GRILLES EN SALADE]

LAMB STEW WITH ARTICHOKE HEARTS
[RAGOUT D'EPAULE D'AGNEAU AUX COEURS D'ARTICHAUTS]

RICE PILAF
[PILAF DE RIZ]

WILD SALAD
[SALADE SAUVAGE]

CHEESES
[FROMAGES]

PEARS IN RED WINE
[POIRES AU VIN ROUGE]

Grilled Pepper Salad

Poivrons Doux Grillés en Salade

The pleasant, clean taste of raw peppers contains no hint of the subtle flavor brought out through grilling. Prepared in a vinaigrette, they not only keep, but improve. Red, yellow and green have distinctly different flavors and a mixture of the three is attractive. Choose them large, firm, smooth, heavy and of regular shape (those tortuously formed cannot be evenly grilled). They are best grilled over hot coals, but may perfectly well be prepared beneath a broiler. If a bed of coals has been prepared for another purpose, one may profitably put peppers to grill afterward and leave them on a plate overnight before preparing them.

The flesh should be semi-cooked. A heat that is too intense will char the skins before the flesh becomes soft; one that is too gentle will dehydrate the flesh before the skins are loosened. Turn them regularly so that all surfaces, including the stem end, are equally grilled. Some surfaces will be charred, others not. Once grilled, they should be transferred immediately to a plate to avoid any loss of liquid.

Remove them, one at a time, to another plate, pull out the stem end and the interior seed cluster to which it is attached, cut the pepper in two lengthwise, carefully remove any remaining seeds, and slip off the skins—peeling is no problem unless they are irregularly shaped or improperly grilled. The light, syrupy natural juice is a precious addition to the sauce.

Prepare a vinaigrette in a garlic-rubbed bowl; for those who prefer a more "aggressive" presence, a clove of garlic may be reduced to purée with the dry ingredients of the vinaigrette before adding the vinegar and the natural juices. Count about 1 part of concentrated Aromatic Vinegar (page 89) to 5 of olive oil. The sauce should be somewhat more salted than for most salads. Add the pepper halves, sliced lengthwise into wide strips. If they are stirred vigorously into the sauce, a semi-emulsion is produced which is, no doubt, less pleasing to the eye than to the palate.

An alternate method is to keep the peppers whole, merely slit down one side, sprinkled with vinaigrette, and folded over fresh branches of thyme and savory. These are often garnished with finely sliced scallions or anchovy fillets. Whole anchovies preserved in salt are best—they must be soaked in cold water to desalt them, the fillets lifted from the bones, soaked again and sponged dry in paper towels. If only canned anchovies are available, they, too, should be soaked first.

THE LAMB STEW WITH ARTICHOKE HEARTS

The shoulder and the lower tip of the leg are the two best braising or stewing sections of the lamb. Both are rich in flavor, lean and gelatinous. Lamb and mutton fats are not only indigestible but strong in flavor. It is their taste which, during the cooking process, penetrates the otherwise delicately flavored flesh and renders these meats repellent to many palates. Although the fat should be removed before cooking, lamb of good quality is naturally covered with a healthy layer of white fat, and the flesh should be a clear, rose-tan color.

The kind of oil used for browning in a preparation of this sort is not terribly important, for although without it onions, meat, sugar and flour could not be properly colored (all essential to the deep color and rich flavor of the sauce), it will ultimately be skimmed and discarded.

Only a heavy copper *sauteuse* is perfect; the next-best method is to execute the first steps in a heavy iron skillet and transfer everything to an earthenware or enameled ironware casserole for the longer braising process. The pot should be precisely the right size to hold the pieces of meat placed side by side, but barely touching; if the pan is too large, its surfaces not contacted by the meat will burn while the meat browns (the flame being necessarily quite high for the meat to brown properly); if it is so small that the pieces of meat have to be packed in, they will boil in their juices rather than brown. Moreover, the eventual quality of the sauce depends on the solid elements' being closely arranged in a pan of the right size so that they may be completely submerged in a minimum of liquid.

Lamb Stew with Artichoke Hearts

Ragoût d'Epaule d'Agneau aux Coeurs d'Artichauts

a shoulder of yearling lamb
4–12 *artichokes, depending on size* (*plus lemon, salt, thyme, butter for their preparation*)
3 *tablespoons butter*
3 *medium-size mild onions* (12–14 *ounces*), *coarsely chopped*
3 *tablespoons olive or other vegetable oil*
salt
1 *teaspoon sugar*
flour
1 *scant teaspoon Mixed Herbs* (*page* 86)
2 *garlic cloves, crushed and peeled*
1 *bay leaf*
1 *cup dry white wine*
2 *large, firm, well-ripened tomatoes, peeled, seeded and coarsely chopped* (*or a* 1-*pound can*)
1 *cup water*
salt, pepper

Ask your butcher to bone the shoulder. Cut it into 8 pieces of approximately equal size, respecting as nearly as possible the natural muscular structure, and remove all surface fat.

Prepare the Artichokes as described on page 77, keeping them quite firm. After having removed the chokes, sponge them dry and leave them whole, or cut them into halves or quarters, depending on their size. Stew them gently in butter for from 20 minutes to 1/2 hour, tossing from time to time or delicately turning them. They should still remain slightly firm. Put them aside.

Cook the onions in the oil over a low to medium flame, stirring them regularly, until lightly browned. Watch them closely, for they burn easily. Remove them, leaving as much oil as possible in the pan. The slightest fragment of onion that remains in the pan at this point will inevitably burn while the meat is coloring and leave a bitter taste in the sauce. Salt the pieces of meat on all sides and put them to cook in the same fat, turning the flame up somewhat. When they are browned on all sides, lower the flame again, sprinkle with the sugar and turn the pieces around in the pan from time to time over a period of a couple of minutes until the sugar has had time to caramelize. Hold a lid over the pan, pour off the excess fat, return to the heat, and sprinkle with the flour. Turn the pieces over again and, when the flour has lightly browned, return the onions to the pan, sprinkle with the mixed herbs and add the garlic and the bay leaf. Lift all the elements and turn them around with a wooden spoon until well mixed together, and pour in the white wine. Turn the flame up, stir and scrape the bottom and sides of the *sauteuse* well to be certain that all adherent frying matter is loosened and dissolved, reduce somewhat, and add the tomatoes plus just enough boiling water to barely submerge the meat. Bring to a boil and cook, covered, at a bare simmer, either over a tiny flame or in a slow oven, for 1½ hours. Skim off the surface fat 2 or 3 times during this period.

Lift out the pieces of meat, discard the bay leaf, and leave the sauce to rest for a few minutes. Skim off all traces of fat that rise to the surface and pass the sauce and onions through a fine sieve into another saucepan. Return the meat to the *sauteuse*, add the artichoke hearts, sprinkle with freshly ground pepper, and leave, covered, in a warm place.

Bring the sauce to a boil and leave it on the side of a small flame, skinning it regularly (page 90) for about ½ hour. It should, at this point, be of a perfect consistency. If it seems a bit liquid, turn the flame up and reduce rapidly, stirring all the while. Taste for salt, pour it over the meat and its garnish, and leave to simmer, ever so gently, covered, for another ½ hour. Serve directly from the cooking pot, accompanied by a pilaf (page 81). For a less "homey" presentation, the rice may be packed into a ring mold, unmolded onto a large, round, heated serving platter, the center filled with stew and sprinkled with chopped parsley. Second helpings, however, with this pretty presentation, are inevitably cold.

Pears in Red Wine

Poires au Vin Rouge

4 *or* 5 *slightly underripe eating pears*
1 *orange*
cinnamon
2/3 *cup sugar*
1 *bottle good red wine*

Cut the pears in two lengthwise, core and peel them and arrange the halves in the bottom of an earthenware or enameled ironware terrine—if they are to be cooked in the oven, Pyrex or porcelain will do as well. Wash the orange to remove any hint of insecticide or preservative, and shave a long spiral from the peel, keeping clear of the white, pithy material. Add it to the pears, sprinkle very lightly with cinnamon, add the sugar and the wine, bring to a boil, and leave, covered, to simmer for about 2 hours (with certain hard varieties of cooking pears, one may allow as much as 6 to 8 hours' cooking time), or until they are coated in a thin syrup. Serve them chilled, accompanied by *Tuiles* (page 94) or other simple cookies.

Four Simple Autumn Menus

This menu will be happily served by a single red wine, young, cool, fruity and plentiful. The first course is not of a nature to flatter a wine, but if one were drinking a white wine as apéritif, it might be continued with the first course.

MENU II (FOR 4)

COMPOSED SALAD
[SALADE COMPOSEE]

BOILED PIGS' TAILS AND EARS WITH VEGETABLES
[POTEE AUX QUEUES ET OREILLES DE COCHON]

GOAT CHEESES
[FROMAGES DE CHEVRE]

PERIGORD PUDDING
[FLAUGNARDE]

THE COMPOSED SALAD

A composed salad may be a combination of any number of things. Lobster, truffles, asparagus tips, chicken breast, crayfish tails and artichoke hearts often enter into the composition of elegant versions. Depending on its makeup and the menu, it may begin a meal, or be the principal course, or replace the usual green salad.

Dill has a rather special taste that does not please everyone. *Fines herbes* may be substituted.

Composed Salad

Salade Composée

1 celery heart
3 pints mussels
3 small new potatoes of nonmealy variety
1/2 cup dry white wine
1 chopped onion
freshly ground pepper
lettuce leaves

Sauce:
1 lemon
1 teaspoon chopped tender fresh dill (or a pinch of dried dill weed)
a scant teaspoon French mustard
salt and pepper
1/2 cup heavy cream (a few days old, if possible)

If the celery is not absolutely crisp, put it to soak in ice water for an hour or so. Scrape the mussels and rinse them well several times in salt water (if sand is imprisoned inside the shells, the bulk of it is usually disgorged this way).

Boil the potatoes in their skins, peel them the moment they are drained, slice them fairly thickly into a soup plate or bowl, pour the white wine over, and leave to cool.

Put the mussels and chopped onion into a large pot, grind in some pepper, pour over them the wine from the cooled potatoes, cover tightly, and place over a high flame, shaking the pot occasionally. Leave only long enough for all the mussels to open (3 or 4 minutes). Remove them from their shells, put them aside, and allow the cooking liquid to settle for a few minutes. Pour it carefully through a couple of layers of muslin into a small saucepan, leaving all the heavy sediment behind. Reduce the liquid rapidly by half. Taste it—fresh mussels often contain a large quantity of sea water and their cooking liquid is intensely salty—and use it accordingly in the seasoning of the sauce. (If the cream for the sauce is not very thick, forget about the cooking liquid.) Cut the celery crosswise into approximately 1/4-inch slices.

SAUCE

Mix together the juice of 1/2 lemon, the chopped dill, the mustard, and some freshly ground pepper (if dried dill is used, allow it to macerate for 1/2 hour in the lemon juice). Stir in the cream and add as much (if any) of the mussels' cooking liquid as the sauce can support without becoming too thin. Taste for salt, lemon and other seasoning and adjust if necessary.

Mix the celery, the mussels and the potatoes into the sauce carefully, so as not to damage the potato slices, turn it out onto a platter or shallow bowl lined with lettuce leaves and sprinkle with chopped fresh dill or *fines herbes.*

BOILED PIGS' TAILS AND EARS WITH VEGETABLES

A *potée* is a mixture of meats and vegetables, boiled, traditionally, in a large earthenware pot. Each province of France has its own. (This, although all its components are found in one or another *potée*, is not traditional; it lacks the preserved goose of one, the smoked sausage of the other, etc.)

Boiled, pork is finer salted than fresh. Salt pork is so little used in America that when one finds it, it is almost always too old, and sometimes rancid. The best solution is to buy fresh pork and salt it. The ears and tails, in any case, are likely to be found only fresh: sprinkle generously with coarse salt (put layers of salt and meat in a large bowl or spread out on a platter), cover and leave for several days. Rinse well before using. Commercially salted or smoked products should be rinsed, parboiled for 15 minutes (starting them out in cold water) and re-rinsed.

If fresh white beans are not to be found, dried beans will serve. They should be precooked for an hour and added at the same time as the first batch of vegetables.

A *potée* for 4 can always feed 6. The unused cooking liquid forms a splendid base for a rough peasant soup.

Boiled Pigs' Tails and Ears with Vegetables

Potée aux Queues et Oreilles de Cochon

1 *small cabbage (preferably green)*
4 *medium leeks*
1 *pound (unshelled) fresh white beans or* 1 *cup dried beans*
1/2 *pound green beans (the large overmature specimens commonly marketed will do very well)*
about 1/2 *pound turnips*
about 3/4 *pound carrots*
4 *pigs' tails and* 2 *ears*
1/2*-pound slice of lean side pork—fresh, salted or smoked*
3–4 *quarts water*
1/2 *teaspoon thyme*
1 *branch celery,* 1 *bay leaf,* 1 *large bouquet parsley, all tied together in a bundle*
1 *whole head of garlic, left intact and unpeeled*
2 *onions, peeled (*1 *stuck with* 2 *cloves)*
small handful of coarse salt

Boiled Pigs' Tails and Ears with Vegetables

Remove the outer leaves from the cabbage, cut it vertically into quarters and pare the core, leaving only enough to keep the leaves of each quarter attached. Reassemble the cabbage in a saucepan, cover with salted boiling water, cook, covered, at a slight boil for 15 minutes, and drain.

Remove the tough dark-green parts from the leeks, slit the upper halves, wash them well and tie them firmly into a bundle, the slit halves folded down.

Shell the white beans, or partially cook dried beans, snap the green beans and break or cut them into short sections, peel the turnips and carrots, leaving the turnips whole or cutting them into halves or quarters, depending on their size, and cut the carrots into large sections.

Cover the meats generously with water, bring to a boil, and skim (see page 90), adding a glassful of cold water at 2 or 3 intervals each time the boil is reached. Add the thyme, the aromatic package, the head of garlic, the carrots, the turnips, the onions and the salt. When the boiling point is again reached, skim; cover, leaving the lid slightly ajar, and adjust to a simmer.

One-half hour later, add the leeks and the shelled white beans, and gently immerse the cabbage quarters. Return to a boil and leave to simmer as before. When the white beans show signs of softening (after 30 or 40 minutes), add the green beans and cook as before for another 1/2 hour, or until everything is done.

Discard the onions and the aromatic bouquet, remove the string from the leeks, split the ears into several sections lengthwise, and cut the side pork into pieces.

Serve, if possible, in a large deep preheated platter, the cabbage quarters placed outside, the meats in the center, and the other vegetables distributed pell-mell around. Pour a couple of ladles of bouillon over the lot.

A pot of mustard, a dish of coarse salt, and a jar of sour gherkins should be at hand. If possible, the accompanying bread should be coarse, heavy, and not too fresh. Each clove of garlic contains a delicious and delicate purée which may be spread on one's bread. Squeeze the skin and the purée plops out.

THE PERIGORD PUDDING

A Périgourdine specialty, a Périgord pudding (*flaugnarde*) is essentially nothing but a dish of baked crêpe batter filled with brandy-soaked prunes and raisins. Those accustomed to leavened pastries may, at first contact, find the custardy texture and the somewhat leathery skin bizarre. Its simple honesty rarely fails to seduce.

Périgord Pudding

Flaugnarde

2 *ounces raisins* (*dried currants*)
1/2 *pound prunes* (*of the year's production, if possible*)
1/4 *cup cognac* (*or eau de vie de prune*)
1/2 *cup sugar*
4 *eggs*
tiny pinch of salt
1/2 *cup flour*
1 *cup milk*
1/2 *teaspoon vanilla extract*
2 *tablespoons* (1 *ounce*) *butter*

Cover the raisins with cold water, bring them only just to a boil, remove from the heat, leave to swell for 10 minutes, and drain them. Cut the prunes in two and remove the pits. Combine the prunes and the raisins in a glass jar with a tight-fitting lid, pour the cognac over and screw the lid tightly. Shake from time to time, turning the jar over. After 6 or 7 hours, the liquid will have been completely absorbed (a few hours more won't hurt, nor will a few hours less be disastrous).

Beat the sugar, eggs, and salt together in a mixing bowl. Sift in the flour, a little at a time, stirring all the while with a whisk. Stir in the milk, the vanilla extract, and the contents of the jar (don't be alarmed by the thinness of the batter). Butter liberally a gratin dish or a Pyrex pie plate, ladle in the bulk of the prune-and-raisin batter and pour the rest of the batter over. Bake in a hot oven (375° to 400° F.) for 20 minutes. Serve lukewarm, directly from the baking dish. It may be eaten cold, although it is less good, but it must, in any case, be served freshly made.

Four Simple Autumn Menus

This menu will be happily served by a single red wine, young, cool, fruity and plentiful. The first course is not of a nature to flatter a wine, but if one were drinking a white wine as apéritif, it might be continued with the first course.

MENU III (FOR 4 TO 6)

FENNEL A LA GRECQUE
[FENOUIL A LA GRECQUE]

FRENCH MOUSSAKA, WATERCRESS
[MOUSSAKA A LA FRANCAISE, VERT-PRE]

FRESH WHITE CHEESES
[FROMAGES FRAIS]

ORANGE CREAM
[CREME A L'ORANGE]

THE FENNEL A LA GRECQUE

Artichoke hearts, small onions, the whites of leeks cut into 1½-inch lengths, celery hearts split in two, or cauliflower, the "flowers" removed from the main stalk, may all be prepared in identically the same way.

Fennel à la Grecque

Fenouil à la Grecque

1½ pounds fennel
3 cups water
⅓ cup olive oil
juice of 2 lemons
1 onion, finely sliced into rings
2 cloves of garlic, mashed and peeled
8–10 coriander seeds
8–10 whole peppercorns
1 pinch fennel seeds
1 large pinch thyme
1 bay leaf
salt
chopped parsley

Garden fennel (sometimes known as Florentine or bulb fennel) has a light, refreshing anise flavor, much less pronounced than that of the wild fennel that enters so often into the seasoning of Provençal cooking. Unless the bulbs are tiny and tender, the outer stalks should be removed and the "strings" pulled from the remaining surface stalks (exactly as with celery stalks). The bulbs should be cut vertically into halves or quarters, depending on their size, and parboiled for from 5 to 10 minutes.

Bring the water to a boil, add all the ingredients except the chopped parsley, and simmer, covered, until the fennel is tender. Arrange the fennel in a deep serving dish, pour over the contents of the saucepan and leave to cool. Serve chilled, sprinkled with chopped parsley.

THE MOUSSAKA

A very pretty presentation and a savory manner of using up leftover roast or braised lamb or mutton, *moussaka* may also be prepared by cooking the eggplant halves in oil, incorporating the flesh into the mixture, and lining the mold with the skins. Transposed to the needs of classic French cooking, it would certainly be unrecognizable to the people who created it (though the taste is suspiciously similar). The Greek version is basically a hash of leftover meats, onions and eggplant, spread into a large baking dish, covered with white sauce and baked until a gratin is formed.

Dishes based on leftovers cannot depend on precise measurements, and those given here should not be taken too seriously. The tomato purée may be made from fresh or canned tomatoes—or leftover tomato sauce will serve perfectly well. Canned tomato juice is also possible, although it requires rather more drastic reduction. The use of tomato paste is to be discouraged, for it has an unpleasantly bitter, metallic taste which neither baking nor the addition of sugar can disguise.

The small, elongated violet eggplant is far better than the large, nearly black variety, which is always pithy and seedy.

French Moussaka, Watercress

Moussaka à la Française, Vert-pré

1 pound eggplant
salt, pepper
olive oil
1 pound lean, leftover cooked lamb
1/2 cup prepared Duxelles (page 76—if not already prepared, use 1 medium onion and 1/4 pound mushrooms. The butter may be replaced by olive oil)

1 clove garlic, mashed, peeled, and chopped
1/2 cup tomato purée
a healthy pinch of Mixed Herbs (page 86) reduced to powder in a mortar
1 handful bread crumbs
1 egg
watercress for garnish

The eggplant will be used to line the mold. The small elongated variety should be sliced lengthwise into 1/3-inch-thick strips. A large eggplant should be peeled, two 1/3-inch-thick disks taken from it to line the bottom of the mold and close the top, and the rest cut into strips approximately 4 inches high by 1 1/2 to 2 inches wide. Salt and pepper the slices, heat about 1/2 inch of olive oil in a skillet, and fry (in 2 or 3 batches) until golden on both sides. Drain on paper towels.

Slice and cube the lamb as minutely as possible, then chop it fine, using a large, well-sharpened knife and a rapid, loose-wristed motion. Sprinkle with salt and cook in olive oil over a medium to high flame, stirring regularly, for about 10 minutes; add the *duxelles* and continue cooking and stirring for a couple of minutes. Add the garlic, the tomato purée and the powdered herbs, turn the flame up as high as possible and stir constantly until the mixture is well blended. Stir in the bread crumbs and leave to cool slightly while preparing the mold.

Line the bottom of a standard charlotte mold (approximately of 3-pint capacity, slightly over 3 inches high) with eggplant strips (or the circular section) and line the sides with strips, vertically placed and slightly overlapping. Press them gently against the sides to be certain that they are firmly in place.

Sprinkle the meat mixture with pepper, mix in the egg, and add it to the mold, a spoonful at a time, being careful not to displace any portions of the lining. Tap the bottom of the mold firmly several times against a wooden table surface or on the chopping board to be certain that the stuffing is well settled and that no air pockets remain. Press down more strips (or the other round of eggplant) on the surface, carefully fold the overlapping ends of the side strips inward, one at a time, and press a buttered or oiled round of kitchen paper over the surface.

Place the mold in a larger pan, pour in enough boiling water to immerse it by two-thirds and poach in a slow oven (or tightly covered over a low flame) for 40 minutes. Remove the mold from the *bain-marie* and leave it to settle for 7 or 8 minutes before unmolding.

Remove the round of paper, place a round serving platter upside down over the mold and, firmly holding a handle of the mold and the edge of the platter between the thumb and fingers of each hand, turn the mold and the platter over together. Wait a few seconds to be certain that the *moussaka* has unmolded and settled onto the platter, and gently lift off the mold. Surround with bouquets of washed and well-dried watercress, the stem ends tucked underneath the edge of the *moussaka.*

Orange Cream

Crème à l'Orange

5 *egg yolks*
1/2 *cup sugar*
1 *cup freshly squeezed, strained orange juice*
juice of 1 *lemon, strained*
1/4 *cup white wine*

Beat the sugar and egg yolks together until the yellow color turns pale. Slowly add the liquids, stirring all the while, and cook over a low flame in a heavy saucepan, continuing to stir. The mixture will never coat the spoon, and it must not boil. When it assumes something more than a liquid consistency and begins to adhere to the sides of the saucepan, remove it from the heat, immerse the saucepan in cold water, and continue stirring until the cream has completely cooled. Pour it into individual serving dishes, chill thoroughly for several hours at least, and serve accompanied by *Tuiles* (page 94) or other simple cookies.

Four Simple Autumn Menus

This menu will be happily served by a single red wine, young, cool, fruity and plentiful. The first course is not of a nature to flatter a wine, but if one were drinking a white wine as apéritif, it might be continued with the first course.

MENU IV (FOR 4)

GARLIC SOUP
[SOUPE A L'AIL (AIGO-BOUIDO)]

GRILLED LAMBS' HEARTS AND BABY ZUCCHINI
[GRILLADE DE COEURS D'AGNEAU ET PETITES COURGETTES]

CHEESES
[FROMAGES]

FRENCH PANCAKE JELLY ROLLS
[PANNEQUETS A LA CONFITURE]

THE GARLIC SOUP

Aïgo-bouido is Provençal for "boiled water." It is believed to be a cure-all. The rustic accompaniment is always dried bread crusts. The simplest version—reserved for those who are seriously ill—is nothing but a couple of cloves of garlic boiled in a quart of water with a branch of thyme and a sage leaf, strained over some olive oil-soaked crusts of dried bread. A step or two up the ladder, a bay leaf and a few more cloves of garlic are added and the strained liquid is beaten into a mixture of olive oil and egg yolk (traditionally, olive oil is cooked in the soup, but its flavor and digestibility both suffer from this treatment). A rich *aïgo-bouido* (more garlic and egg yolks) is an obligatory course (along with the 13 desserts) in every Provençal Christmas Eve menu. The following recipe is a "super" version, as *aïgo-bouidos* go. For those who fear raw garlic, it cannot be too highly recommended. Whether or not one likes raw garlic, there is no doubt that it is powerful and aggressive in flavor and difficult to digest (although good, they say, for the heart). Cooked garlic is delicate and subdued in flavor, an aid to digestion and a "calmative."

Garlic Soup

Soupe à l'Ail (Aïgo-bouido)

1 *quart water*
1 *bay leaf*
2 *or* 3 *sage leaves*
a healthy pinch of thyme
10–15 *cloves garlic, smashed, peeled and chopped*
salt to taste

Binding pommade:

1 *whole egg and* 2 *yolks*
1½ *ounces freshly grated Parmesan cheese* (*or mixed Parmesan and Swiss Gruyère*)

freshly ground pepper
1/4 cup olive oil

Bring the water to a boil and add all the ingredients except those of the *pommade*. Cook, covered, at a gentle boil, for 40 minutes, strain through a sieve, discard the herbs and pass the garlic through into the liquid. Taste for salt.

Combine the egg, the yolks, the grated cheese, and the pepper in a bowl, stir and then beat with a small whisk until creamy. Slowly pour in the oil, beating all the time, then add, continuing to whisk, a ladleful of the bouillon. Stir the contents of the bowl into the bouillon, transfer it to a saucepan and whisk it over a low to medium flame until it thickens slightly—just enough to be no longer watery. Pour it over a handful of broken-up dried-out crusts of bread in a preheated soup tureen and serve immediately.

THE GRILLED LAMBS' HEARTS AND BABY ZUCCHINI

Lamb (or mutton) hearts, alone, have a distinctly individual flavor. The anonymous veal or beef heart is attractive and delicious either roasted or braised whole with a highly seasoned stuffing, but the quality of the dish depends on the supplementary elements. Lambs' hearts may just as well be tossed rapidly in butter or grilled beneath the broiler. The only detail that must be respected to avoid their becoming tough is that they be kept slightly rare.

Zucchini squash, barely deflowered (the wilted flower often still attached to the tip), no more than an inch in diameter, 4 inches long, and firm to the touch, are exquisite. They should always be cooked in the simplest and most rapid manner possible, and should never touch boiling water; try them sliced coin-thin, seasoned, and rapidly tossed in very hot olive oil with a couple of cloves of garlic. Discard the garlic cloves and sprinkle with a few drops of lemon juice and some chopped parsley.

Grilled Lambs' Hearts and Baby Zucchini

Grillade de Coeurs d'Agneau et Petites Courgettes

4 lambs' hearts
pinch of mixed herbs
8 zucchini
olive oil, salt, pepper

Slice through the outer wall of each heart from both sides so that it may be unfolded into a more-or-less regular single slice. Sprinkle with the herbs and enough olive oil to thinly coat them and leave to marinate for an hour or so. Remove the tips and stem ends from the squash, split them in half and sprinkle with oil. Neither hearts nor squash should be seasoned until just before putting them to grill. One should have a fairly vivid bed of hot coals, and the grill should be preheated.

Count 4 or 5 minutes' cooking time for the hearts (once turned, they are done when rose-tinted droplets appear on the surface) and about 10 minutes at a less intense heat for the zucchini. These may be begun, placed face down, at the heart of the grill and, after 3 or 4 minutes, when the face is nicely colored, turned, removed to an area of less intense heat, and replaced by the hearts. The zucchini are done when the flesh offers no resistance to the sharp point of a small knife. Both squash and hearts should be lightly basted with olive oil just after they are turned. Care should be taken that no oil drops onto the hot coals, lending an unpleasant smoky flavor.

THE FRENCH PANCAKE JELLY ROLLS

Crêpes are served folded or flat. When rolled, usually cut in two at a bias, the ends trimmed to match, they become *pannequets*.

French Pancake Jelly Rolls

Pannequets à la Confiture

butter
sugar
12 *Crêpes (page 82)*
jam or jelly, preferably of an acid fruit—currant, apricot, wild plum, raspberry—and not too sweet

Butter a shallow baking dish that will be attractive on the table and sprinkle the bottom with sugar. Butter the crêpes lightly, spread each with a teaspoonful of jam or jelly, roll them up and place them side by side in the baking dish. Sprinkle the surface with sugar and put into a hot oven long enough for the sugar on the surface to melt and form a glaze.

Winter Menus

Appropriate wines for each menu are suggested on the pages indicated below, which mark the beginning of each menu and its recipes.

Two Elegant Winter Suppers

I

PAGE 190

Caviar

Scrambled Eggs with Fresh Truffles

Lobsters à la Nage

Salad with Fines Herbes

Pineapple and Frangipane Fritters

II

PAGE 200

Whole Foie Gras

Fresh Egg Noodles with Truffles

Tossed Green Salad

Cheeses

Striped Bavarian Cream

An Elaborate Formal Dinner Party

PAGE 208

Cream of Artichoke Soup with Hazelnuts
Grilled Fish with Sea Urchin Purée
Timbale of Sweetbreads and Macaroni
Rum Sherbet
Roast Guinea Fowl with Bacon
Chestnut Purée with Celery
Tossed Green Salad with Fines Herbes
Cheeses
Blanc-manger

Two Informal Winter Dinners

I

PAGE 224

Gratin of Stuffed Crêpes

Stuffed Calves' Ears, Béarnaise Sauce

Tossed Green Salad

Cheeses

Molded Tapioca Pudding, Apricot Sauce

II

PAGE 234

Terrine of Sole Fillets

Beef Stew à la Bourguignonne

Steamed Potatoes

Belgian Endive Salad

Cheeses

Floating Island

Three Simple Winter Menus

I

PAGE 245

Celeriac in Mustard Sauce
Cassoulet
Watercress Salad
Fruit

II

PAGE 252

Soufflés à la Suissesse
Skewered Lambs' Kidneys
Saffron Rice with Tomatoes
Lamb's Lettuce Salad
Fresh Goat Cheeses
Crêpes à la Normande

III

PAGE 259

Poached Eggs à la Bourguignonne
Beef Tripe à la Lyonnaise
Composed Salad
Cheeses
Pineapple Ice

A Note on Truffles

I was delighted and relieved to discover, in the course of my research for this book, that not only are fresh black truffles available in America (from December through February), but that the importer (see page 67) will airmail one- or two-pound packages to any place in the United States.

With the exception of the pheasant *salmis* which is placed in the "Autumn" section to coincide with the hunting season, all the recipes requiring truffles have been gathered into the "Winter" section. There are few, for truffles are hard on the purse—although French cookbooks persist in giving the recipe, no one stuffs a turkey with two pounds of truffles any more—and I have tried to present recipe "types" in which the truffle itself is best thrown into relief. It is twice found associated with sweetbreads. Whatever its preparation, the "cooking" should consist only in its being sufficiently heated to liberate the heady perfume. There is nothing in the world like a fresh truffle and no matter what its price, it is worth it. A good fresh black truffles is heavy, firm and resilient in feeling, never either hard or spongy. A cross section reveals a rich blackish-brown color with a distinct grayish-brown grain.

Cooked whole, in a ragoût or *sous les cendres*, truffles are never peeled. For most uses, truffles may or may not be peeled—it is a question of personal taste. They can be chopped finely and added to any number of forcemeats or sauces. Boned chicken legs are delicious stuffed with a purée of truffles peelings (pounded, mixed with some fresh bread crumbs soaked in a garlic-rubbed bowl with a bit of white wine and a few drops of cognac, seasoned, and passed through a sieve), sewn up, colored slightly in butter, and braised on a bed of *mirepoix* with a chicken or veal stock. Chopped peelings added to a potato-croquette mixture, the croquettes floured, dipped in beaten egg, rolled in slivered almonds and fried in deep fat, constitute a particularly handsome garnish to any grilled or roast meat or fowl.

In France one buys truffles coated with the earth from which they have been dug. In America I assume that they are sold brushed and cleaned, ready for use. They may be conserved in a nearly fresh state for many months by heating them in lard, packing them in small earthenware jars (not for aesthetic reasons, but because glass risks being broken by the contact with the hot fat), and pouring the hot, melted lard over so that they are completely covered. When cooled, cover them and store them in the refrigerator. They may be dug out of the solidified lard as needed, making certain that those remaining are not bared to the air. The lard will be perfumed and useful in many a rustic dish.

The two following menus are described as "suppers," with the French Christmas and New Year's *réveillon* tradition in mind (Christmas Eve and New Year's Eve are both celebrated by midnight suppers in which caviar, *foie gras*, truffles, and champagne are rarely absent). The first—the only one of its kind in the collection—has been specifically planned as a "champagne meal." Each menu contains a recipe for fresh truffles. The eggs in the one and the noodles in the other (any pasta lends support) are perhaps the two perfect truffle vehicles, for although both are fine and delicate in their own right, when inundated by the penetrating perfume of their regal companion, they bask in reflected glory.

Two Elegant Winter Suppers

with appropriate wines

MENU I (FOR 4)

CAVIAR

[CAVIAR]

Champagne:
a light nonvintage blanc de blancs

SCRAMBLED EGGS WITH FRESH TRUFFLES

[OEUFS BROUILLES AUX TRUFFES FRAICHES]

Champagne:
a vintage blanc de noirs (any not labeled blanc de blancs is either blanc de noirs or a mixture) brut, 5 or 6 years old

LOBSTERS A LA NAGE

[HOMARDS TIEDES A LA NAGE]

The same as the preceding or one answering the same qualifications but from an earlier vintage

SALAD WITH FINES HERBES

[SALADE AUX FINES HERBES]

PINEAPPLE AND FRANGIPANE FRITTERS

[BEIGNETS D'ANANAS A LA FRANGIPANE]

Champagne demi-sec

This menu is one of extreme simplicity, each element of which is a luxury item. It represents perfectly the ideal of a number of my French friends who claim to admire only *la cuisine simple.*

There is little work involved. The pineapple should be draped in its frangipane hours earlier and need only be dipped in the batter (which also is prepared ahead of time) at the last minute. The *court-bouillon* for the lobsters may be prepared in advance and they need only be thrown in just before one goes to table. The scrambled eggs represent a few minutes' occupation. That is all. The salad will have been prepared ahead of time and the caviar needs only the care of toasting a few thin slices of bread.

THE CAVIAR

Good caviar is large-grained, pale gray and translucent. It should be served, the container embedded in cracked ice, accompanied by thin slices of hot toast folded in a napkin to keep them warm, cold, sweet butter, and neither lemon nor onion. It is the only food I know that finds its perfect accompaniment in champagne.

THE SCRAMBLED EGGS WITH FRESH TRUFFLES

All scrambled-egg recipes are prepared in the same manner, with the exception that, for most, the garnish, ready-cooked and hot, is added just before serving. Other particularly happy marriages are: tiny, green asparagus tips, artichoke hearts stewed in butter, still-pink sautéed chicken livers, and crayfish tails or shrimp.

It is possible, although interminable, to cook scrambled eggs successfully in a heavy-bottomed saucepan or *sauteuse* over a direct, low flame, but wiser and quicker to use a *bain-marie*, the water kept just below the boiling point. Because the hot water contacts the sides as well as the bottom of the saucepan in which the eggs are cooked, they absorb heat through a much more extended surface.

Perfect scrambled eggs are creamy and absolutely consistent in texture, not so thick that they cannot be poured, but thick enough to hold their form, once served. The additional yolks, the passage through the sieve, the quantity of butter used, the addition of cream and the constant stirring in contact with low heat are all details directed toward this end.

Any receptacle with fairly low sides (3 to 4 inches high), enough larger than the saucepan to easily contain it and largely surround it with water, will do well for the *bain-marie*. A large *sauteuse* is perfect, but a high-sided cake tin or the bottom of a covered roasting pan will do as well. Lacking any of these, one may simply use a larger saucepan, but the work is harder, for, because of its high sides, the smaller saucepan must be held constantly, floating, in a larger quantity of water. Fill the chosen receptacle with enough water to immerse the saucepan about halfway or less, depending on the level reached by the eggs.

The croutons may be prepared somewhat ahead of time and kept warm—or rewarmed in a slow oven.

Scrambled Eggs with Fresh Truffles

Oeufs Brouillés aux Truffes Fraîches

Croutons:

3 *thick slices stale white bread*
about 4 *tablespoons* (2 *ounces*) *butter*

at least 3 *ounces fresh truffles*
6 *tablespoons* (3 *ounces*) *butter*
8 *eggs plus* 3 *or* 4 *yolks*
salt, freshly ground pepper
1/3 *cup heavy cream*

THE CROUTONS

But for a slight edge of sweetness, the commercialized "deluxe" type of American white bread, firm, heavy-textured, and unsliced (the slices are too thin)—or, of course, homemade American bread—is perfect material for croutons. The result is best if it is a bit stale—half dried out, but still easy to cut.

Cut 3 slices of bread, each somewhat over 1/2 inch thick, slice off the crusts, and cut the slices into cubes. Melt the butter in a heavy frying pan or *sauteuse*, the bottom surface of which is just the right size to hold the bread cubes comfortably. Cook them over a flame, turning them regularly until they are crisp and golden on all sides, adding more butter if necessary. The butter must absolutely not be allowed to burn (if it is clarified, there is no risk, but this is pointless, since, if the heat is kept low enough and the croutons constantly surveyed, they are better as described).

THE TRUFFLES

These may or may not be peeled. Cut them into slices fully 1/8 inch thick. The quality of the dish remains unchanged, but the presentation is handsomer if one keeps aside a few thinner slices, cooked gently for 2 or 3 minutes in a bit of butter and Madeira, port, sherry, or cognac, to be used as garnish. Even the finest, firmest, blackest fresh truffles are never as jet-black as when cooked in this way.

THE EGGS

Thickly butter the bottom and the sides of the saucepan with about 1/2 of the amount of butter prescribed. Cut the rest into small pieces. Beat the eggs with a fork until thoroughly mixed—no longer—and pass them through a fine sieve, to remove the firm fragments of white which never mix with the rest, directly into the saucepan, add the seasoning, the raw, sliced truffles and the remaining butter. Bring the water in the *bain-marie* receptacle to a boil and immerse the saucepan. The flame may be left high until the water again approaches the boiling point, then adjust it so that the water remains close to a simmer. Stir the eggs with a wooden spoon continuously, being careful to regularly scrape the entire surface of sides, corners, and bottom. Toward the end of the cooking, when they have noticeably begun to thicken, remove the saucepan from the water 2 or 3 times, continuing to stir (this prevents the thickening process, finally very rapid, from "getting ahead of you"). As they approach the proper consistency, remove the pan from the water, continue stirring (for the eggs continue to cook from the heat contained in the pan), pouring in a little cream, which will stop the thickening process and, in case they have become a bit too thick, bring them back to the right consistency. Be gentle with the addition of cream, for if too much is added, the eggs may be irremediably thinned—however, they will still be delicious. Stir in the croutons, pour onto a warmed (but not hot) serving platter, decorate the surface with the cooked truffles slices, and serve immediately.

THE LOBSTERS A LA NAGE

The "purest" way to prepare lobster is simply to boil it in sea water. *A la nage* is "next purest" and better. The replacement of tap water by sea water or, in either case, the use of sea salt for seasoning, is a valid refinement.

Lobsters may be prepared in precisely the same way to be served cold (allowed to cool in the *court-bouillon*). The butter in this case should be replaced by one of the mayonnaise derivatives (*tartare*, Vincent or *rémoulade*).

Although its preparation is not time-consuming, the *court-bouillon* may be prepared in advance and reheated at the last moment. Any that is left over may be strained, refrigerated and used for the poaching of other fish or as a stock base for a bisque or other fish soup or sauce.

Normally the lobsters are decorated with some of the vegetables of the *court-bouillon*, in which case the carrots are more presentable if peeled with a canaliculated knife. The presence of white wine turns them a dirty color and a clever restaurant practice is to replace this garnish by a handful of canaliculated (finely sliced and ridged) carrots and a fresh bouquet of parsley that have been plunged for a couple of minutes in salted boiling water. The bright green and orange splashed against the red-and-white lobster is spectacular, but I prefer the flavorful gray carrots. The unsightly gray straggles of parsley from the bouillon may be replaced by small bouquets of fresh parsley.

Lobsters à la Nage

Homards Tièdes à la Nage

Court-bouillon:

1 *bottle good, dry white wine*
2 *cups water*
2 *onions, thinly sliced crosswise (rings)*
2 *carrots, ridged and sliced thinly*
1 *small handful coarse salt (sea salt if available)*
a large pinch of whole peppercorns
a small pinch of Cayenne pepper
a healthy bouquet of parsley, a pinch of thyme, a pinch of oregano, a branch of fennel (or seeds) and a bay leaf

2 *large or* 4 *small and lively lobsters*
6 *to* 8 *ounces sweet butter*

Prepare the *court-bouillon* in a pot with a tight-fitting lid, just large enough to hold the lobsters easily. A large enameled cast-iron casserole or *marmite* is practical. Bring the liquids to a boil, add all the other ingredients except the lobsters and the butter, and leave to simmer, covered, for 20 to 30 minutes.

Fifteen minutes before going to table, plunge the live lobsters into the pot, make certain that they are as nearly covered with the liquid as possible, bring back to a boil, cover the pot and lower the flame. Turn them over in their liquid halfway through the cooking process (10 to 15 minutes in all, depending on the size of the lobsters). Remove from the heat and leave them, covered, in the *court-bouillon.*

To serve, twist off and crack the claws, but leave them intact. Spread out the body, face down, on the chopping board and, piercing it through the upper part of the carapace with a large, pointed knife, split it in two lengthwise. Tear out and discard the gravel sack ("queen") from the upper tip of the head, and arrange the halves, split surface up, surrounded by the claws, on a large serving platter. Remove the parsley from the *court-bouillon* and pour over the lobsters a ladleful of *court-bouillon* containing onion rings and carrot slices. Decorate with bouquets of fresh parsley and send to table, separately, a sauceboat of melted butter into which several tablespoons of *court-bouillon* have been incorporated. (I usually place a small sauce-pan containing butter and *court-bouillon* directly in the pot with the lobsters after they have finished cooking; it is thus automatically ready.) Lobster crackers and a plate or bowl to receive the shells at the table should not be forgotten. Finger bowls are more or less obligatory, for lobster in its shell cannot be eaten otherwise than with one's fingers.

Pineapple and Frangipane Fritters

Beignets d'Ananas à la Frangipane

The frangipane and the pineapple should be prepared a few hours ahead of time.

Frangipane:

- 1 *cup milk*
- *few drops of vanilla extract*
- 3 *tablespoons sugar*
- 5 *tablespoons flour*
- *small pinch of salt*
- 1 *whole egg and* 1 *egg yolk*
- 2 *dried-out almond macaroons* (*not coconut*)
- 2 *tablespoons* (1 *ounce*) *butter*
- 1 *tablespoon coarsely chopped pistachio nuts* (*first dipped for a minute in boiling water and rubbed in a towel to remove the skins*)

- *half a fresh pineapple*

Frying batter:

- 1 *egg*
- 1/3 *cup flour*
- *pinch of salt*
- 1 *teaspoon sugar*
- 1/3 *cup warm beer*
- 1 *ounce melted butter*
- *a bit of water*

- *oil for deep frying* (*preferably light olive oil, but a tasteless vegetable oil will do*)

(*Continued*)

THE FRANGIPANE

Bring the milk to a boil with the vanilla and sugar and leave to cool slightly. Sift the flour and salt into a saucepan, add the whole egg and the yolk and stir, keeping the motion to the center, with a wooden spoon so that the flour is slowly absorbed into the egg, then slowly add the milk, stirring all the time. Cook over a medium flame, continuing to stir vigorously, until the mixture becomes very thick. Remove from the heat, crumble in the macaroons, add the butter and the chopped pistachio nuts, mix well and leave to cool.

THE PINEAPPLE

Cut the pineapple in slices of from 1/3 to 1/2 inch thick; cut each slice in quarters, slice off the rind and remove the woody core. Butter a plate, spread half the frangipane over the surface, arrange the pineapple sections on top, and cover with the remaining frangipane so that each pineapple section is completely coated. Put to chill until needed.

THE FRYING BATTER

Prepare the batter an hour or so before the meal. It must "relax" to lose its elasticity; otherwise it refuses to properly coat the object to be fried.

Separate the yolk from the white of the egg and put the latter aside. Add the yolk to the dry ingredients and stir in the beer, adding it at 2 or 3 intervals. Stir only until a regular consistency is achieved. Never beat—the more a batter is "worked," the greater its elasticity. Stir in the melted butter and enough water to bring it to the consistency of fresh heavy cream. Kept this thin, there will be a greater loss of batter in the frying oil, but the crispness and delicacy of the fritters will be assured. Leave batter covered with a plate, at kitchen temperature, until needed; it should never be refrigerated, for a slight fermentation should take place. At the last minute, gently fold in the stiffly beaten egg white.

Heat the frying oil; when it sizzles at contact with a drop of batter, it is ready. Do not use a frying basket. Carefully cut loose, one from the other, the frangipane-covered pineapple sections and, one at a time, drop them from a spoon into the batter, lift them out and drop them into the hot oil. Don't try to fry too many at a time. Delicately turn them over in the oil with the prong tips of a fork, and when they are golden and crisp on both sides, scoop them out with a large skimming spoon. Drain them on paper towels and transfer them to the folded napkin in which they will be served. When all are fried, sprinkle the surface with powdered sugar and serve immediately.

Two Elegant Winter Suppers

with appropriate wines

MENU II (FOR 4)

WHOLE FOIE GRAS
[BLOC DE FOIE GRAS]

A great white Burgundy
(Montrachet, Corton-Charlemagne)
or a light-bodied red Bordeaux
(Médoc, Graves, or Pomerol)

FRESH EGG NOODLES WITH TRUFFLES
[PATES FRAICHES AUX TRUFFES]

A Côte de Beaune red (following
a Burgundy white) or, following
a red Bordeaux, an older Médoc

TOSSED GREEN SALAD
[SALADE VERTE]

CHEESES
[FROMAGES]

Following the Burgundies,
one of the great Côte de Nuits or,
following the Bordeaux,
a Saint-Emilion, older
than the preceding wines

STRIPED BAVARIAN CREAM
[CREME BAVAROISE EN RUBANEE]

Sauternes or champagne (demi-sec)

THE FOIE GRAS

The production of *foie gras* is less mysterious than generally believed. It depends, essentially, on two phases of feeding and development in the goose or duck. (In France, the best goose *foie gras* is produced from a Périgord race of geese and the best duck *foie gras*, firmer, smaller and less "melting" than the goose's, from a sterile hybrid of the Barbary duck and a native breed.) The first phase, involving a varied diet and normal exercise, is designed to strengthen the bird and in particular to develop a resistant heart, which will strengthen the bird for the intense no-exercise, force-feeding corn-diet phase, during which the enormous, fat livers are formed. The by-products of this luxury item, the flesh and fat of these birds, are important elements in many of the regional specialties of Alsace, and in particular of Périgord.

For a long time Hungary, and more recently, Israel, have produced quantities of *foie gras*, mostly for exportation to France, who is far from being able to produce a sufficient quantity for her own needs. There is no reason that enterprising American farmers could not launch a *foie gras* industry—traditions of raising and quality feeding would have to be respected, but even in France, the picturesque old peasant lady who moves from one goose to another, force-feeding each through a funnel, has long since been replaced by production-line mechanical force-feeders. Fresh *foie gras*, aside from the many hot preparations to which it lends itself, when served cold (poached, baked or braised, and kept pink throughout) is of a voluptuousness and a subtlety undreamed of by those who know only the preserved variety.

Although the preserving necessitates a longer cooking and a consequent loss in quality, whole *foie gras* at best retains a delicate flavor and melts sensuously across the tongue like nothing else. It should be noted that pure, solid, whole *foie gras* is always described as *bloc de foie gras*. The other products, variously described as "pâté" (a true *pâté de foie gras* is a whole *foie gras* enclosed in pastry), "purée," or "parfait," are pastes containing a certain amount of puréed *foie gras* in combination with other bland meat fillers. A mousse is a purée extended with butter and whipped cream. All may, on their own terms, be perfectly respectable products.

Foie gras should be served well chilled, accompanied by freshly made hot thin slices of toast. Butter is superfluous.

Fresh Egg Noodles with Truffles

Pâtes Fraîches aux Truffes

Noodle paste:

- *1 1/2 cups flour*
- *salt*
- *2 whole eggs and 2 yolks*

a good 1/2 pound of fresh black truffles
2 cloves garlic
1/2 pound fresh, unsalted butter
salt, freshly ground pepper
1–2 tablespoons good cognac (fine-champagne)

THE NOODLES

Sift the flour and salt, either into a mixing bowl or directly onto a pastry board, make a well in the center, add the whole eggs and yolks, work in the flour, a bit at a time, add, finally, a bit more flour or a bit more egg white, if necessary, to bring the paste to a firm but easily malleable consistency. Make a ball of it, roll it on a lightly floured board so that the surface will not be sticky and knead it several times, pushing it out flat, away from your person, with the heel of your hand, gathering it back into a compact mass and repeating the operation. Roll it into a ball, wrap it in wax paper, and leave it to "relax" in the refrigerator for an hour or so.

Divide the paste into 3 or 4 equal portions, flatten each with the palm of the hand into a regularly formed patty on the floured board, turning it over so that it is evenly coated with flour, and roll it out very thin, turning it over 2 or 3 times during the process and patting it with flour to ensure its sticking neither to the board nor to the rolling pin. These sheets of dough should be allowed to dry for a couple of hours before being cut up. The commonest and most practical home-kitchen method consists in hanging them over broomsticks, the two ends of which are supported by chair backs.

Roll up the sheets of dough and, with a good, sharp knife, cut them crosswise into narrow strips approximately 1/4 inch in width. Illogical as it appears, noodles seem to taste very differently depending on their width. Lightly and delicately, with the fingertips of both hands, lift masses of these cut, rolled ribbons, toss them in the air, letting them fall into spread-fingered, open hands, and retoss until all are loosely unspiraled. Be certain that no ends remain coiled, and leave them in a loose mass on the floured board until ready for use.

Cut the truffles into slices from 1/8 to 1/4 inch thick. Peel the garlic cloves without crushing them and rub the bottom and sides of an earthenware *poêlon* or casserole all over and repeatedly until both cloves have been used. Discard any solid fragments that may cling to the interior. Add half the butter and place the earthenware vessel over a very gentle heat, either in hot ashes or over a tiny flame, protected by an asbestos plaque. When the butter begins to melt, add the sliced truffles, sprinkle with salt, and pepper them generously, regulating the pepper mill to the coarsest grind. Sprinkle a bit of cognac over. (Not too much—its presence should not be suspected. Like the garlic, it is there to reinforce the truffle, rather than to assert its own personality.) Cover the receptacle as tightly as possible and leave it for about 15 minutes over gentle heat, shaking it a bit from time to time. The butter should not even be allowed to come to a bubble—it is not a cooking process, merely a slow warming that permits the various perfumes to mingle and that of the truffles to expand.

Bring a large pot of salted water to a boil and, after the truffles have been warming in their butter for about 10 minutes, add the noodles to the water, first tossing them in a large sieve to rid them of as much excess flour as possible. Fresh noodles require no more than 4 minutes' cooking time (it may vary slightly, depending on the stiffness of the dough and the extent to which they have been dried out). Pour them into a large sieve or colander, pour hot water over to rinse, and drain well. Add them to the truffles, toss the contents together lightly, lifting and turning with wooden forks or spoons, and leave, covered, still over low heat, for a few minutes to allow the noodles to become permeated with the truffles and their juices. Toss the contents a couple of times, holding the lid tightly in place and giving an abrupt forward, upward and backward movement to the casserole. Just before serving, bind the noodles by tossing them with the remaining butter, cut into small pieces.

Striped Bavarian Cream

Crème Bavaroise en Rubanée

NOTE: The proportions given will easily serve 6 or 8, but it is impractical to make a smaller quantity.

Raspberry mixture:

- *1/2 pound frozen raspberries (fresh, in season; those frozen whole and unsweetened seem the best of the frozen)*
- *sugar (1/2 cup if unsweetened raspberries are used—otherwise, sugar accordingly)*
- *3/4 cup water*
- 1 *envelope* (1 *tablespoon*) *gelatin*

(*Continued*)

Cream mixture:

1 cup milk
1/2 vanilla bean (or 1/2 teaspoon extract)
4 egg yolks
1/2 cup sugar
1/2 envelope gelatin (1/2 tablespoon)

2 cups heavy cream
2 heaping tablespoons sugar
a few drops of almond oil or a mild vegetable oil

The raspberry mixture should be prepared first so that the two may begin to set coincidentally.

Purée the raspberries through a nylon drum sieve. Bring the sugar and water to a boil, stir in the gelatin; first softened in a bit of cold water, and allow mixture to cool almost completely before stirring it into the raspberry purée. Put into the refrigerator while preparing the "cream." If the raspberry purée should show signs of beginning to set before the "cream" is prepared and cooled, remove it from the refrigerator.

Bring the milk and vanilla bean to a boil and leave to infuse for 10 minutes or so. Stir and beat the egg yolks and 1/2 cup sugar in another saucepan until creamy and light yellow in color, remove the vanilla bean from the milk, and slowly pour the milk into the egg mixture, stirring with a wooden spoon the while. Add the gelatin, first softened in a bit of cold water, and continue stirring constantly over a low-to-medium flame, regularly scraping the sides, corners, and bottom of the saucepan, until the mixture thickens enough to coat the spoon. Under no circumstances should the boiling point be approached. Immerse the saucepan halfway in cold water and continue stirring from time to time to ensure its cooling evenly. When completely cooled, the gelatin will begin to take action. Whip the heavy cream until firm but not stiff, beat in the 2 tablespoons sugar, and incorporate half the whipped cream into each of the two mixtures, stirring and folding thoroughly, but without violence. Oil very lightly the interiors of two decorative quart molds, and carefully, so as to avoid their mixing, pour in the cream and raspberry mixtures in alternating layers. Put to chill for at least 4 hours embedded in cracked ice, or for from 5 to 6 hours in the coldest part of the refrigerator—but not in the deep-freeze.

An Elaborate Formal Dinner Party

with appropriate wines

THE MENU (FOR 6)

CREAM OF ARTICHOKE SOUP WITH HAZELNUTS
[CREME D'ARTICHAUTS AUX NOISETTES]

A young, "flinty" dry white wine:
Loire Valley (Sancerre, Pouilly-Fumé)
or a champagne (blanc de blancs nature)

GRILLED FISH WITH SEA URCHIN PUREE
[POISSONS GRILLES A L'OURSINADE]

The same wine as above

VEAL SWEETBREADS AND MACARONI TIMBALE
[TIMBALE DE MACARONI AUX RIS DE VEAU]

A white Burgundy: Montrachet,
Corton-Charlemagne, Meursault

RUM SHERBET
[PUNCH A LA ROMAINE]

ROAST GUINEA FOWL WITH BACON

[PINTADE ROTIE AU LARD FUME]

A red Côte de Beaune
about 4 years old: Pommard,
Volnay Chassagne-Montrachet,
Pernand-Vergelesses

CHESTNUT PUREE WITH CELERY

[PUREE DE MARRONS AU CELERI]

TOSSED GREEN SALAD WITH FINES HERBES

[SALADE VERTE AUX FINES HERBES]

CHEESES

[FROMAGES]

A Corton or a Côte de Nuits
(Chambertin, Clos de la Roche,
Echezeaux, Bonnes-Mares),
older than the preceding

BLANC-MANGER

[BLANC-MANGER]

A fine old Sauternes

Although by nineteenth-century standards this menu may be relatively simple, it is rare today to encounter one as elaborate. There are none other of its kind in the book, and though I may for one's guests represent a marvelous experience, I feel uneasily almost as if I owed an apology to my readers, who may justly consider it an archaic curiosity but nearly impossible of execution, particularly in a servantless household. The presentation, singlehanded, of such a menu is perfectly possible, but the amount of work, the intricacy of the organization, and the final fatigue represent a heavy expenditure that may to many minds not justify the result, no matter how glorious. Each recipe may, in any case, find its place in a simpler context, and the rum sherbert, once a standard element in nearly every festive bourgeois menu, may serve equally well as a light, refreshing dessert.

The *blanc-manager*, the *oursinade* and the chestnut purée, but for reheating and buttering, may be prepared the preceding day. The bird may be larded for roasting beforehand and the timbale mold lined with macaroni, and, except for the final addition of cream to the mousseline, its various elements prepared in advance. The final organization of the meal, then, depends essentially on putting things to cook at the right time: the fish, depending on their size, should be put to grill just before or during the service of the soup, the timbale should be put to poach just before the soup service, and the roast put in the oven at the end of the fish service.

Cream of Artichoke Soup with Hazelnuts

Crème d'Artichauts aux Noisettes

For 1 *quart thin béchamel sauce:*
- 2 *tablespoons* (1 *ounce*) *butter*
- 1 *heaping tablespoon flour*
- 5 *cups milk*
- *salt*

4–5 *roasted hazelnuts*
8 *good-sized Artichoke Bottoms, precooked* (*page* 77)

Cream of Artichoke Soup with Hazelnuts

4 tablespoons (2 ounces) butter
1 cup milk
salt, freshly ground white pepper
3/4 cup cream
a handful of chervil leaves

THE BECHAMEL

Melt the butter in a saucepan and cook it with the flour over a low flame for about 1 minute, stirring regularly with a wooden spoon. This *roux* should not be allowed to color. Heat the milk and, away from the fire, add it, at first in small quantities at a time, to the *roux*, stirring all the while to ensure a smooth, non-lumpy mixture. Return it to the heat, salt to taste, and when the boil is reached, lower the flame so that a bare simmer is maintained. Leave it to cook stirring occasionally, for about an hour (20 minutes is usually given as a minimum cooking time to rid it of its floury taste). A longer cooking, which depends in part on reduction as a thickening element, produces a better result. (In Lyonnaise cooking, *béchamel* is the basic element in nearly all sauces, and professional kitchens keep great pots of it gently cooking in slow ovens, often for hours on end.) If it is not to be used immediately, melt a lump of butter on the surface to prevent a skin's forming. Ten minutes before removing it from the heat, add the hazelnuts, crushed; if it is made in advance, reheat it and cook the hazelnuts in it for 10 minutes.

Slice 6 of the artichoke bottoms, leave the other two whole, and stew them all in the butter, stirring occasionally, over a low flame, without allowing them to brown, for a good 1/2 hour (use either earthenware or stainless steel—any other metal will discolor artichokes). Put the 2 whole bottoms aside and stir the rest into the *béchamel*. Pass the mixture through a nylon drum sieve, using either a mushroom pestle or one with a flat bottom, like the old-fashioned American potato masher. Reheat the purée, bring it to a light, creamy consistency by the addition of boiling milk, taste for salt, grind in the white pepper and stir in the cream. Add the two artichoke bottoms, cut into small cubes, pour into a heated soup tureen and sprinkle the surface with chervil leaves.

THE GRILLED FISH WITH SEA URCHIN PUREE

An *oursinade* most often accompanies the Mediterranean red mullet. Sea bass or any fish with a firm, fairly moist, white flesh is a good substitute.

Sea urchins (*oursins*) are common in American waters but rarely eaten. I have never seen them in an American fish market. The "tongues" of coral, forming a star against the inside wall of the shell, are slightly sweet in flavor with a trace of iodine and a strong memory of the sea. In the south of France, sea urchins are ranked among the greatest of delicacies and are most often eaten raw, alone, or as part of a mixture on a seafood platter along with raw oysters, mussels, clams, "violets," etc. The puréed corals may also lend their fine color and unique savor to a fish mousseline forcemeat or a *béchamel* sauce to accompany poached fish. The corals are usually more fully developed in the winter and early spring months.

If small fish (about 3 ounces each) are used, they may by wrapped in grape leaves (if these are in season) just before being grilled (out of season, grape leaves preserved in brine, much used in Greek and near-Oriental preparations, may be substituted) and need not be scaled, for the charred leaves, when removed, will take scales and skin with them.

Grilled Fish with Sea Urchin Purée

Poissons Grillés à l'Oursinade

fish—count 2 or 3 small (3 ounces) or one 6- or 7-ounce fish per person. Two or 3 larger fish, depending on their size, will serve 6

Marinade:

1 *tablespoon lemon juice*

1 *scant teaspoon fennel seeds (in season, chopped fresh wild fennel leaves should be used and the cavities of the fish may be stuffed with a healthy bouquet of fennel branches)*

2 tablespoons pastis or Pernod
1/4 cup olive oil
salt and pepper

Oursinade:

15–20 *sea urchins* (*enough to make a good 1/2 cup of coral purée*)
1/2 cup olive oil

Clean the fish, tear out the gills, rinse fish, and sponge them dry with a towel. Large fish should have diagonal and parallel slits cut into the flesh at approximately 1 1/2-inch intervals on either side to permit a regular penetration of heat.

Mix the elements of the marinade and sprinkle the fish, inside and out, with the marinade. Leave them in a cool place for 1 or 2 hours, turning them from time to time.

THE OURSINADE

To open a sea urchin, hold it in one hand (in several thicknesses of cloth for protection against the spines), pierce the orifice with the pointed blade of a pair of scissors, cut outward through the shell about 3/4 of an inch, then cut all the way around in order to be able to lift out a circular "lid." Discard the lid and either rinse the interior out with sea water or give it a shake to rid it of the water and blackish, granular material inside. Remove the corals with the help of a teaspoon and pass them through a sieve. Mix the purée with the olive oil and store in a cool place until ready for use (if stored in the refrigerator, remove it an hour before using as the oil will have solidified through contact with extreme cold). The coral purée is too heavy to remain in emulsion in the oil and the mixture must be stirred well before each serving (it will, of course, remain in emulsion in an olive-oil mayonnaise, which makes a splendid sauce also for grilled fish).

Small fish should be arranged in rows on a heavy steel-wire double-faced grill. Large fish can be dealt with easily only in the special, fish-shaped double grill. If the small fish are wrapped in vine leaves, the heat should be intense, and they need not be basted. Otherwise, grilled fish should be basted often with the marinating liquid, plus additional olive oil, if necessary, using little at a time to avoid its dropping into the hot coals and bursting into flame. The cooking time and the intensity of the heat both depend on the size of the fish, the smallest requiring a very lively bed of coals and only a couple of minutes' exposure on each side. A large fish may take up to 15 minutes on each side, and the intensity of the heat should be proportionately less. The fish is done when the flesh is no longer resilient to the touch.

Lacking a bed of coals, the fish may be prepared in the oven, smaller fish being grilled directly beneath the broiler, larger ones being first baked, repeatedly basted, and browned at the last minute beneath the open flame.

Large fish should be filleted and served at table, the small fin bones being first removed, the fish slit lengthwise along the central line corresponding to the spinal column, and the fillets slipped loose. When the top fillets have been removed, the skeleton may easily be lifted, leaving the two other fillets clean. Serve the sauce separately.

TIMBALE OF SWEETBREADS AND MACARONI

The possible elements in this type of preparation are unlimited. A "dome" mold lined spirally with macaroni, held firmly by an inner lining of mousseline forcemeat and filled with one of any number of thickly bound stews or garnish mixtures, the presentation, both initial and once served out, is of great beauty—and no less impressive on the palate. It may be prepared with a fish mousseline forcemeat and filled with some kind of firm-fleshed fish stew (lobster, scallops, shrimp, etc.), in which case, a sauce *à l'américaine* would be a happy accompaniment, or a game forcemeat (made from the fillets and back legs of wild rabbit, for instance), filled with a *salmis* type of preparation and accompanied by a *salmis* or civet sauce. The blandness of chicken-breast forcemeat allows it to serve with any kind of filling save fish (a personal prejudice, for, classically, chicken and crayfish are not an unusual marriage). In a less elaborate menu, this sort of preparation may form a perfect main course. It belongs, conceptually, to the realm of professional cooking. The time necessary for its preparation in a home kitchen is great, but the result is well worth while.

The forcemeat may be stretched and rendered firmer, if desired, by pounding 3 or 4 ounces of *panade* with the flesh before adding the egg white. The preparation stands well alone, but may be accompanied by a tomatoed *demi-glace* (stock reduced to a syrupy consistency with tomato purée to taste, lightly buttered at the last minute). If fresh truffles are out of the question, canned truffles may be substituted, their preserving liquid being added to the sauce, and the dish may be enriched by the addition of a small package of dried black morels, available in fancy-food shops (first soaked in cold water for an hour or so, or until tender, stem ends trimmed, each cut in 2 lengthwise, and well rinsed under a strong jet of water to rid it of any adherence of sand or earth, then gently stewed in butter for 10 or 12 minutes).

An exquisite and less time-consuming preparation consists in braising the sweetbreads according to the instructions given, slicing them and arranging them in an earthenware *cocotte*, covering them generously with raw, sliced black truffles, masking the whole with the braising liquid and *mirepoix* passed into a purée, sealing the lid hermetically with a ribbon of flour paste, and heating the *cocotte* for 10 minutes in a very hot oven—just the time necessary to develop the perfume of the truffles. The flour-paste seal is broken at table and the emanations are spectacular.

Veal Sweetbreads and Macaroni Timbale

Timbale de Macaroni aux Ris de Veau

2 pounds veal sweetbreads
mirepoix made with 2 medium carrots, 1 medium onion, 2 tablespoons butter, crumbled bay leaf and thyme (see page 75 for method)
1/4 cup dry white wine
2 cups rich gelatinous Veal Stock (see page 72; a blanched calf's foot may be added to the veal to ensure the gelatinous content)
salt and pepper
3 or 4 large fresh black truffles
1/2-pound package of long macaroni
about 3 tablespoons (1 1/2 ounces) butter (to butter the mold)

(Continued)

Mousseline forcemeat:
breast of a large roasting chicken
1 *egg white*
salt, pepper, nutmeg
1¼ *cups heavy cream*

THE SWEETBREADS

Soak the sweetbreads in cold water for a good hour, put them into a large saucepan, well covered with cold water, bring to a boil, leave to simmer for a couple of minutes, drain, and plunge them into a basin of cold water. Peel them, carefully removing all fat and gristly or cartilaginous material and as much of the surface membrane as possible without disturbing the part that holds the many-sectioned sweetbread together. Place them, side by side, on a towel in such a way that they form a neat, evenly surfaced mass, place another towel over them and a board on top with approximately a 2-pound weight on the board (a medium-sized tin of preserves does well). Leave them under this weight until well cooled and firm (a couple of hours).

Spread the *mirepoix* over the bottom of a heavy *sauteuse* or earthenware casserole of just the right size to hold the sweetbreads placed side by side on this bed. Pour in the white wine and over a high flame (using an asbestos pad for protection if heat resistance of earthenware is in question), reduce it almost completely, gently shaking the receptacle from time to time to discourage anything's sticking to the bottom. Add the stock (enough to cover the sweetbreads generously), bring it to the boiling point, and lower the flame so that, covered, a near simmer is maintained. Count about 40 minutes' braising time from the time the simmer is reached. Remove the sweetbreads from the sauce, slice them in regular ½-inch slices, and pass the cooking liquid and *mirepoix* through a fine sieve. If the sauce remains plentiful and liquid, reduce it over a high flame for a few minutes, stirring constantly. Taste for seasoning, add pepper and salt if necessary. Pour it over the sweetbreads, leave to cool, and stir in the truffles, thickly sliced.

Cook the macaroni in a large pot of salted, boiling water and, when nearly cooked but still quite firm, remove from the heat and leave to swell for two or three minutes in the hot water. They should remain somewhat firm. Drain without rinsing and spread the strands of macaroni out, without touching one another, on a towel. Generously butter a 2-quart "dome" mold (dome molds are not easily found and may be replaced by any metal mixing bowl in the form of a half-sphere) and, beginning with a strand of macaroni which has been fashioned first into a compact, flatly spiraled circle or disk and pressed into the central point at the bottom of the mold, continue twining the strands of macaroni end to end in a close-fitting spiral until the entire mold is lined in this manner. Put the mold to chill in the refrigerator until the butter is set firmly enough to hold the macaroni in place. Cut the remaining macaroni into short lengths and stir it into the sweetbreads.

Prepare the Mousseline Forcemeat as described on page 78, incorporating the cream only at the last moment and being certain to work directly over cracked ice. Spread three-quarters of the mixture evenly over the entire surface of macaroni lining, fill the mold with the sweetbread, truffle, and macaroni mixture, pressing it gently into place so as to leave no air pockets, and spread the remainder of the forcemeat over the surface. Press a round of buttered kitchen paper over the surface and put the mold to poach in a *bain-marie* in a slow to moderate oven for 45 minutes (a round metal cookie cutter or other object of support should be placed in the bottom of the larger utensil on which the round-bottomed mold may rest. The mold should be immersed by about three-quarters in nearly boiling water). If oven space does not permit, the poaching may equally well be operated on top of the stove in a large, covered saucepan or other receptacle. The flame should be kept very low to prevent the water's returning to a boil.

Remove the mold from the *bain-marie* and allow it to settle for 7 or 8 minutes before unmolding it onto a round, preheated platter. The bit of liquid that drains onto the platter should be sponged up with a paper towel. The timbale should be cut into pielike wedges at table; a small spatula or pie knife is useful for serving.

Rum Sherbet

Punch à la Romaine

1/2 cup sugar
1 cup water
1 strip each, orange and lemon peel
strained juice of 1 orange and 1 lemon
1/2 cup dry white wine

Italian meringue:
1 egg white
about 1 tablespoon water
1/4 cup sugar

1/4 cup rum

Boil the sugar and water together, add the peels, juice, and white wine, leave to infuse until cool, remove the peels, and put to freeze, either in a mechanical freezer or an ice-cube tray—in the latter case, scrape frozen parts from the sides and bottom of the tray from time to time and stir them into the unfrozen mass.

When consistently frozen without being too firm, prepare the meringue: Beat the egg white until stiff. In a small saucepan, add just enough water to the sugar to dissolve it, bring to a boil, and cook until a drop of the syrup, let fall into a cup of cold water, forms a soft ball, malleable in one's fingers; then pour it evenly, in a tiny thread, into the egg white, beating all the while, until the syrup is completely absorbed. Turn out the frozen fruit-wine mixture into a chilled mixing bowl, stir and fold in the meringue, and return it to the freezer. Just before serving, stir in the rum. The sherbet should be only semisolid—"mushy" in consistency.

THE ROAST GUINEA FOWL WITH BACON

Although bacon is, in America, usually substituted for fresh or salt fat pork in French recipes, its aggressive smoky taste destroys or disguises most other flavors. But the slightly gamy flesh of guinea fowl, flatter and less subtle than that of the pheasant (which, out of season, it often replaces), is enhanced by the smoky caress of bacon.

Roast Guinea Fowl with Bacon

Pintade Rôtie au Lard Fumé

1 *large or* 2 *small guinea fowl (squabs have a finer flavor—an adult should, in any case, not be over* 6–8 *months old)*
salt, pepper
a large pinch of oregano
2 *tablespoons* (1 *ounce*) *butter*
enough thin strips of bacon to completely cover the breasts
1/3 *cup dry white wine*

In France the feet are generally left attached to roasting fowl (first dipped in boiling water or held over a flame, then skinned, the middle toe cut off at the first joint and the others removed). Those unaccustomed to this presentation do not always find it attractive. All roasting birds, if they have not already been badly mangled by the butcher, should be emptied by way of the throat (the intestines having already been drawn out with the aid of a hooked needlelike device), which prevents an important loss of natural juices. Pick and singe the bird, cut off the head at its base, slit the skin of the neck down the back, carefully loosen it, along with the trachea and the esophagus, from the neck, and sever the neck at its base. Gently pull the crop (the food sac attached to the esophagus) loose from the skin and flesh, being careful to tear neither, separate the flesh from the "wishbone" with the tip of a small, sharp knife, and force it loose with your fingers (a bird cannot be neatly carved at table unless the "wishbone" is removed). Reach as far as possible with the forefinger through the throat orifice, loosening heart, liver and gizzard from the cavity walls. It requires a bit of nudging, while gently pulling at the esophagus and trachea, and one must take care not to damage the gall bladder (a small blackish-green sac attached to the liver), for, if broken, its bitterness will ruin the bird.

Once loosened, everything slips out in a coherent mass. Guineafowl liver tends to be strong in flavor; it may be put aside to be added to a terrine or pâté if one likes.

Sprinkle salt, freshly ground pepper and a pinch of oregano into the cavity, force in a piece of butter, and fold the neck skin over the back of the bird like an envelope. Fold the wings backward so that they "pin" the flap of skin in place and, using a large kitchen needle strung with about 2 feet of kitchen string, transpierce the bird, the needle entering just below the bone of one drumstick about an inch from the thigh, and coming out at a corresponding point through the other leg, leaving a generous length of string dangling from the place of entry. Run the needle through the upper joint of the wing on the same side as the leg through which it came out, send it into the body of the bird through the skin flap at that side, out through the skin flap to the other side, and through the other wing. Tie the two ends of string together, tightly but without forcing, and clip off the string tips. With another length of string, transpierce the bird toward the lower ends of the drumsticks and above the bone, then back through the carcass just above the point at which the thigh joins the body, and tie the string ends as before. This operation, once done, becomes simple and automatic. The 2 lengths of string, strung through the bird in this manner, firmly fix its shape, and no deformation is possible during the roasting process.

Rub the bird with a few drops of oil, sprinkle it on all sides with salt, pepper and a bit of oregano, and press bacon strips, lengthwise, over the entire breast, tying around a couple of lengths of string to hold them in place. Roast the bird (or birds) in a fairly hot oven (375° F.), using a heavy, shallow pan (gratin dish, small skillet, etc.) as nearly as possible just the size to contain it, counting from 45 to 50 minutes for an adult bird and 1/2 hour for squabs. Remove the bacon strips for the last 8 to 10 minutes' cooking time to permit the breast to brown lightly. Clip the strings and pull them out, transfer the bird to a heated platter, skim a few tablespoons of excess fat from the roasting pan, add the white wine and scrape and stir over a high flame until all adherent material is dissolved and the wine reduced by about half. Send this juice to table in a heated sauceboat and serve the chestnut purée at the same time.

Chestnut Purée with Celery

Purée de Marrons au Céleri

2 pounds chestnuts
1 quart milk
salt
1 teaspoon sugar
1 celery branch
pepper
1 fresh, crisp celery heart, cut into small dice
about 6 ounces butter

Slice through the hull of the rounded surface of each chestnut, using a small, sharp knife; the hull is tough and resistant and care should be taken not to cut oneself. Plunge them into a pot of boiling water, and after a few minutes remove them, a few at a time, with a skimming spoon, and remove the hull from each as well as the inner, brownish skin. Holding them in a towel protects one's fingers from the heat and rubbing with it helps remove the inner skin. Any which are particularly resistant may be returned for a couple of minutes to the hot water.

Bring the milk to a boil, add the chestnuts, salt, sugar and celery branch, and cook gently, covered, until they crush easily when pressed with the back of a spoon (they may have to cook as long as 1½ hours).

Drain, saving the milk and discarding the celery branch. Pass the chestnuts through a vegetable mill (*moulinette*), using the finest blade and adding a bit of milk from time to time to facilitate their passage. Taste for salt, season with freshly ground pepper, and just before serving, rapidly reheat the purée in a heavy saucepan over a fairly high flame, stirring constantly with a wooden spoon and, away from the flame, stir in the crisp celery dice and the butter, cut into small pieces. Don't add all the butter at one time—just enough should be absorbed to permit the purée to be thickly poured. It should not be stiff, and a great quantity of butter is necessary to counteract its naturally dry texture and lend it a rich, velvety quality.

THE BLANC-MANGER

A *blanc-manger* is a Bavarian cream made of almond milk (when it is not cornstarch pudding). Formed in an elegant old-fashioned jelly mold, trembling, opaque, creamy-white, its delicate purity should never be marred—visually or tastewise—by a sauce or any other garnish. Accompanied by a great Sauternes, both attain sublime heights.

The preparation of the almond milk is hard work and I have often thought (but have never tried it) that the dreary task of pounding almonds with water might be painlessly achieved in a good blender.

Blanc-manger

Blanc-manger

1/2 pound shelled almonds
3 bitter almonds
3/4 cup water
1 1/4 cup light cream
1 1/2 tablespoons gelatin
2/3 cups sugar
1/2 cup heavy cream
almond oil

Plunge all the almonds into boiling water for about 30 seconds, drain them and rub them in a towel to loosen the skins. Pick them over to be certain all skins are removed and put them to soak in cold water for 1/2 hour to whiten them. Drain them and pound in a stone mortar, adding a spoonful of water each time the paste becomes too resistant to work easily. When half the quantity of prescribed water has been used, put the rest aside and continue pounding and turning, adding the light cream in small quantities at a time, until it has an been added. This should be done slowly and thoroughly to produce the finest possible purée.

Line a sieve, placed over a mixing bowl, with a strong linen towel, first dipped in cold water and well wrung out. Pour in the almond mixture, gather together the edges of the towel in one hand and begin twisting. Relax your hold from time to time to mix up the almond paste and then twist again, as tightly as possible, continuing until all the almond milk possible has been wrung from the paste.

Soften the gelatin in a bit of cold water, then add the remaining water, first heated, bring to a boil and add the sugar. Leave until almost completely cooled, stir it into the almond milk, and place the mixing bowl in a larger container of cracked ice. Stir steadily with a wooden spoon until it begins to "take," whip the heavy cream until fairly firm, but not stiff, fold it into the almond mixture, and pour into a mold that has been lightly oiled with almond oil (lacking that, use a tasteless vegetable oil). The jelly mold may be replaced by any other decorative quart mold, preferably with a central tube. Embed the mold in cracked ice, place a plate over the top and keep in the refrigerator for at least 4 or 5 hours. Unmold only just before serving, first dipping the mold for a couple of seconds into hot water and wiping it dry.

Two Informal Winter Dinners

with appropriate wines

MENU I (FOR 6)

GRATIN OF STUFFED CREPES
[GRATIN DE CREPES FOURREES]

*A light, young, very dry white wine:
Muscadet, Quincy, etc.*

STUFFED CALVES' EARS, BEARNAISE SAUCE
[OREILLES DE VEAU FARCIES, SAUCE BEARNAISE]

*A young, fruity red wine: Beaujolais
de cru from the most recent vintage,
Touraine (Chinon or Bourgueuil),
2 or 3 years old, or Pomerol
from a slight and recent year*

TOSSED GREEN SALAD

[SALADE VERTE]

CHEESES

[FROMAGES]

The same as the preceding—or,
following the Beaujolais,
a light Burgundy (Mercurey, Beaune, etc.);
following the others,
an older version of the same
or a Saint-Emilion

MOLDED TAPIOCA PUDDING, APRICOT SAUCE

[PUDDING MOULE AU TAPIOCA, SAUCE AUX ABRICOTS]

THE STUFFED CREPES

Glamorized *cannelloni*, stuffed crêpes may contain practically anything and they represent one of the prettiest and most satisfactory means of disposing of leftovers (odds and ends of meats, vegetables, mushrooms, etc., bound with a bit of stiff sauce—tomato, *demi-glace, béchamel, velouté, duxelles*). Various soufflé mixtures (either dessert or entrée) are commonly used also.

The sorrel in this recipe may be replaced by spinach (often allied with brains, particularly in Italian cooking), first parboiled, well drained, finely chopped, and stewed in butter long enough to evaporate excess moisture.

Gratin of Stuffed Crêpes

Gratin de Crêpes Fourrées

6 large (7-inch) or 12 small (5-inch) Crêpes (see page 83—but replace the milk by room-temperature beer, eliminate the sugar and add a tablespoon of finely chopped fines herbes)
1 calf's brain
about 1/4 pound butter, in all
about 10 ounces sorrel
1 egg
salt, pepper, nutmeg
freshly grated Parmesan cheese
1 medium-size can (2 cups) whole tomatoes, stewed in butter (in season, fresh tomatoes, peeled and seeded before stewing)
parsley

Make Crêpes as per directions.

Soak the brain in cold water for an hour or so, carefully remove the membrane, and soak it again in fresh cold water to "bleach" it. Stew it gently in a small frying pan or saucepan, with 2 tablespoons butter, for about 20 minutes, shaking the pan from time to time to prevent its sticking, and turning it after 10 minutes. Purée it through a fine sieve.

Wash the sorrel in several waters, tear off the stems, pulling them backward to remove any fibrous material in the leaves, gather them into a tight mass on the chopping board, and shred them finely. Stew them, salted, in 4 tablespoons butter, stirring now and then, until they have melted into a purée (15 or 20 minutes).

Combine the brain, sorrel, and egg, whisking or beating with a wooden spoon, taste for salt, add freshly ground pepper to taste, and a tiny bit of freshly grated nutmeg (the whole brain, sorrel, and egg may be combined in a blender). Stuff the crêpes, folding the sides up and over the stuffing and leaving the ends open. The form will be that of a small omelet. Place them side by side in a buttered shallow baking or "gratin" dish, folded side down, sprinkle with grated cheese, regularly distribute the remainder of the butter in fine slivers over the entire surface, and bake in a medium-hot oven (375° F.) for about 15 minutes, or until the cheese has formed a light gratin and the stuffing has become resilient to the touch. Place halved tomatoes over crêpes and sprinkle with parsley before serving.

THE STUFFED CALVES' EARS

Lucien Tendret's little book, *La Table au Pays de Brillat-Savarin* (the most recent edition, long since out of print, dates from 1934), although mainly anecdotal, contains a handful of more or less perfunctorily presented recipes, each of which, once *mise au point*, is a small masterpiece, All are stamped by those special refinements typical of the passionate amateur which, when understood and respected by a professional, produce that rarity, a chef of genius. Alexandre Dumaine, now retired, drew a number of his specialties from this work. The *poularde au vapeur*, necessarily modified—the original recipe requires that the bird be stuffed with whole truffles—figured, *sur commande*, on Dumaine's daily menu. Certain others, the elaboration of which, on a restaurant menu, could only spell bankruptcy, he delighted in preparing for special occasions.

The recipe below, altered in some few details after a number of experiments, remains nonetheless loyal in spirit to Tendret. The result is divine.

Preliminary cooking preparations should be got out of the way the preceding day so that the chilled, stuffed ears may receive their breading a number of hours before the meal. The fragile surface, through drying slightly, is more easily handled and less liable to be damaged during the frying. Last-minute work consists only in the actual frying, and finishing the sauce.

Stuffed Calves' Ears, Béarnaise Sauce

Oreilles de Veau Farcies, Sauce Béarnaise

6 *calves' ears, cut off well into the head*
1 *lemon*
2 *cups dry white wine*
3 *cups rich, gelatinous Veal Stock* (*page 72—if prepared especially, add the trimmings of the ears and chicken breasts, plus a handful of chicken necks*)
1 *veal sweetbread*
2 *heaping tablespoons Mirepoix* (*page 74—if prepared especially, count* 1 *medium onion and* 1 *medium carrot*)
breast and liver of a large roasting chicken
4 *tablespoons* (2 *ounces*) *butter*
3 *large fresh black truffles* (*approximately* 6 *ounces in all*)
1 *heaping tablespoon flour*
2 *egg yolks*
1 *tablespoon cream*
1 *loaf of firm-textured, half-dried-out* (*but not hard*) *white bread*
5 *egg whites* (*the* 3 *extra yolks may be submerged in water to protect them from the air and used later for the béarnaise*)
salt, pepper
1/2 *pound* (8 *ounces*) *clarified butter* (*gently melted over a low heat, allowed to settle, the clear butter poured off for use, leaving the whitish residue behind*)
1 *cup olive oil*

THE EARS

Neatly trim the base of the ears, taking care neither to cut too closely to the joining section at the base nor to cut into the "well" at the ears' point of entry into the head. Cover them generously, in a large saucepan, with cold water, bring to a boil, and leave to simmer for 10 minutes. Plunge them into cold water, drain them, and carefully clean them, rubbing gently with a cloth, scraping here and there to remove any remaining hairs, and cleaning out the canal-like areas in the "well" of the ear with a small stiff brush. Rinse well, sponge them dry, and rub them inside and out with the cut halves of a lemon.

Cut pieces of cloth (an old bedsheet will do) into approximately 8-inch squares, wrap an ear in each, neatly and firmly, taking care to gently force it into its natural position (it will have been warped out of shape during the initial parboiling), and sew the package tightly. Choose a large saucepan or deep *sauteuse* of just the right size to hold the ears placed side by side and touching, but without being packed in. Pour over them the white wine and enough stock to completely cover them, bring to a boil and cook, covered, at a bare simmer for 3½ hours, adding a bit of boiling stock when necessary, to keep the ears submerged. Leave them until almost cool in their cooking liquid, remove them from their cloth envelopes and put them aside.

THE SWEETBREAD

Prepare and braise the sweetbread exactly as described in the Veal Sweetbreads in Macaroni Timbale recipe on page 214, using the ears' cooking liquid, somewhat reduced, as braising liquid. Remove the sweetbread, pass the *mirepoix* and braising liquid through a fine sieve, supplement it with enough of the ears' cooking liquid to make a good cupful, and put it aside.

THE CHICKEN BREAST AND LIVER

Remove the skin and bones from the breast, season it, and cook it in the butter without browning, only until just firm—2 or 3 minutes on each side. A minute before removing from the heat, add the liver.

THE STUFFING

Peel the truffles, chop the peelings very finely, remove breast and liver from pan, leaving the butter, and cut the truffles, chicken breast, liver and sweetbread into approximately ⅓-inch cubes. Reheat the butter in the chicken's cooking pan, add the cubed meats and truffles and the chopped peelings, sprinkle with flour, and, after stirring everything around to permit the flour to cook slightly, stir in the cupful of braising liquid. As soon as the mixture is thoroughly thickened, remove it from the fire and stir in the two egg yolks, first mixed with a spoonful of cream.

When cooled, pack the stuffing into the ears, gently so as not to damage them, but firmly enough to leave no possible air pockets, particularly in the ducts at the base, smooth the surface, mounding it slightly, to the edges and point of each ear, and put them to chill for several hours—or overnight—so that ears and stuffing will be firm enough to be easily workable.

THE BREADING

In order to grate fresh bread crumbs (which, for all breaded, fried objects, gives a finer result than dried crumbs) the bread must be firmly textured and, without being dried out, sufficiently stale to crumble. Remove the crusts, grate the bread, and, if the result is not uniformly fine, pass the crumbs through a coarse sieve. You will need a generous pile.

Sprinkle the naked surface of the ears—but not the surface of the stuffing—with flour. Beat 3 of the egg whites with a pinch of salt until stiff, carefully pass each ear in the beaten whites, making certain that it is evenly coated, and roll it ever so delicately in the crumbs, first placing it on the bed of crumbs and sprinkling the top surface with crumbs. Finally, sprinkle again any parts to which no crumbs have adhered, lightly patting the surface, but never with pressure. Leave them to dry for 2 or 3 hours in the open air (not in the refrigerator), then beat the remaining egg whites, repeat the breading procedure, and leave the ears on a light bed of crumbs to dry for 7 or 8 hours.

Use either 1 pan large enough to hold the breaded ears comfortably without touching or 2 medium-sized pans (in which case the quantity of butter and oil may have to be augmented—the fat should be deep enough for the ears to bathe over halfway, permitting them to become evenly colored on all sides with a single turning). Heat the clarified butter and the oil together until fairly hot but not smoking, and gently put the ears, stuffed surface down, in the fat. Survey them carefully, turning the fire up and down between medium and low, if necessary, to achieve an even, crisp, golden surface without burning.

Turn them over carefully with the prong tips of a fork, taking care not to pierce the crust. Drain them on paper towels, enclose them in a folded napkin on a warmed platter, and serve immediately, accompanied separately by the béarnaise sauce.

THE BEARNAISE SAUCE

Fresh tarragon gives the distinctive quality to a béarnaise. When it is not available, the usual replacement is tarragon leaves "pickled" in vinegar. A superior preserve consists in packing alternate layers of fresh tarragon leaves and salt into jars which, after sealing, are then sterilized. The sauce, mainly an emulsion of butter in slightly cooked egg yolks, is served tepid. Any attempt to heat it beyond this point will result in its separating. It may be prepared somewhat ahead of time and kept in a *bain-marie* of warm, but not hot, water. It is most often served with grilled meats, but can be useful with poached or grilled fish or grilled poultry.

Béarnaise Sauce

Sauce Béarnaise

1/2 cup dry white wine
1/4 cup wine vinegar (preferably tarragon-flavored white-wine vinegar)
2 finely chopped gray shallots (or 1 medium-small onion)
salt, freshly ground pepper, a tiny pinch of Cayenne
a small handful (about 1/2 ounce) tarragon and chervil branches and leaves
3 egg yolks
1/2 pound fresh sweet butter, cut into small pieces and allowed to soften at kitchen temperature
1 teaspoon each of finely chopped tarragon and chervil leaves

Combine white wine, vinegar, shallots, salt, pepper, Cayenne, and the handful of branches and leaves, coarsely chopped and crushed, in a small, heavy saucepan or, better, in a small earthenware casserole protected from the direct heat by an asbestos pad. Boil until only 3 or 4 tablespoons of liquid remain, pass through a fine sieve, pressing the debris, and return the liquid to the saucepan. Add the egg yolks and, over a tiny flame, using a small whisk, stir in a rapid, circular motion. After a few seconds, add about one-third of the butter, continuing to whisk, and, as the butter is absorbed, add another third, and finally the last third, continuing to whisk until the butter is totally absorbed and the sauce begins to thicken. Remove the saucepan from the heat but continue to stir the sauce, which, because of the heat retained in the saucepan, will continue thickening. Taste for seasoning and stir in the chopped herbs.

THE MOLDED TAPIOCA PUDDING

Similar puddings may be made with rice, semolina, vermicelli, noodles, etc. Rather than serve an accompanying sauce, the mold may be lined with caramelized sugar. Served hot or warm, Sabayon Sauce (see Charlotte with Crêpes, page 137) is also a fine accompaniment, and served cold, a fresh raspberry purée is another possibility.

Molded Tapioca Pudding, Apricot Sauce

Pudding Moulé au Tapioca, Sauce aux Abricots

2 *cups milk*
1/4 *cup sugar*
1 *small pinch salt*
1/2 *vanilla bean (or* 1/2 *teaspoon extract)*
6 *tablespoons (*3 *ounces) butter*
4 *ounces tapioca (approximately* 1/2 *cup)*
3 *eggs, separated*

Apricot sauce:
puréed stewed apricots, flavored with a small glass of Madeira or port wine, and sweetened to taste. If the pudding is served hot or warm, the sauce should be heated and 2 *tablespoons of butter may be stirred in when it is removed from the heat*

Molded Tapioca Pudding, Apricot Sauce

Combine milk, sugar, salt, vanilla, and 3 tablespoons butter in a saucepan, bring to a boil, and slowly pour in the tapioca, stirring the while. Stir over direct heat for a minute and put the saucepan, covered, into a slow oven for about 20 minutes. Turn it out into a mixing bowl, remove the vanilla bean, stir in the rest of the butter and the yolks of the eggs, gently fold in the stiffly beaten whites, and pour into a generously buttered mold (quart size), the inside of which has been lightly sprinkled with dry tapioca. Poach in a *bain-marie* in hot, but not boiling, water in a slow-to-medium oven for about 1/2 hour, or until the center of the pudding is elastic to the touch. Remove from the hot water and allow it to settle for about 10 minutes before unmolding. If it is to be served chilled, leave the mold over it to protect the surface from the air until just before serving. Coat it with a bit of sauce and send the rest of the sauce to table in a separate dish.

Two Informal Winter Dinners

with appropriate wines

MENU II (FOR 6)

TERRINE OF SOLE FILLETS
[TERRINE DE FILETS DE SOLE]

A white Burgundy (Chablis, Pouilly-Fuissé, Mercurey blanc, Pinot Blanc)

BEEF STEW A LA BOURGUIGNONNE
[SAUTE DE BOEUF A LA BOURGUIGNONNE]

The same red wine as that used in making the stew: Beaujolais, Mercurey, Mâcon, etc.

STEAMED POTATOES

[POMMES DE TERRE A LA VAPEUR]

BELGIAN ENDIVE SALAD

[SALADE D'ENDIVES]

CHEESES

[FROMAGES]

The same as the preceding, or
an older red wine from the Côte d'Or

FLOATING ISLAND

[OEUFS A LA NEIGE]

THE TERRINE OF SOLE FILLETS

Possible variations are innumerable: the central roll of fillets may enclose bars of truffles rather than the sorrel stuffing; the forcemeat may be replaced by a classic mousseline forcemeat, and pike, salmon, trout, etc., may replace those fish suggested in the recipe that follows; it may be enriched by the addition of cubes of poached lobster or shrimp, chopped truffles peelings, dried morels (soaked, well rinsed, chopped and stewed in butter).

In this particular terrine, the acidity of the sorrel lends a delicious contrast to the fish, and the pretty geometry of the cross-sectional slices, forming a central disk of pale green bound in a ribbon of pure white against the mottled square, would have moved Alberti to admiration.

Terrine of Sole Fillets

Terrine de Filets de Sole

Fish fumet:

sole carcasses, cleaned and rinsed, the gills discarded, 1 coarsely chopped onion, thyme, bay leaf, parsley, salt, 1/2 cup white wine, 1/2 cup water

large handful of fresh white bread crumbs

1/2 pound fresh (not frozen) fish fillets (whiting, lemon sole, flounder)

1 egg, separated

salt, pepper, nutmeg, Cayenne

1 small handful raw, shelled pistachio nuts

3 heaping tablespoons Duxelles (page 76—if made especially, count 1/4 pound mushrooms and 1 medium onion)

1/2 pound sorrel

4 tablespoons (2 ounces) butter

2 soles of approximately 1 pound each, filleted, the carcasses saved (lacking Dover sole, use grey or lemon sole)

THE FUMET

For the *fumet*, cut or break the carcasses into small pieces, combine all the elements in a saucepan, bring to a boil, and simmer, covered, for 1/2 hour. Strain the liquid and rapidly reduce it over a high flame to about 1/3 cup.

Pour the *fumet* over the bread crumbs, mashing with a fork to ensure its being thoroughly imbibed.

Pound the 1/2 pound of fillets to a purée in a mortar, work in the white of the egg, small quantities at a time, with the pestle or a wooden spoon, and, when it is completely absorbed, pound in half the soaked bread crumbs, first squeezed if they are too liquid. Season to taste with salt, freshly ground pepper, a tiny bit of nutmeg, and a pinch of Cayenne, remembering that cold preparations support a sharper seasoning than hot dishes. Pass through a fine drum sieve, a tablespoonful at a time, using the plastic disk.

Drop the pistachio nuts into boiling water for a minute or so, drain them, rub them in a towel to remove the skins, chop them coarsely, and stir them and the *duxelles* into the fish purée.

Pick over the sorrel, tearing off the stems backward, wash it in several waters, drain well, shred it finely, and stew it gently, lightly salted, in the butter until reduced to a near purée. Mix it thoroughly with the yolk of the egg and the remaining bread crumbs, squeezed dry, if necessary, and pass through a fine sieve. Taste for salt, stir in a bit of freshly ground pepper, and put to chill to make it more easily manageable.

Soak the sole fillets in cold water for 15 minutes, spread them on paper towels and pat them dry.

Use an earthenware, porcelain, or enameled ironware terrine, long and rectangular in form. Cut a piece of aluminum foil, in width the same as the length of the terrine, and long enough to line the bottom and the two sides and to fold over the top of the filled terrine; this is to facilitate unmolding it, the fragility of fish terrines rendering them difficult to serve directly. Butter the terrine, butter one side of the foil and press it into place, unbuttered side placed against the buttered walls of the terrine. Make an even bed in the bottom of about 1/3 of the fish forcemeat and arrange the sole fillets on top, slightly overlapping, placed crosswise in a row the entire length of the terrine, the bottom and two long sides, thus, lined with the fillet tips hanging over the edges. Spoon in the sorrel stuffing, even it out, and, beginning with the last fillet to have been placed, pull the ends of the fillets, one after the other, inward, one folded over the other so as to form a "tube" of stuffed fillets through the central length of the terrine. Add the rest of the forcemeat, forcing it gently down each side of the roll of fillets, and covering them. Tap the terrine a couple of times against a wooden surface to settle the contents, fold the buttered foil over the top and press it down. Cook in a 300°–325° F. oven in a *bain-marie*, the terrine immersed two-thirds of the way up in hot, but not boiling, water, for about 45 minutes.

Leave the terrine to cool under approximately 1 pound of pressure (a board the dimensions of the terrine's surface with a weight on top), then put to chill for a day. To unmold, loosen the pâté from the ends of the terrine with the blade of a knife, lift the body of it loose by pulling up on the foil flaps that have been folded over the top, then fold them over the outside walls of the terrine, turn the pâté out onto an oval or rectangular platter, and peel off the foil. Surround it with a *chiffonade* of lettuce or other simple décor, keeping it chilled until the moment of serving.

THE BEEF STEW A LA BOURGUIGNONNE

Probably the most widely known of all French preparations, Beef Burgundy certainly deserves its reputation—or would if the few details essential to its success were more often respected. The meat must be a gelatinous cut—oxtail (which is never larded), shank, heel or chuck are all good. The cooking must be slow and even—stringy, dry, cooked-apart meat and an emulsion of indigestible grease in the sauce are the inevitable results of a too-rapid cooking. The sauce must be strained, well skimmed of fat, slowly reduced and purified by skimming. Properly done, the meat will be firm, moist and tender, and the sauce, a deep, warm brown, will have sufficient body to coat all the solid ingredients. There is nothing difficult about its preparation, but there are no shortcuts.

If good lean salt pork is not available, omit it; do not substitute bacon, the smoky flavor of which, even when first parboiled, distorts and "muddies" the otherwise dean, distinct flavor of the sauce.

As a preparation "type," *bourguignon* is identical to *Coq au Vin* (page 308), *sauté de veau au vin rouge* (veal in red wine), *matelote d'anguille* (eel in red wine), *mou de veau en civet* (calves' lungs in red wine), the only difference residing in the various lengths of cooking time and the consequent difference in reducing time for the sauce. Poached Eggs *en meurette* or *à la Bourguignonne* (page 260) and Brains *en Matelote* (page 334), because of the fragility of the central element, are treated somewhat differently, but the sauce remains identical in concept. *Civet de lièvre* (jugged hare), but for the final thickening with the animal's blood, is the same preparation, and rabbit, either domestic or wild, wild boar and venison, although termed civets, are often prepared exactly like a *bourguignon.* Evidently, once the principles of one of these preparations is understood, the others not only become automatic knowledge, but a world of new and less traditional possibilities is opened out. Pork, goose, squirrel, and squid are good when subjected to this treatment (game birds, because of the dryness of their flesh, do not lend themselves to it). Muskrat (discreetly labeled "marsh rabbit") is commonplace in Baltimore markets and, despite the merchants' claim that the only possible preparation is first to boil it "to get rid of its taste," and then to "fry it like chicken," it is delicious when treated *à la bourguignonne.* A *bourguignon* does not suffer from being prepared in advance and gently reheated.

Beef Stew à la Bourguignonne

Sauté de Boeuf à la Bourguignonne

1 *single 3-pound cross section (bone removed) of heel*
3 *ounces fat fresh or salt pork*
2 *tablespoons finely chopped parsley*
1 *teaspoon thyme (or mixed herbs)*

(Continued)

2 tablespoons olive oil
1 bottle good red Burgundy wine
1/2 pound (2 slices) lean salt side pork
3–4 medium carrots (10–12 ounces)
3 large onions (something less than 1 pound)
3 tablespoons olive or vegetable oil
3 level tablespoons flour
1/4 cup cognac
1 bay leaf and a bouquet of parsley
2 cloves garlic, crushed and peeled
about 1 cup veal stock, pot-au-feu bouillon, or, lacking either, water
1/2 pound small, firm, unopened mushrooms
salt and pepper
6 tablespoons (3 ounces) butter
30 small white onions (between a hazelnut and a walnut in size)

Cut the section of heel (the part of the hind leg beneath the round) in 2, crosswise, and divide each piece into 6 pieces, respecting the muscular structure, each piece remaining intact within its membrane (the heel is so constructed that this may easily be done). Cut the fat pork into small strips about 1 inch long and 1/4 inch square, roll them in the chopped parsley mixed with a pinch of the thyme (or mixed herbs), pierce each piece of meat once or twice, with the grain, and force a strip of fat pork into the slit, making certain that it is well embedded in the piece of meat. Put the meat to marinate for about 3 hours with 2 tablespoons olive oil, the rest of the thyme, and the bottle of wine, turning the pieces around in their marinade 2 or 3 times during this period.

Cut the 2 slices of lean salt pork crosswise into sections slightly over 1/2 inch wide, cover them with cold water, bring to a boil, simmer for 2 or 3 minutes and drain. Peel the carrots and cut them crosswise into 1- or 2-inch lengths. Peel the large onions and cut each into 4 or 6 pieces.

A large *sauteuse* may be used for the entire cooking process, but it is usually more practical to carry out the preliminary steps in a smaller *sauteuse* or skillet, transferring everything to an earthenware or heavy copper or enameled ironware *cocotte*—the latter, impossible for the browning process, serves well during the braising stage. Beginning the braising process in a different vessel with an absolutely clean surface reduces the risk of anything's sticking to the bottom, and the fact of its being smaller but deeper than the *sauteuse* permits one to arrange the meat in such a way that it may be well covered with a minimum of liquid.

Cook the sections of side pork in the 3 tablespoons olive or vegetable oil over a medium heat, turning each (if they are tossed, some are always overbrowned on some sides and untouched on others) until they are golden and the surfaces lightly crisp. Put them aside and, over a lower flame, cook the cut-up carrots and onions in the same oil, stirring regularly, for from 20 to 30 minutes. The onions should be lightly browned—they burn easily and should be constantly surveyed. Remove the vegetables from the pan with a perforated skimming spoon, draining them as nearly as possible of all the fat, and making certain to leave no fragment of onion behind—it would inevitably burn and leave a bitter taste in the sauce.

While the vegetables are cooking, remove the meat from its marinade, drain it well in a colander or large sieve, collecting the liquid, and sponge the pieces of meat with a paper towel until dry. Turn the flame up and, still in the same oil, brown the meat on all sides, adding a bit more oil, if necessary, and salting only after the pieces have been turned once. (If they are not placed closely enough together, the fat will burn, but if they are packed in, their juices will be drawn out rather than being sealed in and they will boil rather than sear. Use an extra skillet, if necessary, or sear them in relays.) Turn the flame down, drain off any excess oil, sprinkle the flour over, and turn the meat 2 or 3 times over a period of 5 or 6 minutes until the flour is lightly browned (the eventual color and flavor of the sauce depends, in large part, on the onions, meat and flour being browned to just the right point). Return the onions and carrots to the pan, stir everything together, and pour in the cognac and the reserved marinade. Stir and scrape the bottom of the pan with a wooden spoon to loosen and dissolve all frying adherents, transfer the pieces of meat to the *cocotte* or casserole, pour the liquid and vegetables over, add the parsley and the bay leaf, tied together, the garlic, and enough boiling stock (or water) to cover. Bring the liquid back to a boil and cook, covered, the surface hardly bubbling, preferably in an oven, for from 2½ to 3 hours, or until the meat is tender but still firm. Skim the surface fat

2 or 3 times during this period and gently displace the pieces of meat in their sauce to ensure that nothing sticks to the bottom.

Rinse the mushrooms rapidly, drain them, dry them in paper towels and toss them, salted and peppered, in half the butter, over a high flame, for a couple of minutes, or until they are lightly colored and their superficial moisture has evaporated. Peel the small onions and cook them whole, seasoned, in the remaining butter, in a pan just the right size to hold them, over low heat, tossing them or turning them from time to time, until yellowed and tender, but not browned.

Remove the pieces of meat and carrot from the sauce (with a spoon, not a fork), discard the parsley and bay leaf, and pass everything else through a fine sieve. Return the meat and carrots to their cooking utensil, add the pieces of browned side pork, the glazed little onions, and the sautéed mushrooms and keep covered while finishing the sauce.

Bring the sauce to a boil and, keeping the saucepan to the side of the flame, simmer and skim regularly for 1/2 hour (see Skimming, page 90). If at this point the sauce seems too thin, reduce it for a couple of minutes over a high flame, stirring constantly. Pour it over the meat and its garnish, slowly reheat, and simmer gently for about 20 minutes. Serve in its cooking vessel, accompanied by freshly steamed potatoes in a separate dish.

FLOATING ISLAND (OEUFS A LA NEIGE)

The name of this dessert creates a great deal of confusion. Its literal translation is "Snow Eggs" but in English it is most often called Floating Island. However, other custard sauces (*crème anglaise*) and meringue desserts also claim a right to that title and, in French, *île flottante* is totally different—an island of alternate layers of alcohol-soaked dessert biscuits and jam, around which a custard or fruit sauce is poured.

One may, for variation, dissolve caramelized sugar into the sauce.

Readers who do not care for baked (or, in the case of certain American pies, half-baked) meringues may be pleasantly surprised at the firm, moist, consistent texture of this poached version.

Floating Island

Oeufs à la Neige

The sauce:

1 *quart milk*
1 *cup sugar*
1 *vanilla bean* (*or* 1 *teaspoon vanilla extract*)
10 *egg yolks*

The meringue:

4 *egg whites*
1 *small pinch salt*
1 1/2 *cups sifted confectioners' sugar*

Bring the milk, sugar and vanilla to a boil in a large *sauteuse* or other low, wide pan, remove it from the flame and leave the vanilla bean to infuse while preparing the meringue.

Add a pinch of salt to the egg whites, beat them until they stand stiffly in peaks, and sift the confectioners' sugar over, folding it in delicately but thoroughly.

Remove the vanilla bean from the milk, bring milk again to a boil, and regulate the heat so that a bare simmer is maintained. Gently drop heaping teaspoonfuls of the raw meringue into the simmering milk, poaching no more than 5 or 6 at a time, for the meringues swell and should not be crowded. After a couple of minutes, cautiously turn them over and leave to poach a couple of minutes longer. Lift them out with a tablespoon or perforated skimming spoon and slip them onto a nylon drum sieve placed over a mixing bowl. Remove them, once drained, to a large, deep serving platter to make room for the following batches.

When all the "eggs" have been poached and drained, pass the poaching milk through the drum sieve to join that which has been drained from the meringues. Beat the egg yolks and slowly pour in the milk, whisking at the same time. Pour the mixture into a heavy saucepan and, over a low to medium flame, stir constantly with a wooden spoon, scraping the sides of the saucepan repeatedly, until the "cream" is sufficiently thick to coat the spoon. It must not approach the boiling point. Remove the saucepan from the heat immediately, pass the sauce through the drum sieve into another container and pour it carefully into the serving platter, around, but not over, the meringues. Serve well chilled.

Three Simple Winter Menus

MENU I (FOR 6 TO 8)

A simple and solid red wine with the entire meal—body is more important than nuance. Traditionally, Cahors or Minervois accompanies a cassoulet. Bandol or a Côtes-du-Rhône (Cornas, Châteauneuf-du-Pape, Gigonadas) are good possibilities. One of the Italian Piedmont wines would also serve well.

CELERIAC IN MUSTARD SAUCE
[CELERI-RAVE A LA SAUCE MOUTARDE]

CASSOULET
[CASSOULET]

WATERCRESS SALAD
[SALADE CRESSIONIERE]

FRUIT
[FRUITS]

A *cassoulet* is a meal. It would be an error to precede it with anything but the simplest of *crudités*, or to serve, at the end, more than a fruit or the lightest of fruit-derivative desserts. The celeriac and the watercress not only frame the *cassoulet* aesthetically, but their rough age is a distinct aid to digestion.

THE CELERIAC IN MUSTARD SAUCE

Celeriac, also known as "celery root," is coming, in recent years, to be better known in the United States. It is one of the most commonly used vegetables in France—most often served raw in a salad like the following. Mustard-flavored mayonnaise often replaces the cream sauce.

Cooked and puréed, its flavor attenuated with one part of potatoes to two of celeriac, plus a certain quantity of onion purée (turnips may also be added), finished with butter and heavy cream, it is an exquisite accompaniment to a roast, particularly to game.

Celeriac in Mustard Sauce

Céleri-rave à la Sauce Moutarde

1 *celeriac (about* 1 *pound)*
salt and pepper
juice of 1 *lemon*
1 *tablespoon strong Dijon mustard*
1 *cup heavy cream*
chopped parsley

Peel the celeriac, cut it into pieces and pass it through the *mouli-julienne* into a fine julienne (or grate it). Mix the salt and pepper in the lemon juice, stir in the mustard and then the cream. Taste for seasoning, mix thoroughly with the celeriac, turn it out onto a serving dish, and sprinkle with parsley.

THE CASSOULET

Cooked fat is, for most people, difficult to digest, and for some impossible. The same may be said for dried beans. Moreover, *cassoulet*, assuming it not to be the dreary bean soup, often canned, served in most restaurants that claim it as a specialty, is so good that only those with the strongest willpower, or those of puritan persuasion, will refrain from overeating. A regional specialty from *foie gras* country (the Languedoc), goose fat naturally lends the *cassoulet* its *onctuosité* (which description suggests a smooth, suave, velvety quality, but does not imply slippery, oily, nauseating or insincere, as does its English equivalent, "unctuousness"). For a peasant people whose life pattern turns, in large part, around hard, out-of-doors physical work, this kind of nourishment "passes"—is, indeed, essential to its well-being. We others are required to expiate the pleasures taken in *cassoulet* (or go back to the farm).

Gastronomic literature, which, although abundant, is rarely able to stumble out of a pathetic morass of pretension and deliberate mystification (happily, a few artists have, incidentally, written brilliantly and with lucid passion of food and wine—Colette, no doubt, leading the twentieth-century contingent), has nearly drowned this good, solid dish of beans in more idiotic odes to its glory, essays on its mystic divinity, etc., even than those dedicated to *la bouillabaisse*; and it is more often read about than tasted, for although rustic in personality, it is long of execution and not particularly economical.

There are said to be three *cassoulets* (Castelnaudary, Carcassonne, and Toulouse), but their definitions vary too much to be taken seriously and it would be more correct to say that there are as many as there are cooks, and to define a *cassoulet*, in a general way, as a slow-cooked gratin made up of two or more separate preparations, one of which is always a pork and bean stew, the others of which may be chosen among preserved duck or goose, braised lamb or mutton, and roast or braised partridge.

The gentle, sweet odor of broom which, in the past, was burned to heat the bread ovens in which *cassoulets* were cooked, lent, no doubt, a dimension to the dish that we shall never know.

In France, where mature mutton is rarely eaten, the terms *mouton* and *agneau* are used interchangeably to designate grass, or yearling, lamb.

Cassoulet

Cassoulet

a healthy pinch of Mixed Herbs (*page* 86)
1/4 *goose* (*breast or leg*) *or* 1/2 *gosling*
salt
goose fat from inside the bird

Bean stew:

6 *ounces fresh pork rind*
1/2 *pound lean salt side pork* (*if necessary, substitute bacon and parboil it longer*)
1 *pig's foot*
1 *good-sized garlic sausage* (*cervelas—a good equivalent is difficult to find in the U.S., but perhaps Polish or German cooking sausages are the best substitute. In any case, only those of impeccable quality are digestible*)
2 *pounds dried beans of a large starchy variety* (*in the U.S. those known as Great Northern are perhaps best*), *of the most recent harvest, if possible*
2 *medium carrots, peeled and cut into pieces*
1 *large onion, stuck with* 2 *cloves*
2 *cloves garlic, crushed and peeled*
a large pinch of mixed herbs
1 *bay leaf*
salt

Lamb stew:

2 *medium onions*
3 *cloves garlic*
2 *medium carrots*
goose fat
1 *lamb shoulder, all surface fat removed, cut into large pieces but not boned*

salt
1 *heaping tablespoon flour*
1 *cup dry white wine*
thyme, bay leaf (or mixed herbs)
1 1-*pound can tomatoes (in season,* 3 *or* 4 *fresh tomatoes)*
cooking liquid from beans

2 *cloves garlic*
freshly ground pepper
white bread crumbs
goose fat

THE GOOSE

Reduce the first pinch of herbs to powder in a mortar, sprinkle the goose with the herbs and salt and leave overnight. Render the goose fat (melt the pieces of fat over a low flame, and when nothing solid is left but the cracklings, strain off the pure fat). Cook the goose gently, well bathed in this fat, until tender, turning it after about 15 minutes. Save the fat. (This is merely the method of preparing preserved goose—*confit d'oie*. Normally it is then packed into earthenware jars, covered with melted goose fat, and kept this way in a cool, dry cellar throughout the year.)

THE BEANS

The beans should be uniform in size and uniformly white in color. Assuming them to be of the most recent harvest, there is no need to soak them.

Roll up the pork rind and tie it with a string. Cover it, the salt pork, and the pig's foot with cold water, bring to a boil, simmer for a few minutes, drain, and rinse them in cold water. Prick the sausage in several places with the prongs of a sharp fork or the tip of a knife.

Cover the beans generously with cold water in a large, heavy saucepan or earthenware casserole. Bring slowly to a boil, drain them and return them to the cooking utensil along with the vegetables, garlic, herbs and pork products, including sausage. Pour in enough tepid water to cover everything by about 2 inches, bring to a boil again, slowly, and adjust the heat so that, covered, the barest simmer is maintained. Do not salt.

The sausage should be removed and put aside after about 40 minutes and the salt pork when it is tender, but still firm—about 1 hour. The foot and rind should remain with the beans until they are done—about 2 hours in all. Taste the cooking liquid and salt to taste. Put the rind and pig's foot aside with the sausage and salt pork. Discard the onion and bay leaf.

THE LAMB STEW

Peel and coarsely chop the onions. Crush and peel the cloves of garlic. Peel the carrots and cut them into 1-inch lengths. Cook the carrots and onions in a couple of tablespoons of goose fat in a heavy *sauteuse* or skillet (just the size to hold the pieces of meat placed side by side) for about 15 minutes, stirring regularly, until lightly browned. Remove onions and carrots, making certain, to leave no fragment of onion behind, and, over a high flame, color the pieces of lamb in the same fat. Salt them just before turning, and when they are browned on all sides, sprinkle with flour, turn the pieces over, return the vegetables to the pan, and when the flour is lightly cooked, add the white wine, garlic, and herbs. Scrape and stir with a wooden spoon to loosen and dissolve frying adherents and transfer the contents to a heavy *cocotte*. Add the tomatoes and enough of the beans' cooking liquid to cover, and leave, covered, at a bare simmer, either in a slow oven or over a tiny flame, for 1½ hours, skimming off surface fat 2 or 3 times during this period. Pour the contents of the *cocotte* into a sieve, carefully pick out the pieces of meat and carrot and put them aside, discard the bay leaf, and pass the rest through the sieve. Bring the sauce to a boil, move it to the side of the fire, regulating to a "bubble," and skim for 15 minutes.

Rub the bottom and sides of a large, medium-deep earthenware oven dish with the 2 cloves of garlic until they are completely absorbed. Untie the pork rind, cut it into small rectangles about ½ inch by 2 inches and distribute them regularly over the bottom of the dish. Cut the goose into two pieces, place them on the bed of rinds, and, after having drained the beans, putting their liquid aside, distribute about ⅓ of the beans over and around the pieces of goose. Split the pig's foot, remove the largest bones, cut each half into 3 or 4 pieces and arrange them, along with the pieces of lamb and carrot (both those from the lamb stew and from the beans), evenly over the surface. Sprinkle generously with pepper, cover everything with half of the remaining beans, and distribute the sausage, cut into thick slices, and the salt pork, cut into 1-inch lengths, on top, pepper again and cover with the remaining beans. Generously sprinkle the entire surface with bread crumbs and, carefully, so as to moisten them without displacing them, pour over, ladle by ladle, the sauce from the lamb stew until the liquid rises just to the surface of the beans. Dust lightly again with bread crumbs, sprinkle several tablespoonfuls of melted goose fat over the surface, and put the dish into a hot oven until it is heated through and the surface begins to bubble. Turn the oven low (275°–300° F.) so that a gentle bubbling is maintained, and, after about 20 minutes, as the liquid reduces, partly by absorption and partly by evaporation, begin to baste the surface, first with the remaining lamb sauce and, when it is finished, with the beans' cooking liquid. Continue in this way every 20 minutes or so and, when a pretty, golden-crisp gratin has formed on the surface, break it regularly all over with a spoon so that part becomes submerged and the rest is moistened by the sauce. The *cassoulet*, in principle, should remain at least 2 hours in a slow oven, and the gratin should be broken a minimum of 3 times, but if the basting liquids should run short before this time, it is better to stop the gratinéing process than to risk the dish's becoming too dry.

The beans retain their form but at the slightest pressure may be reduced to a creamy purée, and all the elements are coated with a succulent sauce whose body is drawn from the gelatinous rind and pig's foot and whose suaveness is enhanced by the discreet presence of goose fat.

Three Simple Winter Menus

with appropriate wines

MENU II (FOR 4)

SOUFFLES A LA SUISSESSE

[SOUFFLES A LA SUISSESSE]

A light white wine:
Burgundy (Mâcon-Viré, Pouilly-Fuissé)
or Loire Valley (Pouilly-Fumé, Sancerre)—
or a rosé with the entire meal

SKEWERED LAMBS' KIDNEYS

[BROCHETTES DE ROGNONS D'AGNEAU]

Following a white wine,
a light-bodied young, cool red wine:
Mâcon, Beaujolais, Côtes-du-Rhône

SAFFRON RICE WITH TOMATOES

[RIZ SAFRANE AUX TOMATES]

LAMB'S LETTUCE SALAD

[SALADE DE MACHE]

FRESH GOAT CHEESES

[FROMAGES FRAIS DE CHEVRE]

The same as the preceding,
or a bigger-bodied wine of the same
region. If a "flinty" Loire Valley wine
has been served with the soufflés,
return it to the table
for those who are interested in
the goat cheeses–white
wine marriage

CREPES A LA NORMANDE

[CREPES A LA NORMANDE]

Although for most of the simple menus
dessert wines have not been recommended,
remember that apple desserts—in
particular those served tepid or hot—
marry especially well with a fine,
well-chilled Sauternes, or a cool
and elegant young Burgundy

THE SOUFFLES A LA SUISSESSE

The composition of these soufflés differs from that of an ordinary cheese soufflé only in that the latter would contain one more beaten egg white. The final result, because the *suissesses* are poached and thoroughly cooked—rather than being rapidly puffed up in a hot oven—and then imbibe a large quantity of heavy cream through a further gratin process, in no way resembles a classic soufflé, but more nearly brings to mind *quenelles.*

Just as artichoke bottoms filled with a classic soufflé mixture and baked in a hot oven provide a light and elegant first course, so will they (first stewed in butter to accentuate their flavor, after having been prepared as indicated on page 77), each "stuffed" with a poached *suissesse* and finished as indicated, afford a unique gratin.

Soufflés à la Suissesse

Soufflés à la Suissesse

1 *cup milk*
2 *heaping tablespoons flour (about 1/3 cup)*
salt, freshly ground white pepper, tiny bit of freshly grated nutmeg
4 *tablespoons (2 ounces) butter*
about 1 cup freshly grated Parmesan cheese
3 *egg yolks*
2 *egg whites*
1 1/2 *cups heavy cream*

Bring the milk to a boil, leave until lukewarm, and pour it slowly into the flour, stirring to avoid lumping. Season with salt, pepper and nutmeg and, stirring constantly with a wooden spoon, cook over a medium flame until thickened. Leave to cool for several minutes, add 2 tablespoons of butter, something over half of the grated cheese and the three egg yolks, and mix thoroughly. Beat the egg whites until stiff and fold them in gently but thoroughly.

Butter individual molds, porcelain ramekins or muffin tins, spoon them about two-thirds full of the mixture, place them in a larger pan (a cake tin, for instance), and pour in enough hot, but not boiling, water to immerse them by two-thirds. Poach in a slow oven (about 300° F.) for 15 or 20 minutes, or until they are firm and spongy to the touch. Unmold them carefully, so as not to damage them, one by one (or, if they are in muffin tins, all at once) onto a large cookie sheet, first running the blade of a knife around the edges to loosen them. This first cooking process may be carried out in advance, if preferred.

Butter a shallow baking or gratin dish of the right size to hold the little soufflés, placed side by side, but not—or barely—touching. Sprinkle the bottom with half the remaining cheese, place the soufflés on top, pour in enough cream to immerse them by half, sprinkle the rest of the cheese over the surface, and bake in a medium oven (about 350° F.) for another 15 or 20 minutes—or until the cream is nearly all absorbed and a light, golden gratin has been formed.

THE SKEWERED LAMBS' KIDNEYS

If rosemary bushes are handy, the branches, sharpened at one end and a tuft of leaves left at the other, not only afford a much prettier presentation than the usual metal skewers but lend their delicate perfume to the meats. Lamb hearts or lean pieces of meat may be mixed with the kidneys, and small tomatoes, slices of small zucchini, small mushrooms, etc., represent alternate vegetable possibilities. The strung skewers may, for variation, be rolled in *duxelles* before being grilled. (This is more often done with calf's liver, the pieces of which are first sautéed just long enough to become slightly firm.) When using *duxelles*, it is more successfully done beneath a broiler than over hot coals, as the *duxelles* that refuses to cling to the skewers is then recovered to be used as a garnish instead of being lost in the coals.

Skewered Lambs' Kidneys

Brochettes de Rognons d'Agneau

8 *lambs' kidneys*
2 *medium-sized sweet onions (Spanish or white) or*
    12 *small fresh white garden onions*
2 *sweet peppers*
6 *bay leaves, preferably fresh, each cut in* 2
few pinches Mixed Herbs (page 86)
about 1/3 *cup olive oil*
2 *cloves garlic, crushed and peeled*
1/2 *cup bread crumbs*
salt, pepper

Remove the fat and the thin surface membrane from the kidneys and cut each into 3 pieces, spokewise, from the point of attachment. If the onions are tiny, leave them whole; otherwise, cut them into quarters, vertically, and separate the sections. Remove all the seeds from the peppers and cut them into pieces approximately 1 1/2 inches square. Combine the kidneys, vegetables, and pieces of bay leaf in a bowl, sprinkle with a couple of pinches of mixed herbs and the olive oil and toss together. Leave to marinate for an hour or so, tossing or turning from time to time.

Reduce the garlic to a purée in a mortar, add the bread crumbs and mix well until they are sticky and permeated with garlic.

Alternate 6 pieces of kidney on each skewer with the peppers and onions, season, and roll the skewers in the garlic crumbs, pressing lightly to ensure their being well coated. Grill them, preferably over hot coals on a preheated heavy welded-iron grill, turning them 4 times, about every 1 1/2 or 2 minutes, depending on the intensity of the heat, and basting them regularly but lightly with the remaining marinade, until all sides are evenly browned. To be tender, moist and flavorful, the kidneys must remain pink inside. Arrange them on a bed of rice which has been turned out onto a heated serving platter.

Saffron Rice with Tomatoes

Riz Safrané aux Tomates

1 *medium onion, finely chopped*
1/4 *pound* (1 *stick*) *butter*
1 *cup long-grained rice*
a pinch (something less than 1/4 *teaspoon) saffron*
salt
2 *cups boiling water*
1 1-*pound can whole tomatoes (in season,* 3 *or* 4 *medium-size tomatoes, peeled and seeded)*

Use an earthenware or heavy copper utensil with a tight-fitting lid. Cook the chopped onion gently in 1 tablespoon butter for about 10 minutes, until soft and yellowed but not browned. Add the rice, saffron and salt, stirring from time to time with a wooden spoon, and after a couple of minutes, when the grains have acquired a "milky" tint, pour in the boiling water, stir once, and leave, covered, over a tiny flame so that the barest possible movement may be detected at the water's surface. Remove from the heat after about 20 minutes (some rices require more or less cooking time), and leave to swell and dry out for 5 to 10 minutes.

Meanwhile, drain the tomatoes, cut them in half to remove seeds and liquid, and stew them gently in 2 tablespoons of butter for a few minutes. Just before serving, mix into the rice the tomatoes and the remaining butter, cut into small pieces, delicately and repeatedly lifting the rice with the prongs of a fork so as to loosen the grains from one another without damaging them. Grated cheese may also be added at this time, if desired.

CREPES A LA NORMANDE

Good cooking apples are, the world over, becoming increasingly difficult to find. Russets are the best (in France, a small and unsightly variety known as *clocharde* is a perfect cooking apple), but the mediocre "golden delicious," because of its tremendous productivity, is replacing them on the market, and one is often obliged to use it.

Crêpes à la Normande

Crêpes à la Normande

12 *Crêpes, prepared as on page* 83, *but substituting Calvados* (*apple-jack*) *for the cognac*
3 *apples, halved, peeled, cored and sliced thin*
4 *tablespoons* (2 *ounces*) *butter*
about 1/2 *cup sugar*

Make crêpes. Stew sliced apples in butter over a low flame, tossing them from time to time, until just cooked but firmly retaining their shape. Roll about a tablespoonful, first sprinkled with a bit of sugar, into each crêpe, arrange the crêpes in a buttered shallow baking dish, sprinkle the surface lightly with sugar, and put into a hot oven for a few minutes—just long enough to heat them thoroughly and to melt and lightly glaze the sugar on the surface.

Three Simple Winter Menus

MENU III (FOR 8)

A Beaujolais (Chiroubles, Brouilly, Saint-Amour, Morgon) from the most recent vintage, served cool, with the entire meal

POACHED EGGS A LA BOURGUIGNONNE
[OEUFS POCHES A LA BOURGUIGNONNE]

BEEF TRIPE A LA LYONNAISE
[GRAS-DOUBLE A LA LYONNAISE]

COMPOSED SALAD
[SALADE COMPOSEE]

CHEESES
[FROMAGES]

PINEAPPLE ICE
[GRANITE A L'ANANAS]

THE POACHED EGGS A LA BOURGUIGNONNE

In a professional kitchen the sauce would be prepared in advance, with a *roux* base to thicken it, simmered for at least 1/2 hour to rid it of its "floury" taste, a spoonful of meat glaze added for extra body and succulence, and lightly buttered at the last moment. Another red wine *court-bouillon* would then be kept on hand for use as poaching liquid. A *beurre manié* is less satisfactory as a thickening agent, but more practical in a home kitchen. The unpleasant floury taste that many people fear in all flour-thickened sauces is present only in a sauce in which the flour has cooked too short a time, but not, mysteriously, in a *beurre manié*-thickened sauce, in which it is subjected to no cooking.

Oeufs en Meurette, also Burgundian and more authentically regional, are similar, but simpler of presentation: A *roux*-thickened red wine sauce is simmered for 1/2 hour or so with little glazed onions and bacon or lean salt-pork *lardons*, first parboiled and cooked in butter, and the eggs are poached, with sauce and garnish, in individual casseroles or ramekins, in the oven. Croutons may be sprinkled over the surface just before serving.

Poached Eggs à la Bourguignonne

Oeufs Pochés à la Bourguignonne

Mirepoix (see page 75 for method):

- *1 large onion*
- *2 medium carrots*
- *1 large pinch mixed herbs*
- *1/2 crumbled bay leaf*
- *parsley (leaves, stems, roots)*
- *salt*
- *1 slice (about 1 1/2 ounces) prosciutto or Bayonne-type ham, finely chopped (not the heavily smoked, sweet-flavored variety)*
- *2 tablespoons (1 ounce) butter*

Poached Eggs à la Bourguignonne

1 bottle red wine (preferably the same as served at table)
8 thick slices firm, close-textured white bread, crusts removed andcorners rounded
about 6 tablespoons (3 ounces) butter
2 cloves garlic, peeled
8 very fresh eggs
freshly ground pepper

Beurre manié:
4 tablespoons (2 ounces) butter and 1 heaping tablespoon flour, mashed with a fork into a uniform paste

chopped parsley

Simmer the *mirepoix* and wine together, uncovered, for a good 1/2 hour, or until reduced by half, taste for salt, and pass the reduction through a fine sieve, pressing the debris well to extract all flavor.

Cook the bread slices in butter in heavy-bottomed skillets or *sauteuses* over a low flame until golden and crisp on both surfaces, adding more butter at the moment of turning, if necessary. Rub 1 surface of each with a clove of garlic and arrange them on a preheated serving platter, garlic sides up.

Bring the liquid back to a simmer and carefully break in the eggs, opening each cracked egg just over the liquid's surface so that it slips gently in (or break them, one at a time, onto a saucer before slipping each into the hot liquid—this permits one to remove any fragment of shell that may remain, or to put aside for other purposes any eggs the yolks of which may have broken). Cover tightly, turn off the flame (or turn it as low as possible—it is a question of how effectively the receptacle retains heat), and leave to poach for a couple of minutes, or until the white is softly coagulated, but the yolk still liquid. (For this quantity of eggs, it may be more practical to poach 4 at a time.) Remove them carefully with a perforated skimming spoon, trim the edge of each, if necessary (very fresh eggs hold their form well—if not absolutely fresh, they tend to spread out, but will hold better if chilled when broken), place one on each crouton and sprinkle with pepper. Bring the liquid back to a simmer, whisk in the *beurre manié*, adding it bits at a time until the sauce is lightly thickened, and pass the sauce through a fine sieve over the eggs. Sprinkle with parsley.

THE BEEF TRIPE A LA LYONNAISE

Gras-double à la lyonnaise is made with a combination of different stomach and intestine parts. Honeycomb tripe is indicated here because the other parts are rarely available in America. Usually onions and tripe are both sautéed in lard rather than in butter and olive oil, and finished with vinegar instead of lemon. The substitutions here represent personal taste.

Beef tripe is sold precooked. If raw, it should be well scrubbed and rinsed in vinegar-water and simmered for about 6 hours in a *blanc* (water ever so slightly thickened with flour—about 1 tablespoon for a large pot of water—onion, thyme, bay leaf, salt and a dash of vinegar or lemon juice).

Chitterlings, or calves' intestines (*fraise de veau*), may be prepared in the same way. The last-minute addition of sautéed onions is characteristic of many sautéed preparations *à la lyonnaise.* It is essential that the onions be neither chopped nor too thinly sliced and that they be added at the last moment in order that their sweetness remain in clean juxtaposition to the flavor of the principle element.

If an accompaniment is desired, a *Paillasson* (Potato Straw Cake, page 392) is perfect, in which case a simple green salad would be more suitable than the composed salad.

Beef Tripe à la Lyonnaise

Gras-double à la Lyonnaise

about 3/4 pound sweet onions, halved and sliced—if only strong onions are available, they should be sliced, parboiled for a few minute and drained

2 *tablespoons* (1 *ounce*) *butter*

Beef Tripe à la Lyonnaise

1½ pounds precooked honeycomb tripe
¼ cup olive oil
salt, pepper
juice of ½ lemon

Cook the onions, salted, in butter, over a low flame, stirring and tossing regularly, until soft and yellowed—about 15 minutes. Just before removing them from the heat, turn the flame up and toss them until lightly browned. Put them aside.

Cut the tripe into bands 2½–3 inches wide, cut each band crosswise into approximately ¼-inch strips, and sponge them dry in paper towels. Heat the olive oil in a large, heavy *sauteuse* or skillet (not enamelware) until it gives of its distinctive perfume, add the tripe, season with salt and pepper, and cook over a high flame, frequently tossing and stirring and scraping the bottom with a wooden spoon, for from 8 to 10 minutes, or until some of the strips show signs of browning and crisping at the edges. (To be sautéed to the point of being dry and lightly browned, the quantity of tripe must be small in relation to the size of the *sauteuse*, but it is a question of opinion whether this result is essential to the quality of the dish.) Add the onions, toss everything together for another minute or so, and turn it out onto a heated serving platter. Squeeze the lemon juice into the hot pan; swirl it around and sprinkle it over the tripe.

THE COMPOSED SALAD

Artichokes, if young and tender, the chokes still undeveloped, are best raw, simply "turned," sliced, and soaked in lemon water, in a salad of this sort. Parboiled fresh, young green beans, precooked salsify (oyster plant) and avocados are other possible ingredients. This salad may either accompany or follow an ungarnished main course.

(*Recipe follows*)

Composed Salad

Salade Composée

3 medium-sized potatoes of a firm, nonmealy variety
about 1/3 cup dry white wine (enough to cover potato slices)
2 medium Artichoke Bottoms (page 77)
1 celery heart
1 heaping tablespoon fines herbes (equal parts of whatever is available: chervil, parsley, chives, tarragon)
Vinaigrette
1 small head lettuce (not iceberg)

Boil the potatoes in their skins, peel them the moment they are drained, slice them into a bowl, cover with the white wine and leave to cool. Slice the artichoke bottoms, slice the celery heart crosswise, and put them, along with the drained potatoes (the white wine may be put aside for other cooking purposes) and half the *fines herbes*, to marinate in the vinaigrette. Loosely place the lettuce leaves, washed and gently sponged dry in a towel, on top, sprinkle with the remaining *fines herbes*, and toss only at the moment of serving.

Pineapple Ice

Granité à l'Ananas

1 large ripe pineapple
about 3/4 cup of sugar (or to taste)
juice of 3 oranges, strained (about 1 cup)

Remove the top of the pineapple, cutting in at an angle all around, so as to form a lid, and pare the inside of its flesh. Remove all the pulp from the inside of the pineapple. To do this, cut around and about halfway down, close to the skin, but being careful not to pierce it, with a long, sharp, pointed knife; then cut all around the core and make spokelike incisions between the two circular cuts. Remove the wedges with the help of a tablespoon and continue scraping around the core until all the pulp has been removed and the shell is empty, except for the upright core. Cut into the base of the core with the point of the knife and break it off as cleanly as possible.

Mash the pulp with a pestle and work it well in a sieve until all the juice possible has been extracted. Mix about 1 cup of the juice with the sugar and boil to form a syrup. When it is cool, mix it with the rest of the pineapple juice and the orange juice, pour the mixture into 2 ice-cube trays and put them to freeze, along with the pineapple shell and lid (lacking a sufficiently large freezing compartment, chill the pineapple separately as well as possible). After an hour or so, stir the mixture, scraping all sol id parts from the sides and bottoms of the trays and mashing it together with the liquid. Repeat this process a couple of times over the course of approximately 3 hours or until, when mixed together, a semifirm but still mushy consistency is achieved; then spoon it into the pineapple shell. It may then be left in the freezing compartment for another hour or so and allowed to become slightly firmer—but if served frozen solid, it loses all its quality.

Spring Menus

Appropriate wines for each menu are suggested on the pages indicated below, which mark the beginning of each menu and its recipes.

Two Formal Spring Dinners

I

PAGE 272

Raw Shellfish Platter

Turban of Sole Fillets with Salmon, Sorrel Sauce

Roast Saddle of Lamb with Herbs

Green Bean Purée, Artichoke Bottoms with Mushroom Purée

Cheeses

Frozen Strawberry Mousse with Raspberry Purée

II

PAGE 286

Crayfish Salad with Fresh Dill

Spring Stew

Poached Chicken Mousseline

Crusts with Fresh Morels

Tossed Green Salad, Fines Herbes

Cheeses

Pineapple Surprise

Two Informal Spring Dinners

I

PAGE 302

Hors d'Oeuvre of Raw Vegetables

Shrimp Quiche

Chicken in Red Wine

Steamed Potatoes

Wild Green Salad

Cheeses

Flamri with Rasberry Sauce

II

PAGE 314

Marinated Raw Sardine Fillets

Grilled Steak, Marchand de Vin

Gratin of Potatoes

Field Salad

Cheeses

Apple Tart

Four Simple Spring Menus

I

PAGE 321

Boiled Beef with Vegetables

Field Salad

Cheeses

Fresh Fruits

II

PAGE 327

Garden Peas à la Française

Blanquette of Veal

Rice Pilaf

Tossed Green Salad

Cheeses

Molded Chocolate Loaf with Whipped Cream

III

PAGE 333

Terrine of Poultry Livers
Deep-fried Beef Tripe, Rémoulade Sauce
Dandelion and Salt Pork (or Bacon) Salad
Goat Cheeses
Strawberries in Beaujolais

IV

PAGE 341

Warm Asparagus Vinaigrette
Calves' Brains in Red Wine
Cauliflower Loaf
Green Salad with Fines Herbes
Cheeses
Molded Apple Pudding

Two Formal Spring Dinners

with appropriate wines

MENU I (FOR 6)

RAW SHELLFISH PLATTER
[PLATEAU DE COQUILLAGES]

A young, light, very dry white wine:
champagne (blanc de blancs, nature),
Riesling, certain of the driest Graves

TURBAN OF SOLE FILLETS WITH SALMON, SORREL SAUCE
[TURBAN DE FILETS DE SOLE AU SAUMON, SAUCE A L'OSEILLE]

A white Burgundy with greater body
and depth than the preceding,
old enough (5 or 6 years) for bouquet
to have begun replacing "fruit":
one of the Meursault or Montrachet growths

ROAST SADDLE OF LAMB WITH HERBS
[SELLE D'AGNEAU ROTI AUX AROMATES]

A red Graves (Haut-Bailly,
Pape Clément, La Mission Haut-Brion),
a Saint-Julien (Ducru-Beaucaillou,
Léoville) or a Saint-Estèphe
(Cos d'Estournel, Montrose),
from a light and fairly
recent year (6 to 8 years)

GREEN BEAN PUREE, ARTICHOKE BOTTOMS WITH MUSHROOM PUREE
[PUREE DE HARICOTS VERTS, FONDS D'ARTICHAUTS
A LA PUREE DE CHAMPIGNONS]

CHEESES
[FROMAGES]
One of the great Pauillacs or
Saint-Emilions, or a first growth
from one of the Côte de Nuits
communities—in any case, from a "big"
year and fully matured (Bordeaux,
10–15 years; Burgundy, 6–10 years)

FROZEN STRAWBERRY MOUSSE WITH RASPBERRY PUREE
[MOUSSE DE FRAISES GLACEE A LA SAUCE MELBA]

The fresh, clean taste of live things from the sea is a welcome opening to any meal and a particularly useful possibility when composing a more or less complex menu in delicate balance, for it adds its dimension without placing restrictions on the choice of dishes to follow, and the light, sharp wine that best accompanies it leaves an equally open field in the *suite* of wines.

The "turban" is highly decorative. The various poached fish-fillet and mousseline preparations count, certainly, among the most delicate and sumptuous in classical cooking and their lightness and fantasy offset perfectly the sobriety of an unadorned roast. The marriage of fresh strawberry and fresh raspberry is one of the most exquisite in the dessert world. The frozen mousse discourages an accompanying wine, but has no other failings.

Much may be prepared in advance: The mousseline forcemeat, but for the final addition of cream, the *fumet* and the sorrel purée for the fish sauce, the vegetable purées, and the artichoke bottoms. The turban should be put to poach about 20 minutes before going to table and the saddle put to roast at the moment one is seated. The precooked artichoke bottoms may be put to stew in butter when the turban is served. Finishing the fish sauce and reheating the vegetable purées are rapid last-minute chores whose timing requires no forethought.

THE SHELLFISH PLATTER

Oysters, clams, mussels and sea urchins form the usual composition of a shellfish platter in France. All should be opened just before being served. A firm, moist, smooth, plump flesh is proof of the freshness of the first three (the ultimate test being their wriggling reaction to a drop of lemon juice at table). The undulating spines and the regular movement of the starlike orifice are sufficient proof of a sea urchin's freshness. (See *Oursinade*, page 213, for the method of opening them.) The traditional accompaniments are lemon halves, wine vinegar with chopped shallot, coarsely broken-up (mignonette) white peppercorns, fresh, unsalted butter and thin slices of firm, fine-textured rye bread.

The northern Pacific Coast of the United States claims to produce a small oyster with a particularly delicate flavor. East Coast oysters tend to be "fatty" and their flavor has much less clarity than European varieties. (*Portugaises* and *claires*, elongated deep-shelled oysters with greenish flesh and delicate black beards, and *belons* and *marraines*, round and flat, the first with tan flesh, the latter, greenish, are the principle French varieties. The very fine oysters often found in England are of the same sort as the last two.) American cherrystone clams are, on the other hand, of a finesse unknown to that general variety of mollusk in France (French clams resemble, in a larger version, the gray-shelled *palourdes* and the little cocklelike *praires*). Razor clams, when they can be found, are a marvelous addition to a shellfish platter.

THE TURBAN OF SOLE FILLETS WITH SALMON, SORREL SAUCE

A fish-fillet and mousseline turban permits endless variations. Unlike certain preparations, its basic qualities suffer in no way through being subjected to the most elegant and formal of *grande cuisine* presentations.

The forcemeat may be made of pike, whiting, sole, trout, etc. A particularly fine forcemeat, somewhat more difficult to manipulate because of the resistance of the flesh and its lack of body when raw, is made of lobster (in which case, the carapace and coral are transformed into an *à l'américaine* sauce—see Squid à l'Américaine, page 377—pounded, sieved, reduced and creamed). The buttered mold may be lined with a décor of truffle slices, diamonds or crescents before the fillets are pressed into place, and chopped truffle peelings or chopped dried morels, first soaked, rinsed, sponged dry and stewed in butter, may be added to the forcemeat. Alternate sole and salmon fillets (the latter sliced lengthwise from a tail section of salmon the same length as the sole fillets) may be used to line the mold, forming a ravishing pink-and-white-striped turban. A spectacularly beautiful and voluptuous presentation and an exquisite assembly of flavors and textures are afforded by a truffle-studded pink-and-white turban, the central well of which is filled with a ragoût of crayfish tails bound by a Nantua sauce. This sauce is, technically, a creamed *béchamel* finished with crayfish butter. It may reasonably he prepared by sautéing the crayfish *à la bordelaise* (see shrimp preparation for Shrimp Quiche, page 305), removing the tails and, except for the emptied shells to be used for garnish, pounding everything remaining, cooking it for 10 minutes in the *béchamel*, passing it through a fine sieve, and buttering it lightly at the last moment. There is a surrounding ribbon of sorrel purée upon which, symmetrically arranged, are placed emptied crayfish shells, filled with forcemeat and cooked for 7 or 8 minutes in a gentle oven, the remainder of the Nantua sauce sent to table apart.

Frozen products never produce a satisfactory mousseline forcemeat, nor will frozen fillets be resilient and moist after the poaching process.

The proportions given are for a classic savarin mold (circular rounded bottom, large central tube), 10 inches in diameter.

Turban of Sole Fillets with Salmon, Sorrel Sauce

Turban de Filets de Sole au Saumon, Sauce à l'Oseille

3 *filleted soles (substitute grey sole, flounder or lemon sole for Dover sole if it is not available), weighing a good pound each, or* 12 *fillets plus the carcasses*

Mousseline forcemeat:

about 10 *ounces fresh salmon (a good* 1/2 *pound, once bones and skin are removed)*
1 *egg white*
1 *cup heavy cream*
1 *small handful shelled raw pistachio nuts*
salt, freshly ground pepper
freshly grated nutmeg

Fish fumet:

the sole carcasses, cleaned, gills removed, chopped or broken up
about 2/3 *cup each dry white wine and water*
1 *onion, finely sliced*
a bouquet of parsley
1 *bay leaf*

1/2 teaspoon Mixed Herbs (page 86)
salt

1/2 pound sorrel
about 6 tablespoons (3 ounces) butter
butter for the mold

Trim the fillets neatly and add the trimmings to the boned and skinned salmon fresh. Prepare the forcemeat base at least 2 hours in advance, using the above proportions, exactly as described on page 79. The pistachio nuts, first dipped for a couple of minutes in boiling water, drained, and rubbed in a towel to remove the skins, then coarsely chopped, are incorporated at the last minute, at the same time as the cream.

Combine the ingredients of the *fumet* in a saucepan (salting very lightly in view of the eventual reduction), bring to a boil, and simmer, covered, for 1/2 hour, mashing coarsely the solid ingredients with a wooden pestle or spoon after about 20 minutes. Pass through a fine sieve, without pressure, and put aside.

Remove the stems from the sorrel, pulling them backward, wash sorrel well in several waters, and parboil for a few seconds—just long enough for it to turn limp and lose its bright-green color. Drain, shred, and stew it gently in 2 tablespoons of butter (adding a bit more after a few minutes if the mixture seems too dry), lightly salted, stirring regularly, for about 15 minutes, or until the sorrel has melted into a near purée. Pass it through a fine sieve and put aside.

Soak the fillets in cold water for about 10 minutes, spread them out on a paper towel, and sponge them dry with more paper towels. Flatten each fillet slightly by pressing against it with the fiat side of a large knife blade (fairly gently, so as not to break the fibers), and line the generously buttered mold, pressing them into place, skin side next to the mold, slightly overlapping, with the narrow tip of each fillet hanging over the inside wall (the central tube) of the mold, and the wider end hanging over the outside. (Slivers may be cut from some of the fillets and a bit of patchwork effected, if necessary.) Spoon in the raw forcemeat (the purée base of which will have been kept embedded in cracked ice, but mounted with the cream only at the last minute), tap the bottom of the mold firmly against a wooden surface 2 or 3 times to settle the filling and eliminate any air pockets, fold the fillet tips over to form the turban, and press a buttered round of kitchen paper over it, a small hole cut in the center and a few shallow slits cut spokewise out from it. (To prepare the paper, fold a square of paper, somewhat wider than the diameter of the mold, in four, round the unfolded corner, clip off the tip of the doubly folded corner, and cut 2 or 3 inch-long incisions in from that point.)

Poach in a *bain-marie*, the mold immersed by two-thirds in hot, but not boiling, water, in a slow to medium oven (325° F.) for 40 minutes, or until the surface is resilient, firm, springy to the touch. The water must not boil or the fillets will be drained of their moisture. The poaching may be conducted over a tiny flame in a large, tightly covered saucepan or *marmite* if it is not convenient to use the oven. Remove the mold from the *bain-marie* and leave it to settle for 7 or 8 minutes before unmolding (the sauce will be finished during this time). To unmold, remove the buttered paper, place a fine wire grill (pastry grill or special grill for steaming vegetables) on top and turn grill and mold over together, as if to unmold. This will drain off the troublesome liquids which must otherwise be sponged up with towels from the serving platter. Turn mold and grill together back over and unmold the turban onto a preheated round serving platter. Surround it with a ribbon of sauce and send the rest to table separately.

THE SAUCE

Reduce the fish *fumet* in a heavy saucepan over a high flame, stirring frequently—and toward the end, constantly—by about two-thirds, or until it begins to acquire a light syrupy consistency. Add the sorrel purée, continue boiling and stirring for a few seconds until a light but distinct "body" is achieved. Remove immediately from the heat and whisk in the remaining butter (about 4 tablespoons), first cut into small pieces (or softened considerably at kitchen temperature).

THE ROAST SADDLE OF LAMB WITH HERBS

The entire saddle in a grass (yearling) lamb is about 1 foot in length. It is limited by the haunch, or upper limit of the leg, at one end and the first rib chops at the other, and comprises the fillets, filets mignons, (muscles corresponding, respectively, to the *faux-filet* and the fillet in beef cuts), and short sections of the side-belly known as "aprons." Butchers often refer to this cut as "double saddle" or "English-cut saddle." It is wise to order it ahead of time, for butchers often cut up the animals in advance, splitting the saddles and cutting them into loin chops. The flesh should be a clear rose-tan color (not a deep brownish-red), the fillet round and well defined, and the saddle should be surrounded by a healthy layer of firm, dry, white fat. It should be sufficiently aged.

Many people prefer to leave a thin coat of fat to protect and nourish the flesh during the roasting process, but the delicate lamb, in this case, risks being tinged with the "woolly" mutton taste that some find disagreeable, and, properly conducted, the roasting will not dry out a saddle from which all traces of fat have been removed.

Roast Saddle of Lamb with Herbs

Selle d'Agneau Rôti aux Aromates

1 *saddle of lamb* 8–10 *inches long* (3–3½ *pounds*)
2 *cloves garlic, peeled*
a large pinch (*level teaspoon*) *Mixed Herbs* (*page* 86)
¼ *cup olive oil*
salt, pepper
⅓ *cup dry white wine* (*or water*)
2 *tablespoons* (1 *ounce*) *butter* (*optional*)

Remove all the fat: That on the inside, next to the filet mignon and at the underside base of the apron, may easily be pried loose with the fingers. Using a small pointed sharp knife, make an incision through the layer of fat, the entire length of die saddle, following the line of the backbone. First on one side, then on the other, gently force the layer of fat loose from the fillet, using your fingers and, when it resists, the point of the knife, being careful to cut neither into the flesh itself, which is protected by a membrane to which the fat is only lightly attached, nor into the thin membrane that connects the apron to the fillet. Begin, now, at the far tip of the apron and, in the same way, loosen its layer of fat up to the connecting point. Slice through the layer of fat, parallel to the connecting membrane, leaving a thin layer of fat next to the membrane to ensure the apron's remaining attached. Cut out the layers of fat and membrane separating the thin layers of flesh in the lower section of the apron.

Rub the garlic cloves repeatedly against the rough surfaces of bone and over the entire surface of the meat, thus impregnating the bone itself, and lightly coating the flesh with garlic essence. Sprinkle the herbs lightly on all surfaces, most sparingly on the underside, and coat with olive oil, rubbing and patting with your hands to ensure an even distribution. Just before roasting, sprinkle the underside of the apron and the filet mignon with salt and freshly ground pepper and roll the aprons under so that the two rolls touch and rest firmly against the filets mignons (the rolls serve as the base of the roast and as protection for the filets mignons, which otherwise would be overdone before the fillets had reached their stage of perfection). The rolls may be skewered together crosswise or the roast held in shape by a couple of rounds of string, but this is not essential.

Place the roast in a heavy, shallow baking dish of just the right size to hold it (otherwise, the drippings risk burning) and count a maximum of 10 minutes per pound of actual roasting time (25 to 30 minutes in this instance), starting with a very hot oven (425° F.) and, after 10 minutes, turning it down to medium (325° F.). Salt and pepper the surface at this time. Baste during the last 10 minutes or so and, after roasting is done, leave it in its roasting pan in a warm but not hot place for from 10 to 15 minutes so that the meat may relax (most practical is to remove the roast from the oven for a couple of minutes to arrest the cooking, at the same time turning off the oven and leaving the door open so that it may cool slightly before returning the meat to the warm, closed oven). Given all these precautions, the meat should be neither rare nor gray in color, but tender rose throughout. Send it to table, vegetable garnishes and juice separately, on a preheated platter (or, better, a special carving board with a well for collecting the juices), large enough to permit the easy distribution of meat slices after carving.

THE JUICE

Skim off the fat from the roasting pan, place pan over a high flame, pour in the white wine and reduce by about two-thirds, stirring and scraping with a wooden spoon to dislodge and dissolve all caramelized adherences. Remove from the flame and swirl in the butter, first cut into small pieces; this transforms the clear juice into a light-bodied velvety sauce. Purists generally prefer a simple juice and may also require that the white wine be replaced by water.

TO CARVE A SADDLE

The carving knife should be long, narrow-bladed, with an upward curve at the point, and razor-sharp. The saddle should be placed endwise directly before the carver. Pierce the left-hand fillet with the fork and hold the roast firmly in place while slicing vertically downward the entire length of the roast, following closely the right-hand contour of the vertical protuberances of the backbone, thus cleanly separating the inner wall of the fillet from the bones. Slice inward, horizontally, removing 5 slices, the 3 center ones of which are regular in form and from 1/4 to 1/3 inch thick. Reverse the position of the platter or plank and carve the other fillet in the same way. Slice off the aprons, cut each into 3 cross sections, turn the roast upside-down and, cutting first downward vertically against the bone, then inward horizontally beneath the filet mignon, still following closely the contour of the spinal bone protuberances, remove the filets mignons, whole, and section each crosswise into 3. This method produces, in a service for 6, 1 slice of fillet plus a fragment, 1 section of filet mignon, and 1 section of apron for each person. Serve on preheated plates and pass the sauceboat only when the carving has been finished and the resultant juices added.

THE GREEN BEAN PUREE

Instead of rice, dried green flageolet beans, cooked until very tender with carrot, thyme, bay leaf and onion, may be used (1 part of cooked flageolets to 2 of green beans) to give the necessary body to the purée. The result is more velvety and the delicate flavor of the flageolets in combination with that of the green beans is exquisite. The rice method is simpler and the flavor more direct. Many people content themselves with passing the beans fairly coarsely through a vegetable mill. The result is palatable, but it is well worth going to the trouble of passing them a second time through a very fine drum sieve—the difference must be tasted to be believed.

Green Bean Purée

Purée de Haricots Verts

2 heaping tablespoons rice
2 pounds fresh, tender green beans
salt, freshly ground pepper, freshly grated nutmeg
about 1/4 pound butter

Parboil the rice for 15 minutes, drain it and rinse it. Wash the beans (it is not necessary to snap them as all the tips will remain to be discarded after the beans have been passed through the sieve) and plunge them, along with the parboiled rice, into a large pot of salted, rapidly boiling water. Keep at a rapid boil, uncovered, until the beans are just tender (a couple of minutes longer than if they were to be served whole, nonetheless). Pour the contents of the saucepan into a colander or large sieve and leave to drain for at least 1/2 hour, then pass beans and rice first through a *moulinette* (vegetable mill), using the medium blade, then, a couple of tablespoonfuls at a time, through a fine nylon drum sieve, using the plastic disk. Season to taste with salt, pepper and a tiny bit of nutmeg, smooth out the surface, and put aside, covered, until the last minute before serving.

Heat the purée in a heavy saucepan over a high flame, stirring rapidly and constantly to prevent sticking or burning. When sufficiently heated, remove from the heat and whip in the butter, cut into small pieces, then softened, using a wooden spoon. Incorporate as much as the beans can absorb without becoming too liquid—the purée, however, should be comparatively thin, not stiff.

THE ARTICHOKE BOTTOMS WITH MUSHROOM PUREE

Artichoke bottoms may be garnished with a variety of purées, among the finest being: broad beans, or *fave*, the skins first removed, the beans boiled until tender for 7 or 8 minutes with a large pinch of dried savory or, preferably, a branch of fresh savory, then drained, passed through a fine sieve, seasoned to taste, reheated, and generously buttered; green peas prepared in the same way, but without the savory—they should be freshly picked, but may be more mature than those simply to be boiled or prepared *à la française*; and *soubise* sliced new onions—but parboil them first if they are old and strong—gently stewed in butter, bound with a bit of thick *béchamel* and passed through a fine sieve. All are perfect accompaniments to roast or braised lamb, veal, beef or fowl.

Mushroom purées, unlike the other purées, may remain slightly rough in texture.

Artichoke Bottoms with Mushroom Purée

Fonds d'Artichauts à la Purée de Champignons

6 large Artichoke Bottoms, precooked and kept somewhat firm (page 77)
1 pound firm, unopened mushrooms
about 1/4 pound (1 stick) butter
juice of 1/2 lemon

(*Continued*)

salt, pepper
chopped parsley

Precook artichoke bottoms as per directions. Pare the stem tips of the mushrooms, rapidly wash the mushrooms, drain them thoroughly and pass them, raw, through the medium blade of the *moulinette*. Melt 4 tablespoons of the butter in a heavy saucepan, add the raw mushroom purée, season, and cook over a high flame, stirring constantly with a wooden spoon until all the vegetable liquid has evaporated. Squeeze in the lemon juice and stew gently, covered, over a tiny flame, for another 5 minutes or so. Add salt and pepper to taste.

Melt 2 tablespoons butter in a heavy *sauteuse* or saucepan of the right dimensions to just contain the precooked artichoke bottoms at their ease. Place them, bottoms down, in the pan, cut 2 tablespoons of butter into 6 pieces, place 1 in each of the artichoke bottoms and stew gently, covered, without browning, for about 1/2 hour, turning them over once or twice.

Remove the artichoke bottoms to a preheated serving platter, carefully spoon each full of the mushroom purée, and sprinkle the surface of each with chopped parsley.

THE FROZEN STRAWBERRY MOUSSE WITH RASPBERRY PUREE

A mousse packed into a soufflé dish too small to hold it, around which has been tied a strip of kitchen paper or aluminum foil rising 2 or 3 inches higher than the brim of the dish, frozen solid, and the paper peeled off just before serving, is called a frozen soufflé, its form being that of a soufflé that has risen high above the borders of the dish. The presentation is elegant, but the firmly frozen, slightly crystallized mass is less pleasant to the palate than the softer and more even-textured mousse described below.

A handful of wild strawberries (*fraises des bois*) scattered over the mousse just before serving is an attractive refinement.

Frozen strawberries will not replace fresh, but frozen raspberries, in particular those frozen whole and unsweetened, are excellent.

Frozen Strawberry Mousse with Raspberry Purée

Mousse de Fraises Glacée à la Sauce Melba

3/4 cup sugar (or more, to taste)
1/3 cup water
1 quart fresh, ripe strawberries
1 cup whipping cream

Sauce:
1 quart fresh raspberries (or 2 packages frozen)
sugar to taste (sweetened, frozen raspberries may need none)

Boil the sugar and water together and let cool. Pass the strawberries through a sieve and mix the purée with the syrup. Pour the chilled cream into a cold bowl, whip it until semi-firm, but not stiff, mix it with the strawberry mixture, and freeze, either in a mechanical ice-cream freezer or in ice trays. If trays are used, scrape the mixture out of the trays into a chilled bowl when half frozen, whip it, and return it to the trays to finish freezing.

Pass the raspberries through a nylon drum sieve, and add sugar to taste. Heap the mousse into a chilled crystal bowl and serve the raspberry sauce separately.

Two Formal Spring Dinners

with appropriate wines

MENU II (FOR 6)

CRAYFISH SALAD WITH FRESH DILL
[SALADE D'ECREVISSES A L'ANETH]

A young, dry white wine with an elegant fruit: Chablis, Riesling, champagne (blanc de blancs, nature), etc.

SPRING STEW
[RAGOUT PRINTANIER]

POACHED CHICKEN MOUSSELINE
[POULARDE POCHEE MOUSSELINE]

A bigger white wine than the preceeding (Montrachet, for instance), 6 to 10 years old, or a "lacy" red Burgundy with a floral bouquet from a light and recent year: Volnay, Chambolle-Musigny, Les Amoureuses, etc., served cool (cellar temperature)

CRUSTS WITH FRESH MORELS

[CROUTES AUX MORILLES FRAICHES]

TOSSED GREEN SALAD, FINES HERBES

[SALADE VERTE AUX FINES HERBES]

CHEESES

[FROMAGES]

One of the great growths from
Vosne-Romanée or a neighboring community

PINEAPPLE SURPRISE

[ANANAS EN SURPRISE]

All the elements of the crayfish salad may be prepared ahead of time. The vegetables for the stew may be cleaned, peeled, etc., and kept fresh in a damp towel in the refrigerator, the chicken may be boned a day in advance, if one likes, and the forcemeat, but for the final mounting with cream, must be prepared in advance. The crusts may be browned ahead of time.

The chicken should be stuffed and put to poach about 1¼ hours before going to table. The vegetable stew should be put to cook just before the crayfish salad is assembled (a question of a minute's time), and the morels only well after the vegetable stew has been served.

Cream occurs in three different preparations in this menu, but these are so different in nature and the cream in each so different in effect that there is no risk of monotony, and the actual quantity of cream allotted per person throughout the entire meal (½ cup) is not excessive.

THE CRAYFISH SALAD WITH FRESH DILL

A slight elaboration on *écrevisses à la nage* (the simplest of all crayfish preparations, cooked in *court-bouillon*, then served—a dish to be shared with unfastidious friends and accompanied by bibs and finger bowls), this salad throws the subtle, delicately sweet flavor into cleaner relief than perhaps any other preparation.

Fresh dill marries particularly well with crustaceans, and in northern European countries it is a usual ingredient. In France it is practically unknown, and if one has the good luck to find it on the market, it is most often mislabeled "fennel" (*Larousse Gastronomique* contents itself with calling it *fenouil bâtard* and referring the reader to the word *fenouil*). The appearance of the young plants is indeed practically identical; the savor is totally different. Should fresh, tender shoots of dill not be available, the dried and bottled dill weed, commonly found in American markets, may be substituted as it retains a great deal of the natural dill taste. Use only a teaspoonful of dill weed, leave it to macerate for a while in the lemon juice before preparing the sauce, and sprinkle the crayfish, finally, with chopped parsley instead of the dried dill.

The *court-bouillon* may be saved to moisten a bisque or other soup, or used as a poaching liquid for other fish.

Crayfish Salad with Fresh Dill

Salade d'Ecrevisses à l'Aneth

Court-bouillon:

- 2 *cups dry white wine*
- 2 *cups water*
- 1 *small handful coarse salt (sea salt, preferably)*
- 1 *small pinch Cayenne*
- 1/2 *teaspoon Mixed Herbs (page* 86)
- 1 *bay leaf*
- 1 *bouquet parsley and fresh dill*
- 1 *large onion, peeled and sliced thinly into rings*
- 1 *medium carrot, peeled and thinly sliced*
- 8–10 *whole peppercorns*

- 36 *large live crayfish (something over* 2 *ounces each), or, if unavailable,* 5 *pounds smaller crayfish*
- 1 *heaping tablespoon finely chopped young, tender, feathery dill leaves (no stems), or chopped parsley if fresh dill is not available*
- *salt, freshly ground pepper*
- *juice of* 1 *lemon*
- 1 *cup heavy cream*
- 1 *medium-size head tender-leafed lettuce (Boston type)*

THE COURT-BOUILLON

Bring the white wine and the water to a boil in a large saucepan and add all the ingredients except the peppercorns (which, with extended cooking, lose their savor and instead lend a bitter taste). Simmer, covered, for 1/2 hour, ad ding the peppercorns after 20 minutes.

The crayfish, because of their quantity, will be cooked in relays. This not only prevents a loss of their valuable liquids, once the intestines have been drawn, but economizes on *court-bouillon*, which is that much more flavorful for having been used for the second batch of crayfish as well.

Starting with the largest, rinse the crayfish (the easiest way is simply to dump them into the sink and let them crawl around while picking up one at a time and holding it for a second beneath the tap before drawing it), and remove the intestine of each, grasping the animal just above the point at which the pincers join the body, to avoid being pinched—or holding it with a towel for protection, and, with an abrupt motion to either side, tear loose the central fin from the tail fan, then pull gently in order to slip out the attached intestinal tract without breaking it. Toss each into the simmering *court-bouillon* the moment it is drawn. When half the crayfish have been added, cover the saucepan and leave to cook over a medium flame, holding the lid tightly and "tossing" the contents of the saucepan (abrupt forward, upward, and backward motion) from time to time, for about 8 minutes. Remove the crayfish to a bowl with the help of a wire skimming spoon and proceed in the same way for the others. Combine the two batches and leave to cool in the *court-bouillon*.

Put aside 6 of the largest and most perfectly formed crayfish to be used as garnish, keeping them moistened in some *court-bouillon* until the moment of presentation. Tear off the tails of all the others, remove and discard the tail shells, and put the flesh aside, covered with *court-bouillon*.

Pound the carapaces (heads, claws, legs, coral), 4 or 5 at a time, in a stone mortar, pass each pounded batch through the medium blade of a *moulinette* (vegetable mill) and, once all the juices are thoroughly extracted, discard the debris of shells. When all have been pounded and puréed, pass this coarse purée, in small quantities at a time, through a fine drum sieve, using the plastic disk (page 62).

Put aside 1/3 of the chopped dill for the décor and mix together the remainder with salt, pepper and lemon juice (the juice of one medium-size juicy lemon should be just right, but it is wiser to begin with too little and rectify the acidity later), add the cream, mix well, and whisk in the crayfish purée. Taste for salt and lemon.

Pick over the lettuce, keeping the leaves whole, wash them and sponge them dry between two towels. Arrange them on the bottom and around the sides of a large, deep serving platter, distribute the drained crayfish tails on top, mask the entire surface with the sauce, place the unshelled crayfish, trussed (pull the tail slowly upward, in an arc, toward the head, ease each pincer under and backward to meet it, and pierce the tail shell near the base, on either side, with the stable prong of each pincer), symmetrically around the border, and sprinkle with the remaining dill.

THE SPRING STEW

In Provençal homes, a vegetable preparation is an automatic precedent to the roast, which most often is served ungarnished. The tradition is unknown to the rest of France, and Provençal restaurants do not maintain it—no doubt because a large part of their clientele is foreign to the region. It is a pity that it is not more widespread, if only as an occasional habit, for, not only is one obliged to treat the vegetables in a manner interesting enough for them to stand alone, but, unattended by meat, the palate not distracted by unrelated sauces, their purity and fragrance is thrown into relief, and because of their lightness, the course is an automatic relaxation point in a meal (perhaps more attractive to many modern-day gourmets than the archaic mid-menu sherbet or the somewhat barbaric *trou normand*, a straight shot of powerful Calvados thrown down halfway through a meal).

In addition to the vegetable trinity presented here, such ragoûts may be prepared from spring carrots, unpeeled garlic cloves, shredded lettuce, tender young peas, baby zucchini, celery hearts, the tender hearts of young bulb fennel, tiny turnips, cauliflower flowerets, etc., taking into consideration different cooking times and adding each accordingly at its right time). Onions should be omitted from none.

The savory finds its place in this recipe because of its particular affinity with broad beans, which in themselves are among the most delicate of all vegetables, but always gain by this marriage. In the past, broad beans figured, probably more often than any other vegetable, as an element in formal spring menus; the only possible explanation for their decline in popularity lies in their interminable preliminary preparation, for which there is no shortcut. Do not confuse broad beans and lima beans. Their only resemblance lies in a vague similarity of appearance.

Spring Stew

Ragoût Printanier

4 *pounds freshly picked young broad beans (Italian fave)*
12 *tiny artichokes (or* 6 *medium Artichokes, precooked—see page* 77)
1 *lemon*
30 *peeled whole new white onions, each about the size of a small walnut*
salt
6 *ounces butter*
2 *tablespoons water*
1 *teaspoon chopped fresh savory leaves, or a large pinch of dried savory*
chopped parsley

The broad beans must not only be shelled (pods removed), but, with the exception of the tiniest, whose skins remain a bright and tender green, the skin of each bean must be removed. This is a simple but tedious task: tear off a "cap" of skin with a thumbnail and press the other extremity of the bean between thumb and forefinger—the bean will slip out. Once skinned, any whose flesh is not tender and fresh green, but yellowing and pale of color, should be discarded or put aside for a soup.

Young artichokes, whose "chokes" remain undeveloped, should not be precooked, but simply "turned" (stems and outer leaves torn off, the upper half of the remaining leaves cut off, and the remainder pared slightly with a stainless steel knife to remove dark-green parts or tough extremities from the outer leaves), and plunged immediately into a bowl of water acidulated with the juice of a lemon.

Use an earthenware casserole or *poêlon* to ensure slow, even cooking and to avoid any metallic contact with the artichokes. Put the artichokes (whole, if chokeless, otherwise halved or quartered, depending on their size) and the onions, lightly salted, to cook, covered, in 1 ounce of butter (separate from direct flame by an asbestos pad), over low heat, shaking the receptacle from time to time. The vegetables should not color. After about 10 minutes, add the water (just enough to moisten the bottom), the broad beans and the savory. Dot the beans with about 2 ounces of butter cut into small pieces, sprinkle with salt, and continue to cook, tightly covered, over a tiny flame, for about 20 minutes, shaking and tossing the receptacle from time to time—avoid stirring so as not to break or crush the vegetables. At this point, the broad beans should remain intact, but crush easily beneath the slightest pressure, and no more than a couple of tablespoonfuls of slightly syrupy cooking liquid should remain. Should there be more, turn the flame high for a few moments, shaking the casserole gently. Remove from the heat and add the remaining butter cut into small pieces, tossing and swirling the contents until it is absorbed. Serve directly from the cooking utensil (if it is presentable), sprinkled with chopped parsley.

THE MOUSSELINE CHICKEN

In France, chickens are bled by thrusting a sharp instrument down the bird's throat. As a result, when bought at the market, the skin is absolutely intact. Chickens are kept in cold storage, but not directly on ice, so that the skin is dry and the flesh has not been drained of its flavor while being permeated with ice water. Happily, it is still practically impossible to find frozen chickens on the French market, although many, thanks to modern raising methods, have little quality other than that of freshness.

A chicken, to be prepared in the following manner, need not be killed *à la française*, but the skin from the base of the head down must be intact.

If the morels were not creamed, a sauce might accompany the chicken. Such a sauce would be based on the poaching liquid, reduced somewhat with some stiff *velouté* (stock thickened with *roux* and simmered and skimmed for at least 1/2 hour to give it body. Lightly tomatoed, or colored by the addition of good sweet red Hungarian paprika, the base becomes *sauce Aurore* (because of the "rose of dawn" hue); finished with egg yolks and cream, it is *suprème*; reduced with cream and meat glaze and finished with cream, it is *ivoire*. All these sauces are delicious—and rich. They are perfect with a garnish of rice or egg noodles, but would detract from the delicate purity of the morels, and the finesse of the mousseline would be masked as well. But there is no doubt that a poached chicken coated in a sauce affords a more impressive presentation.

The forcemeat, were the sauce not based on morels, might be enriched by the addition of chopped truffles, *duxelles*, or chopped morels first stewed in butter. A particularly pretty, clean-tasting and delicate variation involves the addition of tiny raw garden peas and broad beans and cubed, parboiled spring carrots. The preparation is then poetically termed "renaissance," an alternate appellation to *printanière*.

Chilled, either simply left in its terrine, embedded in its jelly, or decorated and coated with jelly (see Jellied Chicken, page 379), it is a perfect principal course for a summer luncheon.

The cooking utensil should be oval and as nearly as possible just the right size to hold the chicken comfortably, thus permitting it to be completely submerged in a minimum quantity of rich gelatinous stock.

Poached Chicken Mousseline

Poularde Pochée Mousseline

1 *large tender* (4–6 *months*) *roasting chicken*

Forcemeat:

breasts from a large chicken (*or* 3 *small chicken breasts*)—*about* 10 *ounces, skin and bones removed*
1 *egg white*
salt, freshly ground white pepper
a tiny bit of freshly grated nutmeg
a small handful of fresh, shelled pistachios
1¼ *cups heavy cream*

1 *lemon* (*juice*)

Poached Chicken Mousseline

Veal Stock (page 72), enriched by the addition of giblets, and carcass, etc., resulting from the boning of the chicken and chicken breasts
chopped parsley

BONING THE CHICKEN

But for the legs and wings, the chicken will be completely boned and the skin pierced at no point except for the slit down the back of the neck.

Singe the chicken, pass the feet, up to the drumstick joint, through an open flame, and remove the skin from the feet, grasping with a towel and pulling downward toward the claws, cut off the extremity of each central "toe" and remove the others. Cut off the wing tips at the second joint (leaving nothing but the small drumstick-like shoulder joint). If the head has not been removed, cut through the neck at the base of the head, slit the length of the neck skin down the back, carefully pull the skin, trachea and esophagus clear of the neck, and sever it at the first vertebra of the spinal column, cutting halfway through and twisting the neck off.

For the principal part of the boning, use a small, pointed, very sharp knife. The bulk of it will be done feeling one's way with fingertips, forcing the flesh away from the bones as one goes. The tip of the knife will serve in the face of resistance and, above all, for severing tendons at bone joints.

Pull the esophagus and trachea loose from the neck skin and loosen them, along with the connecting crop, from the throat entrance to the body cavity. There are 3 bones attached to each wing joint: one tip of the V-shaped "wishbone," the bone corresponding to the clavicle or collarbone, and that bone, the other end of which is free-floating in the flesh of the back, which corresponds to the shoulder blade. Remove, first, the wishbone; making a V-shaped incision with the point of the knife and touching the bone along its entire contour, cut through the tendons or ligaments that connect its pointed end to the skeletal structure, force the flesh loose from the 2 prongs with fingertips and fingernails, and pull it backward, tearing it loose from the wing joints. Remove the clavicles in the reverse sense, first slicing through the tendons connecting them to the wing joints, loosening adhering flesh, and pulling each upward and away from your person (the chicken is, automatically, on its back, legs pointed away from you, as you work) to tear it loose from its connection inside the body. Sever the attachment of each shoulder blade at the wing joint and, holding it firmly between the thumb and forefinger of the left hand, pull it out of the flesh with the other hand, thus forcing it clean of any clinging flesh. Reach inside the body cavity with the index finger, working all around the cavity walls in order to loosen the internal organs completely, then, gently pulling at crop and trachea, remove them by the throat orifice in one mass, taking care not to injure the gallbladder. Force the flesh loose from the breastbone, working along the crest with the point of the knife and forcing that at the sides loose with fingertips. With fingertips, loosen all the way around the rib cage, and finally, at the highest point of the breastbone, cut through the cartilage connecting it to the skin, being careful not to pierce the skin. Remove, in a single piece, the rib cage and connected breastbone.

With the aid of the knife tip, separate the spinal column from surrounding flesh until about the halfway point in the back. Force the flesh and skin loose from the wide, pelvis-like flat backbones to either side of the spinal column, being careful to work down into the shallow cavity to each side, forcing with the index fingernail, to separate the cushions of flesh known as "oysters," leaving them attached to the body of flesh and skin. Slice through the ligaments connecting the pelvic construction to the thigh joints (directly behind each "oyster") and force them loose. From mid-back to the tail, the spinal column is directly attached to the skin by a series of tiny tendons with no intervention of flesh. Pull the skin gently away from the spinal bones while, at the same time, slicing through the tendons, keeping the knife tip as close as possible to the bones so as to avoid piercing the skin. Having arrived at the base of the tail, cut through the spinal column, leaving the last couple of tiny vertebrae in the tail, and remove the remaining part of the carcass, still forcing with fingertips and knife point if there is any resistance. The chicken, at this point, is turned completely inside out. Turn it skin side out again, and put it aside until needed for stuffing.

NOTE: For a less elaborate boning method, see page 380.

THE FORCEMEAT

Prepare the Mousseline Forcemeat as explained on page 79, adding the pistachio nuts, skinned (dip them into boiling water for a minute, drain them, and rub them between two layers of towel to loosen the skins) and coarsely chopped, at the same time as the whipped cream.

Stuff the chicken without forcing (the forcemeat swells during the poaching and the flesh and skin contract somewhat), place it, breast down, neck skin spread out wide, fold the neck skin neatly and tightly over the back, and sew the chicken up, running the needle through the upper part of the wing, near the joint, next to and above the bone, then down through the neck-skin flap and the back, up through again on the other side, and back through the other wing. Return the needle in the same way, lower down toward the wing tips, and tie and clip the string ends. Turn the chicken onto its back and, with another length of string, transpierce the body, just beneath the joints connecting thighs and drumsticks, then return the needle, through the body and just beneath the bones toward the lower ends of the drumsticks; tie and clip the string ends.

Rub the entire surface with lemon juice, re-form the chicken, molding it in your hands, to its original shape, and place it, breast up, in its cooking utensil. Pour in enough veal stock, warmed only enough to be melted, to completely, but only just, submerge the chicken, bring it to a simmer over a medium heat, reduce the heat, and cook, covered, at just under a simmer, for 2 hours.

Remove it from the broth with the help of a wire skimming spoon (or 2) and present it on a large, preheated oval platter. When sprinkled with a ribbon of chopped parsley along the crest of the bird's breast and surrounded by the morel crusts, the presentation is much the prettiest, but the crusts should, in this case, be served out before the chicken is carved.

It may be carved in the traditional way or, wings and legs first removed, cut into cross-sectional slices about 2/3 inch thick. Serve a sauceboat of the cooking liquid separately.

THE CRUSTS WITH FRESH MORELS

There are different schools of thought concerning the superiority of the "white" (beige) or the "black" (dark brown) morel. Both are exquisite. The latter I have never encountered in the United States, but, during its short season (from 3 to 6 weeks depending on the year, the extreme limits being mid-March and mid-May), the white morel abounds, at least in certain areas of the Midwest, and, no doubt, in many other parts of the country. Novice collectors need not fear making a mistake—the spongelike shape of the morel is unique—but it should be remembered that raw, they are toxic. Fancy-food dealers in New York claim to have attempted their commercialization, but have been forced, through lack of interest, to abandon it. On the other hand fresh morels have been known to appear in neat cellophane packages in Des Moines supermarkets, so there is still hope for the future.

Morels share, with *cèpes* and the rare, orange-colored, egg-shaped "amanita of the Caesars," the distinction of being far finer than any other mushroom. Their delicacy of flavor permits of no complicated preparations. They are best simply stewed gently in butter and served just that way, or else creamed.

Although certain qualities are lost, the deep-freeze is nonetheless a boon to morel collectors. Stem ends should be trimmed and the morels should be split and washed rapidly but thoroughly beneath a jet of water to rid them of clinging earth or sand before being frozen. They should be put directly to stew in fresh, unsalted butter while still frozen.

The imported, dried morels, like dried *cèpes*, are useful as flavoring agents in sauces, terrines, etc., but resemble in no way the fresh product.

Crusts have mysteriously fallen from favor and are universally replaced today by the rich little *vol-au-vent* puff-pastry shells. It is a pity, for the texture, flavor and appearance of these nutty, brown-butter-flavored, crisp golden bread-crumb shells are all beautiful. They may be garnished with any number of preparations—scrambled eggs, sautéed kidneys, livers, etc.—and sometimes gain by being caressed with a clove of garlic, notably, when filled with a ragoût of fresh black truffles, prepared initially like those with fresh Noodles—page 203—a bit of Madeira added, bound by the addition of some meat glaze, and lightly buttered at the last minute. "Lids" of bread slices, crusts removed and treated like croutons, may be fitted over the tops.

It is possible, in certain American homes, where even bread is deep-frozen, to prepare good crusts from loaves of otherwise unmanageable light-as-a-feather American bread, by cutting it and putting it to cook in butter while still frozen.

Morels in crusts also provide a distinguished luncheon first course.

Crusts with Fresh Morels

Croûtes aux Morilles Fraîches

Crusts:

enough heavy, close-textured stale white bread in uncut loaves, crusts removed, to be cut into 6 sections, each about 2 inches thick
4–6 *ounces softened butter*

1 *pound fresh morels*
4 *tablespoons* (2 *ounces*) *butter*
salt, freshly ground white pepper
1 *cup heavy cream*
1 *tablespoon finely chopped chervil* (*or if unavailable, parsley*)

Hollow out each section of bread, leaving ½-inch-thick walls and bottom: Using a small, sharp, pointed knife, cut down, all around the sides, ½ inch in from the edge, without penetrating all the way to the bottom, then, ½ inch from the bottom, pierce one side and cut through the inside crumb in a swivel fashion, the point of entry serving as axis, without widening the slit. The inside section of crumb may then easily be lifted out, any uncut extremities tearing loose without damaging the shell. Spread hollowed-out slices generously, inside and out, with butter and put them to color in a slow oven, keeping an eye on them and turning them regularly to ensure their being evenly colored on all sides and no darker than a rich gold at any point. They may, if necessary, be prepared somewhat ahead of time and rewarmed in the oven.

Trim the stem tips of the morels, split each in two and rinse it rapidly beneath a strong jet of water. Sponge them dry between two towels and in a heavy saucepan over a low flame stew gently in butter, seasoned with salt, for about 10 minutes, regularly tossing and stirring with a wooden spoon. Add about 2/3 of the cream, reduce over a high dame, stirring, until it thickens and clings to the mushrooms, remove from the flame, taste for salt, sprinkle with pepper, and stir in remaining cream. Fill the crusts and serve, a pinch of chopped chervil topping each.

THE PINEAPPLE SURPRISE

A surprise anything, culinarily speaking, is, of course, something whose exterior does not prepare one's guests for its contents.

Pineapple marries well with other acid fruits, and in particular with strawberries, raspberries, and orange juice (which may, if one likes, replace the raspberry purée in this recipe). Kirsch or other liqueurs are often added to the maceration liquid, but for many, this sophistication destroys the purity of the fruit.

Pineapple Surprise

Ananas en Surprise

1 *large, ripe pineapple*
1 *pint small, ripe strawberries (or wild strawberries)*
1/2 *cup of sugar (or to taste)*
1 *pint fresh (or frozen) raspberries, puréed*

Cut in and downward at an angle around the top of the pineapple to remove a lid, cut out the flesh from the lid, and discard the core. Cut deeply down and circularly around the core in the main body of the pineapple, and as far down as possible without piercing the shell, all the way around, about 1/2 to 2/3 inch in from the outside. Cut a series of "spokes" between the two circular incisions and force the sections loose with your fingers, emptying out the remaining flesh with a spoon, crushing it as little as possible. Cut inward all around the base of the core (because of its awkward position, it is not possible to slice it cleanly across), break it off at its base and discard it. Scrape the inside of the shell clean with a tablespoon and put the lid and the shell to chill (if the shell has accidentally been pierced, freeze it. This will prevent leakage during the serving). Put aside any mashed pineapple and the juice for another use.

Cut the pineapple flesh into cubes, pick over the strawberries, wash them rapidly, drain them, add them to the pineapple cubes, sprinkle with sugar, and store, covered, in the refrigerator until just before serving. Fill the shell, without packing, with the macerated fruits and pour the raspberry purée over. The pineapple may be served half embedded in cracked ice, which is attractive, ensures its remaining chilled for a second service, and facilitates the service by stabilizing the fruit.

Two Informal Spring Dinners

with appropriate wines

MENU I (FOR 6)

HORS D'OEUVRE OF RAW VEGETABLES
[CRUDITES]

A light, young white wine, neither too dry nor too rich: Pouilly-Fumé, Pouilly-Fuissé, Châteauneuf-du-Pape, Savennières, etc.

SHRIMP QUICHE
[QUICHE AUX CREVETTES]

The same wine as the preceding

CHICKEN IN RED WINE
[COQ AU VIN]

A 4- or 5-year-old Burgundy, neither from a very great year nor a very great vineyard (Côte de Beaune, Nuits-Saint-Georges, Fixin, etc.) or a Touraine red wine (Chinon, Bourgueuil). Should be served cool, but not chilled

STEAMED POTATOES
[POMMES DE TERRE A LA VAPEUR]

WILD GREEN SALAD

[SALADE SAUVAGE]

CHEESES

[FROMAGES]

The same as the preceding, or a greater Burgundy from an older vintage: Côte de Nuits (Chambertin, Bonnes Mares, Vosne-Romanée, Echezeaux, etc.)

FLAMRI WITH RASPBERRY SAUCE

[FLAMRI A LA PUREE DE FRAMBOISES]

A Sauternes

Practically speaking, the presentation of this menu is extremely simple, for nearly everything may be prepared in advance: the *coq au vin* must be put to warm, eggs and cream beaten and the quiche put to bake one hour before going to table, and the potatoes put to steam just before the guests are seated—nothing more.

The visual succession is exciting, as it progresses from the tender, natural garden colors of the *crudités* through the delicate pinks and creams of the quiche, masked by a golden gratin, and the rich, bitter-chocolate-colored velvet of the *coq au vin* sauce, thrown into relief by the green of the parsley and the white potatoes, the deep greens of the salad—which, in season, may be enhanced, both in appearance and taste, by the addition of a handful of brilliantly colored nasturtium flowers—and the pale yellow and cool, transparent red of the *flamri*, recalling, to some extent, the quiche, but with more fantasy and sharper relief. The pale green, ruby, and deep gold of the wines enrich the effect.

The *crudités*, fresh and clean, sharpen the appetite. They do nothing for a wine, but as one's guests' glasses should never be empty, the simplest solution is to serve the same wine that will accompany the quiche. The quiche is delicate in flavor and light in effect. If it were not followed by a rich sauce, it might be accompanied by one, but it stands well without and marries beautifully with a young, fruity white wine.

The high point, culinarily speaking, is the rich and robust main dish, the quality of whose sauce holds the key to the essential success of the meal. It would kill a wine that is elaborate with the nuances of age—therefore, the wine climax follows with the cheeses.

The *flamri* is light. It is refined without being sophisticated, and above all, it is not rich. The Sauternes, though rich, is so totally different in character from the entire gamut of preceding wines that it, too, refreshes, cleanses and relaxes a jaded palate.

THE CRUDITES

Crudités can be any combination of fresh, tender, young raw vegetables: tiny, white heads of cauliflower, little radishes, the small, elongated, light green, sweet Italian peppers, peeled and grated (or better, passed through the medium blade of a *mouli-julienne*), hearts of celery, cherry tomatoes, scallions (if they are not too strong), bulb fennel, Belgian endives, avocados (the tiny, seedless variety, recently developed, provides a very pretty element in a *crudités* still-life presentation). Among the most delicate of *crudités* are very young broad beans (*fèves*, often known in America by their Italian name, *fave*), and violet artichokes, picked before the choke is developed. The former are eaten simply with coarse salt, and the latter with vinaigrette or simply with salt, pepper and olive oil. Both are greatly appreciated in the south of France, where every morning in the beautiful outdoor markets, lines of rough and picturesque ladies try to outbellow each other to sell their freshly picked vegetables *du pays*. The first native *fèves* each year, toward the end of January, bring astounding prices, and it is considered a sacrilege to cook them. In Italy both *fave* and tiny artichokes are often eaten after the main course as a salad replacement, the broad beans sometimes in conjunction with cheese. Both are difficult to find in American markets, but could easily be grown in our more temperate climates.

Crudités should be accompanied by slices of rough peasant bread (in America, where such bread is not easily come by, Jewish sourdough rye bread, although too pronounced in flavor for many dishes, accompanies this kind of thing well), fresh unsalted butter, coarse salt (sea salt, if available), fruity olive oil and wine vinegar.

THE SHRIMP QUICHE

The shrimp and the pastry may be prepared and the pastry shell partly baked several hours in advance, which leaves nothing to be done at

Spring Menus the last minute except to beat together the eggs and cream and put the quiche to bake.

The preliminary shrimp preparation is identical to that of crayfish (*écrevisses*) *à la bordelaise*, which in itself is a fine dish. It is a great pity that in the United States the heads of the shrimp are discarded before they appear on the market, for they contain flavor and material enough to produce a splendid sauce.

Where no fresh seafood is available, frozen shrimp, although never as succulent as the fresh, may serve as a replacement. Do not boil them as recommended on the package, but simply plunge them into cold water to defrost them, sponge them dry in a towel, and proceed as for the others.

Shrimp Quiche

Quiche aux Crevettes

The pastry:

2/3 cup all-purpose flour
pinch of salt
6 tablespoons (3 ounces) butter
2 1/2–3 tablespoons cold water

After sifting the flour and salt into a bowl, you may mix in the butter with your fingers, as do the French, or cut it with knives in the American manner. The essential things to remember are:

1. The butter should be cold and firm so that it does not mash into a purée in the flour. Cut it into pieces before adding it.

2. The dough should be worked as rapidly and as little as possible. Stop the moment you have a pebbled mixture in which the largest pebbles are the size of small peas.

3. The more butter that can be incorporated into the flour, the finer the pastry—flours differ.

4. Add only enough cold water to transform it into an adherent mass, working it deftly and no more than necessary with a fork.

5. Wrap it in wax paper or a plastic bag and leave it for a couple of hours in the refrigerator, so that it may relax and lose its elasticity.

Shrimp Quiche

The pastry takes 2 or 3 minutes to prepare and somewhat less time to roll out.

Flour the ball of dough on a floured board and form it into a patty. Roll it out rapidly. Be certain that the board and the upper surface of the paste remain well floured, turning it over on the board 3 or 4 times during the process to ensure this. Fold the sheet of pastry in two, pick it up gently at the folded edge, drop it gently, once, on the board to rid it of excess flour and slip it into pie dish or tart mold. If you have only American pie tins, it couldn't make less difference—the presentation is not less attractive. Press the dough to the form of the mold and trim the pastry all around the edge, leaving an excess of about 1/2 inch. If, through inexperience, your pastry sheet was not altogether circular, there may be a skimpy point or two at the edge—it is very simple to moisten the edge of a piece of trimming and attach it to the short edge of the pastry. Roll the outer edge under, press it to the border all the way around, and "scallop" it with the side of your thumb, dipped repeatedly in flour. Prick the inside in several places with a fork, line the pastry with a round of kitchen paper or light aluminum foil, pour in enough dried beans, lentils or raw rice to provide sufficient weight to prevent the crust from buckling, and partly bake it for 15 minutes in a medium oven—350°–375° F. Remove the weighted paper and return the shell to the oven for 3 or 4 minutes to dry it out. Put it aside.

The shrimp:

- *2 tablespoons Mirepoix (page 74), or 1 medium carrot, 1 medium onion, thyme, bay leaf, salt, pepper, 2 tablespoons butter*
- *3/4 pound fresh small shrimp*
- *1 tablespoon olive oil*
- *salt, pepper*
- *1 pinch Cayenne pepper*
- *1 tablespoon cognac*
- *1/2 cup dry white wine*
- *1/2 cup heavy cream*

If you have no *mirepoix* on hand, it should be prepared in advance as described on page 75.

Rinse the shrimp and sponge them dry in a towel. Do not shell them.

Heat the oil in a *sauteuse* or frying pan, add the shrimp and the *mirepoix*, salt, pepper and Cayenne, tossing and stirring with a wooden spoon over a high flame until the shrimp has turned pink on all sides. Add the cognac, light it and continue stirring until the flames are extinguished, add the white wine and reduce until the liquid has nearly disappeared. Put aside to cool.

Shell the shrimp, leaving the tail segment of the shell attached to 10 or 12 of them (depending on their size) and pound the shells in a mortar. Stir into the pounded shells 1/2 cup of cream, transfer to a small saucepan, bring to a boil, then pass the mixture through a fine sieve, working the residue well with a wooden pestle in order to extract all the flavorful—and colorful—juices. Reserve.

Arrange the shrimp with the tail segments around the edge of the pastry shell so that they lean against the side with the tail tips protruding above the border of the shell. Cut the rest of the shrimp into pieces and distribute them in an even layer on the bottom of the shell.

The quiche batter:

3 *eggs*
salt, freshly ground pepper
1 *cup heavy cream*
1 *small handful freshly grated Swiss Gruyère*

Combine in a bowl the eggs, salt, freshly ground pepper, the reserved shrimp-flavored cream and the additional cup of cream, beat together with a rotary beater, pour the mixture into the pastry shell, sprinkle the surface with cheese and bake in a moderate oven (350°–375° F.) for approximately 1/2 hour. The quiche is done when the center of the custard is firm. It may be left in the oven with the door ajar for 1/2 hour or so before serving—and it is better warm than hot.

THE COQ AU VIN

The *coq au vin* usually found, whether in cookbooks, in restaurants, or in the home, is a red-wine stew made from young fryer-type chickens. It is not a bad dish when properly done; but it is only logical that a bird no more than 2 months old, though perfect for a sauté (in which flavor, through a fairly rapid cooking process, is concentrated in the seared flesh) should be less satisfactory in a dish whose qualities depend on the flavor and gelatinous material which, over an extended cooking period, may be drawn from the meat into a reduced and concentrated sauce. A *coq au vin* prepared in a Burgundy peasant (which does not mean poor) kitchen is made from a year-old cock, neither too tough nor too tender, that has lived in liberty and been liberally fed on grain. (This beast, incidentally, is no easier to find in a Paris market than in New York.) Its sauce is a concentration of essences that, at the ultimate point of refinement, no more than coats the pieces of chicken, and that depends uniquely on its natural gelatin and the body of the aromatic elements for the thickening—no flour.

The recipe that I give you is a compromise. If you are a farmer or have farmer friends, you may have no trouble finding the perfect bird. If you are obliged to use young, commercially raised chickens, there are several points to bear in mind:

1. Replace the large bird by 2 smaller ones—or buy parts and use only leg and thigh sections, which lend themselves better to this type of preparation than do breasts.

2. Replace half the red wine by a rich gelatinous Veal Stock (page 72) or veal-and-chicken stock.

3. Do not overcook the chicken—30 or 40 minutes is enough, but reduce the sauce radically after having passed it through a sieve.

A *coq au vin* is at least as good reheated, which is obviously an advantage. You have only to add the garnish, gently reheat it and leave it to barely simmer for 15 or 20 minutes before serving it.

Chicken in Red Wine

Coq au Vin

2 *strips lean side pork, salted or smoked, approximately* 2/3 *inch thick*
3 *medium-sized carrots*
3 *medium-sized onions*
1 *bird, preferably a cock weighing around* 6 *pounds,* 10–12 *months old, cut into serving pieces*
salt and pepper

(*Continued*)

2 tablespoons flour
1 bouquet garni (thyme, bay leaf, parsley)
1/4 cup cognac
1 bottle good red wine (the same as served as accompaniment, for instance)

Garnish:
1/2 pound mushrooms
butter (5 or 6 ounces in all)
salt and pepper
25–30 *small white onions*
6 slices firm-textured white bread for croutons
1 clove garlic
chopped parsley

Cut off the rind from the side pork and cut each strip in 2/3-inch sections. Parboil them for 2 minutes, drain, and sponge them dry in a towel. Put them to fry, over a low flame, in a large *sauteuse* or skillet with a bit of oil (butter is nearly always called for, but it makes absolutely no difference—none of its flavor remains, and it is actually skimmed off and discarded at a later stage). When the strips are golden brown on all sides, remove them and put them aside. In the same cooking fat place the carrots, peeled and cut into 1- or 2-inch sections, and the onions, peeled and cut into pieces or coarsely chopped. Keep the flame medium to low and allow them to cook, stirring regularly to avoid overbrowning, for 20–30 minutes. Remove the vegetables, put them aside and replace them by the chicken pieces, previously salted and peppered. Cook them over a somewhat higher flame until gently browned on all sides, sprinkle with flour and continue to cook, turning the pieces as necessary. Return the sautéed onions and carrots to the pan. When the flour has cooked for a few minutes, pour in the cognac, then the wine and raise the heat. Stir the chicken pieces and move them around until the liquid comes to a boil. At this point, unless you are working with a very large, heavy pan, in which all the chicken may remain and continue cooking over a tiny flame, everything may suddenly seem complicated and messy. Don't worry about it. If the skillet is already overfull of the chicken, or if perhaps you have had to use 2 skillets that both seem too full to permit adding the vegetables, keep the carrots and onions aside and add them later when the chicken goes into the oven dish. Transfer the chicken pieces and vegetables to an oven dish of some sort (earthenware, copper, enameled cast-iron casserole, etc.) with a lid, add the *bouquet garni* (or simply sprinkle with thyme leaves and add the bay leaf and parsley branches untied). Stir and scrape the pan with a wooden spoon to loosen and dissolve the frying adherents. Pour the liquid over the chicken pieces. If they are not entirely covered, add enough wine, water or good stock (water is better than indifferent stock) to barely, but completely, cover them. Put to cook, covered, in the oven, regulating the heat so that the sauce hardly simmers. The length of cooking time depends altogether on the bird's age and "past"—from 30 minutes for a fryer that has never exercised to 1½ hours for a 10-month-old rooster, and still an hour longer for one that may be too old to have a fine flesh but will produce a marvelous sauce.

Meanwhile, wash the mushrooms rapidly and sponge them dry. If they are small, leave them whole, otherwise cut each in 2 or 4 pieces. Toss them in butter over a high flame, seasoned with salt and freshly ground pepper, for 2 or 3 minutes. Peel the little onions, leaving them whole, and cook them, seasoned, in butter over a very low flame, shaking the pan from time to time, for 20–30 minutes. Keep them covered and avoid browning them—if the saucepan is not heavy enough, you may have to use an asbestos pad over the flame.

Transfer the chicken pieces and the carrots to a platter, discard the discernible remains of the *bouquet garni* and skim as much fat from the surface as possible. Pass the cooking liquid through a very fine sieve, using a wooden pestle to work it, pour it into a saucepan, bring it to a boil, then place the saucepan over the flame so as to permit its contents to simmer only on one side. A skin will begin to appear on the surface containing fat plus other impurities. Carefully pull it to one side with a spoon, remove it and discard it. Repeat this process regularly for approximately ½ hour. This skimming process, in French called *dépouillement*, is too often avoided because it is time-consuming and boring. It is, however, essential to the purity and digestibility of the sauce. If, at this point, the sauce is still not consistent enough, turn the fire up to create a rapid boil and reduce it rapidly to the right consistency, stirring constantly.

Replace the chicken pieces in the oven dish, distribute the garnish (sautéed mushrooms, glazed little onions, and fried side pork sections) on top and pour the sauce over. Cover and return to the oven to simmer gently for 15–30 minutes.

Trim the crusts from the bread slices, cut slices in half diagonally and brown them in butter over a low flame until golden and crisp. They will absorb an astonishing quantity of butter. They may be prepared ahead of time and rewarmed in the oven.

To serve, dispose the chicken pieces more or less symmetrically on a large, heated platter. Rub the crouton triangles with the clove of garlic, dip one corner of each in the sauce, then in chopped parsley, and arrange them around the edge of the platter, parslied tips pointing out, pour sauce and garnish over the chicken and sprinkle with a bit of chopped parsley. Serve the steamed potatoes separately.

THE FLAMRI WITH RASPBERRY SAUCE

A *flamri*, to my way of thinking, is a perfect type of dessert. It is light, simple, full of nuances, and not rich. The quality and personality of the wine used in its preparation remains to an amazing degree in the final product. Its presentation is attractive and admits endless fantasies. I usually prefer to prepare it in the simplest type of mold (charlotte), but sometimes I do it in a series of decorative molds of different sizes, unmold one on top of the other in a tiered fashion, and decorate with—in addition to the raspberry purée—whipped cream into which a certain amount of raspberry purée has been incorporated, and a few whole raspberries. An apricot sauce accompanies it equally well.

Flamri with Raspberry Sauce

Flamri à la Purée de Framboises

1 *cup water*
1 *cup good dry white wine*
1/2 *cup* (4 *ounces*) *fine semolina*
3/4 *cup sugar*

small pinch of salt
1 *egg*
3 *egg whites*
butter
1 *pint fresh raspberries* (*or* 1 *package frozen*)
sugar to taste

Combine the water and the wine in a saucepan and bring them to a boil. Sprinkle in the semolina in a slow stream and from well above the saucepan, stirring all the time with a wooden spoon. Leave, covered, to cook gently for 25 minutes. (I have never tried the quick-cooking or "minute" products—they are probably satisfactory if you cannot find the other.) Remove from the fire and mix in immediately (if you leave it to stand, a skin forms rapidly on the surface) the sugar, the salt and the whole egg. Beat the egg whites until stiff and fold them delicately into the mixture. Pour it into a buttered mold, cover with a round of buttered kitchen paper, and poach in a *bain-marie* for 40 minutes (a *bain-marie* in this instance may be either a large saucepan with a tight-fitting lid containing enough hot water to reach the 2/3 mark on the mold, kept over a low flame on top of the stove, or an open receptacle containing an equivalent amount of hot water and placed in a medium oven). The water should be close to the boiling point but not allowed to boil during the poaching process.

Allow the pudding to cool until lukewarm, then unmold it onto the serving dish (if it is allowed to chill completely before unmolding, it will stick to the mold), but leave the mold over the pudding to protect it from the air until just before serving, chilled and coated with raspberry sauce. Serve a sauceboat of raspberry purée separately.

For the raspberry purée, pass the raspberries through a fine sieve, preferably nonmetallic (nylon), and add sugar to taste. When fresh raspberries are in season, they should, of course, be used, but, in fact, frozen raspberries are one of the few frozen products that I have found to be altogether satisfactory.

Two Informal Spring Dinners

with appropriate wines

MENU II (FOR 4)

MARINATED RAW SARDINE FILLETS

[FILETS DE SARDINES CRUES EN MARINADE]

A slightly sharp, very dry white wine: Muscadet, Quincy, Pouilly-sur-Loire (Chasselas), etc.

GRILLED STEAK, MARCHAND DE VIN

[GRILLADE DE BOEUF, MARCHAND DE VIN]

A hearty, fruity, young, cool red wine: Beaujolais de cru, Chinon, Saumur-Champigny, Mercurey

GRATIN OF POTATOES

[GRATIN DE POMMES DE TERRE]

FIELD SALAD

[SALADE DES CHAMPS]

CHEESES

[FROMAGES]

The same as the preceding or a Burgundy from either the Côte de Beaune or the Côte de Nuits

APPLE TART

[TARTE AUX POMMES]

A Sauternes

THE MARINATED SARDINE FILLETS

Fresh sardines are stiff, often arched, and glossy in appearance. Their scales reflect a bright metallic blue. They must be absolutely fresh. French fishermen delight in eating them straight from the net, with or without a drop of lemon juice, but preferably accompanied by a bottle of cold white wine.

Marinated raw, they have a frank, clean savor and are more easily digestible than when cooked. The flesh is fragile and so little resistant that they may easily be cleaned simply by tearing out the intestines with one's forefinger, and may be scaled by holding under water and rubbing them from tail to head with the fingers. The fillets may be pried from the skeleton without recourse to a knife.

Marinated Raw Sardine Fillets

Filets de Sardines Crues en Marinade

12 *fresh sardines, filleted*
salt, freshly ground pepper
juice of 2 lemons

Rinse the fillets, sponge them dry in paper towels, salt them and pepper them on each side, and sprinkle the lemon juice over, turning them so that all are evenly moistened. Leave them for several hours or overnight, turning them from time to time, and serve well chilled, accompanied by rye bread and firm, fresh, unsalted butter.

Grilled Steak, Marchand de Vin

Grillade de Boeuf, Marchand de Vin

The commonest cuts of steak in France are taken from the fillet (Chateaubriand and *tournedos*, the tenderest cuts), the rump (rump steak, the most flavorful cut), the section of the sirloin opposite the fillet (called either *contrefilet* or *faux-filet*), and the boned rib section (*entrecôte*, the cut traditionally accompanied by *marchand de vin butter*).

Whether the meat is cut in the French or the American manner, it should come from an animal that is not too young, it should be finely, but not excessively, veined with fat, it must be fresh and not frozen, but sufficiently aged to have gained in tenderness, juiciness and flavor. To be properly grilled, a steak should not be less than 1 inch nor more than 2½ inches thick. Allow approximately ½ pound, boned, per person. It may be lightly sprinkled with herbs and marinated with a bit of olive oil for a couple of hours or so before cooking. It should, in any case, always be rubbed with oil before grilling, sprinkled with salt and pepper on the side first to be grilled, just before placing it on the hot grill, and, on the other, just after turning it.

Steaks may be grilled on heavy cast-iron grills, preheated over a gas flame, or, if very thick, beneath a broiler, but by far the best way of grilling is on a preheated welded-iron grill over hot fruitwood (best of all, grapevine prunings) coals—these should be hotter and the grilling time comparatively shorter than for other meats, but the thicker the steak, the less intense the heat should be. A handful of rosemary leaves thrown into the coals (they will smoke without bursting into flames), a few seconds before removing the meat, enhances the flavor.

The French say that a steak is *à point* ("just right"—the equivalent of medium rare) when, once having been turned, the first "pearl" of transparent, rose-colored liquid oozes up through the seared surface. If it is then removed from the grill and kept warm for a few minutes (on the heated serving platter, for instance, a heated bowl or saucepan inverted above it, or in a warm but not hot oven), the flesh will continue to cook without becoming overdone. Although some people fear rare meat and others require that a steak be *bleu*, that is to say, both sides so rapidly seared that the heat is not permitted to penetrate the interior, an overdone steak is always dry and savorless, and one that is underdone is always rubbery and resistant. (Raw beef can be delicious, but must be prepared in the manner of steak *à l'américaine*: the steak, completely cleared of all fat, is scraped to separate the flesh from all tendons or membranous material and finely chopped. It is usually served with a half eggshell containing a yolk implanted in the center of each portion, and surrounded by small mounds of parsley, sour gherkins, onions and capers, all finely chopped. Olive oil, salt, pepper and sometimes Worcestershire sauce are served separately, and each person doses his mixture to taste. It is nearly always called "steak *tartare*," which technically is raw, chopped beef accompanied by tartar sauce.)

A steak *marchand de vin* is served with the *marchand de vin* butter apart, and each guest spreads a spoonful over his steak. On restaurant menus, *marchand de vin* often indicates a pan-fried steak sauced by sautéing chopped shallots in the pan in which the steak was cooked, washing the pan with red wine and lightly buttering the reduction, which is sometimes strengthened by the addition of meat glaze.

Other "butters" often served with grilled beef are: Bercy (the same as *marchand de vin*, except that white wine replaces the red), chivry (see Grilled Lambs' Kidneys, page 390), *maître d'hôtel* (chopped parsley, seasoning, and lemon juice, mashed with butter), anchovy butter, etc. Except for *sauce béarnaise* (see Stuffed Calves' Ears, page 231), which is served separately, grilled meats are rarely accompanied by sauce, pan-fried or sautéed steaks lending themselves better to this treatment.

MARCHAND DE VIN BUTTER

If meat glaze is on hand, a tablespoonful, melted, may be added to the butter. The butter may be prepared in advance, but should be served semisoft and not chilled.

3/4 cup good red wine
1 *tablespoon finely chopped gray shallot (if unavailable, replace it with onion plus a small, finely chopped clove of garlic)*
salt to taste
a generous pinch of freshly ground pepper
6 *ounces softened butter*
1 *tablespoon lemon juice*
1 *tablespoon chopped parsley*

Reduce the wine and chopped shallot, in a small saucepan over a high flame, to about 1/3 cup, pour it into a mixing bowl and, when it is just tepid, whisk it vigorously with all the other ingredients.

THE POTATO GRATIN

This differs from the classic *gratin à la dauphinoise* only in that in the latter the potatoes are finely sliced. The potatoes are often mixed raw with the other ingredients and put directly in the oven, but one must then count from 45 minutes' to 1 hour's cooking time at medium heat, and the gentle caress of fresh garlic is lost. The potatoes may also (as in the following recipe) be first parboiled in milk. The milk may be replaced by cream in the baking process (the milk serves later for a soup or *béchamel*).

Gratin of Potatoes

Gratin de Pommes de Terre

2 cloves garlic
butter
2 pounds nonmealy potatoes
3 cups milk
1 eggs
salt, freshly ground pepper, a suspicion of freshly grated nutmeg
about 1 cup grated Gruyère cheese (the dry, nutty-flavored Swiss Gruyère, not Emmenthal)

Choose a large shallow earthenware baking or gratin dish. Earthenware, when rubbed with garlic, "takes" it better than any other material and, the larger the dish, the greater will be the surface of the delicious gratin and the more rapidly will the thinner bed of potatoes cook, keeping the perfume of the garlic fresher.

Rub the sides and bottom well with the garlic cloves, wait a couple of minutes for the garlic moisture to dry, and generously butter the dish. Peel the potatoes, pass them through the medium julienne blade of a *mouli-julienne*, rinse them well in a large basin of cold water, and drain them. Bring the milk, lightly salted, to a boil and parboil the potatoes for about 5 minutes. Pour the contents of the saucepan into a sieve, collecting the milk in another receptacle, beat the egg, a pinch of salt, the pepper, nutmeg, and half the grated cheese together in a mixing bowl, and slowly pour in the milk, whisking. Stir the potatoes into the mixture and pour it into the baking dish, smoothing out the surface. Sprinkle with the remaining cheese, distribute paper-thin slices of butter, cut from a chilled block, evenly over the surface, and bake in a hot oven for 15 to 20 minutes, or until the potatoes are cooked and the surface crisp and golden. Should the potatoes be cooked before the gratin is sufficiently formed, place the dish beneath the broiler for a minute or so to brown.

Apple Tart

Tarte aux Pommes

1 *half-baked pastry shell (same ingredients and preparation as for Shrimp Quiche, page* 306)
1 *pound cooking apples, preferably russet, peeled, cored and sliced*
4 *tablespoons* (2 *ounces*) *butter*
pinch of cinnamon
2 *eggs*
1/2 *cup sugar*
1 *cup heavy cream*

Cook the apple slices gently in butter until tender and translucent, but not falling apart (aside from their unique perfume, russets hold their shape best); line the bottom of the pastry shell with the slices and sprinkle lightly with cinnamon.

Beat the eggs and sugar together until the yellow color lightens, stir in the cream, and pour the mixture over the apples. Bake in a medium oven until the custard has set and the crust is golden. Serve warm, but not hot.

Four Simple Spring Menus

All of these menus will, ideally, be accompanied by a single, simple, young red wine (Beaujolais, Côtes-du-Rhône, Cahors, Bandol).

MENU I (FOR 6)

BOILED BEEF WITH VEGETABLES

[POT-AU-FEU]

FIELD SALAD

[SALADE SAUVAGE]

CHEESES

[FROMAGES]

FRESH FRUITS

[FRUITS]

THE POT-AU-FEU

"In France, the *pot-au-feu* is the symbol of family life. . . . A good *pot-au-feu* will always be a comfortable and thoroughly bourgeois dish which nothing may dethrone."—Escoffier: *Ma Cuisine*

If any single preparation merits being termed the French national dish, it is *pot-au-feu*. Technically the word means nothing more than "stewpot" and was originally the pot of soup kept at the back of the stove from one end of the year to the other, regularly supplemented by bones, vegetables, water, meats, etc., to provide a family's daily sustenance. A handsome piece of meat, if the family could afford it, was added on Sundays.

It has long since come to mean boiled beef ("poached" would be more accurate) and vegetables, and there are regional variations: in Provence, mutton is added, elsewhere a hen, often stuffed with rice, may be thrown in (it may then be called *petite marmite*), and veal sometimes lends a more gelatinous quality to the broth). No soup is more succulent than the amber broth, unclarified and imperfectly degreased and poured over dried bread crusts, from a beef *pot-au-feu*.

Pot-au-feu is a meal in itself, and unless it has been prepared specifically with the notion of using the bouillon for another preparation (in which case, the meats and vegetables may be preceded by a simple hors d'oeuvre, but should in any case be accompanied by enough bouillon to moisten them), it would be an error to attempt to correlate it with other dishes.

A perfect bouillon depends, among other things, on the meat's being started in cold water (as low in calcium content as possible—if your tap water is very hard, it is well worth while collecting rainwater or using clean-tasting, bottled mineral water). But the meats, to guard their succulence, should be plunged directly into boiling liquid. Logically, then, a perfect *pot-au-feu* must really be two: the first, begun cold, produces the basic broth; the second, moistened with the boiling broth, permits the meats to retain their maximum qualities.

Cabbage greatly enriches the garnish and, in itself, is never better than when braised in the fat bouillon skimmed from a *pot-au-feu*. Because of its distinctive flavor, it should always be cooked separately so as not to destroy the delicacy of the soup (the cabbage's leftover cooking liquid moistens to perfection a partridge braised with cabbage—see page 155). In the past, a parsnip (*panais*—a vegetable practically unknown in France today) always lent its unique, sweet flavor to the bouillon of a *pot-au-feu*.

Oxtail is an economical cut and lends a fine rich quality to the bouillon. None of the other cuts recommended are irreplaceable, but at least one must be gelatinous (in this instance, the heel—those cuts, known in French as *macreuse* and *paleron*, both from the chuck section, are also excellent gelatinous cuts) and another interlarded.

Leftover *pot-au-feu* meats lose their firmness and savor if allowed to stand in the bouillon. If they are to be used in other preparations, they should be drained and stored separately, covered with a plate. Possibilities for using leftover boiled beef are endless. Simply sliced and served cold, sprinkled with coarse salt, it is delicious—or prepared *à la vinaigrette* as a first course. Perhaps the commonest of the hot preparations is *miroton*: Sautéed onions are sprinkled with flour, moistened with bouillon and vinegar—a couple of tablespoonfuls of the latter for 1½ cups of bouillon—and simmered for 15 minutes with a pinch of herbs; they are then poured over the slices of beef, which have first been arranged in a gratin dish and sprinkled with capers and sliced sour gherkins. The surface is sprinkled with bread crumbs, dotted with butter and gratinéed in a gentle oven.

An earthenware *pot-au-feu* or *marmite* or one of enameled cast iron are perfect cooking vessels. Lacking either, use the largest pot of any kind available—12 to 15 quarts. Leave out any ingredients you can't get, but do not forgo trying a *pot-au-feu*.

Boiled Beef with Vegetables

Pot-au-Feu

The preliminary bouillon:

1 pound carrots
3 large onions, 1 stuck with 3 cloves

(*Continued*)

1 parsnip
1 unpeeled whole head of garlic
1 handful dried mushrooms—cèpes (wild mushrooms), if available
1 or 2 oxtails (about 4 pounds), cut into sections and tied firmly together
1 heaping teaspoon thyme or mixed herbs (if branch thyme is available, incorporate in the bouquet below instead)
1 bouquet containing: parsley stems, leaves and roots, 1 large branch celery, 2 bay leaves, and green parts of 1½ pounds small spring leeks (the whites of which will serve in the 2nd preparation)
1 handful coarse salt (sea salt, if available, or kosher salt)

The pot-au-feu:
3 pounds heel (or preferably a piece cut from heel and bottom round, together), boned, but kept in 1 piece, tied up
about 2½ pounds short ribs, in 3 pieces, tied firmly together
2 small green cabbages
1 pound small spring turnips
1 pound small spring carrots
white part of the 1½ pounds of leeks used in earlier preparation
1 apple

Accompaniments at table:
slices of dried-out French-type bread
grated cheese (Parmesan or half Parmesan, half Gruyère)
dish of coarse salt
Dijon-type mustard (and/or horseradish)
sour gherkins or small dill pickles

THE PRELIMINARY BOUILLON

It is practical, but not necessary, to prepare this bouillon the preeeding day.

The vegetables should be peeled but left whole, the green parts of the leeks slit and washed thoroughly while still attached to the whites, the parsley roots scraped, and the dried mushrooms put to soak in a bowl of cold water.

Place the oxtail in the bottom of the *pot-au-feu* pot, pour water over, and bring to a boil over a medium flame (if earthenware is used, it should be protected by an asbestos pad; the flame may be turned high because of the slowness with which the pad absorbs the heat). As the boil approaches, begin to skim off the rising gray scum, add a glass of cold water, and continue skimming as more rises to the surface. Repeat this procedure several times, adding some cold water each time the liquid arrives at a pronounced boil.

Drain the mushrooms, rinse them well, pare any stem tips to which sand or earth still cling, and add them, along with all the other ingredients, to the pot. As the boil approaches again, skim once more and, over a period of 10 to 15 minutes, regulate the heat until assured that a bare simmer will be steadily maintained, the liquid's surface hardly murmuring, with the lid kept slightly ajar (on the cast-iron surface of an old-fashioned stove or with the gas-flame-heated cast-iron plaques of semiprofessional stoves, the heat regulation is both simpler and more precise). Leave undisturbed for from 3 to 5 hours; if the oxtail is intended to serve in another preparation—simmered in tomato sauce and accompanied by pasta, for instance, or *à la provençale*, with black olives, garlic, sautéed eggplant and sweet peppers added to the tomato sauce—it should be removed after 3 hours; if not, it will continue for another couple of hours to lend its qualities to the broth. Pass the broth through a sieve to remove all solid ingredients (don't discard the head of garlic—the purée, squeezed from the hulls and mixed with a bit of olive oil is a delicious snack when spread on crusty bread or toast).

THE POT-AU-FEU

Skim off any excess fat from the bouillon, bring it back to a boil in the *marmite* or other pot (which has meanwhile been cleaned—if it is earthenware, the bulk of the bouillon may first be brought to a boil in another vessel to save time), taste for salt, add the tied-up meats and, if necessary, just enough boiling water to ensure their being largely covered. Skim again, 2 or 3 times, as before, and regulate the heat again to maintain a bare simmer, the lid kept slightly ajar.

Remove the tough, dark-green outer leaves from the cabbages, cut each vertically into quarters, pare the visible thick leaf ribs and the core, leaving just enough to hold the quarters together, and wash them. Fit them snugly, so that they will retain their form, into a large saucepan, immerse them in salted boiling water and parboil, covered and at a simmer, for from 12 to 15 minutes (even tender, young cabbages should first be parboiled to make them more digestible, to attenuate their aggressive flavor and to rid them of excess water, which, in the braising process, would dilute the rich flavor of the braising liquid). Drain them, pressing gently to force out excess liquid, and, 1½ hours after the meats have been put to cook, replace the parboiled cabbage quarters in their saucepan, skim several ladles of bouillon from the surface of the *pot-au-feu*, taking as much of the fat with the bouillon as possible, pour it over the cabbages (just enough to completely immerse them), and put them to simmer, covered, until ready to serve—a good 1½ hours.

One-half hour later, add to the pot in which the meat has been cooking the whole, peeled turnips and carrots, the whites of the leeks, firmly tied into a bundle, and the apple.

Cooking time depends on the age of the animal and the way in which it has been raised. Usually, today, one may count just under 3 hours for meat to be just right—tender, but still firm enough to be easily cut into slices. In the past, cookbooks recommended from 3½ to 4 hours—the animals were not killed so young as they are today, their diet was more natural, their flesh less tender and more flavorful.

Discard the apple. Leave the cabbage to continue cooking while the soup is being served. The easiest and perhaps the most sympathetic way to serve the soup is directly from the *marmite*, leaving meats and vegetables in the pot to keep hot. Crusts of dried bread should be placed in each soup plate before the bouillon is ladled in and a piece of Parmesan and a grater (or a dish of grated cheese) should be at table for those who require it.

Serve the meats, strings removed, on a separate platter from the vegetables to facilitate carving. Remove the cabbage quarters from their cooking liquid and surround them with all the vegetables from the *pot-au-feu*, first removing the strings from the leeks.

A tureen of bouillon should be kept at table throughout the service to moisten meats and vegetables. The usual accompaniments are a dish of coarse salt, Dijon-type mustard and/or horseradish, and sour gherkins (or small dill pickles), of which the first is obligatory. Gherkins, if not too vinegary, are good with the meat, but will annihilate any wine.

Four Simple Spring Menus

MENU II (FOR 4)

This menu will, ideally, be accompaniedby a single, simple, young red wine (Beaujolais, Côtes-du-Rhône, Cahors, Bandol).

GARDEN PEAS A LA FRANCAISE
[PETITS POIS A LA FRANCAISE]

BLANQUETTE OF VEAL
[BLANQUETTE DE VEAU A L'ANCIENNE]

RICE PILAF
[RIZ PILAF]

TOSSED GREEN SALAD
[SALADE VERTE]

CHEESES
[FROMAGES]

MOLDED CHOCOLATE LOAF WITH WHIPPED CREAM
[GATEAU MOULE AU CHOCOLAT, CREME CHANTILLY]

THE GARDEN PEAS A LA FRANCAISE

Most often, peas *à la française* are prepared with a *chiffonade* of lettuce mixed in and with a certain amount of water added. Although the flavor of the lettuce braised with the peas enhances them, serving the lettuce with the peas detracts from their rare delicacy (the onions and lettuce will make a valuable addition to a soup). Inasmuch as the cooking liquid should be very sparse, and because with this method of cooking there is practically no evaporation, the water contained in the vegetables themselves, plus the humidity of the freshly washed lettuce, is largely sufficient.

The quantity of peas recommended for 4 people may seem overgenerous, but in order for the dish to be prepared to perfection, all the peas must be tiny, tender, and of nearly the same size. A batch of peas picked at the same time, all the pods of which are similar in appearance, never displays an altogether uniform maturity, once shelled, and the larger and harder peas should be put aside for another use (in purées and soups, they are superior to the tiny ones because of their greater starchy "binding" content). The length of cooking time may also seem surprising, but it should be remembered that their cooking is mainly a gentle steaming and that they are not even uniformly heated through until a good 15 minutes after they have been put to cook—the same tiny peas, plunged into rapidly boiling water, would require only about 5 minutes.

It is absolutely essential that the receptacle in which they are cooked be of a heavy material that takes the heat slowly and evenly (earthenware, heavy copper or enameled cast-iron ware), that it be of a size to just hold the ingredients, and that it have a tight-fitting lid.

Garden Peas à la Française

Petits Pois à la Française

1 *medium head Boston-type lettuce*
1 *large pinch thyme (or a couple of branches)*

7 or 8 little new onions
1/4 pound (1 stick) softened butter
salt, pinch of sugar, freshly ground white pepper
3 1/2–4 pounds tender garden peas, picked the day to be used, if possible

Remove the outer leaves from the lettuce, keeping the heart intact, wash the leaves and the heart, and line the bottom and sides of the saucepan with lettuce leaves. Carefully open out the leaves of the heart, imprison the thyme within, close them up again, tie the heart well with thread, and place it in the center of the saucepan, with the little onions, peeled but whole, all around.

Mash the softened butter together with the salt, sugar and pepper, and very gently, with your hands, mix in the peas, being careful to crush none. When they are all uniformly coated with this *pommade*, pack them lightly all around the lettuce heart, cover with more lettuce leaves, fit the lid tightly, and start them out over a high flame for something less than a minute—just long enough for the saucepan to absorb a bit of heat—and leave them to cook over a tiny flame, gently shaking the saucepan from time to time, for 40–45 minutes. After 1/2 hour, lift off the lid briefly to check their progress.

Remove the onions, the lettuce heart and all the leaves, and serve directly from the cooking utensil.

Blanquette of Veal

Blanquette de Veau à l'Ancienne

6 ounces small, firm, unopened mushrooms
juice of 1/2 lemon
1/4 cup water
1 tablespoon (1/2 ounce) butter
salt, pepper
2 pounds breast or rib tips of veal (tendrons—the point at which the ribs become cartilaginous), cut into 3/4-inch slices
salt
3 medium carrots, peeled and cut into 1-inch lengths

(*Continued*)

2 medium onions, peeled, 1 stuck with 2 cloves
a large pinch of thyme or mixed herbs
a bouquet containing parsley, a small celery branch and 1 bay leaf
about 20 small new onions
2 tablespoons (1 ounce) butter
roux made with 1 tablespoon flour (mounded but not heaping) and 2 tablespoons (1 ounce) butter
1/3 cup heavy cream
3 egg yolks
freshly ground pepper
pinch of freshly grated nutmeg
a few drops of lemon juice
chopped parsley

Pare the stem tips of the mushrooms, wash them rapidly, and, if small enough, leave them whole (or cut them into halves or quarters, depending on their size). Combine them with the lemon juice, 1/4 cup water, 1 tablespoon butter, and salt and pepper, and boil, covered, for 1 minute.

Arrange the pieces of meat in a heavy saucepan so that, without packing them in, they take up a minimum of space, add the mushrooms' cooking liquid (put the mushrooms aside), and enough cold water to cover the meat by about 1/3 inch, salt, bring to a boil, and skim 2 or 3 times, adding small amounts of cold water each time the liquid returns to a boil. Add the carrots, the two onions, the herbs, and the aromatic bouquet, making certain that all are submerged, and regulate the heat to maintain a bare simmer, the saucepan covered, for 1 1/2 hours.

During this time, the little onions should be seasoned and gently stewed, whole, in 2 tablespoons of butter, in a saucepan, the bottom of which just holds them side by side. Count about 15 minutes, keeping them covered and tossing them from time to time. They should be soft and slightly yellowed, but not browned.

Pour the contents of the saucepan containing the meat into a large sieve placed over a mixing bowl. Pick out the 2 onions and the bouquet and discard them. Reserve the liquid. Return the meat and carrot pieces to their saucepan, add the mushrooms and the little onions, and put the pan aside, covered. Skim any fat from the surface of the liquid.

In another saucepan, make the *roux*: Melt 2 tablespoons butter over a low flame, add the flour, and leave to cook for a minute or so, stirring regularly, without allowing the flour to brown. Away from the flame, pour in the cooking liquid, slowly, stirring the while. Return to a medium flame, continue stirring until a boil is reached, lower the flame to maintain a simmer, the saucepan uncovered, and, over a period of about 20 minutes, skim the light, fatty skin that repeatedly forms on the surface. Pour this lightly thickened sauce back over the meat and its garnish and leave to simmer, covered, for about 15 minutes.

Mix together in a bowl the cream, the egg yolks, the pepper and very little nutmeg, stir in, pouring slowly, a ladleful of the sauce, and then, away from the flame, stir this mixture into the stew. Return the saucepan to a medium-low flame, stirring constantly, until the sauce is only thick enough to lightly coat the spoon. It must not approach a boil or it will curdle. Squeeze in a few drops of lemon juice (not too much—taste and add more, if necessary), and pour the stew into a preheated deep serving platter. Sprinkle with chopped parsley and serve, accompanied by a Pilaf (page 81).

Molded Chocolate Loaf with Whipped Cream

Gâteau Moulé au Chocolat, Crème Chantilly

1/4 *cup water*
3 *ounces* (3 *squares*) *bitter chocolate*
6 *tablespoons* (3 *ounces*) *softened, unsalted butter*
3 *eggs, separated*
3/4 *cup sugar*
1/4 *cup flour*
1 *scant teaspoon vanilla extract*
1 *small pinch salt*
1 *cup heavy cream*
1/4 *cup sugar*
1/2 *teaspoon vanilla extract*

Stir the water and the chocolate squares together in a round-bottomed metal mixing bowl, over a low flame, until melted, remove from the heat, whip in the butter, then the egg yolks, and finally the sugar, the flour, and the scant teaspoon vanilla. If, at this point, the mixture seems to curdle or disintegrate (it is only the action of the chocolate rehardening in contact with colder ingredients), place the bowl in another bowl filled with warm water, continue stirring, and it will come back together. Beat the egg whites and salt until they stand stiffly in peaks, gently fold about 1/3 of the entire volume into the chocolate mixture, then the remainder. Pour into a buttered quart mold (a savarin or a decorative jelly mold with central tube) and poach in a *bain-marie*, in a medium oven, immersed in hot water to approximately the same level as the pudding's surface on the inside, for 40 minutes. Leave to cool slightly and unmold onto the serving plate, leaving the mold over the pudding until serving time. Whip the cream with the sugar and 1/2 teaspoon vanilla extract. Serve well chilled, either with whipped cream separately, or the central well filled with whipped cream and a decorative ribbon of it piped around the base of the pudding.

Four Simple Spring Menus

MENU III (FOR 4)

This menu, each course of which, to a Lyonnais palate, represents a peak of perfection, is well served by a cool, fruity Beaujolais from the most recent vintage (Beaujolais-Villages, Chiroubles, Morgon, Côte de Brouilly, Fleurie, Saint-Amour, Juliénas).

TERRINE OF POULTRY LIVERS
[TERRINE DE FOIES DE VOLAILLES]

DEEP-FRIED BEEF TRIPE, REMOULADE SAUCE
[GRAS-DOUBLE FRIT, SAUCE REMOULADE]

DANDELION AND SALT PORK (OR BACON) SALAD
[SALADE DE PISSENLIT AU LARD]

GOAT CHEESES
[FROMAGES DE CHEVRE]

STRAWBERRIES IN BEAUJOLAIS
[FRAISES AU BEAUJOLAIS]

THE TERRINE OF POULTRY LIVERS

Technically, a pâté is a preparation like the one below (more often based on game or duck flesh) enclosed in a pastry, into which, after having been cooked and cooled, meat jelly is poured. When the preparation is simply prepared in a terrine (a deep oval or oblong oven dish of earthenware, porcelain, or often, today, enameled ironware), it is named after its container. The terms have become so confused, even in France, that pâtés are often referred to as *pâtés en croûte* and terrines as pâtés; and any sort of meat paste or spread is also termed "pâté."

Chicken livers are the most easily obtainable on the market, but, when duck or goose livers are available, they are even better; don't hesitate to mix up the three. Whatever the bird, if it is fat, the liver (which is then larger, softer, and a creamy-beige color rather than a dark reddish-brown) is better. The result, even with unfattened chicken livers, providing they are not frozen, is very fine indeed. It is among the simplest and best of terrine recipes.

Sour gherkins traditionally accompany terrines, but, inasmuch as wine accompanies them beautifully and suffers from any proximity to vinegar, it is perhaps best to eliminate the gherkins, leaving one's guests with no choice.

This terrine should be prepared the day before it is served, but, unlike many, it does not keep remarkably well, and once cut into, it should be consumed fairly rapidly (within a day or so).

Terrine of Poultry Livers

Terrine de Foies de Volailles

6 *ounces fat salt side pork, rind removed (if it is not impeccable in quality, substitute fresh fat side pork—but not bacon)*
1 *clove garlic*
1 *healthy handful stale (but not dried out) crumbled white bread crumbs, made without crust*
1/3 *cup tepid milk*
1 *medium onion, finely chopped*
1 *tablespoon (1/2 ounce) butter*

- 1 *teaspoon mixed herbs*
- 2 *"heads" of cloves (the tiny round ball attached to extremity of each clove)*
- 1 *pound poultry livers*
- 1 *egg*
- 1 *tablespoon finely chopped parsley*
- 2 *bay leaves*
- *salt, freshly ground pepper*

Put the fat pork to chill, to facilitate cutting it.

Pound the garlic clove to a paste in the mortar, add the bread crumbs and the milk, mix together so that the garlic thoroughly impregnates the whole, and put aside.

Cook the chopped onion gently in butter for 10 minutes or so, or until it is yellowed and soft.

Reduce the mixed herbs and clove heads to a powder in a stone mortar.

Remove any greenish, discolored sections from the livers (they give a bitter taste from their proximity to the gall bladder), and carefully pull loose all of the little, white, threadlike nerve tissue possible (in particular, that connecting the two "lobes"—don't worry about crushing the livers). Gather together the picked-over livers on the chopping board and, with a large, heavy, sharp, French chef's–type knife, cut through the mass several times, then, holding the knife freely above the board and using a rapid "rat-tat-tat" loose-wristed motion, chop them, gathering the mass back together and turning it over with the blade of the knife from time to time.

Remove enough slices (sliced as thinly as possible) from the fat pork to line the bottom and the sides of the terrine and to cover the surface, once filled, and cut the rest into little cubes (cutting it first into 1/4-inch strips lengthwise, and then, cutting them, gathered together, crosswise).

Squeeze the bread to eliminate any excess liquid and, with the exception of the slices of pork fat and the two bay leaves, combine all the ingredients in a large mixing bowl, working them thoroughly together with both hands, squeezing the mixture repeatedly, through clutching fingers, until it is completely homogeneous. Taste for salt and pepper.

Line the bottom and the sides of the terrine with slices of fat pork, pressing them to ensure their adhering, pour in the liver mixture, tap the bottom of the terrine 2 or 3 times against a wooden surface to settle its contents, place the bay leaves on the surface, and lightly press the remaining fat pork slices on top. Cover the terrine (if it does not have a lid, fit over it a piece of aluminum foil) and poach it in a *bain-marie*, either in the oven (the terrine placed in a larger, deep pan, hot water poured in to immerse it by two-thirds) or on top of the stove (in a tightly covered saucepan large enough to contain the terrine, filled to two-thirds the terrine's height with hot water), without allowing the water to boil, for from 1 hour to 1 hour and 10 minutes. (After an hour, test it by pressing in the center—if it is firm, it is done. It should remain, once cut, rose in color.)

Place the terrine on a large platter, in a cake pan, etc., to collect any juices that run over the edge, and remove the lid or aluminum foil (don't be alarmed at the quantity of liquid in which the contents seem to float—it is made up of gelatinous juices which will solidify in the terrine and of fat which will solidify on the surface). Place a board or a plate just the size of the terrine's opening, on the surface, with a weight of from 1½ to 2 pounds on top—a can of conserves, for instance. The weighting lends a firm, close texture to the body, without which it would be impossible to neatly slice and serve the terrine. When cooled, remove the weight and put the dish to chill. Serve it in slices directly from the terrine, the border of fat pork removed from each slice or not, as preferred.

Deep-fried Beef Tripe, Rémoulade Sauce

Gras-double Frit, Sauce Rémoulade

1½ *pounds precooked honeycomb tripe (usually the only part available—if whole tripe can be found substitute it; in France this is always sold precooked), cut into approximately* 2*-inch squares*

Marinade:

1 *tablespoon fines herbes (parsley, chives, chervil, tarragon—or whatever is available)*

Deep-fried Beef Tripe, Rémoulade Sauce

juice of 1 *lemon*
1 *tablespoon olive oil*
salt, freshly ground pepper

flour
3 *eggs*
stale (but not dried out) firm-textured white bread, grated into crumbs (passed, if necessary, through a coarse sieve to render them uniform)
olive oil for frying (a good quart)
1 *handful parsley bouquets (leaf bunches, stems removed, except for the part necessary to hold leaves together)*

Sprinkle the squares of tripe with all the elements of the marinade and leave for an hour or so, turning them from time to time.

Arrange 3 plates before you, the first containing flour, the second, the eggs, beaten as for an omelet, and the third, the bread crumbs. Dip the pieces, one by one, first lightly on both sides in the flour, then on both sides, being certain that they are well coated, in the eggs, then in the crumbs, placing each piece on the bed of crumbs, sprinkling crumbs generously over the surface, and pressing lightly with the palm of the hand to ensure their adhering. Lift each from the crumbs and remove it to a board that has been lightly dusted with crumbs. Should any seem imperfectly breaded, pass them a second time in egg and crumbs. If one has the time, they may be breaded an hour or so before the meal, and are then less fragile when the moment comes to handle them.

Drop them, one at a time, into very hot olive oil. Do not use a frying basket. (The heat may have to be lowered later, to prevent the oil's overheating.) Fry no more than five at a time (if the frying pan is overcrowded, the temperature of the oil drops too radically, and at the same time the articles to be fried risk touching, sticking together, frying unevenly, and having their crisp surfaces damaged). When they are golden and crisp on one side, turn each over carefully with the prong tips of a fork, and, when evenly browned, lift them out with a large wire skimming spoon, sponge them lightly between two paper towels, and remove them to the folded napkin in which they will be served, while treating the others in the same way. When the last are removed from the oil, drop in the parsley bouquets and, as soon as the violent sizzling has stopped (after a few seconds), remove them, drain them, without sponging, on a paper towel, and sprinkle them over the fried tripe. Serve, enclosed in a folded napkin, and accompanied by the following *rémoulade* sauce.

Rémoulade Sauce

Sauce Rémoulade

Mayonnaise:
salt, freshly ground pepper
juice of 1 *lemon*
2 *egg yolks*
something over 1 *cup olive oil*

1 *anchovy fillet*
1 *tablespoon capers*
3 *sour gherkins* (*or small, firm dill pickles*)
1 *teaspoon Dijon-type mustard*
1 *teaspoon chopped fines herbes*

It is said that, with a whip and a whir, all the ingredients thrown in at once, a perfect mayonnaise may instantaneously be produced in a blender. The method described here is the only one with which I am familiar at first hand. The olive oil should be of impeccable quality, and both it and the egg yolks must be at room temperature, not chilled. Vinegar may be used instead of lemon if the dish is not accompanied, for example, by a vinegar-dressed salad.

Put the seasoning into a bowl (or better, a stone mortar, whose weight will prevent it from slipping around), add a few drops of lemon juice, stir, with either a wooden spoon or a wooden pestle, until the salt is dissolved, add the egg yolks, continue stirring until they lighten slightly in color, then start ad ding the oil, drop by drop, evenly and fairly rapidly, turning always in the same direction. As the egg yolks begin to absorb the oil and to show signs of developing "body," the oil may be poured in a steady trickle, and finally in a fine stream. From time to time, the addition of oil should be stopped and a few drops of lemon juice added. Once all the oil has been absorbed (it need not all be added if the desired thickness is obtained before, but a cupful will probably be necessary), taste for lemon. Two teaspoons of hot water may be stirred in if the mayonnaise is not to be used at once—this is a safeguard against its "breaking."

Soak the anchovy fillet in cold water to desalt it, sponge it dry in a paper towel, and chop it finely. Rinse the capers, sponge them dry and chop them. Chop the gherkins finely. Stir these and all the other ingredients into the mayonnaise before serving.

THE DANDELION AND SALT PORK (OR BACON) SALAD

Young dandelions, gathered wild, are better than the giant bleached commercially raised variety, but either will do.

It is absolutely essential that this salad be prepared the moment before it is served, that the salad bowl be hot (otherwise, the hot fat solidifies on contact with the cold bowl, and the result is distinctly unpleasant), and, in order for the dandelions to retain their freshness, that they be placed in the bowl just before the hot fat is poured in.

Dandelion and Salt Pork (or Bacon) Salad

Salade de Pissenlit au Lard

12–14 *ounces young dandelion plants, cut at the base of the root but kept intact*
2 *slices, each about* 1/3 *inch thick, of either slab bacon or lean salt side pork*
1 *tablespoon olive oil*
about 2 *tablespoons wine vinegar*
salt, pepper

Wash the dandelion plants carefully, spreading the leaves at the base where earth often collects. Shake them as free as possible of water and dry them thoroughly between 2 towels.

Slice the bacon or salt pork crosswise into ½-inch sections, cover them with cold water, bring to a boil, simmer for 5 or 6 minutes, drain, and fry them in the olive oil over medium-low heat, turning the pieces around until they are lightly crisp on all sides and have rendered a couple of tablespoonfuls of fat. Put the dandelions into the preheated bowl, pour the bacon or pork and its fat over them, wash out the pan with the vinegar over a high flame and, the moment it boils, pour it over the salad. Sprinkle with very little salt (keeping in mind the saltiness of the pork), generously grind pepper over, toss and serve immediately.

THE STRAWBERRIES IN BEAUJOLAIS

Strawberries in wine are a common and much-loved dessert in all winemaking countries; usually the strawberries are simply presented at table and each guest fills his wineglass with berries, pours some more wine over, sugars to taste and lightly cuts up and mashes the berries so that their juice mingles with the wine. Those who are unfamiliar with the custom invariably shy away from what sounds like a bizarre combination, and one is obliged to exercise a bit of gentle blackmail by presenting the dessert intact.

The extent to which the specific character of a wine comes through in the marriage is remarkable.

Strawberries in Beaujolais

Fraises au Beaujolais

1 *pound fresh, ripe strawberries*
sugar to taste
wine to cover (*the same that has been drunk throughout the meal*)

Pick over the strawberries, rinse them rapidly, drain them, and sprinkle them with sugar. Leave to macerate for an hour or so and, shortly before serving, pour enough wine over to just cover them.

Four Simple Spring Menus

MENU IV (FOR 4)

This menu will, ideally, be accompaniedby a single, simple, young red wine (Beaujolais, Côtes-du-Rhône, Cahors, Bandol).

WARM ASPARAGUS VINAIGRETTE
[ASPERGES TIEDES A LA VINAIGRETTE]

CALVES' BRAINS IN RED WINE
[CERVELLES DE VEAU EN MATELOTE]

CAULIFLOWER LOAF
[PAIN DE CHOUFLEUR]

GREEN SALAD WITH FINES HERBES
[SALADE VERTE AUX FINES HERBES]

CHEESES
[FROMAGES]

MOLDED APPLE PUDDING
[PUDDING MOULE AUX POMMES]

THE WARM ASPARAGUS VINAIGRETTE

Of commercialized asparagus varieties, whether they are cultivated as green or white (generally only the green are available in America; the French tend to prefer the white), the largest and fleshiest specimens are also the tenderest and least fibrous. Wild asparagus is a world apart. Not the kind that abounds in the Midwest, the feathery branches of which so often find their way into bouquets, and which is really cultivated asparagus, degenerated into a wild state—it, too, is very good and, because of its size, perfect for use as "tips" for garnish—but the truly wild variety whose thorny, tortuous tangles of stem cover the Provençal hillsides, and at whose base, during the month of April, dark green, often deep purplish-green shoots push from the earth, some threadlike, none more than a third the size of an ordinary pencil. Their tips, broken at the tender point (1 or 2 inches down), either parboiled for a few minutes and stewed gently in butter, or cooked, raw, directly in butter, and incorporated into an omelet, are marvelous. Eggs are the perfect background for their intense, wild flavor. They exist in Florida and, no doubt, in California and other parts of America with a similar climate.

Hollandaise sauce is a good accompaniment to warm or hot asparagus. Maltaise sauce (Hollandaise, finished with the juice of a blood orange), understandably a rarity, is conceived uniquely as an asparagus accompaniment. Vinaigrette (or, simply, olive oil, salt and pepper) is less an accompanying sauce than an essential seasoning that permits a total appreciation of the asparagus, unadorned.

Although best hot or warm, asparagus may also be served cold, *à la vinaigrette*, but should never be rewarmed.

Warm Asparagus Vinaigrette

Asperges Tièdes à la Vinaigrette

3 *pounds large asparagus*
salt, pepper, wine vinegar, olive oil

Cut off the tough ends of the asparagus, leaving the stalks all approximately the same length (7 to 10 inches, depending on the size of the asparagus), and peel them from the cut end to the point at which the skin becomes tender. Wash them, tie them into bundles of a dozen or so each, and slip them into a large container of salted boiling water (a large oval *braisière* or an American roasting pan are perfect—lacking a container of this sort, they may be stood on end in a high pot and half immersed in boiling water—with the latter method, the tips are steamed). Cook, covered, at a simmer, until the stems are just tender (the tips should remain absolutely intact). After 10 minutes, test stems by piercing a stalk, with the grain, with the point of a sharp paring knife—the moment it penetrates with no resistance, asparagus is done. Remove stalks carefully with a large wire skimming spoon, leave them to drain for a few minutes, remove the strings and arrange stalks in overlapping rows, so that an the tips are exposed, on a large serving platter on which a folded napkin has been placed; this permits asparagus to continue draining. There are especially designed asparagus platters fitted with perforated porcelain false bottoms that allow one to dispense with the napkin; these are attractive but today are hard to come by.

Each guest prepares his own vinaigrette in his plate, first propping the far side of the plate on the arched part of a fork or spoon, and mixing salt and pepper with vinegar before adding the olive oil. Each asparagus, taken in hand, is dipped and rolled repeatedly in the sauce as it is eaten. The addition of coarse white bread, generously spread with unsalted butter, completes a simple perfection.

THE CALVES' BRAINS IN RED WINE

A somewhat richer version of this recipe consists in replacing the water by veal stock or *pot-au-feu* bouillon, thickening the *court-bouillon* by reducing it with some thick *velouté* (*roux*-thickened stock, simmered and skimmed), and, away from the flame, buttering it lightly. For the housewife who cannot always keep stocks and their derivatives on hand, the method described here is simple and the result very good.

Calves' Brains in Red Wine

Cervelles de Veau en Matelote

2 *calves' brains (firm and moist in appearance, and as little stained with blood as possible)*

Court-bouillon:

2½ *cups red wine (the same as that served at table)*
1½ *cups water*
2 *medium carrots, peeled and thinly sliced*
1 *large onion, peeled and thinly sliced*
chopped stems of the ½ *pound of mushrooms to be used as garnish*
½ *teaspoon thyme or mixed herbs*
a few branches and roots of parsley
1 *bay leaf*
salt
8–10 *whole peppercorns*

Garnish:

about 20 *peeled whole, small, new white onions*
salt, pepper
about 5 *ounces butter*
4 *slices stale white bread, crusts removed, each slice cut diagonally into* 2 *triangles (or any other form fancy suggests)*
½ *pound small, firm, unopened mushrooms, rapidly washed and sponged dry in paper towels (stems added to court-bouillon as directed above)*

1 *small pinch Cayenne pepper*
beurre manié made with 1 *tablespoon flour and* 2 *tablespoons softened butter, mashed together into a paste with a fork*
finely chopped parsley

Soak the brains in cold water, carefully peel off the thin surface membranes, and put brains back to "bleach" in cold water for about 1 hour, changing the water a couple of times.

Combine the red wine and the water and bring to a boil, add all the other ingredients of the *court-bouillon*, with the exception of the peppercorns, and simmer, covered, for at least 40 minutes, adding the peppercorns 10 minutes before removing it from the heat. Pass the liquid through a sieve, pressing the solids to extract all the juices, but without passing them through in a purée. Return liquid to a boil, add brains and poach, covered, at a bare simmer, about 25 minutes.

Meanwhile, cook the little onions gently in a heavy saucepan just the size to hold them, placed side by side on the bottom, salted and peppered, in about 2 tablespoons (1 ounce) of butter, tossing them from time to time, for about 15 minutes, or until soft and yellowed, but not browned; cook the triangles of bread in a *sauteuse* or skillet, with about 4 tablespoons (2 ounces) of butter (starting with less and adding more as required), over a very low heat, surveying them carefully, until they are golden—but no darker—and crisp on both sides; cook the mushroom caps in about 2 tablespoons (1 ounce) of butter, seasoned, tossing or stirring with a wooden spoon, over a high flame, for 2 or 3 minutes, or until the liquid they exude has evaporated and they are lightly colored.

Remove the brains, one at a time, from their poaching liquid, with a flat wire skimming spoon, slice them, and arrange them in a preheated shallow baking dish or gratin dish; scatter the mushrooms and onions over them and keep them warm while finishing the sauce.

Over a high flame, reduce the *court-bouillon* by about half, remove from the flame, taste for salt, add a tiny pinch of Cayenne, and whisk in the *beurre manié*. Return the saucepan to the flame, whisking the while, and as soon as a boil is reached, pour the sauce into a sieve held over the brains and their garnish, pass it all through, and put the dish into the oven until the sauce begins to bubble evenly over its surface. Sprinkle with chopped parsley and arrange the croutons around the edge. They may, if one likes, be lightly stroked with a clove of garlic, and a tip of each may also be dipped first into the sauce, then into chopped parsley, for the sake of a more formal presentation. Send the cauliflower loaf to the table at the same time.

THE CAULIFLOWER LOAF

The cauliflower loaf served here with the brains in red wine is also well worth trying as an accompaniment to braised sweetbreads, with or without truffles.

Sauced, a cauliflower loaf may also respectably serve as a course apart. It may be enriched by the addition of such elements as chopped roast almonds, fresh peeled chopped pistachios or *duxelles*, or very pretty fantasies may be created by filling the mold with thin alternate layers of other vegetable fillings (shredded sorrel stewed in butter, or parboiled puréed spinach, one or the other beaten with an egg, grated carrot stewed in butter, etc.).

Similar loaves may be prepared from other vegetables and, for those vegetables richer in starch, the *béchamel* may be omitted.

The parboiled carrot slices and green bean strips are decorative and they relieve an otherwise monotonous whiteness.

Cauliflower Loaf

Pain de Choufleur

a few small, tender green beans
1 *small carrot*
about 3 *tablespoons* (1½ *ounces*) *butter*
1 *good-sized cauliflower*
stiff béchamel made with 1 *mounded, but not heaping, tablespoon flour,* 1 *tablespooon butter,* ½ *cup milk*
2 *whole eggs and* 1 *egg yolk*
salt, pepper, nutmeg

Cut the string beans into approximately 2-inch lengths and split them in half. Peel the carrot either with a serrated vegetable peeler that makes ridges the length of the carrot, and slice it thinly, crosswise, or peel it smoothly, cut it into 2-inch lengths, slice these thinly lengthwise, and cut them into matchlike strips. Parboil the beans and the carrot in rapidly boiling salted water for about 5 minutes, or until they have lost their crispness and are pliable. Drain them and sponge them dry with a paper towel.

Generously butter a quart mold (any form), arrange the carrot and bean fragments in a simple design, pressing them well against the buttered surface, and put the mold to chill (not essential, but the decorative elements are less likely to be displaced when the mold is filled).

Break the cauliflower up into flowerets, cook it in boiling salted water until just tender, not mushy, drain it, "dry it out" for a couple of minutes in 2 tablespoons of butter, tossing and stirring, over a medium flame, and pass it through a fine sieve.

Melt 1 tablespoon of butter in a small saucepan, add the flour, cook gently for a minute or so, stirring with a wooden spoon, and, away from the heat, slowly pour in the heated milk, stirring the while. Return to the heat, continue stirring until it has returned to a full boil, and stir it into the cauliflower purée. Beat in the eggs and the egg yolk, seasoned to taste with salt, freshly ground pepper and very little freshly grated nutmeg, pour the mixture into the mold and tap the bottom a couple of times against a wooden surface to settle the contents. Lightly press a buttered round of kitchen paper against the surface and poach in a *bain-marie*, immersed by two-thirds in hot water, in a medium oven for about 1/2 hour, or until the center is firm to the touch. Once removed from the *bain-marie*, leave to settle for a few minutes before unmolding.

THE MOLDED APPLE PUDDING

Served caramel-coated, as is, the pudding is delicious, but it also may be accompanied by whipped cream, *sabayon sauce* (Charlotte with Crêpes, page 137) or apricot sauce.

Molded Apple Pudding

Pudding Moulé aux Pommes

Caramel:

3 *heaping tablespoons sugar*
3 *tablespoons water*

almond oil or butter
1 1/2 *pounds cooking apples (preferably russet)*
1/3 *cup water*
1/2 *cup sugar (to taste)*
1 *pinch cinnamon*
3 *eggs*

(*Continued*)

For the caramel, combine the sugar and water in a small saucepan, bring it to a boil and adjust the heat to a bubble. Don't take your eye off it, and remove it the instant it is a rich, deep amber color (once it begins to color, it advances very rapidly and 2 seconds may mean the difference between perfect caramel and burnt sugar). Pour in about 1 tablespoon hot water, stirring until thoroughly blended, and pour the caramel immediately into the mold, turning it in all directions to coat the mold as evenly as possible. When cooled, lightly oil or butter any parts of the inner walls of the mold that have not been coated with caramel.

Quarter, peel, core and slice the apples. Cook them with the water, over a high flame, stirring constantly with a wooden spoon, until just cooked—that is, reduced to a near-purée. Stir in the sugar and the cinnamon, pass through a sieve, and beat in the eggs. Pour the mixture into the mold (an old-fashioned jelly mold affords a pretty presentation), tap it on a wooden surface to settle the contents, and poach in a *bain-marie* in hot, but not boiling, water, in a moderate oven, for from 45 to 50 minutes. Leave to cool until tepid; then unmold and, once unmolded, leave the dessert covered by the mold and chill. Remove mold just before serving, well chilled.

Summer Menus

Appropriate wines for each menu are suggested on the pages indicated below, which mark the beginning of each menu and its recipes.

Two Elegant Summer Dinners

I

PAGE 354

Artichoke Bottoms with Two Mousses
Sole Fillets with Fines Herbes
Stewed Cucumbers
Spitted Roast Leg of Lamb
Buttered Green Beans
Cheeses
Peach Melba

II

PAGE 372

Cold Calves' Brains in Cream Sauce
Squid à l'Américaine
Rice Pilaf
Jellied Poached Chicken
Tossed Green Salad with Fines Herbes
Cheeses
Apricot Fritters

A Semiformal Summer Dinner

PAGE 386

Cantaloupe with Parma Ham
Braised Stuffed Artichoke Bottoms
Grilled Lambs' Kidneys with Herb Butter
Potato Straw Cake
Tossed Green Salad
Cheeses
Peaches in Red Wine

Four Simple Summer Luncheons à la Provençale

I

PAGE 397

Provençal Fish Stew

Tossed Green Salad

Fresh White Cheese with Fines Herbes

Fresh Fruits

II

PAGE 405

Fresh Sardines in Vine Leaves

Lambs' Tripes à la Marseillaise

Wild Salad

Fresh Cheeses

Strawberries in Orange Juice

III

PAGE 411

Warm Salad of Small Green Beans
Braised Beef Provençal
Macaroni in Braising Liquid
Tossed Green Salad with Fines Herbes
Cheeses
Fruit

IV

PAGE 417

Cold Ratatouille
Blanquette of Beef Tripe with Basil
Steamed Potatoes
Tossed Green Salad
Cheeses
Cherries and Fresh Almonds

Two Elegant Summer Dinners

with appropriate wines

MENU I (FOR 8)

ARTICHOKE BOTTOMS WITH TWO MOUSSES
[FONDS D'ARTICHAUTS AUX DEUX MOUSSES]

A light, young, dry white wine:
Quincy, Muscadet, champagne nature

SOLE FILLETS WITH FINES HERBES
STEWED CUCUMBERS
[FILETS DE SOLE AUX FINES HERBES]
[CONCOMBRES A L'ETUVEE]

A richer, fuller, but still dry
white wine, several years old:
Burgundy (Chassagne-Montrachet,
Meursault, Corton-Charlemagne),
Loire (Coulée de Serrant,
Pouilly-Fumé), Graves (Laville Haut-Brion)

SPITTED ROAST LEG OF LAMB
BUTTERED GREEN BEANS
[GIGOT D'AGNEAU ROTI A LA BROCHE]
[HARICOTS VERTS AU BEURRE]

A rich, full-bodied, fairly young red wine (3-6 years old): Burgundy (Nuits-Saint-Georges, Fixin), Bordeaux (Pomerol), Côtes-du-Rhône (Hermitage, Côte-Rôtie), Loire (Chinon)

CHEESES
[FROMAGES]

A wine of the same general type as that chosen for the roast, older and from a richer vintage

PEACH MELBA
[PECHE MELBA]
No wine

Everything in this dinner is simple, classical and sober in spirit—no fantasy, no breathtaking presentations, no "guess-what's-in-it" flavors.

The presentation of the first course may advantageously be thrown into relief by a harlequin or mosaic pattern of black (olives), white (the whites of hard-boiled eggs), and bright green (tarragon leaves) against the background of warm tomato red and pale artichoke green whose definitions are softened in the amber suffusion of the jelly. The firm, velvety texture of the liver mousse (which, incidentally, in a simpler meal forms a perfect hors d'oeuvre in itself), the concentrated richness and sensuous quality of a trembling natural meat jelly that melts on the tongue, the refreshing slight acidity of the tomato mousse and the clean savor of the artichoke bottoms form an intricate juxtaposition of flavors and textures in which each retains its identity.

The *suite* represents not only a switch from cold to hot, but from involved to simple and from vibrant to suave and soothing. The fillets are masked in an essence of their own flavor, heightened by the herbs and cucumbers. In effect, it is a unified experience in taste and color.

From simple to radically simple and from delicate to robust, the roast is climactic.

The progression is a particularly happy one for inquisitive palates, and ideal for the presentation of a selection of fine wines, for, with the exception of the dessert, which needs no wine, and the first course, which is accompanied perfectly by the slight, dry white wine that is also an ideal preface to a gamut of finer wines. (If champagne were served as apéritif to "set the tone," it would be better to continue with the same or another champagne with the first course, for the first course wines suggested would suffer by comparison.) Each preparation is of a nature to enhance a wine. The fish alone requires a particular kind of wine; under other circumstances, a *gigot* may be accompanied equally well by a fresh country wine, a 6-months-old Beaujolais, or a venerable *grand seigneur*). If a fine bottle has been chosen for the cheeses, avoid cheeses of the strong-flavored fermented varieties. A good selection would be: a dry, nutty-flavored Swiss Gruyère (but not an Emmenthal), a fresh goat cheese, and a fresh, creamy Reblochon.

Artichoke Bottoms with Two Mousses

The first course and all the elements of the dessert will have been prepared far ahead of time. The preliminary preparations for the fish course (except for the actual poaching and the finishing of the sauce—15 minutes) may be done in advance. The cucumbers may be prepared and parboiled, and the beans and roast prepared for cooking ahead of time. There is little to do at the last minute, but one must organize one's time, for neither the fish nor the green beans can wait. In the recipe I have indicated a 20-minute period of "relaxation" for the leg of lamb, but that time, fortunately, is flexible. The meal may be begun 15 minutes after the roast has been put to cook. Don't try to prepare the fish until the first course is nearly finished (it is good to wait a bit between courses, and as long as the guests' glasses contain wine, everything is all right). It is best to have the boiling water in readiness for the beans, but do not begin to cook them until after the roast has been put to "relax."

Artichoke Bottoms with Two Mousses

Fonds d'Artichauts aux Deux Mousses

8 *medium artichokes*
1 *lemon*
salt, thyme

Veal jelly:

1 *calf's foot*
1 *pound lean gelatinous veal (rib tips and shank)*
about 1/2 *pound chicken parts (necks are good and cheap)*
1 *leek (if difficult to find, eliminate it)*
3 *medium-size onions*
2 *medium-size carrots*
thyme, bay leaf, small branch of celery, bouquet of parsley
coarse salt

Clarification:

small handful of chopped chervil and tarragon
2 *egg whites*
1 *small glass of wine (Madeira, port or Banyuls)*

(*Continued*)

Tomato mousse:

- 1¼ *pounds firm, ripe tomatoes*
- 1 *onion*
- 1 *tablespoon* (½ *ounce*) *butter*
- ⅓ *cup dry white wine*
- *salt, pepper, small pinch of Cayenne*
- 1 *cup veal jelly* (*above preparation*)
- 1 *cup heavy whipping cream*

Chicken liver mousse:

- ½ *pound chicken livers*
- 1 *small onion*
- ¼ *pound butter*
- *salt, pepper*
- 1 *pinch mixed herbs* (*savory, thyme, oregano*)
- 1 *tablespoon cognac*
- ½ *cup heavy whipping cream*

The artichokes may be prepared a day in advance. Prepare them, using the lemon, salt and thyme, exactly as indicated on page 77.

THE VEAL JELLY
(to be prepared the day before)

Cover the calf's foot with cold water, bring to a boil, and simmer for 15 minutes. Drain it, rinse it in cold water, and place it in a *marmite* or large saucepan along with the veal and chicken pieces. Add enough cold water to cover generously (there should be enough so that, when all the vegetables are added, they are just covered), place the pot over a medium flame and, as the boiling point nears, begin to skim off the scum that rises to the top. When the boil is reached, pour in about ⅓ cup of cold water. More scum will rise to the top. Continue skimming and repeat the process 3 or 4 more times, adding cold water in between each skimming—this is absolutely essential for a limpid jelly. Add the vegetables, peeled and cut into pieces, the aromatic elements, tied together, and a small handful of coarse salt (not too much, for evaporation must be taken into consideration, and seasoning may always be adjusted later), and continue to skim as before for a few minutes. Adjust the heat so that the barest simmer is produced at the liquid's surface (if you are working with a gas flame, use an asbestos pad to help disperse the heat so that it may be regulated more meticulously).

Leave to cook for about 6 hours. Don't stir or disturb the contents during this time except to skim off any fat floating on the surface every hour or so. At the end of the cooking time, gently pour the contents of the saucepan into a fine sieve suspended over a large mixing bowl. Remove the sieve without pressing the contents or stirring them around and pass the liquid again—this time through a cloth placed over the sieve. If all of the operations have been carried out as described, the result should be a succulent deep honey in color, and transparent. Taste at this point and add more salt if necessary (remembering that, hot, it will taste slightly more seasoned than when it is cold). Leave to cool and, when jelled, lift off any solid fat that has formed on the surface, then wipe the surface of the jelly with a towel dampened with hot water to remove any traces of fat that may remain. If the jelly is limpid, further clarification may be eliminated. The process is explained below because, despite detailed explanations, first attempts at making jelly often produce a cloudy product. Before clarification, put aside a cupful of jelly to serve in the confection of the tomato mousse.

THE CLARIFICATION

Heat the jelly until melted, add the herbs and the stiffly beaten egg whites. Over a high flame, using a whisk, beat the mixture until it boils. Lower the flame to avoid its frothing over the edge and continue whisking for 4 or 5 minutes. Pass the liquid first through cheesecloth, then through a piece of linen or other finely woven cloth.

If the jelly is to be used immediately, wait until it is nearly cold and add the glass of wine; in any case, wait until just before using to add the wine (the reheating necessary to melt the jelly damages the wine's perfume).

THE TOMATO MOUSSE

Peel and seed the tomatoes and chop the pulp coarsely. Peel the onion, chop it finely and cook it gently in butter for 10 minutes without allowing it to brown. Add the white wine and, over a high flame, reduce by half. Add the tomatoes and the seasoning and leave to cook gently, covered, for 1/2 hour. At the end of this time, if it seems to be too liquid, turn the fire up for a couple of minutes and reduce, stirring constantly with a wooden spoon. Add the cupful of jelly that has been put aside, boil for a couple of minutes and pass through a very fine sieve with the help of a wooden pestle. Taste for seasoning—it should be highly seasoned, for the addition of the cream will sweeten and attenuate it greatly. Immerse the saucepan in a basin of cold water and stir until the tomato mixture is cold, changing the water if necessary, or adding ice cubes to it. Whip the cream until it is good and frothy but not stiff (this way the mousse will be moist and velvety on the tongue—if the cream is whipped stiff, the result will be dry and cottony) and mix it into the tomato sauce. Pour into a deep serving platter or crystal dish and place in the refrigerator to solidify. It is wise to embed the dish in cracked ice to hasten this process.

THE CHICKEN LIVER MOUSSE

Check the livers carefully, cutting off any edges that may be greenish or discolored and consequently bitter from having contacted the gall. Peel and chop the onion finely. Heat 2 tablespoons of butter in a small frying pan, add the livers, salt, herbs and a generous amount of freshly ground pepper. Toss them and turn them around for a minute or two—just the time necessary for them to become firm to the touch. They must remain rare. Add the cognac, set fire to it, and pass the contents of the frying pan through a fine sieve. Mix in thoroughly the remaining butter (which has been kept out of the refrigerator to soften), whip the cream (the directions for the cream in the tomato mousse hold for all mousses) and mix it into the liver mixture. Leave to partly stiffen in the refrigerator and then fill the artichoke hearts (first sponged dry with a paper towel), piling the chicken liver mousse in a dome and smoothing the surface with the concave surface of a spoon.

Arrange the stuffed artichoke bottoms on the jelled bed of tomato mousse. A simple décor may be executed with the help of pieces of hard-boiled egg white, tarragon leaves dipped into boiling water to render them supple, slices of black olive, etc. (these elements should all be dipped first in jelly before placing them in position), or the dish may simply be decorated, after being masked in jelly, with small bouquets of chervil.

If the jelly has been allowed to stiffen, heat it just enough for it to be completely melted, allow to cool slightly and stir in the glass of wine. Place small quantities at a time (1/4 to 1/3 cup) in a bowl embedded in cracked ice, turn it with a tablespoon and, as it begins to thicken, pour it, a spoonful at a time (but deftly, for once the thickening begins, it rapidly turns to solid jelly) over all the elements of the dish, concentrating on the peaks of liver mousse, as much will flow down to coat the bed of tomato mousse. Repeat this process, filling the bowl when necessary, until all the jelly is used and the entire dish is masked evenly in amber transparence.

Sole Fillets with Fines Herbes

Filets de Sole aux Fines Herbes

4 *fish, each weighing from* 1 *to* 1 1/2 *pounds (Dover sole, lemon sole, grey sole, or flounder), or* 12 *fillets and an equivalent quantity of carcasses, heads, etc., from fish of the same varieties*

Fumet:

1 *onion*
1 *small carrot*
1 *clove garlic*
carcasses and trimmings of fish
herbs (thyme, bay leaf, fennel, parsley)
healthy pinch of salt
1 *cup of dry white wine*
water

10 *ounces fresh unsalted butter*
1 *tablespoon each of chopped parsley and chervil*
1 *teaspoon chopped tarragon*
salt, pepper to taste

Genuine Dover sole, unhappily, does not exist in American waters. Dover sole is flown in, but the price is high and it can only be found in fancy fish shops in large cities. Lemon sole, grey sole and flounder cannot compare with it either in delicacy of flavor or in the moist firmness of the flesh, but must usually by substituted. The results, however, are satisfactory.

This is the basic recipe—extremely simple in execution—of its type: poached fish fillets with a mounted butter sauce. There are literally hundreds of variations, but it is only necessary to succeed with one to be assured of success with all of them, for the method never changes—only the poaching liquid and the garnish. The poaching liquid may be a fish *fumet* made from either white or red wine, mushroom cooking liquid, the cooking liquid from mussels, a special wine (port, champagne, Château d'Yquem, Chambertin, etc.), or any combination of these. The preparation may be enriched by the addition of mussels, shrimp, mushrooms, shallots, truffles (certain "chic" restaurants add caviar to the sauce, to the detriment of both caviar and sauce—one, to my knowledge, adds both caviar and whiskey plus a few salmon eggs for color!). The fillets may remain flat, or be folded or rolled. They may be stuffed, usually with a base of mousseline forcemeat (sole, salmon, pike, or whiting) to which may be added a certain amount of *duxelles*, chopped truffles, chopped pistachio nuts, etc. The character of the sauce may be totally transformed by the addition of a special condiment (saffron, curry, etc.). Despite these and many other variations, the basic physical structure of the sauce remains constant.

Assuming a few simple rules to be borne in mind, the miracle never fails to occur, and each time one is left in wonder that butter alone can thicken a sauce. Because it contains neither farinaceous agents nor egg-yolk emulsion, and does not require an extended cooking process, it is perhaps the finest-textured, the purest in flavor, and the most easily digestible of all sauce types.

The following details must absolutely be respected:

(1) The cooking vessel should be of a heavy material that takes heat evenly and slowly and holds it long (heavy copper, earthenware, or enameled ironware).

(2) The fillets must be poached, *not* boiled.

(3) The cooking liquid should be reduced to the consistency of a light syrup and removed immediately from the flame. One must sense the right moment. It must pass, first through a period of frothy "foaming up," then settled into a regular boil, which is soon transformed into a rapid staccato surface bubbling. Several seconds later it will arrive

at the precise consistency desired. There should be but a few spoonfuls of liquid remaining.

(4) The butter should be removed from the refrigerator ahead of time, cut into small pieces and allowed to soften.

A preparation of this nature in a restaurant would be "glazed" just before serving; that is to say, once the sauce is finished and poured over the fish fillets, the serving dish is placed for a very few seconds under a very intense heat, which immediately browns the surface without penetrating the main body of the preparation or altering the sauce. This is hardly to be recommended in home kitchens, for they are never equipped with a grill powerful enough, and a prolonged stay beneath the usual flame could only result in overcooked fish floating in a disintegrated and oily sauce.

If the fish are bought whole, ask the fish merchant to fillet them, saving the carcasses. Or do it yourself—the experience is useful. Make an incision from top to bottom at the base of the tail, loosen the cut edge of the skin and, using a towel to ensure a firmer grip, hold the tail firmly with the left hand while ripping off the skin, the tip of which is also grasped with a towel, with the right hand. Repeat the procedure on the other side. Using a sharp, flexible boning knife, make an incision the length of the fish on each flat side, following the visible central line, corresponding to the spinal column, which separates the fillets. Starting at the head end and holding the knife firmly so that the blade, at an extreme angle, is nearly flat against the bones, slice carefully, but decisively, while lifting the fillet loose with the other hand. Trim the fillets neatly, removing any parts that may have been discolored by contact with blood, and the lacy edges that often contain tiny fin bones. Remove the eyes and gills and discard them, cut each carcass into 4 or 5 pieces and put these aside with the trimmings. Put the fillets to soak in a basin of cold water.

THE FUMET

Peel the onion and the carrot and slice them thinly. Smash the clove of garlic. Combine fish trimmings, vegetables, herbs and seasoning in a saucepan, pour the wine over, and add enough water to just cover. Bring to a boil and leave, covered, to simmer for 1/2 hour. Pour the contents of the saucepan into a sieve, placed over a mixing bowl, and press the solids well with a wooden pestle to extract all the juices.

Spread the fillets out, skin side down, on paper towels and place another towel over them, pressing well to sponge them dry. Sprinkle them with salt and pepper and place a thin slice of butter half the total length of the fillet on the lower (or thicker) half of each. Fold the slender half over and press gently. Butter the bottom and sides of a heavy *sauteuse* or low, wide earthenware casserole just large enough to hold the fillets without having to squeeze them in, sprinkle the bottom with half of the chopped herbs and place the folded fillets side by side on this bed. Pour in enough *fumet* to barely cover, sprinkle the surface lightly with salt and pepper (remembering that the *fumet* will be radically reduced, concentrating the saltiness) and the remaining chopped herbs, and press a round of generously buttered kitchen paper, cut to the dimensions of the cooking utensil, buttered side down, over the fillets. Everything up to this point, assuming the *fumet* to be cold, may be done an hour or so ahead of time, if desired.

Place the casserole, covered, over a medium to high flame (with earthenware placed over an asbestos pad, the flame may be turned to maximum strength). As the liquid heats, check regularly, lifting the edge of the buttered paper, and, the instant the boil is reached, remove from the heat and leave, tightly covered, to poach for 7 or 8 minutes.

Lift out the fillets, one by one, allowing them to drain well, and place them on a heated serving platter. Place another heated plate over them to keep them warm while finishing the sauce.

Reduce the sauce (if earthenware has been used for poaching, the liquid will have to be transferred to a metal saucepan) over a high flame, stirring constantly. Once it acquires a light syrupy consistency, remove it from the heat and, with a small whisk, whip in the remaining butter (which has previously been cut into small pieces and allowed to soften) at 3 intervals, adding more as the preceding batch is absorbed. It is essential that the butter be *unsalted* or the sauce will be oversalted—nor can one "make do" by undersalting the *fumet* and the fillets, for the latter will then be undersalted. Pour the sauce over the fillets and serve immediately, accompanied by the stewed cucumbers in a separate dish. The sauce will be consistent and creamy in texture without feeling "thick."

Stewed Cucumbers

Concombres à l'Etuvée

2 *pounds cucumbers*
salt, pepper
2 *tablespoons* (1 *ounce*) *butter*
chopped chervil (*optional*)

Peel the cucumbers, cut them in 4 lengthwise, scrape out the seeds with a small spoon, and cut them into approximately 1-inch lengths. Each section may, for the sake of elegance, be pared into the form of a large olive, but the quality of the preparation is in no way altered by this refinement. Plunge them into generously salted boiling water for a minute, drain them and sponge them dry, gently, with paper towels. Season them and put them to cook in butter over a low flame for 7 or 8 minutes, tossing them from time to time (turning them around with a spoon risks damaging them). An easy way to toss is to hold a lid over the sautéing pan with one hand while lifting the pan with the other and giving it an abrupt forward, upward and backward movement. The cucumbers should be only slightly yellowed by cooking and should remain slightly firm. Sprinkle with chervil and serve.

Spitted Roast Leg of Lamb

Gigot d'Agneau Rôti à la Broche

1 *leg of lamb*
2 *cloves garlic*
1 *teaspoon mixed herbs—thyme, rosemary, oregano, savory*

(*Continued*)

olive oil or melted butter
salt and pepper

A good leg of lamb is proportionately short and well rounded. The fat is white and plentiful and the flesh a clear rose-tan color. Do not buy dark, brownish-red meat. To be properly served, lamb must be carved at table and, to be properly carved at table, it is essential that a section of the leg bone be left protruding (it should be sawed off just above the hock) and that the upper section be boned to the joint (which is to say that the pelvic bone must be removed). American butchers, unless their origins are Italian or French, refuse to understand this, and one must insist. An American "leg of lamb" usually consists of a piece from which the lower third of the leg has been removed and to which part of the saddle remains attached.

Trim nearly all the fat from the leg. Peel the garlic cloves and slice them lengthwise into 3 or 4 sections each. Pierce the meat with the point of a small knife and insert garlic at either end next to the bone and at several points in the fleshier parts of the leg. Sprinkle with the herbs and rub the leg all over with the olive oil or melted butter. This may be done a couple of hours ahead of time and, if olive oil is used, the leg gains by "marinating" for a while.

Grass, or yearling, lamb (baby milk-fed lamb must be well done) is never so exquisite as when roasted medium-rare (in France it is often roasted so rare that the flesh in the middle remains rubbery and cold; in America it is most often cooked until completely dried out and savorless) on a spit before a well-attended fruitwood fire. One may count approximately 15 minutes' cooking time per pound, but it is impossible to be exact; meat which is too fresh takes longer to cook than meat which has been properly aged, and one fire, no matter how well attended, does not always have the same intensity as another. With a bit of experience, one can "feel" the right moment by pressing the surface of the meat between thumb and forefinger. When properly cooked, it is firm and resilient to the touch. For an average-sized leg of lamb, one may plan on an hour before an open fire (count 10 minutes less in an oven, starting it in a very hot oven that is turned down to medium the moment the roast is put in), during the last 10 minutes of which the turning of the spit should be stopped so that the thick, rounded section of the leg is left facing slightly downward toward the heart of the fire—baste regularly at this point. The roast should not be seasoned until well seared—about 15 minutes after being put to cook and after the actual cooking process, it should be always left in a warm place for a good 20 minutes to "relax." During this period, the flesh becomes firmer and the heat contained in it continues to even out the cooking of the interior. In an oven, one may leave it with the oven turned off and the oven door left slightly ajar. Before an open fire, it may be unspitted and placed, covered, in the dripping pan near the fire, or transferred to the serving platter and removed to a warm oven.

Prepare the fire in the fireplace a good hour before putting the roast to turn so that it will be blazing and a heart of coals will have formed. Nurse the outside edges to keep them flaming—there is always plenty of heat radiated from the center. Try to keep the logs in a vaguely semicircular form so that the heart of the fire is somewhat farther back than the outside parts. Construct a low wall of bricks, a strip of asbestos, etc., directly behind the dripping pan to protect it from the intense heat of the fire bed.

CARVING AND SERVING

There are two basic ways to carve a leg of lamb: the English way (in which the lean side is carved on the slant and the fleshy side perpendicularly to the bone) and the French (everything, starting with the fleshy side, carved at a slant). In any case, a screw-on handle (*manche à gigot*—see Kitchen Equipment, page 65) is essential. The carving knife must be razor-sharp. Screw the handle tightly onto the leg bone and, holding it firmly in hand with the other end of the leg resting on the serving platter, slice, almost flat (at a sharply acute angle to the bone), away from your person. When as many slices as there are guests have been produced, bring the knife back to the shank and, slicing slightly upward and still away from you, cut off as many slices as before (this section, distinctly different in flavor, is, because of its small size, always well done, but thanks to its gelatinous content it remains moist and succulent—in France it is affectionately known as *la souris*, "the mouse"). A great deal of juice will exude from the roast during the carving process. It is finest pure and unadorned, and should be served, a tablespoonful to each guest, over the meat. Return the serving platter to a warm oven in case second servings should be desired. Pass the green beans (below) the moment the roast has been served out.

Buttered Green Beans

Haricots Verts au Beurre

2 pounds tiny, freshly picked green beans
salt
1/4 pound butter

The same general remarks hold as for the green bean salad on page 412. The beans should be snapped at the ends, left whole, and cooked in the largest possible quantity of well-salted, rapidly boiling water until just done—around 8 minutes if they are small and fresh, as they should be. Before being buttered, they should be well drained (but not allowed to cool), returned to their cooking utensil, or to another large saucepan, and tossed (the pan should be held over the flame and the beans tossed constantly to avoid any possibility of sticking or scorching) over a high flame until their superficial moisture has completely disappeared. The butter should be cut into small pieces, and must not be added until the beans have been removed from the flame. Continue tossing and swirling the pan until all the butter has been absorbed. This is absolutely the only way to bind a boiled vegetable such as beans, peas, broad beans or cauliflower. In France, the vegetable is most often merely sautéed with the butter—that is to say, fried. The result is visually unattractive, bitter in flavor, and distinctly "unbound." In America, the butter is added in minuscule quantity to the undried vegetable, the result being a puddle of thin broth with a few globules of grease floating on top.

Peach Melba

Pêche Melba

Vanilla ice cream:
- *2 cups milk*
- *1/2 vanilla bean (or something less than 1 teaspoon of extract)*
- *1 egg yolk*
- *1/2 cup sugar*
- *1 cup whipping cream*

- *8 fresh peaches, poached in syrup*
- *1 quart fresh raspberries, passed through a nylon drum sieve and sugared to taste*
- *slivered fresh almonds (optional)*

The *pêche Melba* of worldwide fame is a scoop of ice cream with the half of a commercially canned peach on top, a spoonful of currant jelly on top of that, and a mound of frothy material shot from a gas-bomb apparatus topping the whole thing off. Each food, although of a different texture, has the same flavor—that of the chemical laboratory. The dessert created by Escoffier to honor the singer Nellie Melba depends on three things only for it to rank among the finest of classical French desserts: the honesty of the ice cream, flavorful peaches that have been freshly poached in a syrup containing only water and sugar, and a sauce that is nothing but a purée of fresh raspberries. The best whipped cream in the world only detracts. The only acceptable refinement is the sprinkling of a few sliced fresh almonds over the surface.

The following ice-cream recipe is only a suggestion, for all vanilla ice-cream recipes are good, provided that the ice cream is made of fresh milk, fresh eggs and fresh cream. The relative richness in egg yolks or cream, whether the basic "cream" is cooked beforehand or the whole thing is frozen raw in the form of a beaten-up eggnog, are all a question of taste, and not quality.

(*Continued*)

THE VANILLA ICE CREAM

Bring the milk to a boil with the vanilla bean (or flavor the hot milk with the extract), remove from the flame and allow it to infuse for about 10 minutes (or simply cool slightly if extract is used). Stir the egg yolk and the sugar together and beat until the yellow lightens in color, then slowly pour in the milk, stirring all the time. Place the saucepan over a low to medium flame and stir constantly with a wooden spoon, making certain to reach all corners of the saucepan, until the "cream" starts to take on a certain consistency (until it lightly coats the spoon). Above all, it must not be allowed to boil. Immerse the saucepan halfway in a basin of cold water, stirring the contents from time to time, and, when completely cooled, whip the cream until fairly firm and frothy, but not stiff, and stir it in. Freeze.

There is no perfect replacement for the old-fashioned hand-turned ice-cream freezer, but the small electrical apparatuses meant to be installed in the freezing compartment of a refrigerator produce respectable results with a minimum of effort. There are also electrical freezers, of the same form as the old-fashioned variety, which freeze by means of cracked ice and coarse salt; still, the movement is not the same. The old method was not that difficult—perhaps we should return to it.

THE PEACHES

Peel the peaches (if the skins resist, dip them for a moment in boiling water). In this age of huge, perfectly formed, beautiful and tasteless fruit, it is perhaps best to taste a tiny slice of each before accepting it for use. Put them into a boiling sugar-and-water syrup, sweetened to taste (1 cup of sugar to 3 cups of water is about right) and allow them to poach, covered, at a bare simmer for 5 or 6 minutes. Leave them to cool in the syrup.

Heap the ice cream in the center of a chilled, deep serving dish (crystal offers the prettiest presentation), surround it with the peaches (cut in half and pitted) and coat lightly with raspberry purée. Sprinkle the surface with peeled, sliced fresh almonds, if available, and send the rest of the sauce to the table in a sauceboat.

NOTE: If fresh peaches and raspberries are out of season, home-canned peaches are respectable and wholesome in taste, and frozen raspberries still recall the flavor of the fresh.

Two Elegant Summer Dinners

with appropriate wines

MENU II (FOR 6)

COLD CALVES' BRAINS IN CREAM SAUCE

[CERVELLES DE VEAU FROIDES A LA CREME]

A young, dry, fruity white wine:
Pouilly-Fumé, Sancerre,
Pouilly-Fuissé, Mercurey blanc

SQUID A L'AMERICAINE—RICE PILAF

[CALMARS A L'AMERICAINE—RIZ PILAF]

The same, or a "spicier," stronger
white wine: Châteauneuf-du-Pape blanc
or Château-Chalon

JELLIED POACHED CHICKEN

[POULE AU POT EN GELEE]

Château-Chalon or a light young
Burgundy red wine, served cool:
Côte de Beaune (Chassagne-Montrachet,
Santenay, etc.) or Mercurey

TOSSED GREEN SALAD WITH FINES HERBES

[SALADE VERTE AUX FINES HERBES]

CHEESES

[FROMAGES]

An older wine than the preceding:
a Côte de Nuits (following
a Côte de Beaune) or a Côtes-du-Rhône
(Châteauneuf-du-Pape, Hermitage)

APRICOT FRITTERS

[BEIGNETS D'ABRICOTS]

A fine Sauternes

This is hardly the menu to serve a group of visiting dignitaries with conventional palates that might object to cold brains and the octopus-like squid in a highly seasoned sauce. But the conception of the menu is not less fine for that. The succession of textures, flavors, colors and temperatures, distinctly different from one dish to another, could not be happier. It is a menu that deserves a fairly formal presentation, but should, no doubt, be shared with friends or guests known to be gastronomically adventurous in spirit.

The most difficult detail is the choice of white wine for the squid, for it should be powerful enough not to suffer from the heady personality of the dish, and at the same time fine enough neither to suffer by comparison with, nor to prejudice the palate against, the wine to follow. That which seems to ideally fulfill these requirements is Château-Cahlon, and whether one chooses either to serve a wine of lesser prestige with the squid and the Château-Chalon with the chicken or to serve Château-Chalon with both, it will answer equally well. The trouble is that it is hard come by and the price tends to be steep. A Burgundy rosé (Marsannay) might be drunk with the squid, followed by a Côte de Beaune red.

Cold dishes like the chicken in jelly (and game terrines, which in more elaborate menus find their place after the roast) are usually accompanied by a salad. For the qualities of the preparation, as well as those of its accompanying wine, to be justly appreciated, it seems best to withhold the salad at least to the halfway point in the service, offering it with second helpings.

Cold Calves' Brains in Cream Sauce

Cervelles de Veau Froides à la Crème

3 *fresh calves' brains*

Court-bouillon:
- 1½ *quarts water*
- ¼ *cup wine vinegar*
- 1 *carrot*
- 1 *onion*
- *thyme, bay leaf*
- *a large bouquet of parsley*
- *salt*
- 10–12 *whole peppercorns*

Sauce:
- *salt, freshly ground pepper*
- 1 *level teaspoon French mustard*
- 1 *lemon*
- 1 *cup heavy cream*
- 1 *heart fresh, crisp celery*
- 1 *tablespoon chopped chives*

Lambs' brains may be substituted, in which case, 1 brain should be counted per person. Choose brains as white as possible (avoiding those that are coated beneath the membrane with clotted blood), firm and moist-looking on the surface. If your plans are made far enough ahead of time, ask your butcher to procure them freshly for the specified day. Only very fresh brains are easily rid of the surface membrane (butchers have assured me over and over again that I am wrong and that it is a mere question of chance whether a brain is easily peeled or not, and yet, curiously, each time that I have bought brains from freshly killed animals and watched them being cut out of the head, the membrane has slipped off like magic).

French *crème-double* is always very thick (although not always impeccably fresh) and more suitable to this sauce than American whipping cream (*crème-double* is pure, unpasteurized separator cream, whereas the heaviest cream available in America today always has a certain percentage of milk homogenized into it). To get a cupful of really thick cream, one must pour a pint of whipping cream into a bowl and leave it, covered, in the refrigerator for 2 or 3 days, then spoon the required quantity off the surface. The remainder will always find a use in some other preparation.

Put the brains to soak in a basin of cold water immediately upon unwrapping them. After 1/2 hour, remove the surface membrane, carefully and delicately—if it resists, return the brain to soak and try another. Occasionally, to one's total desperation, the membrane sticks like glue no matter how much it has soaked. In this instance, one must simply do one's best. After the brains have been peeled, return them to a fresh basin of cold water and leave them to soak for up to an hour, changing the water 2 or 3 times. This last is a blanching process, intended to draw out discolorations from the brains. If they are perfectly white to begin with, it is unnecessary.

THE COURT-BOUILLON

Put the water and vinegar to boil, peel the carrot and onion and slice both thinly, and add all ingredients to the saucepan. Leave to simmer, covered, for 1/2 hour or so—long enough for the aromatic elements to have given their qualities to the liquid.

Slip the brains into the boiling *court-bouillon* and turn down the flame so that they poach at the barest simmer for from 20 to 25 minutes. Lift them out gently, one by one, with a perforated skimming spoon, place them on a plate and cover them with a cloth that has been moistened in the *court-bouillon* (which prevents them from drying out and discoloring on the surface). Put them to chill in the refrigerator until ready for use. Everything up to this point may be done hours ahead of time. The sauce, however, should be prepared no more than 1/2 hour to 1 hour before serving.

Trim the brains, slice them neatly, and arrange them on a chilled serving dish. Put salt, pepper, mustard and the juice of 1/2 lemon together in a bowl and stir until thoroughly combined. Pass the trimmings from the brains through a small sieve, stir them into the sauce, then stir in the cream. Taste and, if necessary, add a bit more lemon juice and additional seasoning. Chop the celery heart into tiny cubes and stir it in. Spoon the sauce over the brains and sprinkle with chopped chives. If one likes, a few of the carrot slices from the *court-bouillon* may be used to enhance the decorative aspect of the dish. In this case, the carrots should have been peeled with a serrated knife that leaves decorative ridges down the length of each carrot.

THE SQUID A L'AMERICAINE

Squid and cuttlefish are very similar and may be prepared in the same way. In America, squid are easier to find on the market. Tiny cuttlefish are very delicate and need a shorter cooking period (about 20 minutes). The dish is incorrectly named, but so generally known as *à l'américaine* that it seems useless to rebaptize it. (Any number of dishes are correctly entitled thusly—the sauce in these cases must be based on lobster. A lobster *à l'américaine*—not *à l'armoricaine*, as many people insist—is prepared in the same way, except that it must be cut up alive, it needs a shorter cooking period—12–15 minutes—and the sauce is finished with a paste of the mashed coral and butter and mounted with a larger quantity of butter.) This squid is often called the poor man's lobster *à l'américaine*. Once tasted, it needs no apology, and, except for those customers who are terrified at the notion of eating anything invertebrate, it never fails to please.

Squid à l'Américaine

Calmars à l'Américaine

2 pounds squid
1 onion
1 pound firm, ripe tomatoes
2 cloves garlic

(*Continued*)

3 *tablespoons olive oil*
salt, pepper, Cayenne
1 *small glass cognac*
1/3 *cup dry white wine*
thyme, bay leaf
4 *tablespoons* (2 *ounces*) *butter*
1 *small handful finely torn up fresh basil leaves*
  (*lacking that, fresh parsley*)

Clean the squid: pull the tentacles apart from the conical body, press the outsides of the tentacles at the mouth opening to force the little pouch of clawlike teeth to pop out, remove the eyes and any soft intestinal material that clings to the base of the tentacles. Clean out the inside of the body well and wash the tentacles and the body in several waters. Cut the conical bodies into sections about 1½ inches long. Put them into a colander and leave to drain.

Peel the onion and chop it finely. Put it to cook gently in a bit of olive oil or butter until it is soft and yellowed in color. Put it aside. Peel and seed the tomatoes and chop them coarsely. Smash the garlic cloves, peel them and chop them very finely.

Sponge the pieces of squid and their tentacles in paper towels to dry them. Heat the olive oil in a heavy *sauteuse* or large saucepan and throw in the squid. Sprinkle with salt and toss the pieces or stir them around regularly for a couple of minutes, keeping the flame high, until they have retracted in size and become firm. Add the cognac, set fire to it and stir constantly until the flames die down. Add the white wine, reduce a minute, still over a high flame, then add the chopped, cooked onion, the chopped garlic, the chopped tomatoes, a bit more salt, pepper, a small pinch of Cayenne pepper, the thyme and bay leaf; these vegetables, herbs, and seasonings may all be combined in a bowl ahead of time—if one is unfamiliar with a recipe, the process is tremendously simplified by having 1 rather than 8 items to add at a given time. Bring to a rapid boil, stir and scrape the bottom with a wooden spoon to be certain that nothing is sticking, and turn the fire down so that, covered, the sauce simmers. After 45 or 50 minutes (the squid is done when the flesh no longer produces a rubbery resistance to pressure) remove the pieces to a heated serving dish, discard the bay leaf and reduce the sauce over a high flame, stirring constantly with a wooden spoon until it becomes fairly consistent. It should not be too thick, but it must lose its watery consistency. Remove the pan from the heat and add the butter, cut into small pieces. Swirl the pan until all the butter is absorbed into the sauce, and pour it over the squid. Sprinkle the surface with the finely torn up basil leaves (torn only at the last minute or they will be discolored and unsightly) or the chopped parsley. Serve accompanied by a Rice Pilaf (page 81).

Jellied Poached Chicken

Poule au Pot en Gelée

1 *large tender roasting chicken with skin intact, including that of the neck (a well-fed, 6-months-old farm chicken, if possible)*

Bouillon:

1 *pound gelatinous lean veal*
broken veal bones (hock, etc.)
1 *pound chicken necks and the boned chicken's carcass*
8 *chicken feet*
3 *onions,* 1 *stuck with* 2 *cloves*
2 *carrots*
2 *leeks*
thyme, bay leaf, parsley, salt

Stuffing:

1 *clove garlic*
1 *small bowl (about* 1½ *cups) half-dried bread from which crusts have been removed*
1 *ladleful of the bouillon above*
10 *ounces chicken livers (plus that of the chicken being poached)*
1 *medium onion, finely chopped*
2 *tablespoons butter*
1 *teaspoon dried Mixed Herbs (page* 86)
1 *tablespoon finely chopped parsley*
2 *eggs*
salt, pepper

(Continued)

Clarification:
- 2 *egg whites*
- 1 *small handful chopped chervil and tarragon*

- *juice of* 1 *lemon*
- 1 *small glass good port (or Banyuls or Madeira)*
- *decorative elements: hard-boiled egg whites, truffle, black olives, blanched tarragon leaves, canned pimento, fragments of tomato, etc.*

The bouillon is prepared like the Veal Jelly on page 358. The calf's foot is replaced by chickens' feet (first turned over a flame until the skin is blistered, then skinned by rubbing them with a towel—the skin and claw nails slip off very easily), the broken-up bones, and the carcass of the chicken. It is this stock that serves as the poaching liquid for the chicken, and subsequently for the jelly.

The bouillon should be prepared and the chicken boned, stuffed and poached the preceding day. The finishing decorative touches may be executed on the morning of the day on which the dinner is planned. (If the dish were intended for a luncheon, it would be wiser to finish it the day before.)

A much simpler presentation is possible. The additional work of clarification, decoration, and painstaking masking with jelly may be eliminated if one simply places the poached, unwrapped fowl in an oval terrine, pours all the bouillon over it and puts it to cool. It may be served directly from the terrine or turned out just before serving. In the latter case, the chicken should be placed breast side down in the terrine in order to be turned out right side up. To me, it seems a pity to sacrifice the more elaborate presentation in this instance, for the dish lends itself so perfectly to it.

THE BONING PROCESS

The chicken is only partially boned, the breastbone, the wing bones and the leg bones remaining. It is possible to remove the breastbone also, if one wishes, but the final manipulations will be more difficult because of the loose consistency of the raw stuffing. The following instructions are for a picked and singed but uncleaned chicken (the only way one may be certain of its skin remaining intact). The usual commercial product often has its skin ripped open across the breast and the abdomen has always been torn into a huge gash. You may still, with a bit of careful patchwork, approximate the preparation, hiding its imperfections beneath the decoration, so don't give up, even if your chicken is less than perfect in appearance.

As the feet, neck, wing tips, and carcass are removed from the chicken, throw them into the pot of stock (which is already cooking) along with the giblets. The boning process goes slowly the first time, but it is simple and logical, and one need only be relaxed and patient. Work seated at a table, in a good light. Remove the feet, and the wing tips at the second joint. Using a small, pointed, well-sharpened knife, cut the skin of the chicken the length of the back, from the top of the neck to the base of the tail, following the line of the backbone. Pull the skin loose from the neck, being careful not to tear it, and cut off the neck at its base. Loosen the flesh adhering to the skin, following the contour of the rib cage, slicing little by little and, when it is possible, forcing the flesh loose from the bones with your fingers. Slice through the ligaments at the leg-bone and wing-bone joints to liberate them from the body of the skeleton. With care, you will be able to lift out the entire spinal column and the rib-cage section containing the heart, liver, gizzard and intestines. Rather than risk tearing the skin at the tip of the tail, clip the spinal column just before. Remove the wishbone, the "shoulder-blade" type of bones reaching to the wing joints, and the few small flexible bones attached to either side of the breastbone, and, with a pair of kitchen shears, cut vertically through the breastbone, being careful not to pierce the skin of the breast. This permits the chicken to swell, while cooking, into a plump, rounded shape.

NOTE: It is perfectly possible to completely bone a chicken without puncturing the skin at any point except for a small slit on the back of the neck (the method is described on page 295), and once one understands the principle, it goes more rapidly than the above method and the results are more elegant. But it seems best to acquaint oneself with a chicken's anatomy by first boning it opened up, rather than to attack the earlier method blindly.

THE STUFFING

Pound the clove of garlic to a paste in the mortar. Add the bread, crumbled or broken up, pour a ladleful of the bouillon over, mix well together, and leave to soak. Pick over the livers carefully, cutting off any parts that are tinged with green and pulling out the whitish membranelike threads that connect the lobes. Place livers in a mound on the chopping board and, with a well-sharpened French chef's knife, chop them finely, turning the mass over several times (the first time through, they have to be cut, rather than chopped, to prevent their flying all over the place—after that, you can land into them, chopping with loose wrist and machine-gun continuity). Put the chopped onion to cook gently in butter without allowing it to brown. Pound the mixed herbs to powder in a mortar.

Press the excess liquid from the soaked bread and put it into a large mixing bowl along with the livers, the cooked onion, chopped parsley, powdered herbs, the 2 eggs, salt, and freshly ground pepper. Mix thoroughly with your hands, squeezing the mixture through your fingers over and over again (there is no other way) until it is completely homogeneous. Taste for salt.

Thread a large needle (a curved upholsterer's needle works most easily) with a good yard of kitchen string. Pierce the skin on either side of the anus. Knot the string, leaving 3 or 4 inches of loose end, and, starting at the tail, sew the chicken about 1/3 to 1/2 the way up the back, folding the skin in such a way as to leave no possible openings (as you would fold or roll the top and bottom edges of a pie crust under before pinching it). Now pour in the stuffing, lifting and pulling gently at the skin and shaking the bird around a bit to settle the stuffing into the pocket formed by the sewn lower half. Continue sewing almost to the top, then run the needle through the center of the underside of the neck-skin flap, fold the flap over the back (as for sealing an envelope) and sew all around the edges. Wrap the remaining length of string once around the upper part of the chicken, piercing through the wings to fix them in place and, drawing the string diagonally across the breast, wrap it 2 or 3 times around the drumstick ends and the tail, then tie the two ends of string together. Rub the surface all over with lemon juice to keep it white, and "mold" the chicken in your hands to ease it into its natural form. Wrap it, firmly but without forcing, in a cloth (or a double layer of cheesecloth) and tie the two ends securely.

Remove the debris from the bouillon with a large skimming spoon (if a few odds and ends remain, it is of no importance—the bouillon will be strained later), and put the chicken into the pot. Leave the cover slightly ajar and, once the liquid returns to a boil, regulate the heat so that there is the barest suggestion of a simmer. One and one-half hours later, remove the chicken and leave it, still wrapped up, to cool. Pass the cooking liquid through a fine drum sieve (or through a strainer lined with a cloth) and leave it to cool.

Unwrap the chicken, place it on the serving plate, and, holding it with one hand, clip the knot in the string and pull one end of it firmly but carefully. It will suddenly give, and the entire length may be slipped out without affecting the chicken's form.

When the bouillon is cold, remove all traces of fat from the surface and clarify it exactly as veal jelly on page 359, adding the wine of your choice when the liquid is nearly cool.

THE DECORATION

Cool small quantities of jelly at a time in a bowl placed over cracked ice. First coat the chicken thinly all over with jelly; then dip each element of the décor into the jelly, affix all to the surface of the chicken, and put the dish into the refrigerator for 15 minutes so that the décor may set. Trickle the semiliquid jelly over the chicken, concentrating on the highest points (leg joints and breastbone) over and over again, until jelly is all used up—or, if there is enough jelly, until the outline of the chicken, softened through the undulating coat of jelly, melts into the mirror of clear jelly at its base. Put to chill until serving. The base may be decorated with small bouquets of chervil or parsley.

Apricot Fritters

Beignets d'Abricots

12 *apricots, ripe but firm*
sugar (3 *or* 4 *tablespoons*)
about 2 *tablespoons cognac*

Frying batter:

1 *egg*
1 *scant cup flour*
1 *pinch salt*
1/3 *cup tepid beer*
about 2 *tablespoons water*
2 *tablespoons* (1 *ounce*) *melted butter*
1 *tablespoon cognac oil* (*preferably a light olive oil*) *for frying*

Cut the apricots in 2, sprinkle them with sugar and cognac and leave them to macerate for an hour or so. Separate the yolk from the white of the egg and put the white aside. Sift the flour and salt into a mixing bowl, make a well in the center, add the egg yolk, the beer and the water and stir from the center outward until the flour is incorporated into the liquid. Stir in the melted butter and the cognac. Do not beat; excessive stirring and beating renders the batter elastic, and it will not adhere properly to the objects to be fried. It is for this reason, no matter how little the batter has been worked, that it is wise to leave it to "relax" for an hour or so before using. It should be fairly liquid (a thicker batter holds its form better, but tends to be spongy, whereas, although a thinner batter disperses threads into the frying oil, it is finer, lighter, and crisper). Leave it to rest an hour or so and, just before using, gently fold in the egg white, beaten stiff. Sponge the excess liquid from the apricot halves, drop 1/3 of them into the batter and, being certain that each is well coated with batter, lift them out, one at a time, with a teaspoon, and drop them into the deep fat. (It should be hot, but not smoking; let a drop of batter fall in, and if it sizzles immediately, the oil is ready.) When the fritters are golden and crisp, lift them out with a large wire skimming spoon and wrap them in a towel while continuing with the other 2 batches. When all have been fried, transfer them to a serving platter on which has been placed a folded napkin, sprinkle them with powdered sugar, and serve, the surface covered with the flaps of the napkin to keep them warm.

A Semi-formal Summer Dinner

with appropriate wines

THE MENU (FOR 8)

CANTALOUPE WITH PARMA HAM

[MELON CHARENTAIS AU JAMBON DE PARME]

A white wine, light in body, but
with a distinct fruit and not too dry:
Vouvray, Savennières, Hermitage blanc, etc.

BRAISED STUFFED ARTICHOKE BOTTOMS

[FONDS D'ARTICHAUTS FARCIS A LA DUXELLES]

The same wine as the preceding

GRILLED LAMBS' KIDNEYS WITH HERB BUTTER

POTATO STRAW CAKE

[ROGNONS D'AGNEAU GRILLES CHIVRY]

[PAILLASSON DE POMMES DE TERRE]

A young, fruity red wine:
Touraine (Chinon, Bourgueuil)
or Beaujolais (Fleurie, Saint-Amour,
Chénas, Juliénas, etc.)

TOSSED GREEN SALAD

[SALADE VERTE]

CHEESES

[FROMAGES]

The same wine as the preceding,
or another of the same general type
(an older Touraine or a Beaujolais,
still from the most recent vintage,
but a different growth)

PEACHES IN RED WINE

[PECHES A LA VIGNERONNE]

In most parts of America, Parma ham may have to be replaced by *prosciutto*, and the Charentais melon by the local cantaloupe.

The Charentais melon—that most raised in France—is a smooth-skinned variety of cantaloupe. It is often served chilled, macerated in port wine, but, except for a slight sprinkling of salt and freshly ground pepper, its natural qualities are best thrown into relief when it is unadorned. (Colette, whose palate was as fine as her pen, was horrified at the idea of chilling melon, for it kills "the taste of the sun.") Melon requires a fairly rich, though not necessarily delicate, wine. It can be nicely accompanied by a semi-dry port or Banyuls, but a wine of this sort lends an unwelcome reception to the following white wine. The reasonable solution is to serve a single white wine that has the necessary body to flatter the melon while remaining sufficiently dry to accompany the following course (melon and raw ham are an Italian marriage and, in fact, are easily washed down by a good Frascati, which could serve as well for the artichokes).

The meal requires a minimum of preparation and, with the exception of the actual cooking of the artichokes, potatoes, and kidneys, everything may be done in advance. The artichokes may be put to cook 15 minutes before the diners go to table, the potatoes at the same time as the artichokes are served, and the kidneys only after the second course is finished.

Braised Stuffed Artichoke Bottoms

Fonds d'Artichauts Farcis à la Duxelles

Artichoke bottoms:

8 medium artichokes
lemon, thyme, salt

Duxelles:

1/2 pound mushrooms
2 medium-size white onions
1 tablespoon chopped parsley

2 tablespoons (1 ounce) butter
lemon, salt, pepper, nutmeg

Mirepoix:

1 medium-size carrot
1 medium-size onion
1 tablespoon (1/2 ounce) butter
thyme, bay leaf, salt

10 thin slices fresh or salted side pork (or bacon)
salt, pepper
6 tablespoons unsalted butter
equal quantities of dry white wine and stock, bouillon, or water (from 1/2 to 1 cup of each, depending on the preciseness with which the artichoke bottoms fit into the utensil)
chopped parsley

The methods of preparation for Artichoke Bottoms, *Duxelles* and *Mirepoix* are given on pages 77, 76, and 75. If the latter two are already made up, count about 8 tablespoons of *duxelles* (enough to stuff each artichoke bottom, well packed but not heaped up) and 2 heaping tablespoons of *mirepoix*.

It is rare, on the American market, to find artichokes sufficiently young and tender not to require precooking. Should they be available, they need only be turned, the chokes removed, and the artichokes then rubbed with lemon and seasoned with salt and thyme before being stuffed and put to cook.

The nature of the preparation is such that in a more elaborate menu it might perfectly serve to garnish a braised or roasted meat. Served as a course apart, its qualities will be better appreciated. For a less delicate version, one may reduce the cooking liquid without removing the *mirepoix*, and buttering the reduction as needed. The result is more rustic in spirit, but still very good.

A good gelatinous veal stock will lend a great deal of support to the sauce, but if you have no natural essences on hand, don't try to "improve" the flavor by the addition of bouillon cubes or other commercial products.

Choose a *sauteuse* or casserole of the exact dimensions, as nearly as possible, to just hold the artichoke bottoms without their being packed in. Line the bottom with the *mirepoix* (which may be prepared in the same pan if it is not enameled).

If the side pork is either salted or smoked, parboil the slices in simmering water for a couple of minutes and drain them. Season the inside of each artichoke bottom with a bit of salt and pepper and place a small piece of butter in each. Stuff them with *duxelles*, with the help of a teaspoon, packing the stuffing in firmly and smoothing the surface. Wrap a slice of side pork around each, tying it in place with a string, cut each of the 2 remaining strips into 4 sections and press 1 over each surface of *duxelles*.

Place the prepared artichoke bottoms, side by side, on the bed of *mirepoix*, pour in the liquids and bring to a boil. Cook, covered, at a bare bubble for about 40 minutes. Remove the artichoke bottoms to a preheated serving dish, discarding the strips and pieces of side pork (or saving them to put into a soup). Pass the cooking liquid through a fine sieve into a small, heavy saucepan, pressing well without rubbing (in order to extract all the juices, without at the same time passing the solids through in purée). Reduce the liquid over a high flame, stirring constantly. The moment it begins to turn syrupy in consistency, remove the pan from the heat and whip in the remaining butter, cut into small pieces. Spoon the sauce over the artichoke bottoms, sprinkle each with a pinch of chopped parsley, and serve.

Grilled Lambs' Kidneys with Herb Butter

Rognons d'Agneau Grillés Chivry

8–12 (*depending on appetites*) *fresh lambs' kidneys*
olive oil or melted butter
salt and pepper

American butchers are prepared to argue the virtue of frozen kidneys. They should be absolutely refused, for there is no comparison between the fresh and the frozen. If the kidneys are not to be used immediately after their purchase, ask your butcher not to remove the protective covering of fat. To remove it yourself, use a sharp paring knife and cut lengthwise across the part corresponding to the top of the kidney, only just touching the surface of the kidney itself. Carefully peel off the heavy layer of fat and the thin transparent skin covering the kidney. Remove the skin, cutting it as closely as possible to its attachment at the base without cutting into the kidney. Beginning at the top, slit the kidneys lengthwise, being careful not to cut them completely in two. Open them out, butterfly-fashion, and, using either sharpened branches of rosemary or small skewers, skewer them across—this prevents their folding up as the flesh becomes firmer through contact with heat. Turn them around in the olive oil or melted butter and, just before putting them to cook, season both sides with salt and freshly ground pepper. Sear the cut surface first (face up beneath a broiler or face down over hot coals). Grilled over hot coals, they are much better, but the essential thing to remember, no matter what the method of grilling, is that, to remain moist, flavorful, and tender, the kidneys must remain pink inside. Once having been turned, the moment a rose-tinged tiny drop of liquid appears on the surface, they are done. Count approximately 2 minutes on each side (more or less depending on the intensity of the heat).

Serve them immediately on a large, round, preheated serving platter, arranged face up in a circle around the potato cake, a teaspoonful of Herb Butter (below) in the center of each kidney, and a tablespoonful on the potato cake. Serve the remaining butter separately.

HERB BUTTER

2 *chopped gray shallots* (*or* 1 *small onion*)
1 *large handful* (*about* 3 *ounces*) *parsley and chervil leaves*
1 *heaping tablespoon chopped chives*
1 *heaping teaspoon fresh tarragon leaves*
1/4 *pound* (1 *stick*) *butter*

Blanch the chopped shallots (or onion) for a couple of minutes in boiling water and drain. Plunge all the herbs into boiling water and, after 1/2 minute, drain and press in a cloth to rid them of excess moisture. Pound the herbs and shallots together in a mortar until reduced to a purée, mix together with the butter (removed ahead of time from the refrigerator and allowed to soften) and pass through a drum sieve, using a plastic disk (or, lacking that, through an ordinary fine sieve, using a wooden pestle). Stir the resultant purée so that the greener parts (the last to pass through the sieve) are thoroughly mixed into the butter. If not used immediately, keep covered and chilled, but remove from the refrigerator ahead of time so that the herb butter will be soft—otherwise it will chill the kidneys on contact.

THE POTATO STRAW CAKE

Simplicity itself to make, this preparation is a splendid standby. It can be whipped together in a few minutes and is a perfect accompaniment to any grilled or roasted meat or fowl. It may be enriched or rendered more fanciful by the addition of another ingredient hidden in a layer between the sealed surfaces of golden crisp potato (a julienne of carrots, stewed first in butter, sliced artichoke hearts sautéed in butter, etc. A julienne of fresh truffles spread in a central layer will lend a penetrating and luxuriant perfume that marries particularly well with roast game birds). For a perfect execution, one must use the little vegetable mill known as *mouli-julienne.* Otherwise, one may simply grate the potatoes. The result is satisfactory, but the interior texture is more compact and less delicate.

Potato Straw Cake

Paillasson de Pommes de Terre

about 1¼ *pounds potatoes, preferably of the nonmealy variety*
¼ *pound* (1 *stick*) *butter*
salt, pepper

Peel the potatoes, cut them into sections so that they fit into the *mouli-julienne*, and grind them directly into a large saucepan filled with cold water. Drain, wash again, and leave to drain for a few minutes in a sieve. Spread them out on paper towels and rub them well with another towel; it is essential that all the surface starch be washed from them, both to ensure the lightness of the interior texture and to prevent their sticking to the pan, and they must be equally well dried to avoid the risk of their turning into a messy soup. If desired, the potatoes may be prepared an hour or so ahead of time and kept, wrapped in a towel, until ready for use.

Use a good heavy iron omelet pan about 9 inches across—it will not suffer from this use and may simply be wiped out with a dry cloth afterwards, exactly as after making an omelet. The flame should be low to medium; every stove is different, and one must judge by experience. It is better that the flame be too low to start with than too high—it can always be turned up if the browning process seems to go too slowly, but once the potatoes are burnt, the damage is irreparable. Melt 3 ounces of the butter in the pan, roll it around so that the bottom and sides are well coated with butter, and empty in the potatoes (don't wait for the butter to bubble or turn brown). Pack them down with a fork, gently and unhurriedly, until the mass is firm and the surface formed in a smooth, shallow dome with no straggly, loose strands around the edges. Sprinkle evenly with salt and freshly ground pepper and place the remaining butter, cut into several pieces, around the edges, against the sides of the pan. Leave to cook, covered, for approximately 18 to 20 minutes. It should not be touched until ready to be turned, but if it is being prepared for the first time, take a look at it from time to time. It is ready to turn when the delicate, nutty odor of the cooked butter fills the kitchen and the very edge of the cake begins to be golden and frizzled. Before turning, make certain that the edges are loose all the way round, then jerk the pan slightly to be assured that the entire cake slides loosely in the pan. Slip a wide spatula or pancake turner beneath it and, with a single, deft movement, turn it over; nothing is easier, but if the idea makes you nervous, it is very simple to slip the half-cooked cake onto a plate, hold the pan upside down over the plate, then turn plate and pan back over (a bit of butter will no doubt be lost in this process and should be replaced with fresh around the edges). Season the cooked side and leave to cook, this time uncovered, for another 15 minutes. Slip the cake from the pan directly onto the heated serving dish.

Peaches in Red Wine

Pêches à la Vigneronne

1 *pound peaches*
sugar to taste
1/2 *bottle good red wine (the same as served with the main course, preferably)*

In wine-making areas, this is one of the commonest summer desserts, peaches replacing the springtime strawberries. Each person prepares his own portion, adding the sliced peaches to his wineglass and sugaring to taste. However, in case some of your guests might be taken aback at the notion of mixing peaches and red wine, they should be prepared in advance, to be certain that the joy is shared by all.

Peel the peaches, slice them, sprinkle with sugar and leave to macerate. Shortly before serving, pour the wine over.

Four Simple Summer Luncheons à la Provençale

Meridional French cooking is a world apart. Although certain typically Provençal dishes have been adopted by classical French cooking, the general spirit remains distinctly different. What it lacks in delicacy and nuance, it largely makes up for in robust vitality, high-spiritedness and color. Its affinities with the food of other Mediterranean countries, and in particular with that of Italy, are obvious, but the refinement is greater. Olive oil, olives, garlic, tomatoes, anchovies, saffron, Cayenne, basil and all those herbs that grow wild in profusion—thyme, rosemary, fennel, savory, oregano and serpolet—are the characteristic elements (with little exception, the only herbs used in France outside of Provence are thyme, bay leaf and *fines herbes*—parsley, tarragon, chervil and chives). Lamb and mutton are more often used in Provençal cooking than veal and beef, for good reason—the flocks are shepherded on mountainsides covered with herbs, with which their flesh is exquisitely perfumed. The little veal and beef produced in this part of the country is mediocre in quality. Rabbit and guinea fowl take precedence over chicken, and eggplant, zucchini, sweet peppers, broad beans and artichokes are typical vegetables.

The wines in themselves are not remarkable, but they accompany perfectly the food, whose aggressive qualities would mask the subtlety of a finer product. This is the only section of France where more *vin rosé* is drunk than either red or white wine (elsewhere rosé is rather looked down on), and logically, Provençal food is probably the only food that is best accompanied by rosé wine.

The Mediterranean verve that typifies most of the favorite specialties of Provence defies any attempt to compose them into elaborate menus, for other dishes in juxtaposition would inevitably suffer. Depending on the dish, it should form the entire body of the meal, with a bit of green salad and fresh fruit to finish, or, at most, it should be preceded by a simple hors d'oeuvre and the salad followed by a fresh cheese. There are few traditional desserts in Provençal cooking and those few are extremely simple in nature. These are dishes that seem to go with the sun, the summer, and the out-of-doors (brightly colored tablecloths and ceramic dishes are in the spirit) and are probably better eaten at lunchtime than at dinner. To properly enjoy them, they should perhaps be reserved for vacation time, for a true, old-fashioned Provençal siesta can be useful after such a luncheon. The following menus are conceived in these terms, and, with each, a light, dry, well-chilled rosé (Bandol, Cassis, La Palette, Tavel, Lirac, Chusclan) would be ideal.

It is not possible to include every characteristic dish here, but I particularly regret the omission of *aïoli* (a garlic-flavored mayonnaise accompanied, in its simplest form, by boiled salt cod, boiled potatoes, and boiled carrots, and in its most elaborate—*le grand aïoli*—by artichokes, cauliflower, beets, green beans, chickpeas, mushrooms, hard-boiled eggs, land snails cooked in white-wine *court-bouillon*, sea snails cooked in herb-flavored sea water, squid *à l'américaine*, black olives, raw celery, etc.), and *bourride* (a simplified *soupe aux poissons* containing slices of two or three varieties of large, white-fleshed fish, the bouillon of which is thickened by the addition of an *aïoli*). Good recipes for both are to be found in all books on Provençal cooking.

Four Simple Summer Luncheons à la Provençale

MENU I (FOR 6 TO 8)

Appropriate wine:
a light, dry, well-chilled rosé

PROVENCAL FISH STEW
[SOUPE AUX POISSONS]

TOSSED GREEN SALAD
[SALADE VERTE]

FRESH WHITE CHEESE WITH FINES HERBES
[CERVELLE DE CANUT]

FRESH FRUITS
[FRUITS FRAIS]

THE PROVENÇAL FISH STEW

Bouillabaisse is, to tell the truth, more a philosophy than a culinary preparation. More gastronomic literature—and quarrels—have centered around it than any other dish (with *cassoulet* running a close second). If most of the recipes for it were to be followed, however, the result could only be the most banal of fish soups (I am thinking of those in French—some that I have seen in American and English cookbooks would make the hair of the most indifferent Marseillais stand on end).

It is not a delicate dish; to be good, it must be highly seasoned, and it is terrifyingly soporific, but it embodies and engenders the warmth, the excitement, and the imagination which, perhaps, of all the Mediterranean peoples, the Provençaux exude in the highest degree. At best, it belongs to the realm of divine things.

There is a perpetual quarrel as to whether *soupe de poissons* (literally, soup of fish) or *bouillabaisse* (which is a *soupe* aux *poissons*, or soup *with fish*) is the finest dish. This is essentially debated among professional eaters and writers on food who are not experts on the technical side of things, for any professional chef knows (though rarely tells) that a really good *soupe aux poissons* is moistened, not with water, but with a fish stock, which is nothing more nor less than a *soupe de poissons*. Another detail little discussed by its practitioners is the addition of a bit of pastis, an anise-flavored apéritif alcohol similar to absinthe. It serves admirably to reinforce the perfume of the fennel in the dish.

A number of circumstantial factors are, no doubt, essential for this fish soup to be translated into a memorable experience. It should be the main dish—and plentiful; it should be shared with friends in a relaxed and informal atmosphere; it marries well with the sea air (in any case, the proximity of the ocean tends to ensure the freshness of the fish); the wine should be kept generously flowing throughout the meal. I, personally, have many sublime memories of entire days devoted to shopping (early in the morning to the fish market to find the freshest fish of the greatest possible variety), everyone preparing fish and vegetables together (accompanied by a few more pastis than wisdom would ordinarily dictate), followed by euphoric hours spent at table.

The following is a list of fish used traditionally in *bouillabaisse*, with English translation where possible (although some may be unobtainable in English-speaking countries), and possible substitutes:

Rascasse: The one fish considered absolutely indispensable. Its appearance is vicious; alone, its flesh is mediocre in quality. The ocean *rascasse*, though retaining the same form as the Mediterranean fish, is without interest. No translation. Substitute red snapper.

Vive: Weaver. I have never seen this fish in American markets, but it or a near cousin likely exists in American waters. It is a sand-burrowing shore fish. Substitute whiting.

Girelle: I find no translation for this gloriously colored fish, and a substitution is difficult. Although wall-eyed pike is a freshwater fish, one might try it.

St.-Pierre: John Dory. A ferocious-looking fish of very delicate flesh which exists in English waters, but, to the best of my knowledge, not in American. Substitute grey sole or lemon sole.

Congre: Conger eel.

Baudroie or *Lotte*: Angler-fish. Substitute sea bass, fresh haddock or fresh cod.

Rouget: Red mullet. The Mediterranean rock mullet (*rouget des roches*) is far finer than any other—it even seems a pity to lose its delicacy in a *bouillabaisse*. Substitute other mullets.

Favouilles: Small crabs. Substitute soft-shelled crabs.

There are others with no translations, and no easy substitutions, some of which the fishermen themselves are not always able to name. The Caribbean is undoubtedly rich in species with which I am unfamiliar that would lend themselves well to this preparation. Mussels are often added and one often finds *langouste* (rock lobsters) added for elegance's sake, but neither the lobster nor the soup gains in this marriage.

The following recipe is entitled noncommittally *Soupe aux Poissons*, out of respect for those purist defenders of the true *bouillabaisse*, which is prepared with fish to be found only on the rocky Mediterranean shores, moistened only with water, and accompanied by *la rouille*, a highly flavored *pommade* made by pounding together Cayenne pepper and raw garlic, and adding olive oil (some mount it, like a mayonnaise, with egg yolks). Generally speaking, the qualities essential to the success of the dish given here are a variety of absolutely fresh fish (at least 5 or 6 different kinds, some of firm gelatinous flesh, others of tender white flesh—avoid, above all, any strongly flavored oily fish such as sardines or mackerel), a very good quality fruity olive oil, and a rapid boil (the word *bouillabaisse* means "boil at top speed"). This rapid boiling, by forming a light emulsion of the oil in the cooking liquid, thickens the soup. If some of the suggested fish are unavailable, substitute others and don't worry about it.

Provençal Fish Stew

Soupe aux Poissons

4 *pounds mixed whole fish of medium size*—5–10 *ounces (small red snappers, grey sole, lemon sole, mullet, whiting, wall-eyed pike, etc.)*
1 *pound sea bass, fresh cod, halibut, etc., cut into thick slices*
1 *pound conger eel, cut into slices approximately* 1½ *inches thick*
1 *pound soft-shelled crabs*
1 *cup olive oil*
herbs: branches of wild fennel (or lacking these, fennel seed), bay leaf, thyme, savory, oregano
approximately ½ *teaspoon powdered saffron and a good pinch of whole saffron (more or less, according to taste)*
1 *small glass of pastis, Pernod* '51 *or Ricard*
1 *pound leeks*
3 *medium onions*
4–5 *cloves garlic*
approximately 3 *quarts water*
1 *pound fish carcasses (ask your fish merchant for carcasses from fish that have been filleted—these replace, albeit imperfectly, the little "soup fish" used on the Mediterranean coast)*
dried orange peel
salt (preferably coarse sea salt—or, if near the ocean, sea water diluted to the right saltiness)
1½ *pounds firm, well-ripened tomatoes*

freshly ground pepper
about 20 slices of French bread, dried out, either in the sun or in a very slow oven, but not toasted
garlic (6–7 cloves) with which to rub the bread

Cut off the fins, remove the gills and scale and clean the fish that are whole, if this has not been done for you. The heads may be removed or not—the presentation is more attractive if the heads remain, but the fish stock is thus impoverished. Trim the slices of larger fish to make them more presentable and put aside the trimmings with the heads and carcasses. Sponge all the fish and seafood, dry with paper towels, spread them out on a large platter and sprinkle them thoroughly with some of the olive oil, then with the herbs, about ⅓ teaspoon of powdered saffron, and finally with half the pastis. Gently rub the fish in your hands, inside and out, until they are all equally yellowed by the saffron, then leave to marinate, turning them around from time to time, while preparing the fish stock and vegetables.

THE FISH STOCK

Cut off the tough, dark-green parts of the leeks and discard them. Slit the remaining parts halfway down to facilitate washing them and, when they are well washed, cut each in 2 in order to separate the greenish parts from the white of the leek. Put the white parts aside and coarsely chop the green parts. Peel the onions, put 2 aside and coarsely chop the third. Crush the 4–5 cloves of garlic.

Heat the water and add the heads, carcasses and trimmings of the fish, chopped leek greens, chopped onion, crushed garlic, a branch of fennel (or seeds), dried orange peel, thyme, bay leaf, and salt. Bring to a boil and cook, covered, over a medium flame, for approximately ½ hour. After 15 to 20 minutes, crush all the solid material with a wooden pestle. Pour the contents of the pot into a fine sieve and press the debris well with a pestle or wooden spoon in order to extract all the flavor possible.

THE FINAL STEPS

Dip the tomatoes in boiling water for a moment to loosen their skins, peel them, cut them in 2 horizontally and squeeze them to rid them of seeds and excess liquid. Chop the white parts of the leeks and the remaining onions finely.

Pour the remaining oil (there should be approximately 2/3 cup) into a very large saucepan (the fishermen in the south of France use a large galvanized tin basin, the same form as a dishpan—if you have no suitable saucepan, an enameled dishpan will serve). Put the chopped leeks and onions to cook gently in the oil, stirring them regularly with a wooden spoon, and, 10 minutes later, add the chopped tomatoes, a pinch of powdered saffron, a pinch of whole saffron (the powdered, assuming it to be pure good-quality saffron, lends more flavor, and the whole saffron lends a decorative aspect), and a piece of dried orange peel. Continue to cook for another 5 minutes or so, salt lightly (bearing in mind that the fish stock has already been salted to taste) and add a generous amount of freshly ground pepper. Place the pan over the highest possible flame and add the fish stock and the remaining pastis. From this moment count 15 minutes' cooking time. The liquid should be kept at a rapid boil and the pan uncovered. The fish should be added at 3 different intervals; those of firm and somewhat gelatinous flesh should be added first along with any crustaceans; 5 or 6 minutes later, the larger specimens of the more tender-fleshed varieties; and 5 minutes after that, the smallest of the soft-fleshed fish. This timing is inevitably somewhat arbitrary, everything depending on the variety, the size, and the kind of fish used. Sometimes only 2 intervals rather than 3 are needed, and it may be that 10 or 12 minutes' cooking time is sufficient.

During the time that the fish is cooking, rub the dried-out bread slices with the 6–7 cloves of garlic. Count 1 medium-sized clove for 3 slices of bread.

Lift out the fish carefully with a large wire skimming spoon and arrange them on a heated serving platter. Moisten them with 2 or 3 ladlefuls of broth and pour the remainder into a soup tureen. Send the fish and the soup to the table at the same time, accompanied by the garlic-flavored crusts, and serve, first, a ladleful of soup poured over a garlic crust, and after, the fish, moistened with an additional ladleful of soup for each guest.

NOTE: Should there be leftovers, the whole thing may be thrown together, boiled up, strained, and served, with a handful of boiled pasta thrown in, as a fish soup, or it may be transformed into a *bouil-*

labaisse en gelée, a light and attractive luncheon first course. The fish themselves do not give sufficient gelatin, so a certain amount of commercial gelatin must be added, and, as all cold dishes need to be more sharply seasoned, its flavoring should be heightened by a bit more salt and a pinch of Cayenne.

Choose a simple mold or use a small mixing bowl. Remove the fillets from the larger fish, bone the sliced fish, and put the debris aside with the crabs or other crustaceans. Line the mold with the more presentable pieces and fill up the center with the remaining cold fish. Carefully skim all the grease from the surface of the cold soup, heat the soup and add some dissolved gelatin (using a bit less than instructions indicate for a given quantity, bearing in mind that the preparation already contains a certain amount of natural gelatin, and that a jellied dish should be only firm enough to hold its shape, once unmolded), a bit of salt and a pinch of Cayenne pepper. Pass the liquid through a fine sieve without pressure. Pound the crabs and/or other crustaceans in a mortar until reduced to a near purée, remove to a saucepan, add the other fish debris and that from the sieve, moisten with about 1/3 cup of the broth and bring to a boil. Reinforce this mixture also with a light addition of dissolved gelatin and pass it first through a *moulinette,* then through a fine drum sieve with the help of a plastic disk (*corne*). When the broth has cooled, add it slowly, using a ladle, so as not to displace the fish, to the mold. Put to jell in the refrigerator, and when it is firm enough not to absorb the other liquid on contact, pour the crab purée over the entire surface. Leave overnight to set thoroughly. Before unmolding, pass the blade of a knife around the edge and dip the mold rapidly into hot water. Decorate the plate with a *chiffonade* of lettuce, bouquets of chervil, nasturtium flowers, etc.

THE CERVELLE DE CANUT

A specialty of Lyons, *cervelle de canut* is basically a fresh white cheese made of cows' milk (homemade cottage or pot cheese—that is to say, freshly curdled milk, put to drain in a cheesecloth), beaten with a whisk, seasoned with salt, pepper, finely chopped *fines herbes,* and enriched by the addition of a certain amount of heavy cream. The essential herb is chives. Parsley, chervil and tarragon may be used, but chives should dominate. Some people add garlic and white wine. To my palate, it is in no way improved by these sophistications, and in any case they would not be indicated after a *bouillabaisse*. Although different in spirit and intention, a *cervelle de canut* is similar to a number of American cocktail dips.

A *canut* is—or was—a worker in a silkworm factory at the time that silk was one of Lyons' important industries. Eaten by poor people with nonetheless a solid gastronomic tradition, this dish might be translated "Poor Man's Brains."

Four Simple Summer Luncheons à la Provençale

MENU II (FOR 4 TO 6)

Appropriate wine:
a light, dry, well-chilled rosé

FRESH SARDINES IN VINE LEAVES
[SARDINES FRAICHES DANS LES FEUILLS DE VIGNE]

LAMBS' TRIPES ("FEET AND PACKAGES") A LA MARSEILLAISE
[PIEDS ET PAQUETS A LA MARSEILLAISE]

WILD SALAD
[SALADE SAUVAGE]

FRESH CHEESES
[FROMAGES FRAIS]

STRAWBERRIES IN ORANGE JUICE
[FRAISES A L'ORANGE]

FRESH SARDINES IN VINE LEAVES

None of the many recipes for sardines, to my way of thinking, can compare with the following preparation, radical in its simplicity. Some, indeed, are far from simple. A particularly fanciful recipe imprisons the rolled fillets of sardines, stuffed with a *duxelles*, in squash blossoms, which are then poached in fish stock, and the reduced sauce finished with anchovy butter. Sardines in vine leaves may, in themselves, constitute the principal preparation for a light luncheon, in which case, 6 or 8 would be served per person. In the context of this menu, they should be served sparingly, for in small quantity they may whet the appetite, but their strong flavor, after a certain point, has the opposite effect.

Any small fish may be prepared in this way, but those of lighter or more delicately flavored flesh should be perfumed with an herb less pungent than rosemary—fennel, oregano, or simply *fines herbes*.

Fresh Sardines in Vine Leaves

Sardines Fraîches dans les Feuilles de Vigne

4 *absolutely fresh sardines per person*
rosemary (fresh, if possible)
olive oil
salt, freshly ground pepper
large grapevine leaves, picked with their stems (1 *for each person*)
lemon

Clean the sardines but do not scale them; as they have very soft flesh, it is only necessary to hold the fish in one hand while opening the length of the abdomen with the index finger of the other. Empty the fish, pull out the gills and rinse fish out. Sponge them dry with paper towels, insert a small sprig of rosemary in the abdomen of each, sprinkle them with a few chopped rosemary leaves and enough olive oil so that, after being turned around in it, they are well coated inside and out with oil, salt and pepper them and leave them to marinate for an hour or so.

Cut the tips of the grape-leaf stems so that they are pointed. Lay each on a flat surface and roll a fish into it, beginning at the pointed extremity of the leaf; pierce the rolled leaf with the stem as if it were a pin. Place them on a large, double-faced grill in two rows and grill them over a very hot bed of embers. When the leaves are charred beneath (after a couple of minutes), turn the grill over and count another couple of minutes; for such a rapid process, a large armful of branches, preferably fruit-tree or grapevine branches, will produce a vivid but short-lived bed of coals. The branches should be all of approximately the same size so that some do not remain flaming while others are completely reduced to ashes. Serve fish directly from the grill. Each guest unwraps his own, the blackened leaf lifting off skin and scales with it, exposing the moist and delicate fillets, not a drop of whose natural juices has been lost. Serve lemon and a small pitcher of olive oil apart.

LAMBS' TRIPES A LA MARSEILLAISE

Although the elements of this preparation may be difficult to find in America (I questioned a number of New York butchers, some of whom told me that the stomachs were often available, but only one, on Bleecker Street, claimed to be able to get the feet), I could not resist giving the recipe, simply because the dish is so marvelous. If you should have the luck to find the stomachs, but not the feet, substitute calves' feet split in 2 (1 calf's foot for 4 lambs' feet). In Iowa, where lambs' tripes are out of the question, I have sometimes substituted chitterlings (whose form does not permit a stuffing) and pigs' feet. The dish is no longer the same, but the result is altogether satisfactory.

The success of the dish, although it demands little surveillance, depends on a long and very slow, even cooking process, and an ideal pot for cooking it is a 4-quart-capacity earthenware utensil with a close-fitting lid. It may profitably be prepared a day or two in advance, for in the slow cooling and reheating the sauce reduces and gains in body (it is never very thick, for its only binding element is the natural gelatin, derived mostly from the feet). Like all dishes in a tomato-flavored sauce, its peak of perfection may only be reached during the months of July and August when the vine-ripened tomatoes are full of the sweet, rich flavor of the sun. Out of season, use canned, rather than "fresh," tomatoes. It may be accompanied by steamed potatoes, but good, heavy, rough-textured sourdough bread with which to mop up the sauce is all that is really necessary.

Lambs' Tripes à la Marseillaise

Pieds et Paquets à la Marseillaise

feet and stomachs of 2 lambs (about 4 pounds)

Stuffing:

7 ounces lean salt pork (substitute fresh side pork if salt pork seems not fresh)
4 cloves garlic
1 handful chopped parsley
salt and freshly ground pepper

Mirepoix:

2 medium carrots
2 medium onions
oregano
salt
1/4 cup olive oil

1 pound firm, well-ripened tomatoes
4 cloves garlic
salt, Cayenne
thyme
bay leaf
bouquet of parsley
1 bottle of good dry white wine

The tripe should be properly cleaned when bought, but, to ensure its being in impeccable condition, you may soak it for 1/2 hour in a pan of warm water to which has been added 1/2 cup of vinegar. Rub it together between your hands and brush it with a soft-bristled brush, then rinse it well.

Cut the side pork into small pieces or chop it coarsely. If it is salted, cut it first into larger pieces, parboil it for a couple of minutes, drain it, and then cut it into smaller pieces. Peel the garlic cloves, pound them into a purée in a mortar, add the pork, the chopped parsley, a healthy amount of pepper, and salt (depending on the saltiness of the pork), and mix well.

Cut the tripe into elongated diamond shapes measuring approximately 3 1/2 inches on each side. Assuming the diamonds to be divided into 2 triangles by an invisible line drawn between the 2 oblique corners, a teaspoon of the stuffing should be placed in the lower triangle and, with a small, sharply pointed knife, a 3/4-inch "buttonhole" cut at a diagonal in the upper corner. The side flaps, terminating in the oblique angles, are folded in, one over the other, partially covering the stuffing, and the lower corner is folded up over the stuffing and the side flaps. The "package" is then rolled up toward the slitted tip, and that corner is gently pulled to one side in order to encircle the package within the slit (which, because of the elasticity of the substance, will stretch to encompass it). The process is extremely simple. If this explanation seems inadequate, simply make a package and tie it with a thread.

Prepare the *Mirepoix* with listed ingredients (see page 75 for method) in the utensil that will be used for cooking the *pieds et paquets* (an asbestos pad will protect earthenware from the direct gas flame and at the same time disperse the heat). Allow it to cook for from 20 to 30 minutes over a low flame without browning, then add the tomatoes, peeled, seeded, and coarsely chopped (the liquid from the squeezed tomatoes, passed through a strainer to eliminate the seeds, may be added at the same time as the white wine) and the garlic, finely chopped, sprinkle with salt, Cayenne, and thyme leaves. Stir well and arrange the feet on this bed. Place the bay leaf and bouquet of parsley, tied together, in the middle, and the packages on top, so that all the elements are touching without being packed in. They must be "at ease," but arranged in such a way that they are completely covered by a minimum of liquid. Pour in the white wine and, if necessary, a little water to cover. Bring to a boil over a medium flame. Never stir, but when the boil is reached, gently reach down the sides of the cooking vessel with a wooden spoon to slightly displace anything that may stick to the bottom; repeat this procedure every couple of hours. Adjust the flame so that only the slightest movement is produced on the surface of the liquid—a near-simmer. (Unless you are accustomed to doing this kind of cooking in that particular vessel over the same flame, the adjustment may take a good half hour of lifting the lid at regular intervals and turning the flame slightly up or down. The dish may equally well be done in an oven heated to approximately 250° F., but the adjustment is still necessary, and cooking time may take even longer.) It should cook like this for 8 hours. Halfway through, carefully skim the fat from the surface, taste for seasoning, and continue, every hour or so, to skim. Skim thoroughly before serving, or, if it is to be cooled and reheated the next day, skim it while cold. Count a good 2 hours for reheating (in earthenware at a very low heat). Discard the parsley and bay leaf before serving.

Strawberries in Orange Juice

Fraises à l'Orange

1 *quart of strawberries*
sugar
juice of 3 *oranges*

Wash the strawberries rapidly without letting them soak, and remove the stems. Place them, whole, in the bowl or deep dish in which they are to be served, sprinkle them generously with sugar, pour the orange juice over, and leave them to macerate, covered, in the refrigerator for a couple of hours before serving. Simple, delicious and refreshing.

Four Simple Summer Luncheons

à la Provençale

MENU III (FOR 6)

Appropriate wine:
a light, dry, well-chilled rosé

WARM SALAD OF SMALL GREEN BEANS
[HARICOTS FINS CHAUDS EN SALADE]

PROVENCAL BRAISED BEEF
[DAUBE AL LA PROVENCALE]

MACARONI IN BRAISING LIQUID
[MACARONADE]

TOSSED GREEN SALAD WITH FINES HERBES
[SALADE VERTE AUX FINES HERBES]

CHEESES
[FROMAGES]

FRUIT
[FRUITS]

Warm Salad of Small Green Beans

Haricots Fins Chauds en Salade

2 *pounds young, freshly picked green beans*

Accompaniments:
olive oil
pepper, coarse salt
cold sweet butter
crusty white bread

For this or any other preparation of green beans served whole to be exquisite, the beans should be tiny (about 3 inches long) and freshly picked. Their great delicacy of flavor is partly lost even if one waits for 5 or 6 hours between the time they are picked and the time they are cooked. Snap off the tips, but leave them whole. If they have been picked in your own garden and have never been sprayed by insecticide, they need not be washed. Otherwise, wash them quickly in cold water. Plunge them into a large quantity of well-salted water at a churning boil and cook, uncovered, at a continued rapid boil, until tender—7 or 8 minutes. (There is a widespread theory that vegetables cooked in a large quantity of water lose in vitamin content—on the contrary, this method permits them to be cooked in the minimum amount of time, and the cooking water may, in any case, always be saved to moisten a vegetable soup. Never should they be cooked either covered or in a small quantity of water—their delicate flavor and their bright-green color are both lost.) Serve them, well drained and undecorated, accompanied by a pitcher of the finest and freshest olive oil available, a pepper mill, a salt mill (containing, if possible, coarse sea salt or, lacking that, coarse kosher salt), cold sweet butter and rough, crusty white bread. The contact of the olive oil with the hot beans produces a delicious olfactory explosion.

THE DAUBE

A *daube*, like most rustic dishes that require a long, slow, even cooking process, is never as good as when prepared in seasoned earthenware, which absorbs heat more slowly and more evenly and holds it longer than any other kitchen utensil. A *daube* is usually prepared in amounts sufficient for several meals. If anything, the dish improves with a gentle reheating the next day, and it also serves as a delicious cold hors d'oeuvre—*la daube en gelée.* For a more attractive presentation, it is only necessary to arrange the more presentable pieces of beef and carrot slices neatly in a simple mold and pour the remainder over before chilling. It may then be turned out and decorated with a bit of green. A *daube* is a good winter dish but has been placed here among the summer menus so that it may profit from fresh tomatoes.

Perhaps the finest cut of meat for this preparation is that known in French as the *macreuse.* This is a small section of the chuck near the shoulder joint, rich both in flavor and gelatin. The other recommended cuts are equally gelatinous. In most *daubes*, the larding process is overlooked and, although the resultant sauce may be decent, the meat tends to be dreary, dry and stringy. Only the triple combination of gelatinous meat, the inserted fat, and slow and even cooking can produce pieces of meat that hold their shape, remain moist, and melt in the mouth—and the discovery of the isolated pockets of parsley and garlic flavor is a supplementary pleasure.

Provençal Braised Beef

Daube à la Provençale

3½ *pounds beef without bones (heel, shank, chuck, or a mixture)*

Larding elements:
- 4 *ounces fresh fat side pork*
- 2 *cloves garlic*
- 1 *small handful finely chopped parsley*

(*Continued*)

5 *ounces pork rind*
1 *small glass cognac*
3 *tablespoons olive oil*
1 *bottle good dry white wine*
8 *ounces lean side pork (or bacon, if not available)*
2 *medium carrots (about* 5 *ounces)*
1 *pound firm, ripe tomatoes*
2 *medium onions*
1/2 *pound mushrooms*
4 *cloves garlic*
1 *large bouquet parsley*
2 *bay leaves*
2 *strips dried orange peel*
1 *healthy handful (about* 1/4 *pound) pitted black olives (unpitted if they are the tiny niçoises)*
1 *healthy teaspoon mixed thyme, oregano, savory*
salt
1 *cup (if available) leftover juice from roast or braised beef or veal, or veal stock, or pot-au-feu bouillon—otherwise a cup of water*

Cut the meat into fairly large pieces of more-or-less regular shape, respecting, as nearly as possible, the natural muscular structure. For 3 1/2 pounds of boneless meat, you should have 15 or 16 pieces.

Remove the rind from the fat pork and save it. Cut the fat into strips approximately 1/3 inch square and 1 to 1 1/2 inches long. Peel the 2 cloves of garlic and reduce it to a paste in a mortar, add the chopped parsley, mix well, then add the strips of fat pork and stir well together.

With a small, sharply pointed knife, pierce each piece of meat completely through, with the grain, being careful not to make a wide and messy gash. Gently force a strip of pork fat, well coated with the garlic-and-parsley mixture, into the center of each piece of meat, and place the pieces in a bowl. Sprinkle the cognac and the olive oil over, turn the pieces around until all sides are equally moistened, pour the white wine over and leave to marinate for 2 to 3 hours.

Remove the rind from the lean side pork, and cut all the pork rind, including the rind reserved earlier, into small pieces approximately 1/2 inch square. Parboil them for 5 or 6 minutes and drain them.

Cut the side pork into ½-inch strips across the grain, and, if it is salted, parboil it for 2 or 3 minutes. If you have been able to find only bacon, use a somewhat smaller quantity and simmer it for a good 10 minutes to rid it as nearly as possible of its smoked taste.

Peel the carrots and slice them thinly. Peel and seed the tomatoes and chop them coarsely. Peel and chop the onions fine, pare off the stem tips of the mushrooms, rinse mushrooms, sponge dry with paper towels, and chop them fine. Smash the 4 garlic cloves, remove their skins, chop them as fine as possible, and mix together with the onions and mushrooms.

Divide the parsley into 2 bouquets, enclose a bay leaf and a strip of dried orange peel in each and tie them up with kitchen string.

Choose a cooking utensil (preferably of earthenware, but enameled ironware or heavy copper will do) of approximately 4-quart capacity to hold the ingredients exactly. The lid should fit as tightly as possible.

The different ingredients must now be arranged in layers—whether 2, 3 or more layers will be necessary depends on the proportionate height and width of the cooking vessel. Begin by sprinkling the bottom with pork rind pieces; remove meat from marinade and arrange on the rind a layer of meat pieces, close together but not packed in, then tomatoes, chopped onions and mushrooms, olives, carrots, side pork strips, mixed herbs and salt. Place the parsley packages on this bed and begin again with rind, beef, etc. Pour the marinade over and add sufficient meat juice (or water) to barely cover.

If the lid to your chosen *daubière* should not fit tightly, tear a long strip of cloth about 1 inch wide, dip it into a thin flour-and-water paste, squeeze out the excess liquid, and, placing the lid upside down, wrap the cloth around the outside of the fitting ridge; then turn the lid right side up and carefully cover the *daubière*.

Install the dish in a medium oven (325° to 350° F.). After about 45 minutes, it should be approaching the boiling point—you will be able to hear it beginning to bubble; turn the oven down (250° to 275° F.) and forget about it for a good 5 hours.

Break the seal, if you have used one, lift off the lid and skim off most of the fat floating on the surface. Discard the parsley packages. At this point the dish may be put aside to be reheated the next day, or kept hot while preparing the macaroni, if served immediately.

Macaroni in Braising Liquid

Macaronade

1 pound short macaroni (elbow, rigatoni, etc.)
salted boiling water
cooking liquid from daube
pepper freshly grated nutmeg
3 ounces freshly grated Parmesan cheese, or a mixture of Parmesan and Swiss Gruyère

Plunge the macaroni into a large pot of salted boiling water and cook it at a simmer, keeping it somewhat underdone (10 to 20 minutes, depending on the size and quality of the macaroni). Drain it well and return it to the saucepan. With a ladle, skim off some cooking liquid from the *daube*, being careful to take with it all the remaining fat floating on the surface, and pour it over the macaroni. Add enough, tipping the *daubière* to make it more accessible, to barely cover the macaroni. Place the saucepan, covered, over a low flame for 10 minutes or so, shaking it from time to time to prevent any possibility of sticking. Taste for salt, stir in the freshly ground pepper and a tiny bit of freshly grated nutmeg—an unaware palate should not be able to detect its presence. Pour 1/3 of the macaroni into a previously heated serving dish (an earthenware casserole is good and appropriate to the dish), sprinkle with grated cheese, and continue in layers, finishing with a layer of cheese. Serve.

Four Simple Summer Luncheons

à la Provençale

MENU IV (FOR 5 OR 6)

Appropriate wine:
a light, dry, well-chilled rosé

COLD RATATOUILLE (MIXED VEGETABLE STEW)
[RATATOUILLE FROIDE]

BLANQUETTE OF BEEF TRIPE WITH BASIL
[BLANQUETTE DE GRAS-DOUBLE AU PISTOU]

STEAMED POTATOES
[POMMES DE TERRE A LA VAPEUR]

TOSSED GREEN SALAD
[SALADE VERTE]

CHEESES
[FROMAGES]

CHERRIES AND FRESH ALMONDS
[CERISES ET AMANDES FRAICHES]

This menu may be prepared in such a way, if desired, that at the last minute only the potatoes have to be steamed and the *blanquette* sauce thickened. The *ratatouille* may be prepared far in advance (for that matter, preserved, in sterilized glass jars, it is altogether respectable), and the *blanquette* may, except for the addition of the final thickening agent, be prepared a day in advance, rewarmed gently, and finished as described.

The high color of the *ratatouille* and the cool, creamy, pale green of the *blanquette* form a very pretty juxtaposition.

THE COLD RATATOUILLE

Ratatouille, although often served hot as an accompaniment to pork and veal dishes, gains through being savored cold as an hors d'oeuvre. It is among those dishes for which everyone has a different recipe, "the only authentic one." Many people insist that all the vegetables must be cooked separately—a refinement, to me, without interest and not at all in keeping with the basic nature of a dish whose origins are simple and unpretentious. A few details must nonetheless be retained to arrive at a perfect result: it should be well laced with thyme and garlic (which, being cooked, will be hardly perceptible); the olive oil must be impeccable; it should never boil, but should cook at a bare simmer; the saucepan should be of heavy material (preferably an earthenware casserole), low and wide of form, to permit maximum evaporation; and the natural vegetable cooking liquid (for there must be no addition of water) should be radically reduced separately (most often, unfortunately, the fire is simply turned up at the end of the cooking process and the contents of the saucepan stirred and reduced rapidly—the result is a messy purée in which the vegetables are no longer distinguishable).

Ordinarily I would finish it with basil rather than parsley, but, in the context of this menu that is impossible, since basil plays a dominant role in the course that follows. As for the other identical elements, the garlic in one dish is cooked, and in the other, raw—two totally different flavors—and the aromatic ingredients lend support to the basic elements without themselves being aggressive.

Cold Ratatouille (Mixed Vegetable Stew)

Ratatouille Froide

1 *pound white onions*
2/3 *cup olive oil*
4 *large, firm, well-ripened tomatoes*
1 *pound sweet peppers (red, yellow and green, mixed, or* 1 *large of each)*
1 *pound eggplant (the small violet elongated variety, if available)*
1 *pound baby zucchini (the smallest available, in any case)*
6 *cloves garlic*
salt
tiny pinch of Cayenne pepper
1 *teaspoon thyme leaves*
a bouquet of parsley and 1 *bay leaf, tied together*
a handful of finely chopped parsley
freshly ground pepper

Peel the onions and cut each in quarters or eighths, depending on their size. Put them to cook gently in 1/3 cup of the olive oil while preparing the other vegetables. Stir from time to time and do not let them brown.

Peel and seed the tomatoes and cut each half into 6 or 8 pieces. Cut the peppers in 2 lengthwise, discard the stems and all the seeds and cut them into pieces 3/4 to 1 inch square; wipe the eggplant and zucchini clean with damp paper towels and cut off the tip ends of both. Cut the eggplant into 3/4-inch cubes without peeling, and cut the zucchini crosswise into 1/2- to 1-inch sections, depending on its thickness. Smash the garlic cloves with the blade of a knife, discard the hulls, and chop the garlic.

When the onions are yellowed and soft from cooking, add the peppers, the eggplant pieces, the garlic, salt, and Cayenne. Continue to cook gently for 10 minutes or so, stirring occasionally with a wooden spoon, then add the tomatoes, the zucchini (if desired, the zucchini may be added halfway through the cooking process, for it cooks very rapidly, and if delayed it remains firmer), thyme, and the parsley and bay-leaf bouquet. At this point, one may turn up the flame until the boil is reached, easing a wooden spoon to the bottom of the cooking utensil and stirring from time to time to prevent sticking. Leave to cook over a tiny flame, at a bare simmer, with the lid ajar, for 2 hours.

Place a colander or sieve over another saucepan, pour in the vegetables and allow to drain well; then return the vegetables to their saucepan and to the fire, leaving the lid off (they will continue to give off liquid, which in this way evaporates in part). Place the saucepan containing the liquid over a very high flame and, stirring constantly with a wooden spoon, reduce it to a light, syrupy consistency (first, the liquid will foam up—it must be rapidly stirred to prevent it from boiling over—then it will settle down to a loose, rapid boil, and finally, as it approaches the correct consistency, it will bubble in a more explosive way. There should be around 1/2 to 3/4 cup of syrupy liquid remaining—pour it back into the vegetables and leave to cool. Add the remaining olive oil, half the chopped parsley, season with pepper (and more salt, if necessary), and mix together thoroughly, stirring carefully to avoid crushing the vegetables. Pour into the serving dish, chill thoroughly, and sprinkle with the remaining parsley before serving.

THE BLANQUETTE OF BEEF TRIPE

The term *pistou* refers to the *pommade* of garlic and basil leaves (this ordinarily contains much more garlic), the flesh of raw tomatoes, and grated Parmesan cheese, the whole thing worked into a thick paste and thinned with olive oil; it is customarily used to add an explosive, last-minute perfume to *la soupe au pistou*, basically a minestrone containing, in addition to the usual vegetables and pasta, white beans, green beans, and a slice of cut-up local squash, somewhat resembling our winter squash, which lends a velvety quality to the soup. *Pistou* was, longer ago than anyone can remember, adopted into Provençal cooking from Genoa, where a somewhat different version, *pesto*, is often used as a sauce for pasta.

In French culinary terminology, *gras-double* refers to the stomachs and intestinal parts of beef (it only becomes *tripes* when the feet are added), and the variety is preferable to the exclusive use of honeycomb tripe, but as far as I know, that is the only section of the *gras-double* available commercially in America.

Blanquette of Beef Tripe with Basil

Blanquette de Gras-double au Pistou

2 pounds honeycomb tripe
2 large onions
2 tablespoons olive oil
1 heaping tablespoon flour
1/2 bottle dry white wine combined with approximately the same quantity of liquid, preferably veal stock, pot-au-feu bouillon, or roasting juices—lacking that, water
salt
thyme
1 bay leaf and a bouquet of parsley, tied together

Pistou:

1 clove of garlic
1 handful of fresh basil leaves
salt, pepper
1 tablespoon olive oil
4 egg yolks

juice of 1/2 lemon

Cut the tripe into pieces approximately 2 inches square.

Peel the onions, chop them finely and cook them gently in the oil, in an earthenware casserole or a large, heavy saucepan, for about 10 minutes, without allowing them to brown. Sprinkle with the flour and leave to cook for another minute or so, stirring several times so that the flour cooks evenly. Away from the flame, add slowly, stirring the while, a ladleful of the wine and stock mixture, then stir in the rest. Return to the fire and, over a medium flame, bring to a boil, without ceasing to stir.

Add the tripe, salt, thyme, and the parsley and bay-leaf package, and leave to cook very gently for approximately 2 hours (tripe actually needs 6 or 7 hours of cooking, but it is precooked when one buys it—the time necessary depends on the extent of its precooking).

Pound together in a mortar the clove of garlic, peeled, the basil leaves, a pinch of salt and some freshly ground pepper, until the mixture is reduced completely into a purée. Stir in the tablespoon of olive oil and the egg yolks.

Remove the pot containing the tripe from the fire and discard the parsley and bay leaf. Set aside a ladleful or small bowlful of the cooking liquid and allow it to cool somewhat, then stir it slowly and thoroughly into the basil-garlic-egg yolk mixture. Pour the contents of the mortar slowly into the pot, stirring the while, and return it to a moderate flame. Stir without stopping until the sauce begins to thicken; it should coat the spoon. Above all, it must never come to a boil after the egg mixture has been added. Stir in a bit of lemon juice, taste for seasoning, and serve in its cooking utensil (if it is presentable), accompanied by the steamed potatoes, served apart.

Steamed Potatoes

Pommes de Terre à la Vapeur

So-called "steamed" potatoes are nearly always boiled. They are far better if really cooked in steam, and this is easy to do if one has a special rack or some other device for steaming vegetables in a pot. Choose potatoes that are small, regular in shape, and of a nonmealy variety. Cook them, peeled, for about 30 to 40 minutes, depending on the quality and type of potato. Sprinkle with chopped parsley to relieve them of their naked appearance.

Cherries and Fresh Almonds

Cerises et Amandes Fraîches

If fresh almonds are not to be found in American markets, certain parts of the country, nonetheless, abound in almond trees. The green almonds in the process of maturing contain a gelatinous material that eventually becomes the nut. Sometime between the months of May and July, depending on the species of almond and the climate, the nut solidifies. At this point in its development the outside hull and the unformed shell are easily cut through with a knife, and the almond, from which one first peels the soft, spongy skin (which later becomes the dried, brown covering of the shelled almond), is of a delicacy unrelated to that of the matured nut.

Serve the almonds whole with the cherries and leave your guests to do the work. It is a fine marriage.

When peeled and macerated in the freshly pressed juice of not-quite-ripe white grapes (*verjus*), and sprinkled with salt and chopped chervil, fresh almonds or fresh hazelnuts may be transformed into a delicious, light and refreshing hors d'oeuvre.

Indexes

General Index

The Recipe Index on page 439 guides the reader to specific recipes. The General Index, beginning on this page, is a guide to preliminary discussions relating to many of the recipes; it refers as well to information about ingredients, to cooking and preparation techniques, kitchen equipment and general culinary observations. Page numbers of appropriate wines to be served with specific dishes are in the Recipe Index; all other references to wines are in the General Index.

Académie des Gastronomes, 20
Agneau, meaning of term, 248
Aïgo-bouido (garlic soup), 178
Aïoli, 396
A la bourguignonne, as preparation "type," 239
Aligoté wines, 50
Almond cookies (*tuiles*), 94–95
Almonds, fresh, 422–423
Alsace, 202
  wines, 49
Aluminum, for pots, 61
"Amanita of the Caesars," 298
America, game in, 102
  pheasants, 226
American clams and oysters, 275
Anchovies, in grilled pepper salad, 161
A point, definition, 317
Appellation Contrôlée d'Origine (A.O.), 36
  applied to Bordeaux wines, 44–45
  applied to Côte d'Or wines, 39–41
Apple pudding, molded, 347
Apples, cooking varieties, 258
Araignée (wire skimming spoon), 65
Arbellot, Simon, 13
Aromatic pepper mixture, 89
Artichokes:
  bottoms, 77
  in composed salad, 263
  purées for garnishing, 283
  raw, 86, 305
Arugula (Italian salad leaf), 87–88
Asparagus vinaigrette, warm, 342
Autumn, gastronomic pleasures in, 102–103

Bacon, in French recipes, 218–219
Bain-marie for scrambled eggs, 192, 193
Banyuls wines, 50
Barbary duck, 202
Barsac, 47
Basil, 87
Baudroie (angler-fish), 399
Bavarian cream, 222
Bazar Français, 67
Béarnaise sauce, 231
Beaujolais, 31, 37–38
  length of time in keg, 29
  in informal and simple menu, 259
  with strawberries, 339
  temperature for serving, 38
Beef, boiled, *see Pot-au-feu*
Beef, raw, 317–318
Beef heart, 179
Beefsteak, *see* Steak

Beef stew *à la bourguignonne*, 238–239
Beef stock, 71, 74
Beef tripe:
  blanquette of, 420–421
  à la lyonnaise, 262
Belons (oysters), 275
Bercy butter, 318
Beurre manié, as thickening agent, 260
Blanc, as liquid for simmering tripe, 262
Blanc de blancs (Champagne), 36
Blanc de noirs (Champagne), 36
Blanc-manger, 222
Blanquette of beef tripe, 420–421
Bleu (very rare), 317
Bloc de fois gras (whole goose liver), 203
Blond de veau (veal stock), 71–72
Boning a chicken, 295–296, 380–381
Bonnes-Mares, label for, 42
Borage, 86
Bordeaux, 36, 44–48
  glasses for, 34
  labeling, 45
  length of time in keg, 29
  rivalry with Burgundy, 44
"Bottle sickness" in new wine, 32
Bouillabaisse, 398–400
  confusion with *soupe de poisson*, 398
  European fish (and American substitutes) used in, 399
Bouquet garni, 85
Bourgueuil, 49
Bourguignon dishes, 239
Bourrache (borage), 86
Bourride (fish soup), 396
Bread, 93
  to accompany *crudités*, 305
Brillat-Savarin, 102
Broad beans (*fave*, *fèves*), 87
  in crudités, 305
  in purées, 283
  in spring stew, 291–292
Broad bean seeds, 69
Broche-filet (spit), 70
Bulbs, *see* Seeds and bulbs
Burgundy, 36, 37–41
  glasses for, 34
Burnet, 86, 87
Butcher, importance of, 70
Butters, for grilled beef, 318
Cabbage, in *pot-au-feu*, 322–323
Cabernet-Franc grapes, 49
Cabernet Sauvignon grapes, 45
Calf's-foot jelly, 107–108
Calvados, 291
Calves' brains in red wine, 343
Calves' ears, stuffed, 227–228
Cannelloni, 226
Carême, Antonin, 19
Carving:
  lamb saddle, 281
  leg of lamb, 367
Cassis (blackberry liqueur), 50
Cassis (wine), 50
Cassoulet, 246, 247–248
  regional variations, 247
Cast-iron enamelware, 61
Cauliflower loaf, 345–346
Caviar, 192
Celeriac in mustard sauce, 246
Celery root (celeriac), 246
Cèpes (wild mushrooms), 70, 102, 122, 298
Cerfeuil (chervil), 86, 87
Cervelle de canut (cheese), 403–404
Chablis, 43
Chambertin, 39
Chambertin en Clos de Beze, label for, 41
Champagne, 36
  throughout elegant, formal menu, 190–191
Champignon (wooden pestle), 62
Charentais melon, 388
Charlotte mold, 64, 137
  for *flamri*, 312
Chasselas grapes, 49
Château Bouscaut (1926), 46
Château-Chalon, 49–50
  length of time in keg, 30
  with squid, 374
Chateau d'Yquem, 39, 45, 47
Château-Grillet, 37
Château Haut-Brion, 45, 46
Château Margaux, 46
Châteauneuf-du-Pape, 37
Cheese:
  assortment for formal menu, 356
  cervelle de canut, 403–404
  goat, 23
  platter, 25
  Pont l'Evêque, 106

Cheese soufflés *à la suissesse*, 254
Chervil, 86, 87
Chicken:
  boning, 295–296, 380–381
  in French markets, 293
  poached mousseline, 293–294
  in red wine (*coq au vin*), 308–309
Chicken livers in terrine recipes, 334
Chicory, 87
Chinon, 49
Chopping, 92
Chopping board, 56
Claires (oysters), 275
Clamart (France), 11, 12, 14
Clam varieties, 275
Climats (wine-growing term), 40
Clocharde apples, 258
Clos des Mouches wine, 39
Club des Cent, 20
Cocotte (pot), 58, 60
Colette, on chilling melon, 388
Composed salad, 166, 263
Confit d'oie (preserved goose), 249
Congre (conger eel), 399
Contrefilet (steak cut), 317
Cooking:
  country cooking, 20–21
  in Iowa, 11
  restaurant, 106
  see also French cooking; Provençal cooking; Menus
Cooking techniques:
  baby zucchini, 179
  baking bread, 93
  boning chicken, 295–296, 380–381
  broad beans, shelling, skinning, 292
  clarification of jellies, 358
  cleaning guinea fowl, 220
  crêpes, 82–83
  grilling peppers, 160–161
  grilling steak, 317
  hanging, cleaning of game, 103
  lamb stew, 161
  larding, 114
  lobsters *à la nage*, 195
  opening, cleaning sea urchins, 213
  peeling garlic, 92–93
  peeling, seeding tomatoes, 92
  preparing artichoke bottoms, 77
  preparing mousseline forcemeat, 78–79
  preparing salads and dressings, 88
  removing fat from lamb, 279–280
  rice, 81
  skimming and skinning, 73, 90–91
  slicing, chopping, 92
  using drum sieve, 91
  see also Carving
Copperware, 58
  beating bowl, 63, 64
  cleaning, 59
  shopping sources, 67–68
Coq au vin (chicken in red wine), 304, 308–309
Coriander (*cilantro*, Chinese parsley), 84
Corne (disk for drum sieve), 62, 91
Côte de Beaune, 38
  white wines of, 39
Côte de Nuits, 38
  great wines of, 39
Côte d'Or wines, 38–39
  Appellation Contrôlée system for, 39–41
Côte-Rôtie, 37
Country cooking, 20–21
Couteaux (knives), 56, 57
Crayfish, 107
Crayfish mousse, 106
Crayfish salad with dill, 288–289
Crème anglaise, 242
Crème brulée cooked in fireplace, 21
Crêpe pans, 60
Crêpes, 82–83
  à la normande, 258
  stuffed, 226
Crottins de chavignol (goat cheeses), 23
Croutons, 193–194
Crudités (raw vegetables for appetizer), 304, 305
Crusts with fresh morels, 298–299
Cucumber salad, 152
Cuisine bourgeoise, 21, 22
Cuisine et Vins de France (magazine), 13, 14
Cul de poule (tin-lined metal bowl), 64
Curnonsky, prince of gastronomes, 13
Custard, coffee, 118
Cuttlefish, 377

Dandelion greens, 87, 339
  and salt pork salad, 339
Daube (Provençal braised beef), 413
Decanting, 34

Decure, Madeleine, 13
Dégraisser (degreasing process), 90
Demi-glace de veau (reduced veal stock), 72
Dépouillement ("skinning"), 90
Desserts:
  blanc-manger, 222
  Charlotte with crêpes, 137
  coffee custard, 118
  flamri, 312
  flaugnarde (Périgord pudding), 170
  floating island, 242
  frozen strawberry mousse, 274
  molded apple pudding, 347
  molded puddings, 232
  orange jelly, 130
  pineapple combinations, 300
  in Provençal cooking, 396
  Sauternes with, 35
  strawberries in Beaujolais, 339
  strawberry mousse with raspberry purée, 284
Dill:
  in salads, 166
  with seafood, 288–289
Dill weed, dried, 288–289
Disks for drum sieves, 62, 91
Domaine de Mont-Redon wine, 37
Domaine Tempier wines, 50
Dome (mold), 64
  fillings for, 214
Dripping pan for turnspit, 70
Drum sieves, 62, 91
Dumaine, Alexandre, 227
Duxelles, 76
  with skewered lambs' kidneys, 255

Earthenware, 59–60
Echalotes grises (gray shallots), 86
Ecrivisses à la nage, 288
Ecumer (removing scum), 90
Eggplant, in *moussaka*, 174
Eggs:
  à la bourguignonne, 260
  en meurette, 260
  scrambled, 192–193
Egg white in forcemeat, 79
Electric mixers, blenders, 66
Electric stove, advantages and disadvantages, 53
Enamelware, cast-iron, 61
Entrecôte (steak cut), 317
Equipment, see Kitchen equipment
Escoffier, Auguste, 11, 18–19, 20

Farce gratin, 127
Faux-filet (steak cut), 279, 317
Fave (broad beans), 87, 283, 291–292, 305
Favouilles (small crabs), 399
Fennel, 86
  à la grecque, 173
Fenouil (fennel), 86, 173
Fenouil bâtard (dill), 288
Fèves (broad beans), 87, 283, 291–292, 305
Field salads, 86, 87
  shopping sources for seeds, 68
Fines herbes, 84, 88
  in salads, 87
Fireplace:
  in modern kitchen, 54–55
  use in regional cooking, 20–21
  at Solliès-Toucas, 51, 52
Fireplace equipment, 54–55, 56
  shopping sources for, 69–70
Fish cookers, 60
Fish and seafood:
  baked lobster Garin, 153
  baked trout, 134
  clam and oyster varieties, 275
  crayfish mousse, 107
  crayfish salad, 288
  fresh sardines in vine leaves, 406
  frozen, 276
  grilled fish, sea urchin purée, 212
  lobsters *à la nage*, 195
  marinated raw sardine fillets, 316
  pike *quenelles* (dumplings), 142
  Provençal fish stew (*bouillabaisse*), 398–400
  shellfish platter, 274–275
  shrimp quiche, 305–306
  squid *à l'américaine*, 377
  terrine of sole fillets, 236
  turban of sole fillets, 275–276
  varieties used in *bouillabaisse*, 399
Flageolet beans, in green bean purée, 282
Flamri, 304
Flaugnarde (Périgord pudding), 170
Floating island, 242

Foie gras, 202–203
Fonds blanc, *Fonds de veau* (veal stock), 71–72
Food:
 autumnal gastronomie treats, 102–103
 visual and textural appeal, 23, 236, 274, 304, 305, 356, 374
 see also French cooking; "Gastronomie aesthetic"; Menus
Forcemeats, 214–215
 variations for poached chicken, 294
Fraises des bois (wild strawberries), 284
Fraise de veau (calves' intestines), 262
French chef's knife, 56, 92
French chickens, 293
French clams and oysters, 275
French cooking:
 classical cooking, 19
 cuisine bourgeoise, 21, 22
 "Grand Palace," bastard *grande cuisine*, 18, 19, 106
 regional, 20–21; *see also* Provençal cooking
 relationship with other cuisines, 17–18
 simplification of, 20
 see also Cooking techniques; Menus
French cuts of beefsteak, 316–317
French Institut National des Appellations d'Origine, 36
French melons, 388
"French national dish" (*pot-au-feu*), 322–323
French wines, *see* Wine
Fritto misto (mixed fritters), 124
Frozen foods:
 chickens, 293
 fillets of sole, 276
 morels, 298
 raspberries, 284
 shrimp, 306
 strawberries, 284
Frozen soufflé, 284

Game, 102–103
 braised and roast partridge, 155–156
 cleaning, 219
 pheasant, 126–127
 salmis of, 126
 venison, 113
Game sauces, 106
Gardens, *see* Kitchen gardens
Garin, Georges, 12, 13–14
Garlic, 178
 peeling, 92–93
Garlic soup (*aïgo-bouido*), 178
"Gastronomie aesthetic," 24
Gewürztraminer, 49
Girelle (fish variety), 399
Glace de veau (veal glaze), 72
Godiveau (*farce* mixture), 142
Grand aïoli, 396
Grande cuisine:
 bastardized, 18, 19, 106
 "turbans" in, 275
"Grand Palace" cuisine, 18, 19
Grape leaves, 212
Grapes:
 pourriture noble in, 47
 teinturiers, 28
 varieties, 38, 39, 45, 48, 49, 50
 see also under individual names
Gras-double, defined, 420, 421
Gras-double à la lyonnaise, 262
"Grass" lamb, 248, 279
Gratin à la dauphinoise, 319
Graves wines, 44, 45, 46
Green bean purée, 282
Grenache grapes, 50
Grills:
 for modern fireplace, 54, 55
 wire, 45
Grimod de la Reynière, 102
Gros Plant grapes, 48
Gros rouge (inferior red wine), 27
Guide Culinaire (Escoffier), 18–19, 20

Ham, Parma, 388
Haut-Médoc wines, 45
Herbs, 84–85, 86
 in Provençal cooking, 12, 395
 in salads, 87
 shopping sources for herb seeds, 69
 see also Fines herbes and under individual names
Hyssop, 84

Ile flottante (as distinct from English "Floating Island"), 242
Iowa, cooking in, 11
Ivoire (sauce), 294

Jellies:
  clarification, 358
  commercial, 130
Jelly mold, 64

Kahn, Odette, 13
Kidneys, veal, 135
Kirsch with pineapple, 300
Kitchen:
  placement of work space, 53
  at Solliès-Toucas, 12, 51–53
  see also Kitchen equipment
Kitchen equipment, 53–66
  cast-iron enamelware, 61
  copper pots, bowls, 58–59, 63, 64
  earthenware, 59–60
  electric stove, advantages and disadvantages, 53
  fireplace and accessories, 54, 55; shopping sources, 69–70
  fish cooker, 60
  gas stove, 53
  knives, knife racks, 56, 57
  manche à gigot, 65
  marble slab, 65
  molds, 64
  mortars and pestles, 62
  needles, 65
  poultry shears, 57
  shopping sources for, 67–68
  sieves and disks, 62
  skillets, crêpe pans, 60
  skimming spoon, 65
  vegetable mills, shredders, 63
  wire grills, 65
  wire whisks, 63
  wooden utensils, 56, 62, 66
Kitchen gardens, 86–87
  see also Herbs; Seeds
Knives, kitchen, 56, 57, 92

Lamb:
  carving, 281, 367
  cuts and quality, 279
  grass (yearling), 248, 279
  hearts, 179
  kidneys, skewered, 255
  moussaka, 174
  in Provençal cooking, 395
  roast saddle of, 279
  for stewing, 161
  tripes *à la marseillaise*, 407–408
Lamb's lettuce, 86, 87, 137
Larding, 114
Larding needle, 65
Lèchefrite (dripping pan), 54
  skillet used as, 56
Leeks, 87
  seeds, 69
Leftovers:
  daube, 413
  pot-au-feu, 323
Lemonnier, Michel, 13
Lettuce, with garden peas, 328
Lettuces, 87
Lobster:
  à l'américaine, 377
  à la nage, 195
  baked, 153
Loire Valley, 36
  wines of, 48–49
Lyons, 37, 403, 404

Mâche (lamb's lettuce), 86
Mâconnais wines, 38
Macreuse (beef cut), 323, 413
Maître d'hôtel butter, 318
Maladie de bouteille ("bottle sickness"), 32
Malbec grapes, 45
Manche à gigot, 65, 113, 367
Marble slab for pastry-making, 65
Marchand de vin butter, 318
Margaux wines, 45
Marmite, 61, 323
Marraines (oysters), 275
Meats:
  bacon, 218–219
  beef tripe *à la lyonnaise*, 262
  blanquette of beef tripe, 420–421
  calves' brains in red wine, 343
  cassoulet, 246, 247–248
  foie gras, 202–203
  grilled lambs' hearts, 179
  lamb stew with artichoke hearts, 161
  lambs' tripes *à la marseillaise*, 407–408
  moussaka, 174
  mutton, 248, 395
  pot-au-feu, 322–323
  potées, 167–168
  Provençal braised beef (*daube*), 413
  roast saddle of lamb, 279
  salt and fresh pork, 167–168

sautéed veal kidneys, 135
skewered kidneys, 255
steak tartare, 317–318
stuffed calves' ears, 227–228
sweetbread and macaroni timbale, 214–215
veal cutlets *à la tapenade*, 144
Mediterranean coast wines, 50
Médoc wines, 44, 45
Melons, 388
Menus:
classical French, example of, 354–355, 356
considerations of efficiency, 24
desserts in, 25
exotic, example of, 372–373, 374
"gastronomie aesthetic" in, 24
for Georges Garin in Clamart, 13
in holiday and party tradition, 150–151, 189, 190–191, 200–201, 208–209, 210
Lyonnais, 333
progression in, 22–23, 24, 356
Provençal luncheons, 397, 405, 411, 417
regional food and wine combinations, 23
selection of wines for, 35
semi-formal, 386–387
truffles in, 188–189
for two, 150–151, 152
visual and textural appeal, 23, 236, 274, 304, 305, 356, 374
Mercurey wine, 38
Meridional French cooking, *see* Provençal cooking
Merlot grapes, 45
Mesclun (mixed wild salads), 86
Meursault wines, 39
Mirepoix, 74–75
Miroton (leftover *pot-au-feu*), 323
Mixed herbs, 85
Molded apple pudding, 347
Molds, 64
dome, 214
for *flamri*, 312
Montrachet, 39
Morels, 298–299
dried, 215
Mortars and pestles, 62
Mouli-julienne (grater and shredder), 63, 392
Moulinette (vegetable mill), 63
Mourvèdre grapes, 50
Moussaka, 174
Mousse, frozen strawberry, 284
Mousseline forcemeat, 78–79
in baked trout, 134
Mouton, meaning of term, 248
Mouton-Rothschild, 46
Muscadet grapes, 48
Mushrooms:
duxelles, 76
frozen, 298
see also Cèpes; Morels
Musigny, 39
label for, 43
Mutton, 248
in Provençal cooking, 395

Nantua sauce, 275
Nasturtiums, 87
Négociants (wine merchants), 40

Oeufs en meurette, 260
Oeufs à la neige, 242
Olive oil, 70, 88
Olney, Byron, 12
Olney, James, 12
Omelet pans, 60
Oregano, 85
Oseille (sorrel), 86
Oursinade (sea urchin purée), 212
Oursins (sea urchins), 212, 274
Ovens, gas and electric, 53
Oyster varieties, 275

Pain de campagne (crusty white bread), 93
Paleron (beef cut), 323
Palourdes (oysters), 275
Panais (parsnip), 323
Pannequets (rolled and cut crêpes), 82, 180
Parefeu (turnspit accessory), 70
Parsley, in lobsters *à la nage*, 195
Partridge, braised and roast, 155–156
Passoire (sieve), 62
Pastis (anise-flavored apéritif), 398
Pâté de fois gras, 203
Pâtés, definitions and confusions, 334
en croûte, 334
Pauillac wines, 45, 46
Peas *à la française*, 328

Pepper, peppercorns, 89
Peppers (sweet), 160–161
Perdreau (young partridge), 156
Perdrix (old partridge), 155
Périgord geese, 202
Périgord pudding, 170
Petite marmite, 74, 322
Pheasant, 126–127
Pied de cuve (heated crushed grapes), 29
Pike dumplings (*quenelles*), 142
Pimprenelle (burnet), 86, 87
Pineapple surprise, 300
Pineau grapes, 48
Pinot Blanc grapes, 38
Pinot Chardonnay grapes, 38, 39
Pistou, *pesto* (basil sauce), 420
Plat à sauter (saucepan), 58
Plats cuisinés (complicated preparations), 74
Poached chicken mousseline, 293–294
Poêlon (low, wide pot), 60
Poissonière (fish cooker), 60
Pomerol, 46, 47
Poireaux (leeks), 87
Poivrade sauce, 106
Pont l'Evêque cheese, 106
Portugaises (oysters), 275
Potatoes, steamed, 422
Potato gratin, 319
Potato straw cake, 392
Pot-au-feu, 74, 322–323
  pots for, 61
Potées, 167–168
Pots:
  for *pot-au-feu*, 323
  for scrambled eggs, 192, 193
  for stew, 161
  see also Kitchen equipment
Pouilly-Fuissé, 38
Pouilly-Fumé, 48, 49
  in crayfish *fumet*, 107
Pouilly-sur-Loire, 49
"Pouilly trinity" (wines), 38
Poule au pot, 74
Poultry livers, terrine of, 334
Poultry shears, 57
Pourriture noble, 47
Pousse au crime (inferior white wine), 27
Praires (oysters), 275
Prosciutto, 388
Provençal asparagus, 342
Provençal braised beef (*daube*), 413
Provençal cooking, 395–396
  aïgo-bouido, 178
  characteristic menus and dishes, 397 *ff*, 405 *ff*, 411 *ff*, 417 *ff*
  pot-au-feu in, 322
  tapenade, 144
  spring (vegetable) stews, 291–292
Provençal fish stew (*bouillabaisse*), 398–400
Provence:
  herbs in, 12
  outdoor markets, 305
Puddings, molded, 232
Purées:
  broad bean, 283
  green bean, 282
  mushroom, 283
Purslane, 87

Quenelles, 79, 142
Quiche, shrimp, 305–306

Rascasse (fish), 399
Ratatouille, 418
Red wine, 28–30
  Burgundies, 37–41
  Châteauneuf-du-Pape, 37
  foods compatible with, 35
  manufacturing techniques, 28–30
  of Graves, 46
  in informal and simple menus, 159, 165, 177, 245, 321, 327, 333, 341
  of Rhône Valley, 37
  sediment in, 34
  temperature for serving, 32–33
  see also Bordeaux
Regional cooking, 20–21
  à la lyonnaise, 262
  à la lyonnaise, typical menu, 333
  cassoulet (Languedoc), 246–247
  see also Provençal cooking and individual dishes
Regional wines, 49–50
  see also under regional names
Rhône Valley wines, 36, 37
  grape varieties in, 37
Rice, 80–81
  in green bean purée, 282
Riesling grapes and wine, 49

Rocket, 86, 87–88
Rolling pins, 66
Romanée-Conti, 39
Roquet (rocket), 86, 87–88
Rosemary, 85
  used as skewers, 255
Rosé wines, 31, 37, 49
  of Bandol, 50
  with Provençal cooking, 395, 396
  in Provençal luncheons, 397, 405, 411, 417
Rouget (red mullet), 399
Rouille (sauce for *bouillabaisse*), 400
Rully white wines, 38

Sabayon sauce, 139
Sailland, Maurice, *see* Curnonsky
Saint-Emilion wines, 46, 47
Saint-Estèphe wines, 45
Saint-Julien wines, 45
St.-Pierre (fish), 399
Salads and salad greens:
  composed, 166, 263
  crayfish, 288–289
  dandelion, 339
  lamb's lettuce and beet, 137
  lemon and cream dressings for, 88
  vinaigrette dressing for, 88
  see also Herbs
Salmis (elegant game bird dish), 127
Salt pork, 167–168
  in beef *à la bourguignonne*, 239
Sancerre, 48
Sardine fillets, marinated raw, 316
Sardines, fresh, in vine leaves, 406
Sauces:
  Aurore, 293–294
  béarnaise, 231
  "butters" for grilled beef, 318
  cream, 152
  custard, 242
  duxelles, 76
  ivoire, 294
  marchand de vin, 318
  Nantua, 276
  for poached chicken, 293–294
  poivrade, 115
  rouille, 400
  sabayon, 139
  suprème, 294
  tapenade, 144
Saumur-Champigny, 49
Sauterne (American-made wine), 35
Sauternes, 30, 35, 47
  with blanc-manger, 222
Sauteuse (saucepan), 58
Sautoir (saucepan), 58
Sauvignon, 49
Sauvignon grapes, 48, 49
Savarin mold, 64
Savennières, 48
Savory, 85, 87
  with broad beans, 283, 291
Sea urchins, 212
  freshness of, 274
Seeds and bulbs (herbs and salad greens), 86
  shopping sources, 68–69
Semillon grapes, 45
Serpolet (wild thyme), 84
Shallot bulbs, shopping sources for, 69
Shallots, gray, 86
Shallots, red, 87
Shellfish, *see* Fish and seafood *also under* individual names
Shellfish platter, 274–275
Shrimp quiche, 305–306
Shopping:
  in Italian neighborhoods, 70
  for meat, 70
Shopping sources for food and equipment, 67–70
Sieves, 62, 91
Skewers, rosemary branches used as, 255
Skillets, 60
Skimming, 90–91
Skinning (*dépouillement*), 90
Slicing, 92
Sole fillets:
  terrine of, 236
  turban of, 275–276
Solliès-Toucas, France, 11, 12
  fireplace, kitchen at, 12, 51–53
  seasons and food in, 14–15
Sorrel, 86
  seeds, 69
  in sole fillets, 236
Sorrel soup, 122–123
Soufflé, frozen, 284
Soufflés *à la suissesse*, 254
Soupe au pistou, 420
Soupe au poissons, 398–400

Southern France, wines of, 50
Soutirage (process for clarifying wine), 30
Spoons:
- wooden, 62
- wire skimming, 65

Spring (vegetable) stew, 291–292
Squid *à l'américaine*, 377
Steak, French cuts, 316–317
Steak *tartare*, 317–318
Stews, importance of proper skimming, 90–91
Stock, in *cuisine bourgeoise*, 21
- *see also* Beef stock; Veal stock

Strainers, *see* sieves
Strawberries, wild (seeds), 69
Strawberries in Beaujolais, 339
Strawberry mousse, 284
Sweetbreads and macaroni, timbale of, 214–215

Table au Pays de Brillat-Savarin, La (Tendret), 227
Tamis (drum sieve), 62, 91
Tapenade, 144
Tarragon, in béarnaise sauce, 231
Teinturiers (red-fleshed grape varieties), 28
Tendret, Lucien, 227
Terrine of poultry livers, 334
Terrine of sole fillets, 236
Thyme, 85
Timbale of sweetbreads and macaroni, 214–215
Tomatoes:
- in *moussaka*, 174
- peeling and seeding, 92

Tournebroche (turnspit), 54, 56
Tripe, cleaning and preparation, 262
Trou normand (stiff shot of Calvados), 291
Trout, baked, 134
Truffles, 188–189
- canned, 215
- in chicken ravioli, 111
- in holiday menus, 189
- in scrambled eggs, 192
- shopping sources, 67
- white, 102

Tuiles (almond cookies), 94–95
"Turbans," 274
- of sole fillets, 275–276

Turnspits for fireplace, 54, 56
- shopping sources, 69–70

United States Department of Agriculture, 69
Utensils, *see* Kitchen Equipment; Pots

V.D.Q.S. label, 36
V.S.R., 40 *fn.*
Veal glaze and half-glaze, 72
Veal heart, 179
Veal stock, 71–72
Vegetable mill, 63
Vegetables:
- artichoke bottoms with mushroom purée, 283
- asparagus vinaigrette (warm), 342
- cauliflower loaf, 346
- celeriac, 246
- with cream sauce, 152
- garden peas, 328
- green bean purée, 282
- *à la grecque*, 173
- grilled pepper salad, 160–161
- potato gratin, 319
- potato straw cake, 392
- purées of, 283
- *ratatouille*, 418
- raw (*crudités*), 305
- spring stew, 291–292
- steamed potatoes, 422
- zucchini (young), 179
- *see also* Salads

Venison, 103
- sauces for, 106

Verjus (juice of white grapes), 423
Vinaigrette salad dressings, 88
Vin blanc cassis (apéritif), 50
Vin de paille (straw wine), 50
Vin de presse, 29
Vinification, 28
Vive (fish), 399
Vouvray, 48

Watercress, 87
White bread, 93
- in croutons, 193–194

Whisks, wire, 63
White wine, 30, 33, 34
- of Alsace, 49
- *blanc de blancs natures*, 36
- of Bordeaux, 45, 46, 47, 48

of Châteauneuf vineyards, 37
of Côte de Beaune, 39
foods compatible with, 35
of Graves, 46
of Jura, 49–50
of Loire Valley, 48–49
manufacturing techniques, 30
with quiche, 304
with seafood, 273, 274
temperature for serving, 33
Whiting, 134
Wine, 27–50
aging, 31, 32
of Alsace, 49
Bordeaux, 44–48; *see also* Bordeaux
"bottle sickness," 32
Burgundy, 37–41; *see also* Burgundy
champagne, 36
with cheese, 25
with dessert, 25
for elegant and formal menus, 120–121, 190–191, 200–201, 208–209, 272–273, 286–287, 354–355, 372–373, 386–387
for festive menu for two, 150–151
geographical divisions, 36
glasses for, 34–35
"*grand seigneurs, les,*" 45–46
grapes, *see* Grapes
influences on quality, 28
for informal and simple menus, 132–133, 140–141, 159, 165, 177, 224–225, 234, 245, 252–253, 259, 302–303, 314–315, 321, 327, 333, 341
of Jura, 49–50
labeling, 40–41
labeling examples, 41–43
laboratory vs. "living," 27
of Loire Valley, 48
manufacturing processes, 28–30, 31
of Mediterranean coast, 50
progression in meal, 35
for Provençal luncheons, 397, 405, 411, 417
of Provence, 395, 396
with quiche, 304
red, 33, 34; *see also* Red wine
regional, 49–50; *see also under* regional names
Rhone Valley, 37
rosé, 31; *see also* Rosé wine
storage, 32–33
sweet, 47
tasting, 35
temperature for serving, 33
uncorking and decanting, 33–34
vinification, 28
white, 33, 34; *see also* White wine
Wine cellars, 32–33
Wooden spoons, 62
Wooden weights for pâtés, 62

Yearling (grass) lamb, 248, 279

Zabaglione, 139
Zucchini, young, 179

Recipe Index

Most recipes in *The French Menu Cookbook* have both French and English titles; the Recipe Index lists these tides alphabetically in both languages. References to the preliminary discussion of each menu and its individual dishes are in the General Index; the cook will find it helpful to read these observations before attempting the recipes. The Contents of the book lists all the menus seasonally. Each menu is again described when its composition and its recipes are specifically considered. Page references to appropriate wines to be served with specific dishes are given below; all other references to wines are in the General Index.

Aïgo-bouido (garlic soup), 178
Almond cookies, 95
Ananas en surprise, 300
Appetizers and first courses:
  artichoke bottoms with two mousses, 357
  calves' brains in cream sauce, 375
  caviar, 192
  celeriac in mustard sauce, 246
  composed salad, 166
  crayfish mousse, 108
  crayfish salad with fresh dill, 289
  crudités, 305
  crusts with fresh morels, 299
  cucumber salad, cream sauce, 153
  fennel *à la grecque*, 173
  fresh sardines in vine leaves, 406
  gratin of stuffed crêpes, 224
  grilled pepper salad, 150
  marinated raw sardine fillets, 316
  pike dumplings (*quenelles*) *à la lyonnaise*, 142
  poached eggs *à la bourguignonne*, 260
  ratatouille, 419
  raw shellfish platter, 274
  scrambled eggs with fresh truffles, 193
  shrimp quiche, 306
  soufflés *à la suissesse*, 254
  terrine of poultry livers, 334
  terrine of sole fillets, 236
  warm asparagus vinaigrette, 342
  warm salad of small green beans, 412
Apple mousse with peaches, 147
  appropriate wine, 141
Apple tart, 320
  appropriate wine, 315
Apricot fritters, 384
  appropriate wine, 373
Aromatic pepper mixture, 89
Aromatic vinegar, 89
Artichoke bottoms:
  basic preparation, 77, 78
  braised, stuffed, 388
  with mushroom purée, 283
Artichoke bottoms with two mousses, 357
  appropriate wine, 354
Artichoke hearts (with lamb stew), 162
Artichoke purée, 146

Asparagus vinaigrette, warm, 342
Asperges tièdes à la vinaigrette, 342

Baked lobster Garin, 154
  appropriate wine, 150
Baked trout stuffed with sorrel, 134
  appropriate wine, 132
Bavarian cream, striped, 205
Béarnaise sauce, 231
Beef stew *à la bourguignonne*, 239
  appropriate wine, 234
Beef stock, *see* Boiled beef with vegetables
Beef tripe, rémoulade sauce, 336
Beef tripe *à la lyonnaise*, 262
  appropriate wine, 259
Beignets d'abricots, 384
Beignets d'ananas à la frangipane, 197
Beignets mixtes, 124
Blanc-manger, 222
  appropriate wine, 209
Blanquette of beef tripe with basil, 421
  appropriate wine, 417
Blanquette de gras-double au pistou, 421
Blanquette of veal, 329
  appropriate wine, 327
Blanquette de veau à l'ancienne, 329
Bloc de foie gras, 202
Boiled beef with vegetables (*pot-au-feu*), 323
  appropriate wine, 321
Boiled pigs' tails and ears with vegetables, 168
  appropriate wine, 165
Bouillabaisse, *see* Provençal fish stew
Braised and roast partridge with cabbage, 156
  appropriate wine, 151
Braised stuffed artichoke bottoms, 388
  appropriate wine, 386
Bread, white, 93
Brochettes de rognons d'agneau, 265
Buttered green beans, 368

Calmars à l'américaine, 377
Calves' brains (in *fritto misto*), 124
Calves' brains in cream sauce, 375
  appropriate wine, 372
Calves' brains in red wine, 344
  appropriate wine, 341
  richer version, 343
Cantaloupe with Parma ham, 388
  appropriate wine, 386, 388
Cassoulet, 248
  appropriate wine, 245
Cauliflower loaf, 346
Caviar, 192
  appropriate wine, 190
Celeriac in mustard sauce, 246
Céleri-rave à la sauce moutarde, 246
Cèpes sautés à la bordelaise, 129
Cerises et amandes fraîches, 422
Cervelle de canut, 403
Cervelles de veau froides à la crème, 375
Cervelles de veau en matelote, 344
Charlotte aux crêpes, sauce sabayon, 137
Charlotte with crêpes, *sabayon* sauce, 137
  appropriate wine, 133
  sabayon sauce, 139
Cheeses:
  appropriate wine, 201, 209, 225, 235, 273, 287, 303, 315, 355, 356, 373, 387
  cervelle de canut, 403
Cheeses, goat:
  appropriate wine, 253, 333
Cherries and fresh almonds, 422
Chestnut purée with celery, 221
Chicken, jellied poached, 379
Chicken breasts, ravioli of, 111
Chicken liver mousse, *see* Artichoke bottoms with two mousses
Chicken in red wine (*coq au vin*), 309
  appropriate wine, 302
Coffee custard, molded, 118
Cold *ratatouille*, 419
Composed salad (mussels, celery, potatoes, wine), 166
Composed salad (potatoes, artichokes), 264
Concombres à l'étuvée, 365
Concombres frais à la crème, 153
Cookies, almond, 95
Coq au vin, 309
Crayfish mousse, 108
  appropriate wine, 104
Crayfish salad with fresh dill, 289
  appropriate wine, 286
Cream of artichoke soup with hazelnuts, 210

appropriate wine, 208
Crème à l'orange, 176
Crème d'artichauts aux noisettes, 210
Crème bavaroise en rubanée, 205
Crème renversée au café, 118
Crêpes, 83
batter variations, 82
charlotte with crêpes, *sabayon* sauce, 137
French pancake jelly rolls, 181
gratin of stuffed crêpes, 226
Crêpes *à la normande*, 258
appropriate wine, 253
Croûtes aux morilles fraîches, 299
Croutons, 193
Crudités, 305
appropriate wine, 302
Crusts with fresh morels, 299
Cucumber salad, cream sauce, 153
appropriate wine, 150
variations, 152
Cucumbers, stewed, 365

Dandelion and salt pork salad, 339
Daube à la provençale, 413
Deep-fried beef tripe, rémoulade sauce, 336
appropriate wine, 333
rémoulade sauce, 338
Desserts:
almond cookies, 95
apple mousse with peaches, 146
apple tart, 320
apricot fritters, 384
blanc-manger, 222
charlotte with crêpes, *sabayon* sauce, 137
cherries and fresh almonds, 422
crêpes *à la normande*, 258
flamri with raspberry sauce, 312
floating island, 243
French pancake jelly rolls, 181
fresh figs with raspberry cream, 158
frozen strawberry mousse with raspberry purée, 285
molded apple pudding, 347
molded chocolate loaf with whipped cream, 331
molded coffee custard, 118
molded tapioca pudding, apricot sauce, 232
orange cream, 176
orange jelly, 130
peaches in red wine, 394
peach Melba, 369
pears in red wine, 164
Périgord pudding (*flaugnarde*), 170
pineapple and frangipane fritters, 197
pineapple ice, 264
pineapple surprise, 300
rum sherbet, 218
strawberries in Beaujolais, 340
strawberries in orange juice, 410
striped Bavarian cream, 205
Duxelles, 76

Egg noodles with truffles, 203
appropriate wine, 200
Eggplant:
French *moussaka*, watercress, 174
Eggs:
poached, *à la bourguignonne*, 260
scrambled, with fresh truffles, 193
Escalopes de veau à la tapenade, 144
tapenade, 145

Fennel *à la grecque*, 173
Fenouil à la grecque, 173
Figues à la crème framboisée, 158
Filets de sardines crues en marinade, 316
Filets de sole aux fines herbes, 361
Fish and seafood:
baked lobster Garin, 154
baked trout stuffed with sorrel, 134
composed salad, 166
crayfish mousse, 108
crayfish salad with fresh dill, 289
fresh sardines in vine leaves, 406
grilled fish, sea-urchin purée, 212
lobsters *à la nage*, 196
marinated raw sardine fillets, 316
pike dumplings *à la lyonnaise*, 142
Provençal fish stew, 400
raw shellfish platter, 274
shrimp quiche, 306
sole fillets with *fines herbes*, 361
squid *à l'américaine*, 377
terrine of sole fillets, 236
turban of sole fillets with salmon, 276

Flamri à la purée de framboises, 312
Flamri with raspberry sauce, 312
appropriate wine, 303
Flaugnarde, 170
Floating island, 243
Foie gras (whole), 202
appropriate wine, 200
Fonds d'artichauts aux deux mousses, 357
Fonds d'artichauts farcis à la duxelles, 388
Fonds d'artichauts à la purée de champignons, 283
Forcemeat, mousseline, 79
Fowl, *see* Poultry and game
Fraises au Beaujolais, 340
Fraises à l'orange, 410
French *moussaka*, watercress, 174
appropriate wine, 172
French pancake jelly rolls, 181
Fresh egg noodles with truffles, 203
Fresh figs with raspberry cream, 158
appropriate wine, 151
Fresh sardines in vine leaves, 406
Fritters:
mixed, 124
pineapple and frangipane, 197
Fritto Misto, 124
appropriate wine, 120
Frozen strawberry mousse with raspberry purée, 285
variations, 284

Game, *see* Poultry and game
Garden peas *à la française*, 328
Garlic soup, 178
Gâteau moulé au chocolat, crème Chantilly, 331
Gelée à l'orange, 130
Gigot d'agneau rôti à la broche, 365
Gigue de chevreuil à la sauce poivrade, 113
Granité à l'ananas, 264
Gras-double frit, sauce rémoulade, 336
Gras-double à la lyonnaise, 262
Gratin de crêpes fourrées, 226
Gratin de pommes de terre, 319
Gratin of stuffed crêpes, 226
appropriate wine, 224
Green bean purée, 282
Green beans, buttered, 368
Green beans, warm salad of, 412
Grillade de boeuf, marchand de vin, 316
Grillade de coeurs d'agneau et petites courgettes, 180
Grilled fish with sea urchin purée, 212
appropriate wine, 208
Grilled lambs' hearts and baby zucchini, 180
appropriate wine, 177
Grilled lambs' kidneys with herb butter, 390
appropriate wine, 386
Grilled pepper salad, 160
Grilled steak, *marchand de vin*, 316
appropriate wine, 314
marchand de vin butter, 318
Guinea fowl with bacon, 219

Haricots fins chauds en salade, 412
Haricots verts au beurre, 368
Herb butter, 391
Herbs, mixed, 86
see also General Index
Homard au four, façon Garin, 154
Homards tièdes à la nage, 196
Hors d'oeuvre of raw vegetables, 305
appropriate wine, 302
Hors d'oeuvres, *see* Appetizers and first courses

Jellied poached chicken, 379
appropriate wine, 372

Kidneys:
lambs', skewered, 256
veal, sautéed with mushrooms, 135

Lamb:
roast saddle with herbs, 279
spitted roast leg, 365
stew with artichoke hearts, 162
Lambs' kidneys, grilled, with herb butter, 390
Lambs' kidneys, skewered, 256
Lamb's lettuce and beet salad, 137
Lamb stew with artichoke hearts, 162
appropriate wine, 159
Lambs' tripes *à la marseillaise*, 408
appropriate wine, 405
substitute ingredients, 407
Lobster Garin, baked, 154

Lobsters *à la nage*, 196
  appropriate wine, 181

Macaronade, 416
Macaroni in braising liquid, 416
Marchand de vin butter, 318
Marinated raw sardine fillets, 316
  appropriate wine, 314
Meats:
  beef stew *à la bourguignonne*, 239
  beef tripe *à la lyonnaise*, 262
  blanquette of beef tripe with basil, 42
  blanquette of veal, 329
  boiled pigs' tails and ears, 168
  calves' brains in cream sauce, 375
  calves' brains in red wine, 344
  cassoulet, 248
  deep-fried beef tripe, rémoulade sauce, 336
  French *moussaka*, watercress, 174
  fritto misto, 124
  grilled lambs' hearts, zucchini, 180
  grilled lambs' kidneys, herb butter, 390
  grilled steak, *marchand de vin*, 316
  lambs' tripes *à la marseillaise*, 408
  lamb stew with artichoke hearts, 162
  pot-au-feu, 323
  Provençal braised beef, 413
  roast saddle of lamb with herbs, 279
  sautéed veal kidneys with mushrooms, 135
  spitted roast leg of lamb, 365
  skewered lambs' kidneys, 256
  stuffed calves' ears, béarnaise sauce, 228
  veal cutlets *à la tapenade*, 144
  veal sweetbreads and macaroni timbale, 215
  whole *foie gras*, 202
Melon *charentais au jambon de Parme*, 388
Mirepoix, 75
Mixed herbs, 86
Mixed vegetable stew (*ratatouille*), 419
Molded apple pudding, 347
Molded chocolate loaf with whipped cream, 331
Molded coffee custard, 118
  appropriate wine, 105
Molded tapioca pudding, apricot sauce, 232
Moussaka à la française, 172
Mousse d'écrivisses au champagne, 108
Mousse de fraises glacée à la sauce Melba, 285
Mousse de pommes aux pêches, 147
Mousseline forcemeat, 79
Mushrooms:
  cèpes à la bordelaise, 129
  crusts with fresh morels, 299
  duxelles, 76
  mushroom purée with artichoke bottoms, 283

Noodles with truffles, 203

Oeufs brouillés aux truffes fraîches, 193
Oeufs à la neige, 243
Oeufs pochés à la bourguignonne, 260
Oreilles de veau farcies, sauce béarnaise, 228
Orange cream, 176
Orange jelly, 130

Paillasson de pommes de terre, 392
Pain de choufleur, 346
Pannequets à la confiture, 181
Partridge, braised and roast, with cabbage, 156
Pâtes fraîches aux truffes, 203
Peaches in red wine, 394
Peach Melba, 369
Pears in red wine, 164
Pêche Melba, 369
Pêches à la vigneronne, 394
Pellmènes de blancs de volaille, 111
Perdrix aux choux, 156
Périgord pudding (*flaugnarde*), 170
Petits pois à la française, 328
Pheasant *salmis*, 127
  appropriate wine, 120
Pieds et paquets à la marseillaise, 408
Pigs' tails and ears with vegetables, 168
Pike dumplings *à la lyonnaise*, 142
  appropriate wine, 140
Pilaf, rice, 81
Pineapple and frangipane fritters, 197
  appropriate wine, 191
Pineapple ice, 264
Pineapple surprise, 300

Pintade rôtie au lard fumé, 219
Plateau de coquillages, 274
Poached chicken mousseline, 294
  appropriate wine, 286
Poached eggs *à la bourguignonne*, 260
Poires au vin rouge, 164
Poissons grillés à l'oursinade, 212
Poivrade sauce, 116
Poivrons doux grillés en salade, 160
Pommes de terre à la vapeur, 422
Potage Germiny, 123
Potatoes, steamed, 422
Potato gratin, 319
Potato straw cake, 392
Pot-au-feu, 323
Potée aux queues et oreilles de cochon, 168
Poule au pot en gelée, 379
Poultry and game:
  braised and roast partridge, 156
  coq au vin, 309
  jellied poached chicken, 379
  pheasant *salmis*, 127
  poached chicken mousseline, 294
  ravioli of chicken breasts, 111
  roast guinea fowl with bacon, 219
  roast leg of venison, *poivrade* sauce, 113
Poultry livers, terrine of, 334
Provençal braised beef (*daube*), 413
  appropriate wine, 411
Provençal cooking, *see* General Index
Provençal fish stew, 400
  appropriate wine, 397
Poularde pochée mousseline, 294
Pudding moulé aux pommes, 347
Pudding moulé au tapioca, 232
Punch à la romaine, 218
Purée d'artichauts, 146
Purée de haricots verts, 282
Purée de marrons au céleri, 221
Purée de patates douces, 118

Quenelles de brochet à la lyonnaise, 142
Quiche aux crevettes, 306

Ragoût d'épaule d'agneau aux coeurs d'artichauts, 162
Ragoût printanier, 292
Ratatouille (cold), 419
  herbs for, 418
Ratatouille froide, 419
Ravioli of chicken breasts, 111
  appropriate wine, 104
Raw shellfish platter, 274
  appropriate wine, 272
Rémoulade sauce, 338
Rice pilaf, 81
Rice, saffron, with tomatoes, 257
Riz safrané aux tomates, 257
Roast guinea fowl with bacon, 219
  appropriate wine, 209
Roast leg of venison with *poivrade* sauce, 113
  appropriate wine, 104
  poivrade sauce, 116
Roast saddle of lamb with herbs, 279
  appropriate wine, 272
  carving, 281
Rognons d'agneau grillés chivry, 390
Rognons de veau sautés aux champignons, 135
Rum sherbet, 218

Saffron rice with tomatoes, 257
Salade composée, 166
Salade composée, 264
Salade d'écrivisses à l'aneth, 289
Salade de mâche et betteraves, 137
Salade de pissenlit au lard, 339
Salads:
  composed (celery, mussels, wine), 166
  composed (potatoes, artichokes), 264
  crayfish with fresh dill, 289
  cucumber, cream sauce, 153
  dandelion and salt pork, 339
  greens and herbs for, 87–88
  grilled pepper, 160
  lamb's lettuce and beet, 137
  warm salad of green beans, 412
  see also Vegetables
Salmis de faisan, 137
Sardines fraîches dans les feuilles de vigne, 406
Sauces:
  béarnaise, 231
  herb butter, 391
  marchand de vin butter, 318
  poivrade, 116
  rémoulade, 338
  sabayon, 139

tapenade, 145
vinaigrette, 88
Sauté de boeuf à la bourguignonne, 239
Sautéed *cèpes à la bordelaise*, 129
appropriate wine, 120
Sautéed veal kidneys with mushrooms, 135
appropriate wine, 132
Scrambled eggs with fresh truffles, 193
appropriate wine, 190
Seafood, *see* Fish and seafood
Selle d'agneau rôti aux aromates, 279
Shrimp quiche, 306
appropriate wine, 302
Skewered lambs' kidneys, 256
appropriate wine, 252
Sole fillets, terrine of, 236
Sole fillets, turban of, 276
Sole fillets with *fines herbes*, 361
appropriate wine, 354
Sorrel soup, 123
Soufflés *à la suissesse*, 254
appropriate wine, 252
Soupe à l'ail, 178
Soupe aux poissons, 400
Soups:
cream of artichoke, with hazelnuts, 210
garlic (*aïgo-bouido*), 178
pot-au-feu, 323
Provençal fish stew, 400
sorrel, 123
veal stock, 72
Spitted roast leg of lamb, 365
appropriate wine, 355
Spring stew, 292
Squid *à l'américaine*, 377
appropriate wine, 372, 374
Steamed potatoes, 422
Stewed cucumbers, 365
Stewed tomatoes, 146
Stock, beef, *see Pot-au-feu*
Stock, veal, 72
Strawberries in Beaujolais, 339
Strawberries in orange juice, 410
Striped Bavarian cream, 205
appropriate wine, 301
Stuffed calves' ears, béarnaise sauce, 228
appropriate wine, 224
Sweet potato purée, 118
Tapenade, 145
Tarte aux pommes, 320
Terrine de filets de sole, 236
Terrine de foies de volailles, 334
Terrine of poultry livers, 334
Terrine of sole fillets, 236
appropriate wine, 234
Timbale de macaroni aux ris de veau, 215
Tomatoes, stewed, 146
Tomato mousse, *see* Artichoke bottoms with two mousses
Trout stuffed with sorrel, 134
Truffles, 188
with fresh egg noodles, 203
with scrambled eggs, 193
Truites à l'oseille au four, 134
Tuiles, 95
Turban de filets de sole au saumon, sauce à l'oseille, 276
Turban of sole fillets with salmon, sorrel sauce, 276
appropriate wine, 272

Veal cutlets *à la tapenade*, 144
appropriate wine, 140
Veal kidneys, sautéed, with mushrooms, 135
Veal stock, 72
Veal sweetbreads and macaroni timbale, 215
appropriate wine, 208
Vegetables:
artichoke bottoms, 78
artichoke bottoms with mushroom purée, 283
artichoke bottoms with two mousses, 357
artichoke purée, 146
braised stuffed artichoke bottoms, 388
buttered green beans, 368
cauliflower loaf, 346
celeriac in mustard sauce, 246
chestnut purée with celery, 221
crudités, 305
crusts with fresh morels, 299
duxelles, 76
fennel *à la grecque*, 173
fritto misto, 124
garden peas *à la française*, 328

Vegetables: (cont.)
à la grecque style, 173
green bean purée, 282
green beans, warm salad of, 412
mirepoix, 75
potato gratin, 319
potato straw cake, 392
ratatouille, 419
saffron rice with tomatoes, 257
sautéed *cèpes à la bordelaise*, 129
spring stew, 292
steamed potatoes, 422
stewed cucumbers, 365
stewed tomatoes, 146
sweet potato purée, 118
warm asparagus vinaigrette, 342
warm salad of small green beans, 412
zucchini (with grilled lambs' hearts), 180
see also Salads
Venison, roast leg of, 113
Vinaigrette sauce, 88
Vinegar, aromatic, 89

Warm asparagus vinaigrette, 342
Warm salad of small green beans, 412
White bread, 93
Wines, *see* General Index

Zucchini, with grilled lambs' hearts, 180

About the Author

Richard Olney was born and raised in Iowa, one of eight children. After moving to a Parisian suburb in 1951 and then buying a run-down property in Provence, Olney settled in France permanently. Chief consultant to the Time-Life Good Cook series, Olney was author of eight books, including *Simple French Cooking* and *Lulu's Provençal Table*. He passed away at his Provençal home in 1999.